*101 Masterpieces
of Music and
Their Composers*

101 Masterpieces of Music and Their Composers

Revised and Updated

MARTIN BOOKSPAN

Dolphin Books
Doubleday & Company, Inc., Garden City, New York

Portions of some of the biographical material have been quoted verbatim from *The Music Lover's Encyclopedia* compiled by Rupert Hughes and revised and re-edited by Deems Taylor and Russell Kerr.

This book is based upon a series of articles by the author which were first published in *Stereo Review*, copyright © 1960, 1961, 1962, 1963, 1964, 1965, 1966, 1967, 1968 by Ziff-Davis Publishing Company. Permission has been granted by Ziff-Davis Publishing Company, publisher of *Stereo Review*.

Introduction

The Ziff-Davis publication *Hi Fi & Music Review* was just a few months old in the summer of 1958 when its music editor of the time, David Hall, phoned me to ask if I would prepare a continuing series of monthly articles, each one focusing on a different work from the standard repertoire and assessing the various available recordings of it. The starting point was the much-quoted statement by Virgil Thomson, made when he was the music critic of the New York *Herald Tribune*, that the backbone of the orchestral repertoire was made up of "50 pieces" repeated year after year. Indeed, our original plan was to inaugurate a five-year Basic Repertoire project in the magazine, during which time fifty backbone items from the symphonic literature were to have been treated.

Certain limitations in the original plan became evident very early in the game. In the years since Thomson had made his statement, the literature of the concert hall had expanded greatly and the figure of "50" was now no longer valid. And so the Basic Repertoire series has continued uninterruptedly in the pages of *Stereo Review*—the name of the magazine was changed long ago—every month since November 1958. Doubleday became interested in publishing the articles as a book as we approached the magic figure of 100 subjects—and at the last minute we decided to improve upon the 100 figure—hence 101 *Masterpieces of Music and Their Composers*.

For the purposes of the present volume I have greatly expanded upon the original material, incorporating biographical sketches of the composers, amplifying the historical and analytical information concerning each piece, and completely re-evaluating all the available recordings of every work.

A word or two about the recommended recordings: since a performance's availability is of such a transitory nature, my guide has been the invaluable Schwann Long Playing Record Catalog, published each month by W. Schwann, Inc., in Boston and the Schwann Supplementary Catalog of imported and monophonic recordings; similarly, the Harrison Catalog of Stereo Tapes, published in New York, has served as index to the available tape performances. Most importantly, the judgments concerning quality of performances necessarily reflect my own subjective tastes. I am not as much concerned with a note-perfect projection of the printed score as I am with a direct and passionate involvement of the performer with the music he is re-creating. This elusive quality is a rare experience in the music-making of our time—rarer, perhaps, in the recording studio than on the concert platform—and its absence in the work of certain respected conductors and performers creates a void that cannot be filled by superior craftsmanship: human warmth and communicative spontaneity are far more important to me than meticulous technical refinement. Except in the extraordinary case of a performance of unusual merit that may no longer be available, all the recommended recordings are readily obtainable through normal retail channels; the deleted performances, where they are mentioned, are so identified in the text.

In listing the catalog numbers of the various recordings, the name of the manufacturer is given first, followed by the stereo number. Where a recording is available in monophonic sound only, it is so identified.

This book should not be construed as a definitive listing and analysis of *the* 101 most basic staples of concert literature—though any such compilation would of necessity have to include many of the works covered in these pages. But there are others ignored here that might legitimately be considered to be just as "basic" as are any of those included among the present 101: Schubert's Fifth Symphony, for example, or Mozart's "Linz" or Schumann's Fourth or Stravinsky's *The Firebird*. As you may already have guessed, a sequel to this volume is a distinct possibility.

Without the devoted and considerate co-operation of the executive officers of the Ziff-Davis Publishing Company this volume could never have come into existence. I should like to single out for special thanks the president of Ziff-Davis, Mr. William Ziff, and the following *Stereo Review* executives: Mr. William Anderson, editor; Mr. William Livingstone, managing editor; Mr. James Goodfriend, music editor; and Mr. Robert S. Clark, associate editor. My editor at Doubleday, Mr. Harold Kuebler, has been most helpful with suggestions, patience and wisdom.

Finally, my wife, Janet, and our three children have been most understanding and indulgent of the many hours over the years when I have retreated into my own little "Basic Rep" world in order to listen to dozens of different recorded performances of the same music. That they have emerged from the ordeal with an undiminished love for the staples of our musical culture is a tribute to their fortitude. It is to them—Janet and the three B's (Rachel, David and Deborah)—that I dedicate this book with thanks and love.

MARTIN BOOKSPAN
Eastchester, New York
June 1972

Contents

Contents

Contents

Johann Sebastian Bach

Born: Eisenach, March 21, 1685
Died: Leipzig, July 28, 1750

The Bachs were probably the most musically prolific family in the history of the art. Johann Sebastian was certainly the greatest of them—as indeed he was one of the greatest of all musicians—but a whole host of uncles, cousins, nephews and sons preceded and followed "The Great Bach" in shaping the course of European musical thought. Johann Sebastian Bach was born in the town of Eisenach in Germany on March 21, 1685. Both his parents died when he was ten years old. His father had started giving him lessons on the violin, and Johann Sebastian continued his musical studies at the home of his brother, Johann Christoph, with whom he went to live. While he was still a young boy he damaged his eyes permanently by copying by moonlight some manuscript scores by "radical" and "forbidden" composers of his period.

When he was fifteen his fine soprano voice won him a tuition-paid scholarship at St. Michael's Church in Lüneburg. One of the greatest musical figures of the time was the Dutch organist Reinken, and more than once Bach went on foot from Lüneburg to Hamburg to hear Reinken play. In the decade between 1707 and 1717 Bach moved from one German court to another, holding positions as organist in Arnstadt, Mühlhausen and Weimar, and appearing as concert organist in Leipzig and Dresden. Bach married for the first time in October 1707 and this marriage, to his cousin Maria Barbara Bach, produced seven children. Four of them died in infancy, but three survived—a daughter and two sons, Wilhelm Friedemann and Karl Philipp Emanuel, both of whom became notable composers on their own.

Between 1717 and 1721 Bach served as principal musician at the court of Prince Leopold at Anhalt-Cöthen. The Prince himself was an accomplished amateur musician and Bach's situation at the court was a highly privileged one. In 1719 Bach visited Halle hoping to meet Handel, but he had just missed him: Handel had already left for England.

Bach's wife died in 1720 and the following year he remarried. His second wife, Anna Magdalene Wülcken, was the daughter of the court trumpeter at Weissenfels. The union produced thirteen more children, nine of them sons. Again, several of them became composers, the most notable being Johann Christian. Anna Magdalene was herself an accomplished musician and she wrote out the parts of many of Bach's cantatas. In 1723 he became the organist and director of music at the St. Thomas Church in Leipzig and he retained that honored post for the remaining twenty-seven years of his life.

He was allowed considerable leeway in traveling by his Leipzig employers and he often visited Dresden to hear the latest in Italian opera. In May 1747 he journeyed to Potsdam at the invitation of Frederick the Great. He improvised upon the various Silbermann pianos in the palace—all his own keyboard music was written for organ, harpsichord or clavichord—followed from room to room by the king and his musicians. The next day Bach tried the principal organs in Potsdam, improvising a six-part fugue on a theme proposed by the king. He later wrote a three-part fugue on this theme, a ricercare in six parts, several canons and a trio for flute, violin and bass. These pieces, together, are known as Bach's *The Musical Offering* and they are dedicated to Frederick the Great.

In 1749 Bach was forced to undergo two operations to restore his sight, weakened by copying his own and other men's works and engraving his *Art of the Fugue*. But the operations failed and Bach was left totally blind. Also, his previous robust health began to fail rapidly. On July 10, 1750, his sight was suddenly restored but within three weeks he was dead of a brain hemorrhage.

Bach was little known as a composer during his life and few of his works were published then. It was not until 1829, when Mendelssohn conducted the first performance since Bach's death of *The Passion According to St. Matthew*, that Bach began to be recognized as the great creative genius that he was. In 1850, a hundred years after his death, the Bach Gesellschaft began to publish his complete works.

His enormous output includes hundreds of sacred, secular and comic cantatas; masses, motets, Magnificats and Passions (of which the *St. Matthew* and *St. John* are the greatest); and a huge body of instrumental music, including the forty-eight preludes and fugues of *The Well-Tempered Clavier*, the Goldberg Variations and numerous other works for keyboard; a vast output for organ—solo and in concert with other instruments; sonatas, both accompanied and unaccompanied for violin, cello, flute and other instruments; concertos for one, two, three and four keyboard instruments; violin concertos; and the six Brandenburg Concertos and the Four Suites for Orchestra.

Musicians of the twentieth century have found a new formal and harmonic interest in Bach's music and it is unquestionably true that never before in history has there been such a widespread and clearly focused understanding of stylistic and performing principles in Bach's music as exists today.

BRANDENBURG CONCERTOS (S. 1046/51)

The period of a half-dozen years between 1717 and 1723, when Johann Sebastian Bach served as Kapellmeister to the young Prince Leopold of Anhalt-Cöthen, was one of the most fruitful periods of the composer's creative life. The Prince himself was a talented musician with an abiding devotion to the arts and Bach's relationship with him was warm and friendly from the beginning. In this atmosphere were created some of Bach's most significant and attractive instrumental works, for at the court he had at his disposal some excellent solo instrumentalists and a fine orchestra.

In view of this background, it may seem strange that during the Cöthen period Bach produced six superb orchestral concertos that he dedicated not to his beneficent employer but to the Margraf Christian Ludwig, the youngest son of the Grand Duke of Brandenburg, whom Bach had met in Berlin in 1718. Scholars today seem to have rejected the older theory that Bach composed these works in fulfillment of a commission from the Margraf; rather, the general feeling now is that by 1721 Bach's relationship with Prince Leopold was no longer quite so cordial as it had been at first. The German musicologist Heinz Becker has suggested that Bach, having heard that the Margraf had a splendid small ensemble in Berlin, selected six concertos from among a larger number of similar works and published them with a dedication to the Margraf. In effect, Bach offered these six works as testimonials to his ability as an orchestrator, with the clear implication that he would welcome an opportunity to go to Berlin and become the Margraf's Kapellmeister. This was not to be, however, and in 1723 Bach left Cöthen to take up his duties as cantor of the St. Thomas Church in Leipzig, the post he was to hold until his death, nearly thirty years later—years that shaped the main power of his later creative energy toward the composition of music for the church.

In the six Brandenburg Concertos, Bach left the world a veritable syllabus of the art of Baroque instrumentation and a matchless demonstration of the varied textures and sonorities possible to the Baroque orchestra. Through the years, these superb works have come to be the best-known and most-recorded instrumental works of their period. Each of the concertos is scored for a different combination of instruments, and except for the Third and Sixth, which call for strings only, they each conform to the normal Baroque concerto grosso pattern of pitting two contrasting groups of instruments against each other: a small group of solo instruments (called the concertino) contrasted with the larger body of players (called the ripieno).

The concertino instruments in the First Brandenburg Concerto are two "hunting" horns (without valves and capable of playing high-lying harmonics), three oboes, bassoon (which almost always doubles the cello part) and the now-obsolete violino piccolo (also called a Quartgeige). This "small violin" was a three-quarter-sized instrument tuned a third higher than the normal violin. Its small size effectively reduced the carrying power of its tone, and the great English composer, pianist and scholar Sir Donald Francis Tovey spoke of the "struggling *violino piccolo*, that has more difficulty in getting the upper hand than any other solo in the whole classical repertoire." Modern performances of the First Brandenburg Concerto generally employ a regular violin. In the first movement the solo violinist plays along with the first violinists of the ripieno; he emerges as an individual voice in the slow movement, marked *Adagio*, and so continues for the remainder of the work. Another distinguishing feature of the First Brandenburg Concerto is the third movement, a Minuet with no fewer than three contrasting Trios; the first of them is scored for two oboes and bassoon only, the second, a polonaise, is for strings, and the third is for the horns and oboes.

The solo instruments in the Second Brandenburg Concerto are trumpet, flute, oboe and violin, with the trumpet part a real virtuoso tour de force. It is written in the highest register of the clarino, the highest-playing trumpet of Bach's time, and obviously was intended for a master of the instrument. Clarino players of the time were able to produce their high notes through special training of the lips and breath and through concentration of exclusive attention upon the required techniques. In our own time there have been several different approaches to solving the problem: some players employ specially designed instruments, and there have been various substitute instruments that certain conductors have called for. Toscanini, for example, substituted an E-flat clarinet for the trumpet on occasion and at one of his Prades Festivals Pablo Casals replaced the trumpet with a soprano saxophone. The concerto itself is a vigorous, extroverted work in three movements. One of the more unusual features of its structure is the absence in the second movement of both the ripieno instruments and the solo trumpet. The movement is a three-part meditation for the solo flute, violin and oboe, all over the harpsichord bass.

The Third Concerto is the shortest of the six, consisting of only two movements, for strings alone, separated by two chords in B minor to create a tonal contrast between the prevailing G-major tonality of the two *Allegros*. It is clear that Bach expected his performers to embellish those two chords, in accordance with common Baroque practice. While this is becoming the common procedure in contemporary performances, there still remain some conductors who prefer the unadorned two chords. (On the other end of the scale are conductors who interpolate a whole movement from another of Bach's works: Yehudi Menuhin replaces the two chords with a Benjamin Britten arrangement of the slow movement from one of the composer's organ trio sonatas, and Serge Koussevitzky used to introduce a movement from one of Bach's cantatas.)

Two so-called flauti d'eco—echo flutes—and a solo violin form the *concertino* instruments in the Fourth Brandenburg Concerto. It now seems likely that the flauti d'eco were recorders rather than flutes; in any case, recorders are rapidly replacing flutes as the solo instruments in this work, and the resulting sound texture certainly seems more stylistically appropriate.

In the Fifth Concerto Bach elevates the harpsichord from its recessive role as accompanist and harmonic filler to that of principal solo instrument in the concertino. Indeed, the long and tension-laden cadenza for the harpsichord in the first movement of the Fifth Brandenburg Concerto is one of the most breath-taking moments in all music. The other two solo instruments, the flute and violin, are completely overpowered by the importance of the harpsichord part. In the slow movement Bach again dispenses with the ripieno instruments (as he did also in the Second Concerto) and the entire musical argument is given to the three solo instruments. The concluding movement is a sprightly gigue for the full forces.

The Sixth and last of the works is scored for the lower and darker-hued stringed instruments. Where the bright and incisive tone of the violins predominated in the texture of the Third Concerto, it is the characteristically deeper, more velvety sound of the violas that gives the Sixth Concerto its particular flavor. Bach's original scoring of the work called for two violas da braccio (regular violas held in the upright arm position), two violas da gamba (cello-like instruments held upright between the legs) and cello, with double bass and harpsichord supplying the bass accompaniment. Conductors not too terribly concerned with real performance authenticity will assign the viola da gamba parts to cellos, but the proper instrumental forces in the performance of Baroque music has by now become the norm rather than the exception, for the most part. The British scholar Sir Hubert Parry has written that the Sixth Brandenburg Concerto "is a kind of mysterious counterpart to the Third Concerto; as the singular grouping of two violas, two *viole da gamba* and a cello and bass prefigures. The color is weird and picturesque throughout, and the subject matter such as befits the unusual group of instruments employed."

Among the dozen and a half or so currently available integral recordings of these works, my own favorites are those by the Vienna Concentus Musicus under the direction of Nikolaus Harnoncourt (Telefunken S 9459/60, two discs), and the English Chamber Orchestra under the direction of Benjamin Britten (London CSA 2225, two discs; London D 80223, reel-to-reel tape; London D 10223, cassette).

Harnoncourt strives for more period authenticity than does Britten, even to the point of employing instruments of Bach's own time. But Britten's basically Romantic approach to the music works rather convincingly also, largely due to the composer-conductor's driving energy and powerful personality.

CHACONNE (FROM VIOLIN PARTITA NO. 2, S. 1004)

Along with the Brandenburg Concertos, many others of Bach's most important instrumental works belong to the six-year period (1717–23) when he was conductor of the court orchestra at Anhalt-Cöthen. The Four Suites for Orchestra and the concertos and sonatas for violin came into being during this period, along with sonatas for cello, flute and viola da gamba. In addition, Bach also composed much keyboard music at Anhalt-Cöthen, including the first part of *The Well-Tempered Clavier*, the English and French Suites, The Little Preludes and The Inventions.

In musical intricacy and structural complexity the three sonatas and three partitas for unaccompanied violin are perhaps the most daring works of the Anhalt-Cöthen years. Not that music for unaccompanied stringed instruments was such a rarity during the Baroque period. But Bach brought to these six works all the re-

sources of his relentless musical logic. As Paul Henry Lang has put
it:

> Bach waves aside all restrictions and all conventions, unloosens all ties
> to the rational and empirical, plunging us, with the aid of a little
> wooden box with four strings on it and a thin rod with horsehair
> stretched from end to end, into the irrational and timeless. . . . Crea-
> tive imagination fetes in them its absolute triumph over all limitations
> imposed upon it by form, material, and medium of expression.

The celebrated Chaconne from the D Minor Partita represents
one of the highest peaks of Bach's creation in this medium.
The D Minor Partita begins with four very short dance movements—allemande, courante, saraband and gigue. Then the whole
is capped with the stupendous Chaconne, consisting of more than
sixty variations on a descending ground bass—D, C, B flat, A.
Philipp Spitta, the German Bach scholar, has written a vivid description of this music:

> The overpowering wealth of forms displays not only the most perfect
> knowledge of the technique of the violin, but also the most absolute
> mastery over an imagination the like of which no composer was ever
> endowed with. . . . From the grave majesty of the beginning to the
> thirty-second notes which rush up and down like very demons; from
> the tremulous arpeggios that hang almost motionless, like veiling
> clouds above a gloomy ravine, till a strong wind drives them to the
> tree tops, which groan and toss as they whirl their leaves into the
> air, to the devotional beauty of the movement in D major where the
> evening sun sets in the peaceful valley. The spirit of the master urges
> the instrument to incredible utterances; at the end of the major
> section it sounds like an organ and sometimes a whole band of violins
> might seem to be playing. This chaconne is a triumph of spirit over
> matter such as even Bach never repeated in a more brilliant manner.

Before we continue, we must briefly touch upon the "Great Bow
Controversy." There are many chords in Bach's music for unaccompanied violin in which the performer who uses the modern violin
bow cannot play all the notes simultaneously because the different

notes lie sometimes on three and sometimes on all four of the violin's strings. In such cases the performer must arpeggiate the chords. Because of this some Bach experts—Albert Schweitzer, most notably —have advocated the use of the early-eighteenth-century type of curved bow in the performance of the music so that all the notes of the written chords can be played together as chords. The trouble with this is that when the bow hair is loose enough so that all the notes of the chords can be sounded together, it is too loose to allow the single notes to be played crisply. Several years ago both Columbia and London had recordings (now deleted) of the six Sonatas and Partitas by Rolf Schröder and Emil Telmanyi, respectively, and featuring the curved bow. I have never heard the Schröder performances, but I remember Telmanyi's as flabby and dull. General practice these days is to stick to the modern bow, since it is not at all certain that Bach *wanted* the chords to sound as chords; he wrote them that way, to be sure, but we are learning through research that the musical notation of the Baroque period often meant different things to the performers of the time than it does to us.

Szigeti's integral recording of the Six Sonatas and Partitas for Unaccompanied Violin remains unsurpassed—and the Chaconne performance included in the set (Vanguard-Bach Guild 627/8/9, three discs, mono only) is visionary and monumental in its grandeur and passion. Among stereo recordings of the Chaconne, those by Heifetz (RCA LSC 3266) and Ricci (Decca DL 710151) are the most recommendable. The Heifetz performance, taken from the remarkable television program that documented his unique art in the spring of 1971, is testimony to his continuing Olympian stature among violinists. His Chaconne is on a cooler emotional level than are those of either Szigeti or Ricci, but it has its own kind of controlled dynamism and tension. A performance not to be missed!

There exists a hoary tradition of transcribing this music for other performing media. Soon after the violinist Ferdinand David performed the then recently discovered Chaconne in the winter of 1840, his composer-friend, Felix Mendelssohn, produced a piano accompaniment that was published in London in 1847. Seven years later Robert Schumann published keyboard accompaniments for all six of Bach's Partitas and Sonatas. Later still, Brahms made a solo arrangement of the Chaconne for piano, left hand (once recorded by the one-armed Austrian pianist for whom Ravel wrote his Left Hand Concerto, Paul Wittgenstein). Raff made one for piano, two hands, and Jeno Hubay, a noted violinist himself, produced a version for full orchestra. One of the most famous non-violinistic performances of the Chaconne in our time is that of Andres Segovia on the guitar (Decca DL 79751; cassette C739751). It is amazing how well it sounds. For one thing, there is no problem with arpeggiated chords. With a single stroke Segovia is able to sound all the notes simultaneously. For another, the guitar is able to provide a deep bass, an octave lower than written, so that the music is enhanced in its majesty. Here is a superb performance of real art, and as such the transcription here becomes its own justification.

MAGNIFICAT IN D MAJOR, S. 243

The Song of the Blessed Virgin Mary, a hymn of praise recorded in Chapter One of the Book of St. Luke in the New Testament, served several times to fire the creative imagination of Johann Sebastian Bach. The ultimate demonstration of the strength of this inspiration is the brilliant and joyous Magnificat in D Major.

Albert Schweitzer, in his comprehensive biography and guide to Bach's music, mentions an earlier Magnificat for soprano solo, supposed to have been studied by one of the first editors of the Bach Gesellschaft about 1855, more than a hundred years after Bach's death. This score disappeared, apparently right from under the noses of the Bach scholars of the nineteenth century, and to this day its problematical existence defies and frustrates the best musical sleuths. There is also an earlier version of the D Major Magnificat, composed, it is thought, for the Christmas Day service in Leipzig's Thomaskirche in 1723, Bach's first year as cantor there. This setting of the text is in E-flat major, and several sections have been inserted between the verses that are not part of the traditional text. Some students of Bach have conjectured that he composed this version as stage music to accompany the representation of the scene in the manger at Bethlehem. Sometime during the next decade

Bach completed the final version of the score, omitting the interpolations and transposing the music down to D major.

The Magnificat, which was placed just after the sermon in the
Lutheran service of the time, is a confident, exultant outburst—the
opening words are *Magnificat anima mea Dominum* ("My soul doth
magnify the Lord"). Because it was the climax of the service, the
Magnificat had to be relatively brief to have the proper effect, and
the spare concentration of Bach's score is one of its most extraordinary features. Although short in duration, the work creates an effect of splendor and magnificence. It is written for five-part chorus,
five vocal soloists, and the full, colorful orchestra of Bach's time:
three trumpets, two flutes, two oboes, strings, timpani and continuo
instruments. In form and substance, the Magnificat may well have
served Bach as a preliminary exercise for the mighty task of composing the Mass in B Minor.

Of the Magnificat's twelve sections, five are for chorus, and another—the setting of *Suscepit Israel* ("He has helped His servant
Israel in remembrance of His mercy")—calls for sopranos and
altos in choir. The opening chorus, written for five parts, is one
continuing jubilation, developed and repeated in the spirit of the
first words. Following this is an aria for the second soprano, *Et
exultavit*, accompanied by a contrapuntal line of melting sweetness
and tenderness in the strings, and then the aria *Quia respexit*, a
moving dialogue between the first soprano and the oboe. At its
conclusion comes an extraordinary dynamic contrast: a headlong
intrusion by the chorus intoning the *Omnes generationes* ("Generation after generation will bless the Virgin Mary").

Next comes the first appearance of the bass soloist, in the slow,
florid aria *Quia fecit*, and after it the duet for alto and tenor, *Et
misericordia*, one of the chief glories of the score. Its gently rocking
rhythm gives it the character of a lullaby, and the flutes and muted
strings of the orchestral accompaniment impart to it a particular
poignancy. Again there is a sharp contrast as the music continues
without pause into the brilliant chorus *Fecit potentiam*, a magnificent exposition of the might of the Lord. The momentum is
suddenly arrested, and a descending chromatic passage for solo
violin leads to the tenor aria *Deposuit potentes* ("He has put down

the mighty from their thrones"). In the accompaniment of the succeeding number, the alto aria *Esurientes*, the flutes return to the foreground. Near the end of the aria the soloist sings the word *inanes* ("empty") and Bach at this point dispenses with accompaniment altogether, leaving the word to be heard unadorned.

The next section is the *Suscepit Israel*, one of the most haunting of all the Magnificat's movements, with a particularly memorable use of unison oboes above soprano and alto voices. This is followed by the two concluding choruses, *Sicut locutus est* and *Gloria Patri*. The former is the only full-fledged fugue in the work, and the concluding chorus is again a magnificently vibrant and exciting expression of unbounded joy. One of its chief features is the alternation between the sound of the massed chorus and the imitative entries of the individual choirs. The concluding words are *Sicut erat in principio* ("As it was in the beginning"), and here Bach brings back the music of the opening chorus.

Concerning the available recordings, the performances for Vanguard and Deutsche Grammophon, conducted respectively by Felix Prohaska (BG S 5005) and Karl Richter (ARC 73197) are solid, tasteful accomplishments, with better solo vocalists in the DGG-Archive recording. The technical aspects of both are good without being exceptional.

An exceptional recording is the performance conducted for Columbia by Leonard Bernstein (MS 6375). Together with the New York Philharmonic, the Schola Cantorum directed by Hugh Ross, and five distinguished vocal soloists, Bernstein turns in a reading of sustained grandeur, excitement and exuberance. The choice of soloists is surprising: the second soprano part is sung by mezzo-soprano Jennie Tourel, and the alto solos are given to the countertenor Russell Oberlin. Miss Tourel has a little trouble with some of the higher-lying passages, especially in her first solo, *Et exultavit*, but it is difficult to think of another singer who could invest the part with such perceptive and sensitive musicianship. The other soloists are soprano Lee Venora, tenor Charles Bressler and bass Norman Farrow. All contribute to the success of the performance, and the Columbia engineers have produced recorded sound of clarity and brilliance.

There is now available an even more rapturous and joyful account of this work than Bernstein's, and more stylish, too: Münchinger's, with soloists including Elly Ameling, Werner Krenn, Helen Watts and Tom Krause, the Vienna Chamber Choir and the Stuttgart Chamber Orchestra (London OS 26103).

Of the available recordings on reel-to-reel and cassette tape, my own preference is for the imaginative account conducted by the late Karl Ristenpart (Nonesuch E 1011, 3¾ ips; N5 71011 respectively).

Béla Bartók

Born: Nagyszentmiklós, Hungary, March 25, 1881
Died: New York, September 26, 1945

After studying music at the Budapest Academy, Bartók developed an intense interest in the folk music of his native Hungary. Together with his countryman Zoltán Kodály, another leading figure of twentieth-century music, Bartók made intensive studies of Hungarian folk music in the field, journeying to remote areas of the country in order to hear and transcribe the color and flavor of the local musical tradition. His interest in Hungarian folk music soon was extended to the music of other cultures and he retired from composition for a time in order to collect and study the music of other peoples.

His first major recognition came in 1917 when the Budapest Opera produced his dance-play *The Wooden Prince*. For the next twenty years Bartók was something of an *enfant terrible*, producing music that was for the most part harshly dissonant and violent. Chief examples are his first two piano concertos, his ballet *The Miraculous Mandarin*, the Third and Fourth String Quartets and the two Sonatas for Violin and Piano.

Beginning with the Music for Strings, Percussion and Celesta, commissioned by Paul Sacher for the Basel Chamber Orchestra in 1936, there is a new and less frenzied element in Bartók's music. Instrumental color is most sensitively and delicately exploited and the classical principles of structure and architecture are part and parcel of Bartók's musical impulse. The principal works of the late 1930s, in addition to the Music for Strings, Percussion and Celesta, were the Second Violin Concerto, the Sonata for Two Pianos and Percussion, Contrasts for Violin, Piano and Clarinet, the Divertimento for String Orchestra and the Sixth String Quartet.

As the Hungarian alliance with the spreading cancer of Nazi Germany began to become increasingly pronounced in the late 1930s, Bartók became increasingly critical of the Hungarian political authorities. As early as 1938 he began to make plans for the removal of his manuscripts from Hungary. Beset with ambivalent feelings—to remain in Hungary in face of the Nazification of all life was clearly intolerable; on the other hand, it was impossible to protest in any meaningful way at home—Bartók and his wife left Hungary for America in the fall of 1940. As soon as they arrived, they set out on concert tours as a two-piano team. For an appearance with the New York Philharmonic, conducted by Fritz Reiner, in January 1943, Bartók rescored his Sonata for Two Pianos and Percussion and transcribed it for two pianos and orchestra. Soon after his arrival in this country Bartók was made an Honorary Doctor of Music at Columbia University and given a small grant to carry out folk music research there. This lasted for only two years and when the grant expired, the Bartóks were left with literally no income. To make matters worse, the composer's health—which had never been robust—soon became dangerously poor. Bartók spent much time in hospitals in 1943, helped out financially by friends and a modest allowance from ASCAP. When Serge Koussevitzky visited Bartók in his New York hospital room in the fall of 1943 and delivered a thousand-dollar commission to Bartók on behalf of the Koussevitzky Music Foundation, which the conductor had recently established in memory of his wife Natalie, the symbolism of the event signaled a spiritual and healthful rally for Bartók. For Koussevitzky he created the Concerto for Orchestra, the first work he composed in the United States, and then others began to take shape—a Sonata for Unaccompanied Violin, composed for Yehudi Menuhin; a Third Piano Concerto; a Viola Concerto commissioned by William Primrose. Bartók completed and scored all but the last seventeen measures of the piano concerto (these final bars were deciphered from Bartók's sketches and scored by his friend and colleague, Tibor Serly); the Viola Concerto was left in sketch form only—and it, too, was reconstructed and completed by Serly.

Bartók worked on these last scores until the very end. In September 1945 his condition had deteriorated again so that hospitalization became mandatory. On September 26, 1945, Béla Bartók died in New York of leukemia. To a doctor attending him just before the end Bartók said, "The trouble is that I have to go with so much still to say."

CONCERTO FOR ORCHESTRA

On December 1, 1944, Serge Koussevitzky conducted the world premiere of the Concerto for Orchestra by Béla Bartók at Symphony Hall in Boston. I was present at those initial presentations of the score and I recall being struck even then with the masterly quality of the music. Since then, of course, Bartók's Concerto for Orchestra has become a genuine classic of symphonic literature, an acknowledged masterpiece with a secure and lasting place in the international concert repertoire.

Despite the fact that we still are very close in time to the period when the work was created, an amazing welter of misinformation has already formed around its genesis:

Item: No less authoritative a source than the published score itself blandly states that the Concerto for Orchestra was given its first performance by Koussevitzky and the Boston Symphony Orchestra in New York's Carnegie Hall. Actually, not only the first but also the second, third and fourth performances of the music occurred in Boston's Symphony Hall, with Koussevitzky conducting, on December 1, 2, 29 and 30. The two latter performances were scheduled by Koussevitzky for the same subscription series immediately after the premiere, when the Boston reviews of the first performance were less enthusiastic than he thought the work merited. It was not until January 10, 1945—six weeks after the premiere—that Koussevitsky and the Boston Symphony introduced the work to New York at a Carnegie Hall concert.

Item: Some informants state that Bartók did not hear the Concerto for Orchestra until he attended the Carnegie Hall performance, illness having prevented him from journeying to Boston to attend the premiere. Now it is true enough that Bartók was not present at the performances on December 1 and 2; he *did* come to

Boston, however, for the performances on December 29 and 30 and he was accorded a tumultuous ovation by the audiences. I know—I was there both times!

Item: There are conflicting accounts concerning the hospital in which Bartók was being treated in the spring of 1943 when he was visited by Koussevitzky and offered the commission that resulted in the Concerto for Orchestra. Some sources say it was Doctors Hospital in New York City, others, Mount Sinai Hospital. Doctors Hospital it apparently was.

Item: One source states that the Concerto for Orchestra was written largely in Asheville, North Carolina, where the Bartóks are supposed to have spent an idyllic summer in 1943 away from the sweat and squalor of their Manhattan apartment on 57th Street. Agatha Fassett, in her engrossing book about the last five years of Bartók's life (*The Naked Face of Genius*), states that Bartók did not go to Asheville until the winter months of 1943–44, that during August of 1943 Bartók was in a private sanitarium at Lake Saranac in the Adirondacks and that it was there that the Concerto for Orchestra was largely composed.

For the first performances of the score Bartók prepared a description of the music for the concert bulletin of the Boston Symphony Orchestra. "The general mood of the work," he wrote, "represents, apart from the jesting second movement, a gradual transition from the sternness of the first movement and the lugubrious death-song of the third, to the life-assertion of the last one." The Concerto is in five movements and has all the characteristics of a noble and heroic symphony. In explaining why he did not call it a symphony, Bartók wrote:

The title of this symphony-like orchestral work is explained by its tendency to treat the single instruments or instrument groups in "concertant" or soloistic manner. The virtuoso treatment appears, for instance, in the fugato sections of the development of the first movement (brass instruments), or in the "perpetuum mobile"-like passages of the principal theme in the last movement (strings), and, especially, in the second movement, in which pairs of instruments consecutively appear with brilliant passages. As for the structure of the work, the first and fifth movements are written in a more or less

regular sonata form. The development of the first contains fugato
sections for brass; the exposition in the finale is somewhat extended,
and its development consists of a fugue built on the last theme of the
exposition. Less traditional forms are found in the second and third
movements. The main part of the second consists of a chain of
independent short sections, by wind instruments consecutively introduced in five pairs (bassoons, oboes, clarinets, flutes and muted
trumpets). Thematically, the five sections have nothing in common.
A kind of "trio"—a short chorale for brass instruments and side
drum—follows, after which the five sections are recapitulated in a
more elaborate instrumentation. The structure of the fourth movement is likewise chain-like; three themes appear successively. These
constitute the core of the movement, which is enframed by a misty
texture of rudimentary motifs. Most of the thematic material of this
movement derives from the Introduction to the first movement. The
form of the fourth movement—"Intermezzo interrotto" ("Interrupted
Intermezzo")—could be rendered by the letter symbols ABA-interrup-
tion-BA.

It is interesting to note that at the time of the first performance
Bartók had not yet composed the brilliant coda which concludes
the work; as Koussevitzky conducted it during those December
days in 1944 the music came to an abrupt and unprepared ending.
Later, Bartók wrote the few measures that bring the score to its
logical and inexorable conclusion.

Many recordings of Bartók's Concerto for Orchestra have been
made over the years. My own favorites are the performances conducted by Bernstein (Columbia MS 6140), Leinsdorf (RCA LSC
2643), Reiner (RCA Victrola VICS 1110) and Solti (London CS
6469). Bernstein offers a highly personalized account of the music,
with the various instrumental voices microscopically exposed. If
you want to hear what is going on inside the music, Bernstein's is
the version to get, especially as Columbia's engineers have contrived
an extremely close-to yet well-balanced sound, with extraordinarily
vivid bass response. Be warned, however, that the conductor lays on
some of the Hungarian goulash elements with a rather lavish hand.
Leinsdorf's is altogether more objective, but with equally fine playing
and recording. It is perhaps no coincidence that the Leinsdorf-

Boston Symphony collaboration in Bartók's Concerto for Orchestra was the first recording by these forces to be released after Leinsdorf assumed the music directorship in Boston in the fall of 1962. The Reiner-Chicago Symphony performance dates from 1956 and it is one of hair-trigger precision and virtuosity, with an undeniable feeling of tension, but also with an uncommonly expert shaping of the tonal architecture of the score. The microphoning is more distant than the norm that has prevailed more recently in recordings of the Chicago Symphony, but Reiner's authority and command still make a striking impression. And at the budget price of the Victrola issue, it is certainly a bargain. Solti presents a performance of enormous power and sweep, splendidly played by the great London Symphony Orchestra and superbly recorded by the engineers.

RCA has now withdrawn the reel-to-reel tape edition of the Leinsdorf performance, leaving the tape and cassette field virtually unchallenged to the Angel recording of the score by Seiji Ozawa and the Chicago Symphony Orchestra (M 36035 and 4XS 36035 respectively). The performance is meticulously organized and spectacularly played, but the disc versions by both Bernstein and Solti offer longer-lasting pleasure: Bernstein's has a searing intensity, and Solti's, power and a strong dramatic quality.

Ludwig van Beethoven

Born: Bonn, December 16, 1770
Died: Vienna, March 26, 1827

The first Beethoven to leave his fingerprints on the pages of musical history was a Flemish singer named Louis van Beethoven. Installed at the Rhineland city of Bonn in 1733 with an appointment as a bass singer to the electoral chapel, Louis van Beethoven rose slowly in rank and power until 1761 when he was appointed Kapellmeister of Bonn, with complete supervision over the entire musical activity of the principality.

Of the several children born to him and his wife, only one survived—a son, named Johann, who was born in 1739 or 1740 (the exact date is not known). The youth was groomed by his father for a musical life and he was taught the violin and the clavier. The elder Beethoven was an honored and respected member of the court until his death in 1773; his wife was dissolute and an alcoholic who spent her later years in an institution. Hers was the dominant influence in the life of her son, and Johann van Beethoven led a generally shiftless, irresponsible existence as a ne'er-do-well. In 1767, in his late twenties, he married a widow, Maria Magdalena Keverich, who was his direct antithesis: she was gentle and compassionate, affectionate and devoted.

This, then, is the family background and heritage that produced Ludwig van Beethoven, the composer of some of the most noble, spiritual and heroic music ever written.

Ludwig van Beethoven was the oldest of three surviving children born to Johann and Maria Magdalena. His birth date is variously given as either December 15 or 16, 1770—all that is known definitely is that he was baptized on December 17. He exhibited extraordinary musical gifts at an early age and his father was quick to seize upon and exploit the boy's talents. Ludwig's general education appears to have stopped at about age eleven, with the result that he was never able to express himself clearly or easily in words, and even the most elementary mathematical problems found him hopelessly helpless. Musically, however, he developed at an astonishing rate; by the time he was twelve he was "cembalist to the orchestra in Bonn," and when he was fourteen he was made assistant court organist, with much of the responsibility for maintaining high standards in all the court's musical activities.

In the spring or summer of 1787—here again the history is vague —Beethoven, then a sixteen-year-old, journeyed to Vienna and there met some of the outstanding musical figures of the time, including Mozart. There is reason to believe that Mozart even gave Beethoven a few lessons in composition, but the Viennese sojourn was interrupted by the news from Bonn that Beethoven's mother was seriously ill. He hastily returned to her bedside and was with her when she died, at the age of forty, in July 1787.

Beethoven remained in Bonn another five years, but they were years of deep personal trauma: his father now became completely derelict and the responsibility of raising and supporting the two younger sons fell entirely upon the shoulders of Ludwig. His duties at the court were constantly expanding and he was absorbing the best musical literature he could find. However, the cosmopolitan excitement and challenge of the life he had tasted but briefly in Vienna exerted a powerful pull on him; as soon as his brothers were old enough to make their own way, Ludwig van Beethoven returned to Vienna—there to spend the remaining thirty-five years of his life.

By 1792, when he settled in Vienna, Beethoven had already composed a considerable body of music: three piano quartets; a piano trio; a string trio, Opus 3; several sets of variations for piano; and the String Trio in D Major, Opus 8. Beethoven made his first public appearance in Vienna in March 1795, playing his First Piano Concerto. For the next five years he was much in demand—and not only in Vienna—as a piano virtuoso: in 1798 in Prague, for example, he played two highly acclaimed recitals. The year 1800 ends what is called Beethoven's "first period" of composition (after the book by von Lenz, *Beethoven and His Three Styles*); the "second period" extended to 1815 and the "third" to the year of his death, 1827. To this "first period" belong a whole host of works: the six string quartets of Opus 18; nine piano sonatas; many sets of variations; the concert aria *Ah, perfido!*; and many others.

Now a severe liver ailment began to affect his hearing. Though he had always been brusque—especially with the aristocracy, among whom he had an astonishingly long list of friendships and love affairs—his former generosity and warmth quickly developed into an uncontrollable suspiciousness and jealousy toward his best friends. Also, the wild life of a nephew whom he supported brought him great bitterness. Until the beginning of the "third period," however, he had large stores of joy in life—and he exulted in his creative powers. His sketchbooks, which he kept with him constantly, are a unique testimony to the mind of a creative genius at work. They reveal that the perfected scores that today seem to have sprung whole in the imagination of their creator through some kind of mystical or divine inspiration are the results of the most diligent and painstaking labor, with much revising and rewriting every step of the way.

In the arbitrary but admittedly convenient classification of von Lenz, the works of the "second period" include Symphonies 3 through 8; the opera *Fidelio*; the incidental music for Goethe's drama *Egmont*; the Fourth and Fifth Piano Concertos; the Violin Concerto; the three string quartets of Opus 59; fourteen piano sonatas; and many other of Beethoven's best-known scores.

With the single exception of the so-called "Battle" Symphony, or "Wellington's Victory," the years between 1813 and 1818 were largely unproductive ones—and there are those of us who would prefer to forget the "Battle" Symphony also. Beethoven composed it for the panharmonicon, an invention of Johann Nepomuk Mälzel, who also invented the metronome. The panharmonicon was a mechanical wind band and the Battle Symphony is an unconditional surrender to musical gimmickry. And yet there is something strangely reassuring in Beethoven's capitulation to circus pandering and his production of a score that surely must take pride of place in any chamber of musical horrors.

In 1817, the beginning of the last decade of his life, Beethoven began to work on two scores simultaneously. They were to occupy him uninterruptedly for the next six years, as he painfully scrubbed and polished each of them. The two works, the Ninth Symphony and the Missa Solemnis, are without parallel in their stature and nobility, their devotion to the spiritual qualities of humanity. By now his deafness was complete, and at the first performance of the Ninth Symphony in 1824, one of the singers had to turn him around so that he could see the clapping hands that he could not hear.

Soon after, Beethoven began to lead the life of a recluse. He began to appear in shabby clothing and once while walking in the country he was even arrested as a tramp. And yet it was during this period that his spirit seems to have undergone its ultimate purging: his appearance began to take on a beatific glow and the feeling of cosmic wisdom that pervades his last five string quartets (1824–26) shone through on his face. In 1825 he was described as follows: "Suffering, melancholy and goodness showed in his face, but not a sign of harshness."

In December 1826 Beethoven caught a chill in the raw winter weather as he was returning from a long visit with his nephew Karl, who had attempted suicide six months earlier. Pneumonia developed quickly and dropsy followed. To the doctors who three times tapped him and drew out the water Beethoven is supposed to have remarked, "Better from my belly than from my pen."

An illness of three months followed, and as news of his worsening condition spread, a steady stream of friends and well-wishers visited him. On March 16, 1827, his doctors despaired of saving him, and when a good bottle of Rhine wine arrived a week later from his publisher, Schott, Beethoven shook his head and murmured, "Pity, pity; too late." These were the last words he spoke. For three days he was locked in a fierce struggle with death. On the evening of March 26, 1827, there was a violent thunderstorm in Vienna. A particularly loud clap of thunder momentarily roused Beethoven from his coma. Bedside bystanders reported that he raised his right arm, clenched the fist and, with a very "earnest expression" in his eyes, shook the clenched fist back and forth several times. Then the arm fell back, and Beethoven was dead.

CONCERTO NO. 3 IN C MINOR FOR PIANO, OP. 37

In March 1795 a little more than two years after he had left his native Bonn to settle in Vienna, the twenty-four-year-old Ludwig van Beethoven made his first public appearance, in a charity concert. For the next five years he continued to compose, to teach and to play concerts. On April 2, 1800, Beethoven presented the first public concert in Vienna devoted wholly to his own music.

Until that time Beethoven had made his principal mark as a pianist. According to contemporary accounts, he was an extraordinary performer, with an ability to produce particularly subtle dynamic shadings and an awesome gift of improvisation. After that concert of April 1800, however, word spread quickly throughout Vienna that a striking new composer was beginning to assert himself. Over the next few years it was as a creative musician, rather than as a performer, that Beethoven captured the imagination of Viennese music connoisseurs.

During the year 1803, a rivalry developed between the two leading theaters in Vienna—the Kärntnertortheater, an imperial theater run by a Baron von Braun, and the Theater an der Wien, managed by Emanuel Schikaneder, author of the libretto for Mozart's *The Magic Flute*. The rivalry soon extended even to the hiring of the musical staffs of the two theaters. No sooner was Luigi Cherubini engaged for the staff of the Kärntnertortheater than Schikaneder went Baron von Braun one better by engaging none other than Beethoven for *his* theater, in the hope that some hitherto untapped operatic inspiration might be stimulated in Beethoven. Nothing much came of this hope, though it appears likely that during this period Beethoven did begin to think seriously of writing for the operatic stage. The most tangible result of Beethoven's appointment to the musical staff of the Theater an der Wien was the free residence he received at the theater and his opportunity to use the hall for another all-Beethoven program in April of 1803.

The program consisted of the first two symphonies, plus the first performances of the oratorio *Christ on the Mount of Olives*, and the Third Piano Concerto. The story goes that even on the day of the scheduled concert Beethoven had completed neither the oratorio nor the concerto. A rehearsal was scheduled for eight o'clock in the morning, and only three hours earlier Beethoven was still busy copying out the trombone parts of the oratorio. After a grueling six and a half hours of rehearsal, during which the orchestra members were scarcely given time to eat lunch, the concert began as scheduled at six o'clock in the evening.

Beethoven's friend Ignaz Ritter von Seyfried, who turned pages for the composer at the performance of the Third Concerto, has left a vivid account of the affair:

Heaven help me, turning the pages was easier said than done. I saw almost nothing but empty leaves; at the most on one page or the other a few Egyptian hieroglyphics wholly unintelligible to me scribbled down to serve as clues for him; for he played nearly all of the solo part from memory. He gave me a secret glance whenever he was at the end of one of the invisible passages and my scarcely concealed anxiety not to miss the decisive moment amused him greatly and he laughed heartily at the jovial supper which we ate afterwards.

The Third Concerto, in the words of Sir Donald Francis Tovey, is "one of the works in which we most clearly see the style of Beethoven's first period preparing to develop into that of his second." The opening orchestral statement is the longest of all Beethoven concerto tuttis, and Tovey characterizes it as "something that dangerously resembled a mistake" because the contours and key relationships established by the orchestra "rouse no expectation of the entry of a solo instrument." All is soon put right, however. "Suddenly the orchestra seems to realize that it has no right to take the drama into its own hands; that its function is not drama but choruslike narrative." When the solo piano enters, it does so with three ascending scale passages. Throughout the movement the music alternates between the dramatic and the lyrical; the form is bold, the outline, Romantic. The slow movement is a *Largo* whose principal subject is a broadly flowing melody that lends itself to intricate development. It is a profound movement that is deeply affecting. The last movement is a rollicking rondo, full of wit and energy and with an especially whimsical coda that brings a brilliant climax.

In its power and breadth and in the welding together of orchestra and solo instrument as partners in the musical discourse, the Third Concerto is an amazing advance over the gentler, more traditional format of the C Major Concerto (the No. 1) that Beethoven had revised in its final form only a year earlier.

Leon Fleisher's excellent disc edition of this concerto (formerly released by Epic Records) has been transferred to the Columbia label (M4X 30052, four discs), where it is part of a specially priced set devoted to the established five Beethoven piano concertos played by Fleisher with Szell and the Cleveland Orchestra. It remains one of the best of the available performances. A bold, vigorous, heroic account of the score is to be had from Barenboim, with Klemperer conducting the New Philharmonia Orchestra (Angel S 3752, four discs embracing the other four concertos and the *Choral Fantasy*). An unusually light-textured and intimate account is to be had from Gilels, with Szell and the Cleveland Orchestra (Angel S 36029)—by far the most successful of that team's integral account of the Beethoven concertos.

Among the reel-to-reel versions, the Rubinstein-Leinsdorf edition (RCA TR3 5038, 3¾ ips) has an impressive breadth and elegance; and in the cassette field, the Arrau-Haitink team (Philips 750 5006) delivers an impressively thoughtful and solid performance.

CONCERTO NO. 4 IN G MAJOR FOR PIANO, OP. 58

Beethoven completed his Fourth Piano Concerto in G Major in 1806, one of the most fantastically productive years during the composer's entire lifetime. To 1806 belong also the Fourth Symphony, the Violin Concerto, the Third Leonore Overture and the three "Rasoumovsky" String Quartets of Beethoven's Opus 59. As far as one can tell, the G Major Concerto was played only twice during Beethoven's lifetime and in both cases Beethoven himself was the soloist. The first occasion was at a private concert at the Palais

Lobkowitz in Vienna in March 1807, on a program that also included the *Coriolan* Overture and the composer's first four symphonies. (They went in for marathon concerts in those days!)

Nine months later Beethoven was organizing a public concert and he hoped to include the Fourth Concerto on the program, but with someone else playing the solo part. He turned first to Ferdinand Ries (who later was to write a biography of Beethoven), but the timid Ries tried to persuade Beethoven that there was not time enough for him to learn the new concerto. In anger Beethoven turned to another young protégé of his, Friedrich Stein. Stein took on the assignment and tried desperately to cope with the piece in five days. He gave up in despair on the eve of the concert, however, and at the last minute Beethoven's C Minor Concerto (the Third) had to be substituted. The Fourth Concerto was not performed again until the evening of December 22, 1808, when Beethoven again was the soloist. The concert was given at the Theater an der Wien in Vienna and included the first performances of several of Beethoven's most recent compositions—among them the Fifth and Sixth Symphonies and the *Choral Fantasy*. The occasion, incidentally, marked Beethoven's last public appearance as a piano virtuoso; he performed in subsequent years in some chamber music presentations, but the deafness that was rapidly enveloping him prevented any further solo appearances.

The piano concerto as an artistic expression had been brought to a pinnacle of perfection by Mozart in his many works in the form. Mozart's classical-formal design was the one followed by Beethoven in his own first three piano concertos: each begins with a lengthy statement of the essential musical materials from the orchestra, after which the solo instrument enters to comment upon the subject matter, to engage in dialogue with the orchestra, and—most importantly—to be the chief spokesman for the composer's deepest, most personal message. Early in his piano concertos Mozart did vary the format once: the Concerto in E-flat Major (K. 271) opens with a six-note orchestral flourish, whereupon the solo piano enters immediately to complete the phrase.

In his Fourth Piano Concerto Beethoven threw established tradition out the window in even more spectacular fashion. Instead of the usual opening orchestral statement, the music begins with five measures of subdued, lyrical contemplation from the solo piano in the "home" key of G major; then the orchestra enters, playing in the remote key of B major. But how sublimely Beethoven sets the mood of the concerto at the very start: this is to be music of quiet, personal introspection.

Following the pensive, chordal opening by the solo piano, and the answer and elaboration from the orchestra, the first movement emerges as a true dialogue between the two. The character throughout is one of friendly give-and-take; the mood is generally a gentle one, but there are episodes of contrasting drama and excitement. The slow movement, just seventy-two measures in length, is one of the great spiritual experiences in all music, with the stern, inflexible accents of the orchestra (strings only, in this movement) gradually softening before the gentle pleading of the solo piano. At the end of the movement the music arrives at a peace and serenity of ineffable beauty. The final movement is a joyous rondo of sparkling wit and prodigal inventiveness, yet possessing a warm poetic feeling that perfectly caps this marvelous artistic creation.

Many of us grew to know and love Beethoven's G Major Concerto from the recording made in the early 1930s by Artur Schnabel with Malcolm Sargent. A subsequent Schnabel recording made in this country about a decade later with Frederick Stock and the Chicago Symphony Orchestra failed to match the combination of lyrical grace and emotional sureness that distinguished Schnabel's earlier recording. In 1946, however, Schnabel recorded the concerto a third time (with the Philharmonia Orchestra conducted by Isaay Dobrowen). This last Schnabel recording is one of the treasures of the disc literature; intellectually and emotionally it is a deeply satisfying experience. Unfortunately, the termination of the Great Recordings of the Century series on the Angel label has removed from currency the Schnabel set of the Beethoven piano concertos. Will it return on the lower-priced Seraphim label? Only time will tell. In the meantime, RCA has reissued in its budget-priced Victrola line the wartime Schnabel-Stock recording of this work (VIC 1505, mono only). It is hardly the most representative example of Schnabel's playing, and the recorded sound is dim in the extreme.

Of the recordings of more recent vintage, the Barenboim-Klemperer collaboration (Angel S 3752, four discs, devoted to the four other concertos plus the *Choral Fantasy*) is a massive (some may say ponderous) account that will not be to everyone's liking. I find it sheds a new and by no means unwelcome light on this score. Other, more conventional but first-rate performances are those by Istomin-Ormandy (Columbia MS 7199) and Rubinstein-Leinsdorf (RCA LSC 2848).

The Rubinstein-Leinsdorf account is also available on a tape reel (RCA TR3 5019, 3¾ ips) and there is a good cassette version of the Kempff-Leitner performance (DGG 923014).

CONCERTO NO. 5 IN E-FLAT MAJOR FOR PIANO, OP. 73, "EMPEROR"

In May 1809 Austria was being invaded by the armies of Napoleon. The vanguard of the approaching French forces reached the outskirts of Vienna early in the month and an ultimatum was delivered to the Archduke Maximilian. When he refused to capitulate, the French set up a battery and, during the night of May 11, they opened fire on the city with twenty howitzers. The population of Vienna crowded into every available underground shelter as houses burst into flames and the streets were strewn with the wounded and the dead. Among those crouched in an underground cellar for protection against the all-night rain of shells was Ludwig van Beethoven, who half a dozen years earlier had inscribed a symphony to Napoleon and then had angrily withdrawn the inscription when the fanatic personal ambition of the Little Corporal became evident in the proclamation of himself as Emperor. Beethoven huddled in the cellar of his brother's house on the Rauhensteingasse, clutching a pillow to his deafened but still sensitive ears. The following afternoon Vienna surrendered and the forces of Napoleon began their occupation of the city.

In our own time occupation procedure has been refined to an exact science, but Napoleon, too, knew pretty well what to do in the circumstances. First, he set himself up in Schönbrunn Palace.

Then he had a deputy issue a proclamation assuring the Vienna populace of the warm humanitarianism of the Emperor Napoleon. After that soldiers of the victorious army were promptly billeted in every lodging in Vienna and high taxes levied against the inhabitants. Vienna's glorious parks were closed to the citizenry and a state of stern military occupation became the order of the day.

If ever external circumstances should have inhibited the creation of enduring works of art, the time was then. Yet it was against this very backdrop that Beethoven chiseled into a state of perfection three of his most significant compositions: the "Farewell" Piano Sonata; the "Harp" String Quartet, Opus 74; and the "Emperor" Piano Concerto. Significantly, all three works are in the tonality of E-flat major, a bold, noble, heroic key. Here, then, is another example—and the history of the arts is full of them—of the artist transcending his immediate environment and achieving his catharsis in the act of creation. The "Emperor" Concerto may be martial, imperious in its externals, but it is even more a radiant, superbly self-confident work which boldly proclaims the invincibility of the individual human spirit.

It was at the first performance of the work in Vienna, in February 1812, that a French soldier in the audience is supposed to have cried *"C'est l'Empereur!"* at an especially majestic passage. However the nickname "Emperor" happened to be tagged onto the music, the glamour of such a title has helped in no small measure to crystallize appreciative audience awareness of the work. Today, more than a century and a half after its creation, the "Emperor" Concerto remains a cornerstone of the repertoire, its lofty and exultant nobility a continuing and self-renewing phenomenon.

A singularly interesting aspect of the "Emperor" Concerto is to be found in its combination of classical nobility of utterance with its anticipation of virtuosic solo piano writing of a type most fully exploited by Franz Liszt some forty years later. Heretofore, the so-called virtuoso piano concerto had emphasized high-velocity running passagework, very much in the harpsichord tradition, and with little attention to the potentiality of the pianoforte for rich chordal textures and wide dynamics. Here in the "Emperor" Beethoven seems to have envisioned every possibility of the modern concert grand in all its glorious brilliance. We say envisioned, because there is no reason to believe that any piano Beethoven himself played on —save perhaps the English Broadwood given to him in his last years—could produce anything like the sounds we hear on today's high-fidelity recordings.

The concerto begins with three emphatic chords from the orchestra, each of which is followed by passages from the solo piano of extended and improvisatory virtuosity. Nearly a hundred measures follow in which the orchestra alone sets forth the two main themes of the first movement and elaborates upon them. From the moment when the piano re-enters until the conclusion of the movement, however, it is always in the forefront with a solo part of immense display. Beethoven wrote out his own cadenza right into the score in order to prevent any weaker interpolations.

The slow movement is relatively brief, and like the slow movement of the composer's Fourth Concerto it consists largely of a duet between the solo instrument and the orchestra. A hushed feeling of expectancy and tension is built up until finally, over a sustained horn note, the solo piano gives a soft intimation, still in slow tempo, of the exuberant theme of the rondo which then immediately erupts into a joyous and exultant statement. The movement proceeds in this brilliant fashion and ends in a glorious blaze of fireworks. Before the final flourish Beethoven introduces one of his most masterful inspirations of orchestral color: he pits the ruminating commentary and summation of the solo instrument against repeated soft strokes from the solo tympani. The effect is magical.

Though he lived for nearly twenty years after completing the "Emperor" Concerto, Beethoven never again returned to the concerto form. Did he feel that he had said all he had to say on the subject?

Strength is the one commodity indispensable to any noteworthy performance of the "Emperor" Concerto, and strength is the hallmark of several excellent recordings of the music: Fleisher-Szell (Columbia M4X 30052), Gieseking-Galliera (Seraphim 60069, stereo only), Fischer-Furtwängler (Odeon STE 90048, ASDW 9105), Horowitz-Reiner (RCA Victor LM 1718), Rubinstein-Leinsdorf (RCA LSC 2733) and Serkin-Bernstein (Columbia MS 6366).

The Serkin-Bernstein collaboration remains outstanding for brilliance, intensity and spontaneity. Both soloist and conductor are unabashedly overcome with the grandeur of the music. Serkin throws himself into the score shamelessly. The stentorian heroics of the concerto strike a particularly responsive chord in his make-up and he luxuriates in their re-creation. Completing the happy picture is sound reproduction that matches the vigor of the performance. And tape fanciers need settle for no other performance, for the Serkin-Bernstein version is one of the highlights of the Columbia tape catalog (MQ 489).

Of the several performances available to the cassette collector, my own nod would go to the RCA edition of the uneven but stimulating performance by Van Cliburn with Fritz Reiner and the Chicago Symphony Orchestra (RK 1008).

CONCERTO IN D MAJOR FOR VIOLIN, OP. 61

One of the exploited prodigies of the late eighteenth century was a child violinist named Franz Clement. From the age of nine Clement toured all over the continent of Europe as a Wunderkind. His accomplishments on the violin were solid enough to impress no less a figure than Beethoven, who wrote to the fourteen-year-old instrumentalist the following effusive letter in 1794:

Dear Clement,
Proceed along the path which you have hitherto trodden so splendidly and so gloriously. Nature and art vie in making you one of the greatest artists. Follow both, and you need not fear that you will fail to reach the great—the greatest goal on earth to which the artist can attain. Be happy, my dear young friend, and come back soon, so that I may hear again your delightful, splendid playing.
Wholly your friend,
L. v. Beethoven

Ten years later Beethoven and Clement were thrown together in very close association. Beethoven's opera Fidelio was given its first performance in Vienna in November 1805 at the Theater an der

Wien and the concertmaster of the orchestra was none other than Clement. After the *Fidelio* premiere, which proved to be less than a smashing success, a group of Beethoven's friends gathered at the residence of Prince Lichnowsky to discuss ways of salvaging the situation. One of those attending the meeting was Clement, whose chief contribution was apparently an impromptu performance of the entire *Fidelio* score from memory. The tenor, Joseph Röckel, who was also present, reported: "The extraordinary memory of Clement having been universally known, nobody was astonished by this. . . ."

The renewed friendship between Beethoven and Clement produced, in the following year, the work that has been called by Charles O'Connell "perhaps spiritually the richest of the four or five greatest works for the instrument"—Beethoven's Violin Concerto in D Major. It was written for Clement, who played its first performance in the Theater an der Wien in late December 1806. The story goes that Beethoven was so late in delivering the concerto that Clement had to play the part at sight at the premiere. That he was also not above a bit of charlatanism is indicated by another feat he is reported to have performed at the concert: the performance of a work of his own played while holding the violin upside down! Clearly Clement, were he alive today, would be a natural for the Ringling Bros. circus.

The concerto had a great popular success at its premiere, but there were some grumblings from critics caught unprepared to accompany Beethoven on his rarefied flight into the sublime. The publication *Theater zeitung* published this critique by one Johann Nepomuk Möser: "Concerning Beethoven's concerto, the judgment of connoisseurs is unanimous; its many beauties must be conceded, but it must also be acknowledged that the continuity is often broken, and that the endless repetitions of certain commonplace passages may easily become tedious to the listener." But successive generations of listeners have found Beethoven's Violin Concerto far from tedious, and it has become, by common agreement, the measure of all other violin concertos. Nowhere else in the literature for violin and orchestra is there a work to equal its radiant purity, glowing spirituality and disarming humor.

It remains to be added that in April 1807 Beethoven was visited in Vienna by Muzio Clementi, the composer-turned-publisher, who wished to secure exclusive English rights for the publication of a number of Beethoven's works. During the course of their negotiations Clementi suggested to Beethoven that he transcribe the violin concerto into a more salable concerto for piano and orchestra. Beethoven agreed to this and converted the work by the simple expediency of transferring the solo line, nearly intact, to the piano while leaving the orchestral parts absolutely unchanged. The one major innovation in the conversion was the first movement cadenza: in the piano concerto setting Beethoven wrote out a cadenza for the instrument that also employs a fanciful and highly effective tympani accompaniment. I have long harbored a pet project for some pension fund or other similar gala concert: the performance of the D Major Concerto in both its versions on the same program *played by the same artist*. No pianist I know could do it, but there are a number of violinists who might, among them Jascha Heifetz and Arthur Grumiaux. How about it, gentlemen?

The basic pattern of the entire first movement of the concerto is established immediately by five drum taps. This rhythm, measured and constantly recurring, sets the on-the-beat character insistently. The violin and orchestra have a running dialogue throughout the movement and there is a broad sweep to the over-all musical invention that is quite disarming. The slow movement, a sustained *Larghetto*, turns most of the principal thematic material over to the orchestra, with the solo instrument musing upon and embellishing the discourse with arabesques and other graceful ornaments. In the last movement, by contrast, the violin carries the main melodic interest. The principal theme of the movement has a folk-dance quality about it and since the form is a rondo, the theme is brought back many times. The end is pure bravura.

Tape collectors are at a disadvantage here: the only currently available version in the reel-to-reel format is a curiously disengaged performance by Christian Ferras with Karajan and the Berlin Philharmonic (DGG L 9021). Disc and cassette fanciers have a choice from among several distinguished performances: Francescatti and

Bruno Walter (Odyssey Y 30042) for tender, loving care; Stern and Bernstein (Columbia MS 6093) for impassioned but no less loving intensity; and Menuhin with Furtwängler (Seraphim 60135, mono only) for a highly personal, warmly Romantic account—all on disc. Cassette collectors' choicest options are between the fleet and chiseled performance by Heifetz with Munch and the Boston Symphony (RCA RK 1045) and the weightier—both intellectually and emotionally—version by Menuhin with Klemperer and the New Philharmonia Orchestra (Angel 4XS 36369).

PIANO SONATA NO. 14 IN C-SHARP MINOR, OP. 27, NO. 2, "MOONLIGHT"

Beethoven's "Moonlight" Sonata is far and away the most popular of his thirty-two works in this form. Indeed, it is probably the most popular piano sonata ever written. How did it get that way? To the German music critic and novelist Heinrich Friedrich Rellstab belongs no small measure of the credit, for it was he who tagged the sonata with its "Moonlight" title. Rellstab, for some reason, associated the sonata with Lake Lucerne—as if that lake had a particular and special kind of moonlight! Beethoven never even saw Lake Lucerne, and whatever subjective meaning the sonata may have had for him, an association with moonlight seems pretty farfetched. But the soubriquet has stuck through the years and the opening *Adagio sostenuto* is perhaps the single most familiar piece of concert music in the entire literature.

The "Moonlight" Sonata is the second of the two works for piano solo that make up Beethoven's Opus 27. They were completed in 1801, the year after the First Symphony; Beethoven called them both *Sonatas quasi una fantasia*—Sonatas like a fantasy. The description is apt, for in both works we find Beethoven rebelling against the classical concept of separate and individual movements. The poet-philosopher in Beethoven found these movement boundaries too restrictive; what he wanted was a continual flow from one movement to the next and so he marked an attacca from one movement to the next. The problem of form is more neatly solved in the "Moonlight" than in its companion piece. While it is the opening movement of the Opus 27, No. 2 that has stamped itself into the musical conscience of the civilized world, it is the Finale that is the remarkable crown of the conception. Here is a stormy, tumultuous outburst that heralds many another such *Sturm und Drang* explosion in the later sonatas.

The first movement, *Adagio sostenuto*, begins with its familiar undulating figure in the bass, followed soon by the prayer-like theme in the right hand. There is a middle section that changes the prevailing figuration but not the mood. There is a recapitulation and then a coda that draws upon some of the figures from the middle section.

The second movement, *Allegretto*, has properties of a scherzo. Its first section is a bright, easygoing melody that has a real feeling of exhilaration to it. The contrasting Trio is accented strongly off the beat, but in mood it is merely a continuation of the main *Allegretto* section.

The *Presto agitato* last movement is a headlong rush into the unknown. There are breathless arpeggio figures punctuated by an explosive accent at the end of each one. The entire exposition in this sonata-form movement is then repeated and there is a concise development of the material. There is a perfectly normal recapitulation and then an inventive, fanciful coda, which itself offers further development of some of the material and also includes a freewheeling cadenza. Passionate agitation and an irresistible forward drive are the hallmarks of this music; played well, it never loses its impact.

Until RCA released a performance of the sonata played by Artur Rubinstein in 1963, the pick of a very abundant "Moonlight" Sonata crop was the version recorded for Westminster (XWN 18255, mono only) by Egon Petri when the pianist was in his seventies. Though he never achieved the success in this country which his extraordinary musicianship merited, Petri nevertheless contributed to the repertoire of recorded piano music some of its most rewarding performances. His account of the "Moonlight" Sonata is distinguished by a commanding and solid nobility—akin somewhat to Klemperer's way with the symphonies. If Petri drops a note here and there, the playing is still admirable for its clean articulation, its well-shaped phrasing and the warmth of his personal involvement with the music.

Rudolf Firkusny and Vladimir Horowitz are two other pianists with arresting recorded accounts of the "Moonlight" Sonata to their credit. Firkusny plays impeccably and with a great deal of sensitivity and grace if without the nobility of Petri. Firkusny receives mellow sound reproduction (Pickwick S 4024). Horowitz presents a sensitively calculated and poetic account (RCA LM 2009, mono only), but the sound is unduly lifeless and cramped. (The performance stems from the period in the 1950s when Horowitz recordings were made in the pianist's living room.)

Two splendid accounts of the sonata are those by Ivan Moravec (Connoisseur Society CS/C 1566) and Rudolf Serkin (Columbia MS 6481). Both are fanciful, committed performances that are expertly played and recorded.

All of which leads us to the Rubinstein recording (RCA LSC 4001), which retains all its remarkable freshness and spontaneity. No other pianist communicates the subdued but passionate melancholy of the first movement with the force of Rubinstein; the second movement is all grace, charm and tenderness and the last movement is a whirlwind of blazing, kaleidoscopic motion. Rubinstein has contributed some of the most colossal recorded performances to the literature; nothing is more enduring than his playing of Beethoven's "Moonlight" Sonata. Now it has also been made available on a tape reel (RCA TR3 1016, 3¾ ips). Its eventual release as a cassette likewise seems assured. Until it is, though, cassette collectors should be content with the Serkin performance (Columbia 16 11 0088).

SYMPHONY NO. 1 IN C MAJOR, OP. 21

On the eve of his departure for Vienna in November of 1792 Beethoven's friend and benefactor Count Waldstein inscribed the following words to him:

Dear Beethoven! You are going to Vienna in fulfillment of your long-frustrated wishes. The Genius of Mozart is mourning and weeping over the death of her pupil. She found a refuge but no occupation with the inexhaustible Haydn; through him she wishes to form a union with another. With the help of assiduous labor you shall receive Mozart's spirit from Haydn's hands.

Whatever flowery emotions may have triggered Waldstein's sentiments, the words nevertheless do have about them the powerful ring of prophecy.

Vienna in the closing years of the eighteenth century was the unrivaled music capital of the world. Music was a vital part of the fabric of life there and the art was cultivated in its highest forms in the princely palaces of the aristocracy. Some of the more devoted nobles maintained their own orchestras and chamber music entertainments were regular features of the society. Beethoven spent the rest of his life in Vienna and there is no doubt that the prevailing artistic climate of the city helped to shape the Herculean development of Beethoven the creator.

For the first few years of his Vienna residence Beethoven concentrated upon his studies and the need to earn a livelihood. In short order, thanks to the introductions which Waldstein had given him, he succeeded in penetrating into the very core of Vienna's musical life. Stories of his lack of grace and roughhewn manner are legion, and yet he seems to have had a remarkable gift for inspiring devoted personal loyalty: the essential nobility of his character quickly attracted friends and admirers whose allegiance remained steadfast through the years.

Beethoven made his first public appearance in Vienna in March 1795 at a charity concert at which he played a piano concerto of his own—probably the B-flat Major Concerto (No. 2), which was a product of the years 1794—95. For the next five years Beethoven continued to compose, to teach and to play concerts; he also did a fair amount of traveling, with trips to Prague, Dresden and Berlin. It was on April 2, 1800, that Beethoven undertook his first concert in Vienna under his own auspices and for his own benefit. The concert, which began at 6:30, offered a veritable orgy of music. Consider this line-up:

1. Grand symphony by the late Kapellmeister Mozart.
2. Aria from Haydn's *The Creation*.
3. A grand concerto for piano, played and composed by Beethoven.
4. A septet for four strings and three wind instruments, composed by Beethoven and dedicated to Her Majesty, the Empress.
5. A duet from Haydn's *The Creation*.
6. Improvisation by Beethoven on Haydn's *Emperor's Hymn*.
7. A new grand symphony for full orchestra by Beethoven.

The final item on this formidable program was Beethoven's initial exercise in the form and format that over the ensuing quarter century he was to transform into the most noble and heroic in all music—the symphony.

A contemporary correspondent of the *Allgemeine Musikalische Zeitung* reported that Beethoven's "new grand symphony" contained "much art, and the ideas are abundant and original." The correspondent states further that "the wind instruments are used far too much, so that the music is more for a band of wind instruments than an orchestra." The critic chose to remain silent about another aspect of the symphony that must have been perplexing to its first hearers: its ambiguous hovering in two other tonalities (F and G) before the very opening settles comfortably into the "home" key of C major. Once we arrive at C major though, Beethoven insistently hammers the tonality home again and again. The second theme offers a contrasting, "feminine" quality that was to become a hallmark of Beethoven's symphonic style. The slow movement, marked *Andante cantabile*, focuses on a main theme that has been described as "kittenish." The third movement, a so-called Minuet, marks Beethoven's most significant break with symphonic tradition. Of this movement the great Beethoven enthusiast and biographer, Sir George Grove, wrote that the composer here abandoned the spirit of the minuet of his predecessors, "increased its speed, broke through its formal and antiquated mould, and out of a mere dance-tune produced a Scherzo, which . . . needs no increase of style or spirit to become the equal of those great movements which form such remarkable features in his later symphonies. . . . When he wrote this part of his First Symphony he took a leap into a new world." The last movement begins with five playful bars marked *Adagio* in which the violins play with fragments of an ascending scale before the body of the movement erupts in a joyous *Allegro molto*. The pace is brisk, the spirits high and the whole feeling is one of restless energy and motion. Beethoven's First Symphony is a vigorous, extroverted proclamation of a young but emerging composer intent upon placing his own stamp on his chosen art.

Two distinguished accounts of this score are by conductors no longer alive—but whose extraordinary powers of dynamic music-making live on imperishably in their recordings: Toscanini (RCA Victrola VICS 1654—electronic stereo) and Szell (included in his integral set of all the Beethoven symphonies: Columbia M7X 30281, seven discs). Toscanini's is one of the most successful of all his Beethoven symphony recordings. In addition to the well-known Toscanini virtues of clarity and hair-trigger precision, one finds here a relaxed good humor that did not always mark his music-making. The resulting performance has all about it an irresistible feeling of spontaneity. Szell's account of the score resembles Toscanini's in its basic outlines, with the exception that he doesn't seem to be having as much fun with the score as Toscanini did.

Another excellent recording of the symphony is available as conducted by Klemperer (Angel S 35657). Klemperer sees the score as a much more imposing one, and he successfully infuses it with his own special kind of weight and power. None of the above-mentioned performances exists either on tape or cassette. My recommendations in those departments, then, would be Ansermet's neat but rather prim account for the reel-to-reel collector (London J 80065) and Leinsdorf's efficient but routine performance (RCA RK 1149) in the cassette field.

SYMPHONY NO. 2 IN D MAJOR, OP. 36

Romantic chroniclers have often sought to establish a direct link between the prevailing circumstances of a composer's life at any given time and his creative output of the moment. Berlioz' *Symphonie fantastique* is for them an ideal instance: it was written in the white heat of the composer's unrequited love for the Irish actress Harriet Smithson (who did later become Madame Berlioz for a short time). Berlioz himself could not have been more explicit: in his memoirs he wrote that the *Symphonie fantastique* told "the history of my love for Miss Smithson, my anguish and my distressing dreams." For every such direct connection between life and creative endeavor, however, there are at least as many instances of the complete dissociation of a composer's personal circumstances from his artistic endeavors of the time. No more dramatic illustration exists than the Second Symphony of Ludwig van Beethoven, a vigorous, boisterous, confident score produced during the summer of 1802, when Beethoven's encroaching deafness led him to contemplate suicide.

During the summer of 1802, Beethoven poured out his anguish in the famous Heiligenstadt Testament, a document carefully sealed and labeled "to be read and executed after my death." In it he lamented his failing hearing in language so extravagant that there have been some who have tended to be skeptical of the depth of Beethoven's inner turmoil and to ascribe the document's emotional excesses to the inclination of a young Romantic toward self-dramatization. That the turmoil was real enough cannot be doubted, however; there are too many other evidences of his profound distress. His friend Ferdinand Ries wrote movingly of an episode that occurred one afternoon while the two of them were walking in the country.

On one of these wanderings Beethoven gave me the first striking proof of his loss of hearing, concerning which Stephan von Breuning had already spoken to me. I called his attention to a shepherd who was piping very agreeably in the woods on a flute made of a twig of elder. For half an hour Beethoven could hear nothing, and though I assured him that it was the same with me (which was not the case), he became extremely quiet and morose. When occasionally he seemed to be merry, it was generally to the extreme of boisterousness; but this happened seldom.

And in a letter to a friend in Bonn, Beethoven wrote:

I may truly say that my life is a wretched one. For the last two years I have avoided all society, for it is impossible for me to say to people "I am deaf." Were my profession any other, it would not so much matter, but in my profession it is a terrible thing: and my enemies, of whom there are not a few, what would they say to this?

Nevertheless, Beethoven continued to work at a feverish pace during 1802. "I live only in my music," he wrote, "and I have scarcely begun one thing when I start another. As I am now working, I am often engaged on three or four things at the same time." In addition to the Second Symphony, 1802 was the year of the three violin sonatas of Opus 30, the first two piano sonatas of Opus 31, the Opus 33 Bagatelles, the two sets of Variations (Opus 34 and Opus 35) and other works.

A vivid description of the "action" of Beethoven's Second Symphony was written by none other than Berlioz himself. These are the salient points:

In this symphony everything is noble, energetic, proud. The Introduction is a masterpiece. The most beautiful effects follow one another without confusion, and always in an unexpected manner. The song is of touching solemnity, and it at once commands respect and puts the hearer in an emotional mood. The rhythm is already bolder, the instrumentation richer, more sonorous, more varied. An Allegro con brio of enchanting dash is joined to this admirable Adagio. The Larghetto slow movement is not treated after the manner of the First Symphony. It is not composed of a theme worked out in canonic imitations, but is a pure and frank song, which at first is sung simply by the strings, and then embroidered with a rare elegance by means of light and fluent figures. Their character is never far removed from the sentiment of tenderness which forms the distinctive character of the principal idea. It is a ravishing picture of innocent pleasure, which is scarcely shadowed by a few melancholy accents. The Scherzo is as frankly gay in its fantastic capriciousness as the second movement has been wholly and serenely happy; for this symphony is smiling throughout; the warlike bursts of the first Allegro are wholly free from violence; there is only the youthful ardor of a noble heart in which the most beautiful illusions of life are preserved untainted. . . .

The closing movement is of like nature. It is a second Scherzo, in 2-2 time, and its playfulness has perhaps something still more delicate, more piquant.

The Second Symphony has fared extremely well on records over the years. In pre-LP and pre-stereo days there were excellent recordings of the score by such conducting giants as Sir Thomas Beecham, Serge Koussevitzky, Erich Kleiber and Fritz Reiner. Beecham's (Angel S 35509) and Bernstein's (Columbia MS 7084) are invigorating accounts of this rollicking score among the several currently available recordings of it. The Klemperer performance (Angel S 35658) seizes upon the heroic aspect of the score to make of it a remarkably invigorating experience. If I tend to favor the Beecham recording over all the others, it is perhaps because I have been listening to Beecham's interpretation of the music through successive recordings for more than three decades.

In the tape field, the choice is the same as prevails in the First Symphony: Ansermet's (London K 80057) for reel-to-reel enthusiasts and Leinsdorf's (RCA RK 1152)—by default—for the cassette collector.

SYMPHONY NO. 3 IN E-FLAT MAJOR, OP. 55, "EROICA"

"One of the most incomprehensible deeds in arts and letters, the greatest single step made by an individual composer in the history of the symphony and in the history of music in general," is the way Paul Henry Lang (in *Music in Western Civilization*) describes the work which sprang into Ludwig van Beethoven's consciousness and which occupied him through all of 1803 and into the following year. This, the mighty "Eroica" Symphony, is perhaps the most personal and characteristic work that Beethoven ever composed.

For the source of such a creative outburst, we must recall the spring of 1802, when a Dr. Schmidt suggested to the then thirty-two-year-old Beethoven that he take up lodgings in a quiet place where his failing hearing might be spared. The distraught composer thereupon rented a small peasant house in Heiligenstadt, a peaceful suburb of Vienna. Here was an ideal location; for in the mornings he could take long walks in the woods and meadows of the surrounding countryside and return refreshed to his music sketchbooks. He was alive with music that summer as never before. To a friend he wrote "I live only in my notes and when one composition is scarcely ended, another is already begun. As I work at present I am frequently occupied with three or four compositions at the same time."

To his friends Beethoven presented an outward appearance now high-spirited, now sullen; none knew, however, of the calamitous battle he was waging within himself: he had become aware that his deafness was a progressive and incurable affliction, that he was doomed to a life apart from his fellow men. Among the papers found after his death there was a large, folded sheet dated Heiligenstadt, October 10, 1802, and addressed to his two brothers, Karl and Johann, "to be read and executed after my death." This, the soul-baring Heiligenstadt Testament, tells of the composer's tortured state of mind. Near the end of the document is this significant sentence: "I almost reached the point of putting an end to my life —only art it was that held me back, ah, it seemed impossible to leave the world until I had brought forth all that I felt called upon to produce."

By Beethoven's own admission, then, it was the irresistible, Herculean drive to compose that saved him from suicide. Notebooks from that summer are full of sketches for much piano music, violin sonatas, and most important of all, the Second Symphony, which was completed at Heiligenstadt. Indeed, this work may have served as a catharsis for Beethoven, giving him an inner peace which allowed him "to take a new road." The "Eroica" Symphony was to be its most monumental milestone.

One can sympathize with the listener at the symphony's first public performance in April 1805 who is said to have shouted: "I'd give another kreutzer if the thing would only stop!" In length (the "Eroica" runs about twice as long as the average Haydn or Mozart symphony), in formal design, in complexity and in harmonic daring, the "Eroica" marks a complete break with the musical past. Much has been said and written about Beethoven's original dedication of the symphony to Napoleon Bonaparte, a dedication which was angrily withdrawn when the full impact of the fanatic personal ambition of the then First Consul impressed itself upon the composer. Now, more than 150 years after the events and circumstances surrounding its creation, the "Eroica" is seen to look far beyond Napoleon. Even the published dedication—"Heroic Symphony to celebrate the memory of a great man"—imposes a temporal and personal significance which the music itself far transcends. The "Eroica" is about *the* heroic, about how it can liberate mankind from inward and outward oppression. This is the message of the symphony—and of Beethoven. It is a message which sounds as a pedal point sustained throughout his entire output, whether the works be *Fidelio*, the *Egmont* music, or the Ninth Symphony.

In his first two symphonies Beethoven followed the Haydn pattern of prefacing the whole with a slow introduction. Not so in the "Eroica," however. Two imperious E-flat chords plunge us immediately into an atmosphere of nervous excitement. As more of the orchestra is brought into play, all the pent-up energy of the music is triumphantly unleashed. While broadly adhering to the outlines of sonata form, the architectural plan of the movement is of unprecedentedly vast proportions and the music seems to pour itself out in a white heat, as though a divine hand were behind its creation. In a movement replete with moments of magic, perhaps the greatest of all is the start of the recapitulation section, where the horns mysteriously sound the E flat of the returning "home" key against a lingering chord in the tremolo strings.

The slow movement, the famed Funeral March, opens with a sigh of utter desolation from the strings. The prevailing mood is one of heavy sorrow. The gloom is dispelled for a while with an oboe theme in the bright sunshine of C major, but the mood of the opening soon returns. Throughout the movement there is a repeated alternation of despair and hope until a deep and abiding sense of peace is finally realized in the coda.

With the Scherzo we return to the kinetic excitement of the first movement, but here it is a whispered, demonically controlled excitement. The horns, in three-part harmony, have the bulk of the contrasting Trio section to themselves. When the Scherzo proper returns, Beethoven exultantly does the unexpected: duple meter replaces the syncopation of an earlier passage. The effect is electric.

The Finale opens with an exuberant flourish in the full orchestra, which is followed by the bass of the theme to come, assigned to the strings, pizzicato. When the theme itself appears, it turns out to be one that Beethoven had used three times previously: in the ballet *The Creatures of Prometheus*, as one of the set of twelve contra-dances, and as the basis for the piano Variations, Opus 35. Out of this theme there grows a tremendous set of variations which culminate in a long and pensive slow section. The end is a brilliant repeat of the movement's opening flourish followed by a triumphant outburst of brass and tympani.

Over the years the "Eroica" has been recorded and re-recorded by every major conductor (and some minor ones!) of the past half century. Notable performances have been recorded by Klemperer (Angel 35328—his first one, mono only, not to be confused with his later and less good stereo version), Toscanini (RCA Victrola VICS 1655), Szell (included in Columbia M7X 30281) and Walter (Columbia MS 6036). But my own favorites among the many "Eroica" recordings are the performances conducted by Barbirolli (Angel S 36461), Bernstein (Columbia MS 6774) and Schmidt-Isserstedt (London CS 6483). Barbirolli's, in fact, is the finest "Eroica" performance I have ever heard, on or off records: it is noble, visionary and truly heroic, with playing and recorded sound to match. The performance has lost none of its power and impact with the passage of time. If anything, its stature has grown as far as I'm concerned. Bernstein, too, turns in one of the best performances of his career, despite a first movement tempo that seems rather too brisk for the over-all concept. From the Funeral March onward, however, this is a deeply moving and committed performance, extremely well played by the New York Philharmonic and superbly recorded by the Columbia engineers. Schmidt-Isserstedt's is also deeply satisfying, supremely well played by the Vienna Philharmonic Orchestra and with rich, warm sound reproduction.

Happily, Angel has made Barbirolli's performance available in all three reproduction configurations: disc S 36461; tape L 36461; and cassette 4XS 36461. These are first choice, unquestionably, but for an alternate tape choice there is Bernstein's (Columbia MQ 775).

SYMPHONY NO. 4 IN B-FLAT MAJOR, OP. 60

It has often been remarked that Beethoven's even-numbered symphonies represent their creator in his gentler, softer aspect, and the odd-numbered ones represent the fist-shaking, heaven-storming Beethoven. It is almost as if some inner compulsion demanded a kind of equilibrium as he moved from one symphony to the next, the balancing of fiery and defiant passion with easier, more lyrical expression. And it may be significant that, although in 1805 Beethoven drafted two movements of a symphony in C minor, which ultimately became part of his Fifth, he set them aside and devoted himself in the following year to the more relaxed contours of the B-flat Major Symphony, published in 1806 as his Fourth.

Robert Schumann characterized Beethoven's Fourth Symphony as a "Greek maiden between two Norse giants"—referring, of course, to the two colossal symphonies on either side of the Fourth, the "Eroica" and the Fifth. Though the Fourth Symphony may present a more serene countenance than the two flanking it, it is nonetheless a work of astonishing power and freshness. Hector Berlioz wrote a perfect description of the score: "The character is generally lively, nimble, joyous, or of a heavenly sweetness." Beethoven's biographer A. W. Thayer referred to the "placid and serene Fourth Symphony —the most perfect in form of them all." And that irrepressible Beethoven enthusiast Sir George Grove found in the symphony "something extraordinarily *entraînant*—a more consistent and attractive whole cannot be. . . . The movements fit in their places like the limbs and features of a lovely statue; and, full of fire and invention as they are, all is subordinated to conciseness, grace and beauty."

A popular Romantic theory of the late nineteenth century tied the

Fourth Symphony to the mysterious "Immortal Beloved" to whom
Beethoven pledged his undying love in his diaries and notebooks.
Beethoven spent much of the summer of 1806 visiting his friend the
Count of Brunswick at his ancestral estate in Martonvásár, Hungary.
Among the adornments at Martonvásár were the Count's sisters,
Therese, Josephine and Caroline. Beethoven was especially charmed
by Therese and Josephine ("Tesi" and "Pepi"), and there has even
been speculation that he and Therese became engaged during that
summer; the slow movement of the Fourth Symphony has been
seen by some as the composer's declaration of love for her.

Subsequent examination of Therese von Brunswick's diaries, however, has revealed that there was nothing more between her and
Beethoven than a deep and abiding mutual esteem. Josephine, on
the other hand, is mentioned by Therese as evincing a rather "dangerous" interest in the composer; this testimony has been taken by
some to indicate that it must have been Josephine whom Beethoven
called his "Immortal Beloved."

Whatever may be the truth about Beethoven's emotional involvement at the time, the summer at Martonvásár was perhaps the calm-
est period in the composer's life. Days and nights were spent in
joyful communion with dear friends, and the beauty of the estate
and the surrounding countryside is echoed in the pages of the symphony then in the making.

An air of mystery pervades the expansive introduction to the first
movement, but when the principal theme explodes in a vigorous
ascending scale passage the mood quickly changes to one of boisterous exuberance. Throughout the remainder of the movement the
prevailing feeling is one of joyous merriment. The second movement, an *Adagio*, is a broadly lyrical song with an undulating
rhythmic pulse that gives the music a constant forward impetus. It
is music of calm serenity for the most part, with particularly infectious sections scored for the bassoon and the tympani. The third
movement is a rustic Scherzo that has a rollicking, bouncy quality.
As was to be the case in the Seventh Symphony, Beethoven repeats
the Trio section twice and the Scherzo proper is repeated each time.
The last movement is a playful *Allegro* with whirring figures and

infectious gaiety. The scoring is light in texture but rich in over-all impact. The symphony ends with a slower reminiscence of the bustling theme that opened the last movement, followed by a vigor-ous sequence of peremptory chords.

The first great recording of the Fourth Symphony appeared in the mid-1930s, a performance by the BBC Symphony Orchestra con-ducted by Arturo Toscanini. On these eight 78-rpm sides (RCA Victor album 676) the distinguished conductor, then at the height of his powers, shaped a reading of total communication, the orchestra's musicians outdid themselves, and the British recording engineers in this and other London-originated recordings of the time gave Tosca-nini the finest sound reproduction he was to enjoy for years. The one catch was that Toscanini refused to accommodate the musical con-tinuity to the break imposed every four and a half minutes or so by the limitations of the 78-rpm recording process. The result was that the original issue of the performance had several very abrupt side breaks. To celebrate the centennial year of Toscanini's birth in 1967, Angel Records collected together many of the Toscanini-BBC Sym-phony recordings and issued them on its budget-priced Seraphim line (IC 6015, three discs, mono only). Included in the album are the Toscanini-BBC Symphony performances of three Beethoven sym-phonies, the First, Fourth and Sixth. In the Fourth, the abrupt side changes of the original 78s have been joined together by tape editing and the performance has a dazzling quality of impetuosity—and the slow movement a serenity—that is quite remarkable. This is one of the finest of all Toscanini recorded performances—demonstra-bly superior to his later recording of the symphony with the NBC Symphony Orchestra—and I recommend it wholeheartedly.

Of the other recordings available, there are several that are first-class: Ansermet (London STS 15055), Ormandy (included in the set of his complete recordings of the Beethoven symphonies—Colum-bia D7S 745), Steinberg (Command 11016SD), Szell (included in Columbia M7X 30281) and Walter (included in Odyssey Y7 30051). All these conductors bring to their performances a healthy and extro-verted vigor, and all are very well recorded. The Ansermet and Ormandy performances may be the surprises among the lot, for whatever other good qualities these conductors have, they are not generally considered to be among the leading Beethoven conductors of our day. Yet both deliver readings of the Fourth Symphony that are extremely winning, sensitive and satisfying.

Ansermet's (London K 80057) is the recommended tape version, with Leinsdorf's (RCA RK 1154) the cassette nomination.

SYMPHONY NO. 5 IN C MINOR, OP. 67

The six years between 1806 and 1812 were astonishingly productive ones in the output of Beethoven. To these years belong five symphonies (Nos. 4 through 8); the Fourth and Fifth ("Emperor") Piano Concertos; the Violin Concerto; the Mass in C Major; the *Coriolan* Overture; the Incidental Music to Goethe's *Egmont*; and a whole body of sonatas, including the most famous of those for piano solo and violin and piano.

Until 1808, despite his growing deafness, Beethoven continued to make public appearances as a pianist. During the Christmas season of 1808 Beethoven made what was to be his final concert appearance, playing the first performance of his Fourth Piano Concerto at a marathon concert in Vienna's Theater an der Wien. Like the concert in Vienna's National Court Theater in April 1800 that served to introduce Beethoven's First Symphony to the world, this one, too, began at 6:30 in the evening and was of elephantine proportions. In addition to the Fourth Piano Concerto the audience was also regaled by these other Beethoven compositions: the Choral Fantasy for piano solo, chorus and orchestra (described in the program as a work into which "the full orchestra enters little by little and at the end the chorus joins in the Finale"); the aria *Ah, Perfido!*; excerpts from the C Major Mass; a Fantasy for piano solo; and the first performances of two new symphonies by Beethoven—the Fifth and Sixth.

Even when it was new, the Fifth caught the fancy of performers and listeners alike. Something about the onrushing drive, the compelling energy of the first movement converted even the anti-

Beethovenites. In its triumphant struggle to ultimate victory, its absolute logic at once massive and compact, its confident swagger and heroism, this symphony has served as a clarion call to victory over tyranny through the years. Surely there is a kind of divine coincidence in the fact that the rhythmic motive that is at the heart of the entire symphony—three short beats and one long one—should also be the international Morse code symbol for the letter "V." During the years of the Second World War this symbolism was seized upon by the Allied powers and the opening notes of Beethoven's Fifth Symphony became the musical embodiment of the impending victory. Similarly, when the Israel Philharmonic Orchestra played a victory concert in Jerusalem to celebrate the unification of the city and the imposition of a cease fire following the lightning Six-Day Arab-Israeli War in June 1967, Beethoven's Fifth Symphony was the central work on the program.

The entire first movement of the symphony evolves from the opening four-note motto. The headlong rush pursues a relentless course to the very end of the movement; matter and ideas are reduced to their absolute essence and a pervading inevitability takes hold of the entire structure. Contrasting with the stark brusqueness of the first movement is the confident song of the second movement, marked *Andante con moto*. This is a gentler, more lyrical music but no less heroic in its cast and outlook. The pulse quickens near the end and a mood of a mystery is introduced, but then at the very end of the movement the prevailing atmosphere of bold triumph returns again. The third movement, the Scherzo, opens with the strings and winds rather ambiguously tossing phrases back and forth. Then suddenly the motto rhythm reappears in a dynamic proclamation from the horns and the movement is off on its course cutting a triumphant swath through the underbrush. The music subsides to a whisper at the end of the movement before Beethoven then slowly builds to a shattering crescendo from which emerges uninterruptedly the ultimate and triumphant hymn that forms the main musical material for the last movement. The end of the symphony is one of unquestioned glory and ecstasy, and Beethoven hammers the point home with repeated chords of triumph at the conclusion.

One of the most unreconstructed of Beethoven's antagonists during the early years of the nineteenth century was Lesueur, a professor of music at the Paris Conservatory. When he was finally persuaded by the youthful Berlioz, one of his pupils, to listen to Beethoven's Fifth Symphony, Lesueur was overcome: "Ouf! Let me get out!" he exclaimed. "I must have air. It is unbelievable! Marvelous! It has so upset and bewildered me that when I wanted to put on my hat, *I could not find my head!*"

Beethoven's Fifth Symphony has sent men's heads and emotions spinning for more than a century and a half now. It will continue to do so, assuredly, for as long as mankind responds to artistic creation.

The finest performance of Beethoven's Fifth Symphony I have ever heard, on or off records, is the 1953 recording of the score made by Erich Kleiber and the Amsterdam Concertgebouw Orchestra. Released originally on the London label, the recording was out of circulation for some years during the 1960s but it was then reissued on London's budget-priced Richmond label (19105, mono only). The sonics are now pretty shopworn, but the impact of Kleiber's performance remains undiminished. Here is a fine sense of proportion, a plastic molding of phrase and a keen dramatic urgency which never descends to nervous hysteria. But the performance has now once again been withdrawn, though an occasional copy may still be found on dealers' shelves.

Admittedly, the Kleiber recording will not satisfy the listener in search of up-to-date, stereo sound. My own choice among all the stereo versions is the performance by Fritz Reiner and the Chicago Symphony Orchestra. The tape of Reiner's performance is no longer available (RCA FTC 2032), but otherwise one can have Reiner's driving, headlong account of this most popular of all symphonies in any one of three different configurations: disc (RCA LSC 2343); eight-track cartridge (RCA R8S 1005); and cassette (RCA RK 1005). A recommended alternate choice is the Stokowski recording—a remarkable example of this conductor's unique ability to find fresh meaning in even the most overplayed repertoire. Stokowski's performance is available every which way: disc (London SPC 21042); tape (London L 75042); eight-track cartridge (London M 95042); and cassette (London M 94042).

SYMPHONY NO. 6 IN F MAJOR, OP. 68, "PASTORAL"

When Beethoven's first three piano sonatas were published in Vienna in 1796, the printed edition carried an advertisement for a "Grand Symphony" subtitled "A Musical Portrait of Nature" by a Swabian composer named Justin Heinrich Knecht. The symphony by Knecht had first been published about a dozen years earlier, and Sir George Grove has speculated that Beethoven "must often have read Knecht's suggestive titles on the cover of his own sonatas. If so, they lay dormant in his mind . . . until 1808." This was the year in which Beethoven turned from the tension and drama of his Fifth Symphony and composed his own musical portrait of nature— the Sixth, or "Pastoral," Symphony.

There would seem to be little doubt that Beethoven was influenced, at least subconsciously, by the general programmatic scheme that Knecht had outlined for his five movements:

1. A beautiful countryside where the sun shines, the soft breezes blow, the streams cross the valley, the birds twitter, a cascade murmurs; a shepherd pipes, the sheep leap, and the shepherdess lets her gentle voice be heard.

2. The heavens are suddenly darkened, all breathe with difficulty and are afraid; the black clouds pile up, the wind makes a rushing sound, the thunder growls from afar, the storm slowly descends.

3. The storm, with noise of wind and driving rain, roars with all its force; the tops of the trees murmur, and the torrent rolls down with a terrifying sound.

4. The storm is appeased little by little; the clouds scatter, and the sky clears.

5. Nature, in a transport of gladness, raises its voice to heaven, and gives thanks to its Creator in soft and agreeable song.

Beethoven's program is considerably less detailed in its reference to particular sights and sounds, but it does have a similar pattern:

1. Awakening of serene impressions on arriving in the country.
2. Scene by the brookside.

3. Jolly gathering of country folk.
4. Thunderstorm; tempest.
5. Shepherd's song: gladsome and thankful feeling after the storm.

It is interesting to note that Beethoven scaled his instrumental forces in the "Pastoral" Symphony to suit the basic mood of each movement. The first two movements, with their serenity and un-ruffled calm, call into play only the woodwinds and strings, with no brass except for the horns and no percussion. In the Scherzo the texture is brightened by the addition of a trumpet. A piccolo and two trombones, instruments that Beethoven used in a symphony for the first time when he wrote his Fifth, heighten the effect of the storm music in the fourth movement of the "Pastoral," and the trombones are retained, but used sparingly, in the final movement. The tympani make their only appearance in the "Pastoral" in the fourth movement, where Beethoven uses them to evoke the rolls and claps of thunder. Beethoven was later, in "Wellington's Victory," to indulge in blatant pictorialization, but in the "Pastoral" Sym-phony his means are at once more subtle and more effective.

Berlioz, that incurable Romantic, wrote a highly personal and fanciful blow-by-blow description of the mood and character of Beethoven's Sixth Symphony:

First Movement—This astonishing landscape seems as if it were the joint work of Poussin and Michelangelo. The composer of *Fidelio* and of the *Eroica* wishes in this symphony to depict the tranquillity of the country and the peaceful life of shepherds. The herdsmen begin to appear in the fields, moving about with their usual nonchalant gait; their pipes are heard afar and near. Ravishing phrases caress one's ears deliciously, like perfumed morning breezes. Flocks of chattering birds fly overhead; and now and then the atmosphere seems laden with vapors; heavy clouds flit across the face of the sun, then suddenly disappear, and its rays flood the fields and woods with torrents of dazzling splendor. These are the images invoked in my mind by hearing this movement; and I fancy that, in spite of the vagueness of instrumental expression, many hearers will receive the same impressions.

Second Movement—Next is a movement devoted to contempla-tion. Beethoven without doubt created this admirable scene while reclining on the grass, his eyes uplifted, ears intent, fascinated by the thousand varying hues of light and sound, looking at and listening at the same time to the scintillating ripple of the brook that breaks its waves over the pebbles of its shores. How delicious this music is!

Third Movement—In this movement the poet leads us into the midst of a joyous reunion of peasants. We are aware that they dance and laugh, at first with moderation; the oboe plays a gay air, accompanied by a bassoon, which apparently can sound but two notes. Beethoven doubtless thus intended to evoke the picture of some good old German peasant, mounted on a cask, and playing a dilapidated old instrument, from which he can draw only two notes in the key of F, the dominant and the tonic. Every time the oboe strikes up its musette-like tune, fresh and gay as a young girl dressed in her Sunday clothes, the old bassoon comes in puffing his two notes; when the melodic phrase modulates, the bassoon is silent perforce, counting patiently his rests until the return of the original key permits him to come in with his imperturbable F, C, F. This effect, so charmingly grotesque, generally fails to be noticed by the public. The dance becomes animated, noisy, furious. The rhythm changes; a melody of grosser character, in duple time, announces the arrival of the mountaineers with their heavy *sabots*. The section in triple time returns, still more lively. The dance becomes a medley, a rush; the women's hair begins to fall over their shoulders, for the mountaineers have brought with them a bibulous gayety. There is clapping of hands, shouting; the peasants run, they rush madly . . . when a muttering of thunder in the distance causes a sudden fright in the midst of the dance. Surprise and consternation seize the dancers, and they seek safety in flight.

Fourth Movement—I despair of being able to give an idea of this prodigious movement. It must be heard in order to appreciate the degree of truth and sublimity which descriptive music can attain in the hands of a man like Beethoven. Listen to those gusts of wind, laden with rain; those sepulchral groanings of the basses; those shrill whistles of the piccolo, which announce that a fearful tempest is about to burst. The hurricane approaches, swells; an immense chromatic streak, starting from the highest notes of the orchestra, goes burrowing down into its lowest depths, seizes the basses, carries them along, and ascends again, writhing like a whirlwind which levels everything in its passage. Then the trombones burst forth; the thunder of the tympani redoubles its fury. It is no longer merely a wind and rain storm: it is a frightful cataclysm, the universal deluge, the end of the world. Truly, this produces vertigo and many persons listening to this storm do not know whether the emotion they experience is pleasure or pain.

Fifth Movement—The symphony ends with a hymn of gratitude. Everything smiles. The shepherds reappear; they answer each other on the mountain, recalling their scattered flocks; the sky is serene; the torrents soon cease to flow; calmness returns, and with it the rustic songs whose gentle melodies bring repose to the soul after the consternation produced by the magnificent horror of the previous picture.

The history of the "Pastoral" Symphony on records is, in its most significant aspects, a chronicle of Bruno Walter's way with the score. There once existed a Victor black-label album (G-20, long discontinued) recorded in the 1930s that preserved a performance in which Walter conducted the Vienna Philharmonic Orchestra. His reading was ideal: serene and simple, and obviously the product of loving identification with the music. In 1946 Walter re-recorded the symphony for Columbia with the Philadelphia Orchestra; the reading was basically the same as the earlier one, but the Philadelphia players were not so sensitively responsive to his beat as the Viennese had been, nor was the recorded sound anything exceptional. Nevertheless, the Walter-Philadelphia recording had values that made it the best available "Pastoral" for about a dozen years—until Walter once more re-recorded the symphony, this time on the West Coast with the hand-picked orchestra that Columbia assembled for his recording sessions during the last four or five years of his life. More successfully than any other conductor in my experience, Walter was able to deal with the gentle, lyrical aspects of the symphony without making them sound slightly namby-pamby. Walter's third recording of the "Pastoral" Symphony (included in Odyssey Y7 30051) is one of the great accomplishments in the history of the art and I recommend it without qualification. Another fine performance of the symphony, though not quite on the same level of high inspiration, is the Pierre Monteux-Vienna Philharmonic account (London STS 15161). Monteux is sensitive to the subtle shadings of nuance and balance, and his reading is distinguished by serenity and sure command. The orchestra plays the music magnificently, as it probably always has, but the recorded sound is neither as vivid nor brilliant as that accorded Walter.

Close on the heels of the Walter and Monteux performances is a recent recording by the Vienna Philharmonic Orchestra conducted by Karl Böhm (Deutsche Grammophon 2530 142). Since none of the three is available on reel-to-reel tape or cassette, however, one must look elsewhere for versions in these configurations. Ansermet's (London K 80052) is my preferred tape edition from among the three available—he, too, responds intuitively to the simplicity and relaxation of the music. And Klemperer's strongly personalized account would be my recommendation in the cassette format (Angel 4XS 35711).

SYMPHONY NO. 7 IN A MAJOR, OP. 92

After producing six symphonies in the years between 1800 and 1808, Beethoven waited four more years before giving the world his next one. When he again turned to the symphony, he was secure in his fame and his fortunes were prospering. It was during the summer of 1812 that Beethoven finished his Seventh Symphony, but it was not until the end of the following year that the music was performed for the first time, with Beethoven himself doing the conducting.

The affair was a charity concert, with the proceeds going to benefit the "Austrians and Bavarians wounded at Hanau" while defending their native country against the armies of Beethoven's one-time hero, Napoleon. The concert featured Beethoven's new A Major Symphony and "Wellington's Victory."

The *Allegretto* of the A Major Symphony met with enthusiasm at that first performance, but it was "Wellington's Victory"—its topical interest further compounded by the inflammatory drum rolls and fanfares of Beethoven's music—which roused the audience to a wild and abandoned ecstasy. Today we regard "Wellington's Victory" (or the Battle Symphony as it is also sometimes called), as a laughable if not ridiculous potboiler. But the A Major Symphony long ago came to be recognized for what it is: one of those astonishing works of art so universal and transcendent in its communicative intensity that one has no other choice but to conclude that the hand of its creator was guided by a higher power.

Though the symphony is scored for the standard classical symphony orchestra (woodwinds in pairs, two trumpets, tympani and strings), and is not particularly imposing as to length (thirty-seven–thirty-eight minutes is a good average time, though some conductors get through it in about thirty-four minutes), it nevertheless conveys a feeling of immensity. John N. Burk has written that "Beethoven seems to have built up this impression by wilfully driving a single rhythmic figure through each movement, until the music attains (particularly in the body of the first movement and in the Finale) a swift propulsion, an effect of cumulative growth which is akin to extraordinary size."

And yet this is only one aspect of the Seventh Symphony. An element too easily forgotten is its soaring lyricism, even in the Finale, where the irresistible forward motion is carried along on the wings of a melody of sheer exuberance and drive. And the architectural proportions of the symphony are awesome in their inevitable rightness. Wagner called the symphony "the Dance in its highest conditions; the happiest realization of the movements of the body in an ideal form." The parallel is an apt one; the fluid and easy motion of an athlete's body finds its counterpart in the organic unity, perfect integration and finely honed tooling of Beethoven's Seventh Symphony.

The symphony begins with another long, slow introduction. The second theme of this introduction, first played by the solo oboe, is one of Beethoven's most engaging melodies. The main body of the movement is dominated by the dotted rhythmic figure that is first heard from the solo flute. This first movement exudes a tripping, dance-like quality.

The second movement, mainly in the minor, opens on a long-held, ambiguous inverted chord, and then the main theme appears, stated first in the violas, cellos and basses. The movement, with its serene and solemn dignity, has been likened to a procession in the catacombs.

The third movement is an ebullient Scherzo (though it is not so marked). The Trio, which is repeated twice, has as its main thematic material a melody that Beethoven appropriated from the pilgrims' hymn of Lower Austria, according to the French composer and teacher Vincent d'Indy.

The last movement almost bursts at the seams with energy and rhythmic vitality. D'Indy likened this music to the rough merrymaking at a peasants' celebration; others have compared the movement to a Bacchanalian revel. Whatever metaphor suggests itself, this movement is one of the great whoops in symphonic literature.

The finest of the currently available recordings of the Seventh Symphony is Bruno Walter's, for my taste—but apparently it is no longer available as a single disc; instead, one must purchase the seven-disc Odyssey album (Y7 30051) devoted to Walter's performances of all nine Beethoven symphonies if one wishes to acquire the conductor's blend of athletic vigor and dynamism in the Seventh. Walter's pacing of the music throughout is masterful and he builds to a final movement of overwhelming buoyancy and *élan*. Though a relatively early product of stereo recording technology, the sound is still eminently satisfying.

Also commendable are the versions by Bernstein (Columbia MS 6112) and Steinberg (Command 11014SD). Among the most uniformly recommendable of currently listed performances is Reiner's (RCA LSC 1991; cassette RCA RK 1150)—a beautifully crafted performance with an exciting spark of kinetic energy. Among the four available reel-to-reel releases, Ansermet's (London K 80052) is for me the most satisfying.

SYMPHONY NO. 8 IN F MAJOR, OP. 93

Listening to the effervescent Eighth Symphony of Beethoven, one might imagine that the score represented a particularly happy time in Beethoven's life. Such was not the case. The Eighth Symphony is a product of the summer of 1812. What was Beethoven's life like during those months? He suffered from a persistent digestive ailment and rushed from one spa to another in hopes of easing his discomfort: in July he was in Töpliz, in August he went to Karlsbad and then to Franzensbad, but he felt no better in either place, and so it was back to Töpliz once again. In late September, Beethoven impulsively decided to hie himself off to Linz and meddle in the affairs of his brother Johann. It seems that that worthy gentleman had entered into an alliance with a young lady of whom Beethoven thoroughly disapproved. Once in Linz, he voiced his objections to the situation in no uncertain terms. Johann, in effect, responded that it was a joy to have his older brother visit him—but the circumstances of his personal life were his own concern. In a rage, Beethoven then went to the police and to the bishop and arranged for the forcible expulsion from Linz of the errant young lass. Johann, however, foiled the plan by marrying the girl—and for the rest of his life he was able to blame his brother for forcing him into an unfortunate marriage!

Beethoven's presence in Linz was the cause of considerable local pride. Early in October a musical journal in Linz wrote: "We have had the long-wished-for pleasure of having within our metropolis for several days the Orpheus and greatest musical poet of our time . . . and if Apollo is favorable to us, we shall also have an opportunity to admire his art and report upon it to the readers of this journal." A few days after this story appeared, Beethoven completed the symphony he had begun some weeks earlier in Töpliz and worked on in Karlsbad. It was, of course, his Eighth, but it was not in Linz that the symphony had its premiere; rather, some sixteen months elapsed before the score was finally performed for the first time, in Vienna.

Only four months passed between the completion of the Seventh Symphony and that of the Eighth; for Beethoven this was a remarkably short time. Four years had intervened between the Sixth and Seventh, and a full decade was to pass before Beethoven set himself to work in earnest on his Ninth. The Seventh and Eighth, then, can be said to constitute a pair in Beethoven's output. The English pianist, composer and music historian Sir Donald Francis Tovey wrote: "The Eighth Symphony reflects the unique sense of power which fires a man when he finds himself fit for a delicate task just after he has triumphed in a colossal one." Comparing the Seventh and Eighth Symphonies, Richard Wagner wrote:

> Nowhere is there greater frankness, or freer power, than in the Symphony in A [the Seventh]. It is a mad outburst of superhuman energy, with no other object than the pleasure of unloosing it like a river overflowing its banks and flooding the surrounding country. In the Eighth Symphony the power is not so sublime, though it is still more strange and characteristic of the man, mingling tragedy with force and a Herculean vigor with the games and caprices of a child.

Beethoven himself called his Eighth Symphony "my little symphony in F," but he was infuriated when the public reception of it was lukewarm compared with the wide enthusiasm for the Seventh. In a fit of pique he said that the Eighth was "much better" than the Seventh. "Better" than the Seventh it is not, but it is completely disarming on its own robust and exuberant terms. In the words of Pitts Sanborn, who used to write the program notes for the concerts of the New York Philharmonic, it is a symphony of laughter—"the laughter of a man who has lived and suffered and, scaling the heights, achieved the summit."

The symphony plunges immediately into the rollicking tune that sets the character of the entire work. This is to be a symphony of sunshine and joy. The second theme is an amiable tune built on an upward-rising sequence. The mood of joyful merrymaking is carried through to the end of the movement.

The second movement has a constant ticking rhythm which once gave rise to the legend that Beethoven wrote it as a tribute to Johann Maelzel, the inventor of the metronome. Whether or not there is any substance to the legend is really of no consequence; what *is* important is the fact that the music is one of the most disarming sections in Beethoven's entire orchestral output. Berlioz wrote of this movement: "It is one of those productions for which neither model nor pendant can be found. This sort of thing falls entirely from heaven into the composer's brain."

In the third movement, Beethoven returns to the stately outlines of the eighteenth-century minuet and abandons, for the moment,

the Scherzo that had been such an indispensable part of his previous symphonies. Unlike the symphonic Minuet in his First Symphony, the Minuet in the Eighth is a rather typical country-dance
movement.

The last movement is an unconfined and "unbuttoned" expression
of pure joy. The music roars with a vigorous, boisterous laughter and
there are numerous hearty explosions. Just before the end there
is a rather whimsical coyness but the mood of explosive jest returns
and the symphony ends in a blaze of good humor.

The Eighth Symphony presents relatively few problems to the
conductor. The score probes no great depths, nor is its musical
argument an elusive one. Basically, there are two approaches: one
emphasizes its robust masculine vigor; the other, its gentler feminine grace. This alternation of elements that are perhaps best
described as "masculine" and "feminine" is a distinguishing feature of Beethoven's entire output. Indeed, in the symphonies one
can generalize that the odd-numbered ones are the masculine
defiances, the even-numbered ones the feminine charmers. In the
Eighth the two disparate qualities are perhaps more evenly balanced
than in any of the others.

Many different recordings are available of the music. What is remarkable about the situation is that there is such a uniform excellence among them all. Very recommendable are the performances
conducted by Casals (Columbia MS 6931), Klemperer (Angel
S 35657), Barbirolli (Vanguard Everyman S 146—a budget-priced
label), Monteux (RCA LSC 2491), Steinberg (Command S 12001—
included in the two-disc set that also offers Steinberg's performance
of Beethoven's Ninth Symphony), Szell (included in Columbia
M7X 30281) and Walter (included in Odyssey Y7 30051). All of
them have in common a robust thrust in the outer movements and a
lyrical ease in the two inner ones. All are very well played and recorded, too. If I were forced to make an absolute first choice, I would
select the Casals. Recorded during an actual performance at the
Marlboro Festival, Casals' reading has a headlong impetuosity that
is quite special. The athletic vigor and dynamism of the recording
produces a performance of compelling vitality. The sonics captured
in the Marlboro concert hall are harsher than those in some other

recordings, but this is a relatively small blemish. (A bonus rehearsal record, "Casals, A Living Portrait" is included free.)

Cassette collectors have available only the routine Leinsdorf-Boston Symphony Orchestra performance (RCA RK 1149); while reel-to-reel fanciers must make do with the only available recording in that configuration, the undistinguished Karajan-Berlin Philharmonic performance (DGG K 8807).

SYMPHONY NO. 9 IN D MINOR, OP. 125

Beethoven's first eight symphonies were produced in great spurts over the twelve-year period between 1800 and 1812. Between the Eighth and Ninth, however, a full twelve years more elapsed. Part of the reason for the long delay, surely, was the long period of gestation required by the tradition-shattering Ninth. Just as surely, another contributing element to the long delay was the state of Beethoven's personal affairs at the time. He was involved in an ugly lawsuit with his erstwhile friend, Johann Maelzel, who had commissioned from Beethoven the so-called "Battle" Symphony or "Wellington's Victory," scored for another of Maelzel's inventions, a huge mechanical "orchestra" called the panharmonicon. Referring to the lawsuit, Beethoven wrote to his attorney: "Such things exhaust me more than the greatest efforts in composition." There was also the protracted five-year court battle to gain custody over his nephew, Karl, following the death of Beethoven's brother Kaspar in 1815. Along with these problems, Beethoven was constantly enmeshed in the mundane business affairs of organizing concerts, negotiating with patrons and publishers, and otherwise expending time and energy in non-creative ways.

Thoughts of a Symphony in D Minor were noted by Beethoven in his sketchbooks as early as 1812, when the Seventh and Eighth Symphonies were being honed to perfection. In one of the sketchbooks for 1815 there is notated a subject for a fugue which was destined to become the theme of the Scherzo of the Ninth Symphony. Finally, in 1817 he seriously began making drafts for the first movement. By 1818 he was allowing his musical imagination full sway:

he had recently begun work on his Mass in D Major, the great Missa Solemnis, and this served as a further stimulus to thoughts about the symphony. He imagined a religious symphony, and then the idea of employing a chorus began to take shape.

As early as 1793, Beethoven had announced that he intended to set the noble verses of the "Ode to Joy" by the eighteenth-century German playwright and poet Friedrich Schiller. The theme of universal human brotherhood espoused in Schiller's verses was a subject close to Beethoven's own heart. He considered setting the poem as a concert aria and then considered introducing the words as sung interludes in an overture. It was not until 1822, however, when work on the Ninth Symphony was already well along, that he made a free outline of the last movement of the symphony using Schiller's poem as the text for a choral setting with four vocal soloists and orchestra.

Beethoven's biographer Schindler wrote: "When he reached the development of the last movement [of the Ninth Symphony], there began a struggle such as is seldom seen. The object was to find a proper manner of introducing Schiller's ode. One day entering the room he exclaimed, 'I have it! I have it!' With that he showed me the sketchbook bearing the words 'Let us sing the song of the immortal Schiller, Freude.'" Beethoven's sketchbooks show that these introductory words were arrived at only after many trials and frustrations—and they, too, were ultimately changed. By the end of 1823 the symphony was completely sketched out; by February 1824 Beethoven had scored the entire work. The first performance was given at the Kärntnertortheater in Vienna on May 7 of 1824 and there was a repeat on May 24.

For more than a hundred years there was a swirl of controversy that surrounded the choral Finale. There were those who felt that the intrusion of the human voice in the last movement completely dispelled the atmosphere that had been built up in the first three—that, indeed, the choral Finale was a monstrous mistake, an element grafted onto the other three movements that in reality had no relation to them. This point of view was articulated as recently as March 1929 by no less distinguished a scholar than Boston's great Philip Hale, critic for many years of the Boston *Herald* and the program annotator of the Boston Symphony Orchestra for a generation. Hale wrote: "Better to leave the hall with the memory of the *Adagio* than to depart with the vocal hurry-scurry and shouting of the final measures assailing ears and nerves." Another who took a somewhat similar position was the great Beethoven scholar and biographer Sir George Grove, who maintained that the last movement really did not need to be reconciled with the emotional content of the first three.

Violently dissenting from this view was another distinguished American critic and program annotator, Lawrence Gilman of the New York *Herald Tribune*, and a one-time annotator for the concerts of the New York Philharmonic. Gilman labeled as "an amazingly frivolous thesis" the idea that an organic work of art could be built of completely unrelated and irreconcilable parts. Gilman contemptuously dismissed the idea that the Ninth Symphony was a symphonic mongrel, "three-fourths absolute music and one-fourth cantata."

Today all this controversy is seen as a tempest in a teapot. Beethoven's Ninth Symphony, choral Finale and all, stands as one of the most incredible accomplishments of the mind of man. No matter that Beethoven imposes upon his performers demands that are really beyond the limits of human ability to fulfill. If ever there has been a cosmic musical creation, this is it—a score so overwhelming in its vision and breadth that it transcends temporal, worldly affairs.

Richard Wagner, himself no stranger to rarefied flights of inspired composition, described the "vision of life" of Beethoven's Ninth Symphony in these words:

First Movement—A struggle, conceived in the greatest grandeur, of the soul contending for happiness against the oppression of that inimical power which places itself between us and joys of earth appears to be the basis of the first movement. The great principal theme, which at the very beginning issues forth bare and mighty, as it were, from a mysteriously hiding veil, might be transcribed not altogether inappropriately to the meaning of the whole tone poem, in Goethe's words: "Renounce, thou must—renounce!"

Second Movement—Wild delight seizes us at once with the first rhythms of this second movement. It is a new world which we enter, one in which we are carried away to dizzy intoxication. With the abrupt entrance of the middle part there is suddenly disclosed to us a scene of worldly joy and happy contentment. A certain sturdy cheerfulness seems to address itself to us in the simple, oft-repeated theme.

Third Movement—How differently these tones speak to our hearts! How pure, how celestially soothing they are as they melt the defiance, the wild impulse of the soul harassed by despair into a soft, melancholy feeling! It is as if memory awoke within us—the memory of an early-enjoyed, purest happiness. With this recollection a sweet longing, too, comes over us, which is expressed so beautifully in the second theme of the movement.

Fourth Movement—A harsh outcry begins the transition from the third to the fourth movements, a cry of disappointment at not attaining the contentment so earnestly sought. Then, with the beginning of the ode, we hear clearly expressed what must appear to the anxious seeker for happiness as the highest lasting pleasure.

Beethoven's Ninth Symphony has been recorded many times over the years, especially since the 1950s. One of the most eagerly awaited recordings ever to be released in the history of the art was the performance of the Ninth Symphony that Arturo Toscanini recorded in April 1952 with the NBC Symphony Orchestra and the Robert Shaw Chorale. After the recording was completed, Toscanini is reputed to have remarked, "I'm almost satisfied"—a statement that epitomizes the conflict between the gratification of achievement of aims and purposes as best one can, and discontent with the inadequacy of human means for striving after the infinite. The Toscanini performance (available now as RCA Victrola VIC 1607) is a highly charged account of the score, electrifying in its intensity and nervous energy. One of the most impressive sections is the introduction to the last movement, where the recitative passages of the cellos and bases take on the communicativeness of human speech. The solo quartet—Eileen Farrell, Nan Merriman, Jan Peerce and Norman Scott—do their work dutifully but they are pushed to the limit (and sometimes beyond the limit) by the insistent demands of their conductor. By present standards the recorded sound is overloaded and shrill, but the performance is a representative likeness of

Toscanini's way with the Ninth Symphony and if his way is your way, then nothing more need be said.

Toscanini's way happens not to be my way. I prefer a more broadly expansive performance, one in which there is greater relaxation and poise. Such performances are given by Reiner (RCA LSC 6096) and Schmidt-Isserstedt (London CS 1159). Reiner's occupies three sides, with the fourth given over to a much less successful Reiner recording of Beethoven's First Symphony. Schmidt-Isserstedt's is contained neatly on two sides, hence it is less expensive than Reiner's. The London recording also boasts a superior vocal quartet, headed by Joan Sutherland and Marilyn Horne. To these virtues must also be added sound reproduction of the highest quality, superb playing by the Vienna Philharmonic and especially fine singing from the Vienna State Opera Chorus. There is no question, then, that the Schmidt-Isserstedt recording is my first choice—on tape, also, since a superb tape edition of the performance has been made available (London 90121).

I cannot conclude without mentioning briefly two other recorded performances of Beethoven's Ninth Symphony: Klemperer's (Angel S 3577) and Furtwängler's (Seraphim 6068, mono only). Klemperer's has a stupendous monolithic thrust in the first two movements, but a somewhat antiseptic slow movement and a curiously restrained Finale. The recording is low-level and distant-sounding and the soloists are utterly lacking in distinction.

Furtwängler's is at once the most provocative and most infuriating of all Ninth Symphony recordings. The performance was taped in 1951 at a concert rededicating the annual Bayreuth Festival presentations at that shrine of Wagnerian splendor. The tempos are prevailingly slower than what has come to be considered the norm. Sometimes, as in the slow movement, there is a sublime improvisational quality that seems to suspend time completely. At other times, however—as in the Scherzo—the music is robbed of much of its inherent punch and rhythmic tension. The reproduced sound, considering the circumstances, is quite good. In spite of the eminence of the individual singers the solo quartet—Elisabeth Schwarzkopf, Elisabeth Höngen, Hans Hopf and Otto Edelmann—is little more than adequate. There probably can be no uncommitted reaction to this performance; depending on the viewpoint, it is either thoroughly absorbing or thoroughly perverse. Make your own judgment!

In the tape and cassette fields I would recommend Stokowski's account (London L 75043 and M 94043 respectively); Furtwängler-like in its idiosyncrasies, it is nevertheless a compelling statement of the music.

TRIO NO. 6 IN B-FLAT MAJOR, OP. 97, "ARCHDUKE"

Between the years 1803 and 1806 Beethoven gave music lessons to a chubby, unattractive young man named Rudolph, whose older brother happened to be the Emperor of Austria. Rudolph Hapsburg was not an untalented musician; he composed some pieces and even achieved a sufficient mastery of the piano to enable him to perform some of Beethoven's concertos.

In 1809 Archduke Rudolph was instrumental in securing for Beethoven a regular annuity that gave him a measure of financial security and independence. Quite apart from his gratitude, Beethoven seems to have been genuinely fond of his noble benefactor, referring to him sometimes as "my little archduke," sometimes, with playful solemnity, as "my revered archduke."

Beethoven more than repaid his debt in the form of a series of dedications that immortalized the archduke's name. Conspicuous among these were the Fourth and Fifth Piano Concertos; the E-flat Major Piano Sonata (called *Les Adieux et le Retour* because it was composed when the archduke was forced to flee from Vienna before the advancing troops of Napoleon); two late piano sonatas, including the final one in C minor; the *Grosse Fuge* for string quartet; and the great Missa Solemnis in D Major, which was begun as a ceremonial piece to celebrate the installation of the archduke as the Archbishop of Olmütz. This work was not completed, however, until three years after that event.

In addition to these works, Beethoven also dedicated to the archduke the Trio in B-flat Major for Violin, Cello and Piano. This is the score that has come to be known as the "Archduke" Trio. Like his quartets, Beethoven's piano trios can be classified according to the three creative periods in his life. The first three of them were published collectively in 1795 as his Opus 1. Three years later came a Trio in B-flat Major scored for piano, clarinet (or violin) and cello. These four works belong to Beethoven's so-called early period. Not until fourteen years later, after he had produced his first six symphonies, did Beethoven return to the piano-trio format, producing the two works of his Opus 70—his middle-period trios. The "Archduke" Trio belongs to the year 1811, the year of the Seventh and Eighth Symphonies.

Two more trios were published posthumously: the Trio in E-flat Major, which was apparently composed in 1791 (the composer's twenty-first year), and one in B-flat major, written in 1812 and consisting of a single movement. In effect, then, there are only three piano trios that reflect the ripened maturity of Beethoven's genius, the two of the middle period and the "Archduke."

Like the Seventh Symphony, the "Archduke" Trio displays a buoyant and joyful vitality. The work is in four movements: a broad and lyrical opening *Allegro moderato*; an impish Scherzo marked *Allegro*; a theme-and-variations *Andante cantabile* for the third movement; and a concluding rondo, which grows without pause out of the third movement. Throughout the concluding rondo, incidentally, the writing for the piano is much more difficult than that for the strings.

It is not too surprising to discover that the "Archduke" Trio is the most-recorded of Beethoven's ensemble chamber works. The performance by the trio of Isaac Stern, Leonard Rose and Eugene Istomin (Columbia MS 6819) is for me the supreme statement of this music. More successfully than any other performance I have ever heard this one captures the excitement and *élan* of the music, at the same time that the gentler moments are given their full due. In short, Stern-Rose-Istomin meet the trio head on and reveal it to us in its entirety. Two other very good performances—though not really challenging the supremacy of Stern-Rose-Istomin—are the vintage recordings by Cortot-Thibaud-Casals (Angel COLH 29, mono only) and Heifetz-Rubinstein-Feuermann (RCA LM 7025, mono only, a two-disc set that also contains performances by these same artists of Brahms' B Major Trio and Schubert's Trio in B-flat Major).

The Stern-Rose-Istomin performance has not yet, unfortunately, made an appearance in either reel-to-reel or cassette tape format. Reel-to-reel collectors have available to them the performance by the team of Pinchas Zukerman, Jacqueline du Pré and Daniel Barenboim (included in Angel U 3771, devoted to all Beethoven's music for violin, cello and piano trio). The younger musicians' performance, strangely, lacks the youthful impetuosity of the Stern-Rose-Istomin presentation, but it is a thoroughly respectable performance nonetheless. As yet, no performance of this repertory staple exists in the cassette medium.

Hector Berlioz

Born: La Côte Saint-André (near Grenoble),
December 11, 1803
Died: Paris, March 8, 1869

The "father of modern orchestration" was intended by his parents
for a career in medicine. Sent to Paris to pursue his medical studies,
however, Berlioz promptly abandoned them and enrolled in the
Paris Conservatory of Music; one of the first consequences of this
act was immediate disinheritance. He quickly rebelled against the
formal dictates of some of his Conservatory teachers and thereupon
left the Conservatory and plunged with characteristic energy into the
cause of Romanticism. In 1828, when he was not yet twenty-five, he
produced two overtures—*Waverley* and *The Judges of the Secret
Court*—and the *Fantastic Symphony*. The following year he re-en-
tered the Conservatory over the objections of its director, Luigi
Cherubini, and in 1830 he was awarded the Prix de Rome for a
cantata, *Sardanapale*.

After eighteen months in Italy, Berlioz returned to Paris and took
up journalism with spectacular success. The next several years were
marked also by outstanding successes for a number of new works:
Harold in Italy in 1834; the Requiem in 1837; the Dramatic Symphony, *Romeo and Juliet*, with vocal solos and chorus, in 1839; and
the overture *The Roman Carnival*. However, his two-act opera
Benvenuto Cellini was a failure both in Paris and in London in 1838.
In 1839 he was made conservator of the Paris Conservatory; thirteen
years later he was appointed librarian of the Conservatory but he
never achieved the position there he really wanted—professor.

Berlioz traveled widely and his concert tours through Germany
and Russia in the years 1843–47 are described in his book *Voyage
musical.* Other important works he produced are the oratorio *The
Damnation of Faust* (1846); the sacred trilogy *L'Enfance du Christ*

(The Childhood of Christ) (1854); the operas *Beatrice and Benedict* (1862) and *The Trojans at Carthage* (1863). This latter work is the second part of a mammoth eight-act opera titled *The Trojans* (the first part is called *The Fall of Troy*). The entire work was not given complete until an 1897 production at Karlsruhe. With the Berlioz revival of the 1950s and 1960s attempts have been made to mount viable productions of the colossus in this country and elsewhere. Despite the productions in Boston and San Francisco in recent years, however, *The Trojans* still cries out for satisfactory treatment on an American operatic stage.

Along with his importance as a composer and conductor, Berlioz was also one of the most important literary figures on the French musical scene in the nineteenth century, as critic, and writer of verse and electric prose. His *Treatise on Instrumentation* is a classic in orchestration and among his other books are *Soirées d'orchestre*; *Grotesques de la musique*; *A travers Chants*; and an autobiography, *Mémoires*.

HAROLD IN ITALY, FOR VIOLA AND ORCHESTRA, OP. 16

In 1834, four years after he produced the *Symphonie fantastique* (at the age of twenty-seven), Hector Berlioz completed another large-scale symphony with a descriptive title. It was *Harold in Italy*, a four-movement work with an important viola solo part that was originally intended to be played by Niccolò Paganini at the first performance.

And thereby hangs a tale that began in the final days of 1833 at a concert at the Paris Conservatory. The *Symphonie fantastique* was performed on that occasion, for a wildly enthusiastic audience. In his memoirs Berlioz recalled what followed:

To crown my happiness, after the audience had gone out, a man with a long mane of hair, with piercing eyes, with a strange and haggard face, one possessed by genius, a colossus among giants, whom I had never seen and whose appearance moved me profoundly, was alone and waiting for me in the hall, stopped me to press my hand, overwhelmed me with burning praise, which set fire to my heart and head: it was *Paganini!*

Berlioz goes on to report that some weeks after this initial meeting Paganini came to visit him and proposed that he compose a solo piece for viola—Paganini intended it as a vehicle for a treasured Stradivarius instrument he owned.

Berlioz wrote of his commission from Paganini:

> I tried then to please the illustrious virtuoso by writing a solo piece for the viola, but a solo combined with the orchestra in such a manner that it would not injure the expression of the orchestral mass, for I was sure that Paganini, by his incomparable artistry, would know how to make the viola always the dominating instrument. His proposal seemed new to me, and I soon had developed in my head a very happy idea, and I was eager for the realization. The first movement was already completed, when Paganini wished to see it. He looked at the rests for the viola in the allegro and exclaimed: "No, it is not that: there are too many rests for me; I must be playing all the time." "I told you so," I answered; "you want a viola concerto, and you are the only one who can write such a concerto for yourself." Paganini did not answer; he seemed disappointed, and left me without speaking further about my orchestral sketch.

When the completed score was played for the first time—in November 1834, at the Paris Conservatory—it was not Paganini but an obscure violist named Chrétien Urhan who played the solo part.

The over-all title *Harold in Italy* and the descriptive titles for the four movements of the score are from Lord Byron's poem *Childe Harold's Pilgrimage,* about a melancholy dreamer who in his poetic wanderings about the Italian countryside seems to epitomize perfectly the goals, aspirations, and internal conflicts of the early Romantics. But like so many nineteenth-century musical works with supposed literary programs, Berlioz' *Harold in Italy* depends not one whit on its literary associations: it can be heard and enjoyed purely for itself without knowledge of its extra-musical implications.

The score directs that the viola soloist "must stand forward, near the public and apart from the orchestra"—thus clearly indicating that

Berlioz had a concerto-like arrangement in mind. The first movement, "Harold in the Mountains," begins with a somber and melancholy introduction in the basses. The theme is serpentine, weaving up and down the scale. The viola enters with what is to be the motto theme that recurs through each of the movements. The general character of this opening movement is cumulative drama rising to an exciting climax. The second movement, "March of the Pilgrims," is a slow crescendo, a climax, and a slow diminuendo, as if the marching pilgrims are approaching from a distance, passing and disappearing into the distance. The march theme is varied constantly throughout the movement, its initial repetitions being punctuated by an echoing horn note. Toward the middle of the movement the solo viola plays a long series of arpeggios in the peculiar metallic timbre of *sul ponticello* bowing (near the bridge of the instrument). The third movement is titled "Serenade of an Abruzzi Mountaineer to His Sweetheart." It is a lively, dance-like movement that opens with a frisky theme in the oboe and piccolo. In the middle, the characteristic viola motto is given to the English horn, and then the viola itself does some fancy footwork with the melody. The final movement is a bombastic orgy titled "Orgy of the Brigands." The full glory of the Berlioz orchestra is unleashed in this movement, and there is a long section in which themes from earlier movements are recalled. Near the very end there is a suspenseful silence; then two violas and a cello, offstage, bring back another reminiscence of the pilgrims' march theme. The conclusion is a brilliant outburst for the full orchestra.

The standing of *Harold in Italy* in today's record catalogs and concert halls derives from the championing efforts of two conducting giants of the recent past—Serge Koussevitzky and Arturo Toscanini. Both of them conducted *Harold in Italy* repeatedly a generation ago, when the score was considered little more than a curiosity and a museum piece. Indeed, it was Koussevitzky who conducted the first recording of the music in this country, in November 1944, with William Primrose as violist and the Boston Symphony Orchestra. After its distinguished career as a five-disc set of RCA Victor 78-rpm recordings, the performance was made available for a short time as an RCA Victor Vault Series long-playing record. The performance, unfortunately, has long since passed into that limbo of withdrawal to which RCA, scandalously, has assigned most of the Koussevitzky recordings. The performance—a stunning one, with a passionate commitment that all too frequently is the missing element in the music-making of today—clearly deserves to be heard.

William Primrose has dominated the recordings of *Harold in Italy* ever since that pioneer performance with Koussevitzky. About half a dozen years later he recorded the score again, with another pre-eminent Berlioz conductor, Sir Thomas Beecham, for American Columbia (ML 4542, mono only); and in 1958 Primrose returned to Boston for another recording of *Harold in Italy*, this time with Charles Munch conducting the Boston Symphony Orchestra (RCA LSC 2228); finally, it was only illness that prevented Primrose from performing the viola solo in Leonard Bernstein's 1962 recording of the music with the New York Philharmonic (Columbia MS 6358)— in his place, William Lincer, the Philharmonic's principal violist, took over for Primrose. Another recording of the score—by Yehudi Menuhin, with Colin Davis conducting the Philharmonia Orchestra (Angel S 36123)—has won high praise in certain quarters. Granting the curiosity value attached to hearing Menuhin as a viola player in so extended a role, his performance strikes me as conspicuously undernourished. It is difficult to say how much of this is his fault and how much the conductor's. But in a score that has drawn sparks from other performers, the Menuhin-Davis collaboration is a distinct letdown; the sound reproduction is fine, however. Similarly a letdown is the Soviet-originated recording with Rudolf Barshai as soloist and David Oistrakh conducting (Angel/Melodiya S 40001). Here again the drama and excitement of the score emerge pale and diluted.

Much more satisfying are the Primrose-Munch and Lincer-Bernstein recordings; both are highly charged, dramatically oriented performances. Primrose is the more assured and suave violist of the two. Nevertheless, the team of Lincer and Bernstein has been given somewhat better reproduction and their performance emerges with cleaner, more sharply defined textures.

The recent Columbia release (M 30116) of the performance by

Joseph de Pasquale with his colleagues of the Philadelphia Orchestra
under Eugene Ormandy's direction sweeps the entire field before it.
De Pasquale is a past master of the viola solo part, dating from his
many collaborations with Koussevitzky and Munch in this work in
the concert hall. And Ormandy provides a vibrant account of the
score, superbly played and well engineered. No tape version—either
reel-to-reel or cassette—is currently listed.

SYMPHONIE FANTASTIQUE, OP. 14

In December 1830 Ludwig van Beethoven had been dead less than
four years and his "Pastoral" Symphony and Leonore Overtures were
then the most radical descriptive program music known to the world.
In December 1830 a twenty-six-year-old composer named Hector
Berlioz was waiting anxiously for the first performance—scheduled
at the Paris Conservatory for the fifth of the month—of his new
"great symphony," the first part of a work in two sections called
"Episode in the Life of an Artist."

One of the earliest mentions of the score was in a letter Berlioz
wrote to his friend Humbert Fernand in February 1830:

I am again plunged in the anguish of an interminable and inextin-
guishable passion, without motive, without cause. She is always at
London, and yet I think I feel her near me; all my remembrances
awake and unite to wound me; I hear my heart beating, and its
pulsations shake me as the piston strokes of a steam engine. Each
muscle of my body shudders with pain. In vain! 'Tis terrible! O
unhappy one! if she could for one moment conceive all the poetry,
all the infinity of a like love, she would fly to my arms, were she to
die through my embrace. I was on the point of beginning my great
symphony ("Episode in the Life of an Artist"), in which the
development of my infernal passion is to be portrayed; I have it all in
my head, but I cannot write anything. Let us wait.

The object of all this unrestrained outpouring of passion was a
Junoesque Shakespearean actress from Ireland named Harriet (Hen-
rietta) Smithson, whom Berlioz had seen only on the stage but never

met! He tells of trembling at her performances in the roles of Ophelia and Juliet and says in his *Memoirs* that his "Episode in the Life of an Artist" is a "history of my love for Miss Smithson, my anguish and my distressing dreams." (Elsewhere in the *Memoirs* he states, "It was while I was strongly under the influence of Goethe's poem *Faust* that I wrote my *Symphonie fantastique*." But don't let this seeming contradiction throw you. Harriet Smithson and Goethe's *Faust* are only two of the many forces in Berlioz' psyche which all together conspired to force the creation of such a work as the *Fantastic Symphony*, as the first part of "Episode in the Life of an Artist" has come to be universally known.)

For this *Fantastic Symphony* Berlioz concocted a fantastic program. Printed in the score it reads like this:

A young musician of morbid sensibility and ardent imagination [what a marvelous self-description!] poisons himself with opium in a fit of amorous despair. The narcotic dose, too weak to result in death, plunges him into a heavy sleep accompanied by the strangest visions, during which his sensations, sentiments and recollections are translated in his sick brain into musical thoughts and images. The beloved woman herself has become for him a melody, like a fixed idea which he finds and hears everywhere.

The five movements of the symphony then proceed to describe for us the different emotions and situations which Our Hero experiences in the course of his drugged dreaming. No more revealing a portrait of a creator exists in the realm of art—and make no mistake, a sovereign work of art the *Fantastic Symphony* assuredly is. It is the direct musical ancestor of spooks and rogues from Liszt's *Mephisto* to Moussorgsky's *Bald Mountain* to Strauss' *Till* to Malcolm Arnold's *Tam O' Shanter*. But perhaps its most secure artistic merit is its proportion, sure-handedness, unity and—yes—discipline, which all combine to make the *Fantastic Symphony* as remarkable a forward step in the history of symphonic music as the "Eroica" was. A renowned interpreter of the score, Sir Thomas Beecham, once told me that there have been "no surprises given to us in orchestration since the *Symphonie fantastique* of Berlioz," and as I've thought of this statement over the years I have found myself agreeing more and more with these words.

The composer's own vivid description of the sections of the *Fantastic Symphony* serves as an ideal guide to the "action" of the music:

First Movement: Dreams, Passions—At first [our young musician hero] thinks of the uneasy and nervous condition of his mind, of somber longings, of depression and joyous elation without any recognizable cause, which he experienced before the Beloved One had appeared to him. Then he remembers the ardent love with which she suddenly inspired him; he thinks of his almost insane anxiety of mind, of his raging jealousy, of his reawakening love, of his religious consolation.

Second Movement: A Ball—In a ballroom, amidst the confusion of a brilliant festival, he finds the Beloved One again.

Third Movement: Scene in the Fields—It is a summer evening. He is in the country, musing, when he hears two shepherd lads who play, in alternation, the *ranz des vaches* [the tune used by the Swiss shepherds to call their flocks]. This pastoral duet, the quiet scene, the soft whisperings of the trees stirred by the zephyr-wind, some prospects of hope recently made known to him—all these sensations unite to impart a long-unknown repose to his heart and to lend a smiling color to his imagination. Then She appears once more. His heart stops beating, painful forebodings fill his soul. "Should she prove false to him!" One of the shepherds resumes the melody, but the other answers him no more. . . . Sunset . . . distant rolling of thunder . . . loneliness . . . silence. . . .

Fourth Movement: March to the Scaffold—He dreams that he has murdered his Beloved, that he has been condemned to death and is being led to execution. A march that is alternately somber and wild, brilliant and solemn, accompanies the procession. . . . The tumultuous outbursts are followed without modulation by measured steps. At last the fixed idea returns, for a moment a last thought of love is revived—which is cut short by the death-blow.

Fifth Movement: Dream of a Witches' Sabbath—He dreams that he is present at a witches' revel, surrounded by horrible spirits, amidst sorcerers and monsters in many fearful forms, who have come together for his funeral. Strange sounds, groans, shrill laughter, distant yells, which other cries seem to answer. The Beloved Melody is heard again, but it has lost its shy and noble character; it has become a vulgar, trivial, grotesque dance tune. She it is who comes to attend the witches' meeting. Riotous shouts and howls greet her arrival. . . . She joins the infernal orgy . . . bells toll for the dead . . . a burlesque parody of the *Dies Irae* . . . the Witches' round dance. . . . The dance and the *Dies Irae* are heard together.

One of the most widely honored performances of our time has been the reading of the *Fantastic Symphony* by Charles Munch. The score, when he conducted it in concert, triggered a magic spark in his make-up and he responded to it with irresistible drive and impetuosity. The final two movements were whipped up to an emotional fare-thee-well, achieving a frenzied and neurotic excitement of pure inspiration. And he also communicated the kaleidoscopic nature of the first three movements more successfully than any other conductor I've ever heard. Munch included the *Fantastic Symphony* on his first series of guest appearances with the New York Philharmonic in January 1947, and I remember Olin Downes devoting one of his full Sunday columns in the New York *Times* to an analysis of the Munch alchemy with this score.

Munch had the deserved privilege of recording the *Fantastic Symphony* on four different occasions: first, with the French National Radio Orchestra in Paris in the late 1940s; then twice in Boston with the Boston Symphony Orchestra, in 1954 and again in 1960; his final recording of the music was again accomplished in Paris, this time during the last weeks of 1967 with the newly formed Orchestre de Paris. His second recording of the score with the Boston Symphony Orchestra (RCA LSC 2608) is a superb document. The orchestra plays magnificently, the sound reproduction is excellent and there is a contagious vitality to the performance that captures the essence of what was the spontaneous music-making of Charles Munch.

Ansermet's (London CS 2101) is perhaps the most provocative of all the available performances. It takes him the better part of the first two movements to warm to his task, but from the third movement onward his is a completely convincing account that emphasizes the diablerie of the music to bone-chilling effect. Davis (Philips 835188) represents the opposite polarity from that of Munch: Davis is the more formal, Munch the more flamboyant. Of the performances currently available on tape, Stokowski's (London L 75031; cassette M 94031)—with its many unique moments of tender and reflective poetry—would be my prime recommendation for a version in those configurations.

Georges Bizet

Born: Paris, October 25, 1838
Died: Bougival, June 3, 1875

Bizet became a pupil at the Paris Conservatory of Music at the tender age of nine. Ten years later, after he had composed several works including a symphony, he was awarded the Offenbach First Prize of the Conservatory for an opera buffa, *Doctor Miracle*. He also was awarded the Grand Prix de Rome and went to Italy to further his studies. A steady stream of works flowed from his pen, including a two-act Italian opera buffa, *Don Procopio*, a product of the years 1858–59. In all, Bizet composed a total of twenty-seven operas or fragments of operas, of which the principal ones were *The Pearl Fishers* (1862–63); *The Fair Maid of Perth* (1867); and *Djamileh* (1871). Not until 1872, however, with his *Patrie* Overture and incidental music to Daudet's play *L'Arlésienne*, did Bizet realize a popular success.

In the years 1873–74 Bizet worked on an opera set to a story by Prosper Mérimée. The first performance was given on the evening of March 3, 1875; that morning, Bizet's appointment as a chevalier in the Legion of Honor was announced. The new work shocked and puzzled the audience—but there was no open hostility as has sometimes been claimed. The chief complaint apparently centered on the realism of the story and its characters; Bizet's music was variously charged with being undistinguished, unoriginal and devoid of color. Always sensitive to public reaction, Bizet was especially crushed by this reception afforded his latest work, *Carmen*, which he himself considered quite the best he had yet produced. An acute mental depression ensued, occasioned by the generally negative reaction to *Carmen*, and his condition was further complicated by the recurrence of an old throat ailment. Bizet failed to bounce back with

his usual resilience and exactly three months after the first performance of *Carmen*—and on his sixth wedding anniversary—Bizet
died. In the intervening years *Carmen* has come to be recognized as
the supreme achievement of the French lyric theater and one of the
greatest of all creations for the operatic stage.

SYMPHONY NO. 1 IN C MAJOR

At a concert in Basel, Switzerland, in February of 1935, Felix Weingartner introduced to the world a symphony that had been written
nearly eighty years before by one of the best-known figures in the
history of opera, Georges Bizet. How the symphony came to be
written and why it languished unperformed for so many years is,
and probably will remain, a mystery.

In November 1855, when the seventeen-year-old Bizet wrote the
work, he was enrolled at the Paris Conservatory of Music and was a
student in counterpoint classes held by Charles Gounod, whose
music and personality were both to have a profound effect on Bizet.
Earlier that year, Gounod had had an enormous success with his
own First Symphony in D Major. It is not surprising to find that,
as Howard Shanet, Associate Professor of Music at Columbia University, has pointed out, the Bizet Symphony in C Major is modeled
in all its most conspicuous features on the First Symphony of
Gounod. Perhaps Bizet was obliged to write a symphony for his
composition teacher at the Conservatory and chose to pattern it after Gounod's work; perhaps the younger man spontaneously followed the lead of his friend and mentor. In any case, Bizet apparently forgot about the piece immediately after completing it. Opera
beckoned: it was in the very air around him. Halévy, his composition teacher at the Conservatory, was a successful composer of
operas. This was the period of Meyerbeer's greatest vogue; Ambroise
Thomas and Léo Delibes were beginning to impress the public; and
after 1855, Gounod too almost completely turned away from symphonic composition in favor of the theater. It is little wonder that
Bizet was similarly inclined.

The impetus for Weingartner's 1935 premiere of the C Major

Symphony seems to have come from a Mr. D. C. Parker of Glasgow, the author of the first English biography of Bizet. Parker had seen the manuscript in the Paris Conservatory and had urged Weingartner to investigate it. Within a year after the premiere the score was taken up by Sir Hamilton Harty, who introduced the symphony in England with the London Symphony Orchestra in December 1936, and in the United States six weeks later with the Rochester Philharmonic. Since then the piece has become a staple of the symphonic literature.

The marks of many composers other than Gounod are to be found in Bizet's delightful symphony: Haydn, the early Beethoven, Schubert, Mendelssohn and Rossini. Yet, despite these influences, the distinct musical personality of the composer is everywhere in the music. The first movement is a playful *Allegro vivo*, characterized by rhythmic snap and forward-pressing vitality. The second-movement *Adagio* features a sinuous oboe solo that has something of the character of an operatic intermezzo. The Scherzo is a vigorous and energetic movement that contains in its trio a drone bass accompaniment beneath a more expansive treatment of the basic musical material. The Finale, *Allegro vivace*, is like a whirlwind, constantly challenging the strings, especially the violins, to ever more mercurial feats of articulation and speed.

The first recording of Bizet's symphony appeared in the early 1940s as a 78-rpm album of four records, with Walter Goehr conducting the London Philharmonic Orchestra. This RCA Victor release had the field to itself until the mid-1940s, when Columbia issued a performance by Artur Rodzinski and the New York Philharmonic. The Rodzinski performance was one of the finest of all his recordings, and it was one of the first transfers to the long-playing medium in 1948. Not many years later, RCA Victor released its second recording of the music, this one with a most unlikely conductor at the helm—Leopold Stokowski. But the unpredictable Stokowski turned in a performance that was pure magic: spontaneous vitality fairly leapt out of the record grooves, and the playing of the hand-picked ensemble of orchestral musicians was awesome in its virtuosity. Unfortunately, neither the Rodzinski nor the Stokowski performance remains in the current catalog. The Stokowski recording (RCA LM 1706) may still be available on some dealers' shelves, and it is worth looking for.

Three excellent recordings of the symphony are currently available; the conductors are Ansermet (London CS 6208), Beecham and Munch (Nonesuch 71183). Ansermet's is full of good humor and spontaneity. Beecham has a better orchestra (the French National Radio Orchestra) and he is even more successful than his distinguished Swiss colleague in securing a delicate yet pointed interplay between the contrasting sections of the score. Beecham's jaunty and invigorating performance has recently been reissued in Angel's budget-priced Seraphim line (S 60192). It would be my first recommendation at any price. Munch's is a romp from beginning to end, mercurial in its pacing, bracing in its impact.

A rather quixotic performance is the one conducted by Bernstein (Columbia MS 7159). Brilliantly played by the New York Philharmonic and robustly recorded by the engineers, there are interpretative quirks—ritards and small pauses in the last movement, for example—that may prove irritating on repeated hearings.

On tape, only Ansermet's more sober account is available (London L 80090)—and nothing at all exists for the cassette collector.

Johannes Brahms

Born: Hamburg, May 7, 1833
Died: Vienna, April 3, 1897

Brahms first studied music with his father, who played double bass in the orchestra of the Hamburg City Theater. As a youth Brahms earned his livelihood playing the piano in some of Hamburg's more notorious bordellos. His first important professional appearances were as accompanist to the distinguished Hungarian violinist Reményi, with whom Brahms toured in 1853. It was at a concert with Reményi that Brahms met another distinguished Hungarian-born violinist, Joseph Joachim, who was to become a lifelong friend and champion. Joachim gave the two an introduction to Liszt at Weimar and strongly recommended to Brahms that he also visit Schumann. The two received a cordial welcome from Liszt, who also expressed keen interest in some of Brahms' music. For his part, Brahms was little impressed either by Liszt or by his general musical ideals. In Schumann, however, he found a much more congenial and kindred spirit, and Schumann, for his part, hailed Brahms as the new musical messiah in the influential publication that he edited, the *Neue Zeitschrift für Musik*.

Despite the early championing of his cause by such arch-Romantics as Schumann and Liszt, Brahms nevertheless abandoned Romanticism with a capital R and took up a determined classicism in the matter of form. He made many modifications, however, to suit his own intellectual and technical demands. This early acceptance by Schumann and Liszt also set Brahms up as a hero in opposition to Richard Wagner in the eyes of certain belligerent parties, most notably the critic Hanslick. For his own part, Brahms valued Wagner's scores and owned several Wagner autographs. But Wagner once said of him: "Brahms is a composer whose importance lies in not wishing to create any striking effect."

After serving for a time as conductor to the Prince of Lippe-Detmold, Brahms retired for study to Hamburg (1858–62), then Vienna (1862), then to various other cities, finally returning to Vienna in 1869 and remaining there for the rest of his life. The first complete performance of his *A German Requiem* in the Bremen Cathedral in April 1868 established him on a peak where he has remained ever since while the storms of debate rage below him. He wrote in almost every form but opera—and he had considered that at one time. His First Symphony, for which the musical world had waited eagerly for many years, created a sensation when it was finally produced in 1876. From then on, a respectful and admiring public awaited every new work that came from his pen and to the end he was accorded a public reverence such as few composers before him enjoyed.

As Brahms was helped early in his career by Schumann, Joachim and other distinguished musicians, so did he later prove helpful to many of his fellow composers. He had a particularly high regard for Dvořák and Grieg. He was on friendly terms with Tchaikovsky though there was little musical sympathy between them. He had a deep affection for Bizet's *Carmen*, for the waltzes of Johann Strauss and for Verdi's Requiem, which he called a work of genius when most of his fellow German composers were fiercely attacking it. He also had a deep reverence for the second part of *L'Enfance du Christ* by Berlioz and he had a thoroughly comprehensive knowledge of the classics.

In the 1890s many of Brahms' closest friends began to die. Elisabeth von Herzogenberg died in 1892, von Bülow and Billroth in 1894. The worst blow came in 1896, with the death, after two strokes, of Clara Schumann. Now his own health began to fail. After a fruitless visit to the baths at Karlsbad, it was discovered that Brahms was suffering from cancer of the liver. His death in 1897 was mourned by all Vienna and among the pallbearers at his funeral were Dvořák and the scholar Mandyczewski.

Brahms' output was prodigious—for orchestra, four symphonies;

two serenades; two concert overtures, the *Tragic* and *Academic Festival;* Variations on a Theme by Haydn (the theme, it turns out, is not by Haydn at all but is an old Austrian peasants' hymn); and four concertos, two for piano, one for violin and one for violin and cello. In the realm of chamber music Brahms composed three string quartets; three quartets for piano and strings; a trio for horn, violin and piano; two string quintets; a quintet for piano and strings; a quintet for clarinet and strings; and two string sextets. In addition there are numerous works for solo piano; three sonatas for violin and piano; two sonatas for cello and piano; and many songs and choruses.

CONCERTO IN A MINOR FOR VIOLIN AND CELLO, OP. 102

Brahms spent three consecutive summers during the late 1880s vacationing in the small Swiss town of Thun. Something about its atmosphere and environment served as a powerful stimulus to his creative impulse. During these years Brahms composed some of his most heartfelt and personal works, among them the violin and piano sonatas in A major (called the "Thun" Sonata) and in D minor, the F Major Cello and Piano Sonata and the C Minor Trio for Violin, Cello and Piano.

Why this outpouring of music for the violin? One answer, unquestionably, lies in the friendship, renewed at this time, between Brahms and Joseph Joachim, the distinguished violinist and conductor. A decade earlier these two had been on close terms. Brahms composed his Violin Concerto for Joachim, and the latter was the soloist when the concerto was given its premiere, the composer conducting, at a New Year's Day concert in Leipzig in 1879. But in the intervening years Joachim became embroiled in a bitter divorce proceeding. A letter from Brahms that completely refuted some of Joachim's charges against his wife was introduced in court and opened a gulf between the two friends that was years in the bridging. Finally, by 1886, Joachim and Brahms were reconciled.

The following summer in Thun, Brahms composed a strange hybrid of a work—a concerto for violin, cello and orchestra. Brahms himself conducted the premiere of the piece in Cologne in October 1887; the soloists were Joachim and another friend of Brahms, a cellist named Hausmann. When the music was published the following year, Brahms presented the score to Joachim. On it was the inscription: "To him for whom it was written."

About a year and a half after the world premiere, the Double Concerto, as it has come to be called, was introduced to the United States at a concert in New York conducted by Theodore Thomas. The cello soloist on this occasion, a musician of uncommon artistry, was to become one of America's most successful composers of operettas—Victor Herbert.

The Double Concerto was to be Brahms' last orchestral score. During the final decade of his life, he composed some chamber music and some songs, and the autumnal quality of these works is a characteristic of the Double Concerto too.

The concerto is in three movements, and the writing for the two solo instruments is a matched discourse of perfect fusion. The opening *Allegro* is a dramatic movement rich in lyrical warmth. Brahms' biographer, Walter Niemann, describes the *Andante* slow movement as "a great ballad, steeped in the rich, mysterious tone of a northern evening atmosphere." The concluding *Vivace non troppo* is a jolly rondo with a Hungarian flavor.

The need for two soloists of matched artistic temperaments makes the Double Concerto still rather infrequently encountered in our concert halls. In the world of recorded music, however, the Double Concerto is a perennial favorite. Two of the many available recordings are reissues of performances released many years ago. The pioneer version by Jacques Thibaud and Pablo Casals, with Alfred Cortot conducting the Barcelona Symphony Orchestra, is one of the items in Angel's Great Recordings of the Century series (COLH 75). The performance by Jascha Heifetz and Emanuel Feuermann, with Eugene Ormandy conducting the Philadelphia Orchestra, is in the RCA Treasury series (LCT 1016). Both, of course, are available on monophonic discs only. The Cortot-Thibaud-Casals team brought a strong feeling of dedication and perceptive musicianship to everything it played, but I have always found the performance of the Brahms Double Concerto overintellectualized and more than a little antiseptic; and the sound, of course, is now antique. The Heifetz-Feuermann collaboration is altogether a different matter. Both artists were at their blazing best at the time of the recording (circa 1941), and the performance throws off sparks of artistic excitement. Ormandy and the orchestra are superb, and the sound is on the whole acceptable.

My own favorite among all recorded versions of the concerto is the one with Zino Francescatti and Pierre Fournier, with Bruno Walter conducting (Columbia MS 6158). The two soloists are perfectly matched and they bring to the music an elegance and polish that are extremely winning. Walter's rather broad tempos permit the noble assurance and grandeur of the score to emerge. The recorded sound is good, with rich resonance and fine stereo placement.

To the aforementioned fine versions can now be added the finely-honed performance by Oistrakh and Rostropovich with Szell (Angel S 36032; tape M 36032; cassette 4XS 36032).

There is a recording by Heifetz and Piatigorsky (RCA LSC 3228) with Alfred Wallenstein conducting that is at the opposite pole in interpretation. Everything is hectic and rushed and there are bits of ragged ensemble, orchestral as well as solo. The sound, too, has an unpleasant pinched, wiry quality. Chalk this one up as an off day for all hands.

Also a disappointment is the performance by Isaac Stern and Leonard Rose with Eugene Ormandy and the Philadelphia Orchestra (Columbia D2S 720—a two-disc set that also contains Stern-Rose-Istomin performances of Beethoven's Triple Concerto and Brahms' Trio in C Major, Opus 87). Stern and Rose once participated in a recording of the Double Concerto with Bruno Walter conducting the New York Philharmonic (Columbia ML 5076—withdrawn) that was a beautifully Romantic, highly personal treatment. In the newer performance with Ormandy there is not the freedom and easy give-and-take that so marked the version with Bruno Walter.

CONCERTO NO. 1 IN D MINOR FOR PIANO, OP. 15

In studying the life of Johannes Brahms, one is struck repeatedly by
the complete involvement of the composer's circle of friends in his
creative process. Many of Brahms' most important works were heard
for the first time in two-piano reduction at private gatherings of the
Brahms circle, and Brahms himself would constantly seek the advice and suggestions of his intimates. It is quite possible that the
work we know today as Brahms' First Piano Concerto would never
have come into being without the perceptive encouragement of
Clara Schumann, Julius Grimm and Joseph Joachim.

The D Minor Concerto, Brahms' first full-blown venture in the
orchestral field, began life as a symphony. The twenty-one-year-old
composer had completed sketches for three movements in 1854 and
had even orchestrated the first of them. The more he lived with the
piece, however, the more he squirmed in discomfort. The musical
materials just did not seem right for a symphony. Brahms' experience up to that time was largely as a pianist and as a composer of
piano pieces; the two-piano reduction of the symphony too readily
betrayed the fingerprints of the composer's orientation. At one time
he planned to recast the score as a sonata for two pianos, but the
music far outstripped the scope of this medium.

Florence May, Brahms' pupil and biographer, has written most
interestingly of the evolutionary process that transpired:

Johannes had quite convinced himself that he was not yet ripe for
the writing of a symphony, and it occurred to Grimm that the music
might be rearranged as a piano concerto. This proposal was entertained by Brahms, who accepted the first and second movements as
suitable in essentials for this form. The change in structure involved
in the plan, however, proved far from easy of successful accomplishment, and occupied much of the composer's time during two years.

Brahms sought the support of his friend, the violinist and conductor Joachim (who was destined to serve a similar advisory capacity

some twenty years later when Brahms composed his violin concerto). The original third movement of the symphony was rejected and eventually became the chorus "Behold all flesh" in the *German Requiem*. In its place, Brahms composed the rondo Finale that serves as the perfect capstone for the concerto. As it finally evolved, the D Minor Piano Concerto has about it an air of Herculean triumph, and the ordeal of its difficult birth has left upon it an indelible imprint of relentless power and youthful passion.

That this tumultuous music is the product of a young man in his twenties is one of those miracles of the creative process. Brahms produced a truly symphonic organism with the solo instrument indivisibly joined with the orchestra, each an equal partner in the musical discourse. The concerto was slow to make its way in the musical world, and even so sympathetic a listener as Clara Schumann found the opening movement "wonderful in detail, yet not very vivifying." Even today, Brahms' more graceful and lyrical Second Piano Concerto is heard far more frequently than the First. There remain few more deeply satisfying experiences, however, than a penetrating, perceptive performance of the First Concerto with its defiant *Sturm und Drang*, its melting poetry and its noble heroism.

In at least two places in the score Brahms is supposed to have paid homage to his recently deceased friend and mentor, the composer Robert Schumann. The high drama and tragedy of the first movement, according to Joachim, is a direct musical outcome of Schumann's mad plunge into the river Rhine. Further, Max Kalbeck, a friend and biographer of Brahms, maintained that an inscription over the slow movement was a direct reference to Schumann. The motto reads *Benedictus qui venit in nomine Domini*, "Blessed is he who comes in the name of the Lord," and Brahms apparently often addressed Schumann as "Mynheer Domine."

Florence May in her biography of Brahms relates the First Piano Concerto to the composer's practical needs at the time:

> The desire attributed to the composer . . . to create a new form, to compose a symphonic work with a piano obbligato, did not exist. Brahms simply wished to use what he had already written, and did not feel that the time had come when he could successfully complete a

symphony. . . . How successfully he accomplished his task is today apparent to accustomed ears, for which the first movement, though it contains slight deviations from conventional concerto form, has no moment of obscurity. The imagination of this portion of the work is colossal. It has something Miltonic in its character, and seems to suggest to the mind issues more tremendous and universal than the tragedy of Schumann's fate, with which it must be associated. No one will assert that it contains what are termed "brilliant piano passages," the very existence of which is unthinkable in a movement of such exalted poetic grandeur; but that its performance brings due reward to capable interpreters has been proved by the enthusiasm of many a latter-day audience. After all that has been said, the reader will have no difficulty in understanding the fervent intensity of mood which impelled the composition of the slow movement, or in realizing something of the emotions which suggested the motto, *Benedictus qui venit in nomine Domini,* written above it in the original manuscript.

In the Finale, the difficult task of treating something which should relieve the tension of feeling induced by the preceding movements, without impairing the unity of the concerto as a whole, has been well achieved. If it is somewhat more somber in color than the usually accepted finale in rondo form, it is abundant in vigor and impulse, whilst, on the other hand, though written with a view to the concert room, it never descends towards the trivialities of mere outward glitter.

Brahms created the D Minor Piano Concerto while he was in his twenties; interestingly, there are four pianists whose recordings of the score were made while they themselves were still in their twenties: Daniel Barenboim (Angel S 36463), Van Cliburn (RCA LSC 2724), Leon Fleisher (Epic BC 1003) and Gary Graffman (RCA Victrola VICS 1109). Fleisher's is the most successful of the lot, but unfortunately it has now been withdrawn—to reappear, perhaps, in Columbia's low-priced Odyssey line? With George Szell conducting the Cleveland Orchestra, this is a performance of towering strength, impassioned poetry and flowing lyricism. The performance is as much Szell's as Fleisher's, for he was also the conductor for a recording of the score made in the 1930s by Artur Schnabel to which the same descriptive phrases could be applied. (And as we shall see, Szell is also the conductor for Clifford Curzon's record-ing.) Fleisher's playing here is a throwback to the grand manner of another era—doubly welcome because it is a rare commodity these days. The stereo edition—a product of the early days of the art— is rather more directional than current usage dictates.

Barenboims's performance is an individual one. He and his con-ductor, Barbirolli, tend to linger over passages unduly at times, and some of the tempi are extremely deliberate. Withal, the performance has much to recommend it and it is very well recorded. Both Cliburn and Graffman turn in well-organized, careful performances, but both are rather impersonal and antiseptic.

Of the recordings by older, more seasoned pianists, the outstand-ing performances are those by Curzon Szell (London CS 6329) and Rubinstein-Reiner (RCA LM 1831, mono only). Both deliver readings of impassioned fire and poetry, and both are well re-corded. The Rubinstein-Reiner collaboration is much more vital and committed than is Rubinstein's later stereo recording with Erich Leinsdorf and the Boston Symphony (RCA LSC 2917).

In the tape field, Curzon (London L 80126) is recommended. No cassette performance of this repertory staple has yet been issued.

CONCERTO NO. 2 IN B-FLAT MAJOR FOR PIANO, OP. 83

In July 1881 Johannes Brahms, in a letter to Elisabeth von Herzo-genberg, wrote: "I don't mind telling you that I have written a tiny, tiny *pianoforte concerto* with a tiny, tiny wisp of a *scherzo*. It is in B-flat, and I have reason to fear that I have worked this udder, which has yielded good milk before, too often and too vigorously."

Brahms' "tiny tiny *pianoforte concerto*" turned out to be nothing less than the *colossal* Concerto in B-flat Major and the "tiny, tiny wisp of a *scherzo*" is a monumental *Allegro appassionato* movement which Brahms inserted between the opening and slow movements, thus giving it the aspect of a four-movement symphony. Indeed, the critic Hanslick dubbed the piece "a symphony with piano *obbligato*."

According to Brahms' friend and traveling companion Dr. Theo-dor Billroth, the B-flat Major Piano Concerto first began to take shape in the composer's mind in April 1878, during Brahms' first journey to Italy. He put his sketches on paper the next month when he returned home with the Italian air and fragrance still fresh in his lungs. Three years later the spring again called Brahms to Italy and when he returned this time, the B-flat Major Concerto occupied him almost constantly until he completed it in early July.

In the early years of the existence of the B-flat Major Concerto, the presence of that "tiny, tiny wisp of a *scherzo*" puzzled its auditors. The aforementioned Dr. Billroth wrote to Brahms that he found the "charming *scherzo* hardly in keeping with the simpler form of the first movement." He also advised a prospective performer of the concerto that "the *scherzo* could be omitted without injury." The great English musicologist, pianist and composer Sir Donald Francis Tovey brilliantly answered the question of the relevance of the Scherzo to the other three movements:

Of all existing concertos in the classical form this is the largest. It is true that the first movement is shorter than either that of Beethoven's E-flat Concerto or that of his Violin Concerto; shorter also than that of Brahms' own First Concerto. But in almost every classical concerto the first movement is as large or larger than the slow movement and finale taken together, and there is no scherzo. Here, in his B-flat Concerto, Brahms has followed the first movement by a fiery, almost tragic *allegro* which, though anything but a joke, more than fills the place of the largest possible symphonic scherzo; the slow movement is easily the largest in any concerto, while the finale, with all its lightness of touch, is a *rondo* of the most spacious design. We thus have the three normal movements of the classical concerto at their fullest and richest, with the addition of a fourth member on the same scale.

If there ever could be any doubt as to the purpose of that stormy second movement, the first notes of the *andante* should settle it. The key is B-flat, the key of the first movement, and its emotion is a reaction after a storm, not after a triumph. Thus both in harmony and in mood it would be fatally misplaced immediately after the first movement. After the second, its emotional fitness is perfect, while the harmonic value of its being in the tonic of the whole work is the value of a stroke of genius. It gives this slow movement a strangely poetic feeling of *finality*, though the slow tempo and lyric style make it obviously unlikely that it can really be the end. The first movement had it storms; the second movement was all storm, and here we are not only enjoying a calm, but safe at home again.

And now we have the finale. What tremendous triumph shall it express? Brahms' answer is such as only the greatest of artists can find; there are no adequate words for it (there never are for any art that is not itself words—and then there are only its own words). But it is, perhaps, not misleading to say here, as can so often be said with Beethoven, something like this:—"We have done our work—let the children play in the world which our work has made safer and happier for them."

"Massive" and "monumental" are the two adjectives which are most frequently applied to characterize the Brahms B-flat Major Concerto, and with good reason. As Tovey pointed out, the entire conception of the work is on the grandest of grand scales—even to the nearly fifty minutes required playing time. Any performance which really comes to grips with the score must convey a feeling of monolithic power and invincibility. Anything less than this does Brahms a disservice.

Fortunately, there are several recorded performances of the score which meet it on its own terms and give it back to us in truly heroic proportions. The oldest of the recordings still currently available is the one RCA recorded in 1940 with Vladimir Horowitz and the NBC Symphony Orchestra conducted by Toscanini (RCA LCT 1025). The performance still sparkles with an electric excitement generated by the fantastic facility of Horowitz' ten fingers and the razor-sharp precision of the orchestral ensemble. The recorded sound, not surprisingly, is harsh and brittle (even though the recording was made in Carnegie Hall rather than in NBC's old Studio 8-H) and the balance between piano and orchestra is not good, but the B-flat Major Concerto has seldom had a more dynamic presentation than this one.

One of the newest, and far and away one of the best, of the recorded performances of the B Flat Concerto is the version by Daniel Barenboim, with Sir John Barbirolli conducting the New Philharmonia Orchestra (Angel S 36526). Where the collaboration by these same artists in Brahms' First Concerto was, for me, on the disappointing side, their version of the Second is nothing less than revelatory. For one thing, Barenboim seems much more at home with the gentler contours of the B Flat Concerto than with the heaven-storming anger of the D Minor. And yet the demonic pages in the first two movements of the B Flat Concerto find him in full control of the passion inherent in the music. The serenity of his playing in the slow movement is a marvel, and the last movement has a grace and easy flow that bring the performance to an exhilarating conclusion. Barbirolli is a perfect collaborator for Barenboim, giving the entire enterprise a remarkable sense of cohesion and co-operation. The players of the New Philharmonia Orchestra give of their very best and the recorded sound is warm, clear and well-balanced. In short, the Barenboim-Barbirolli recording of Brahms' B Flat Concerto is one of the glories of recorded music and I heartily recommend it as a unique spiritual experience.

Another outstanding exponent of the solo part of this work is Rudolf Serkin, who has recorded the concerto for Columbia Records no fewer than four different times. The most recent of Serkin's recordings is a collaboration with George Szell and the Cleveland Orchestra (Columbia MS 6967) that is masterful. The emotion is intense and febrile in the first two movements, reposeful in the slow movement and gracefully lyric in the finale.

Excellent also are the recordings by Ashkenazy-Mehta (London CS 6539), Backhaus-Böhm (London CS 6550), Gilels-Reiner (RCA Victrola VICS 1026) and Rubinstein-Krips (RCA LSC 2296). Each of these artists responds individually to the mixture of power and poetry so magically inherent in the music and they are all very well recorded, for the most part. The Gilels reproduction, a product of the early days of stereo technology, is on the cavernous side—big and somewhat boomy—but it doesn't get in the way of enjoying the performance.

In January 1968 André Watts, with Leonard Bernstein and the New York Philharmonic recorded the score for Columbia (MS 7134). It is one of the finest of all Brahms B-flat Major Concerto recordings available. At the age of twenty-one, Watts plays the work with the maturity of a born artist and musician.

Rubinstein's re-recording of the score with Ormandy and the Philadelphia Orchestra (RCA LSC 3253) presents a more introspective account of the music than was the pianist's earlier wont. Riper, more richly Romantic accounts of the score are those from the teams of Barenboim-Barbirolli, Fischer-Furtwängler (Turnabout 4342, mono only), Serkin-Szell and Watts-Bernstein. My preferred choice from among the reel-to-reel versions—in the absence of any of these four—is the Ashkenazy-Mehta performance (London L 80206), with Cliburn-Reiner (RCA RK 1098) leading the field of available cassette performances.

CONCERTO IN D MAJOR FOR VIOLIN, OP. 77

The Violin Concerto by Brahms, in its expansively woven melodies, its rhythmic robustness and warm flow of harmony, seems to carry the imprint of the idyllic surroundings in which it was created: the blue Wörthersee in the southern Austrian Alps where Brahms spent the summer of 1878 at the town of Pörtschach, one of his favorite retreats.

Commentators ever since have linked the character of Brahms' two D major works of that period, the Second Symphony and the Violin Concerto. Both are regarded as sunny, idyllic works abounding in melodic simplicity and charm. Yet this is not by any means the whole story of the Violin Concerto. It is also a work of rugged and noble grandeur, symphonic in its integration of the solo part with the orchestra and a challenge to the new breed of performer who was just beginning to emerge in Brahms' time—the musically intelligent virtuoso.

One of the oft-repeated legends concerning the Brahms Violin Concerto holds that the work was largely molded and shaped by the composer's friend, the great Hungarian violinist, Joseph Joachim. It is certainly true that Brahms sought the advice of Joachim while he was working on the concerto, but it now seems pretty clear that Joachim was helpful to Brahms only in such workaday matters as suggesting the most idiomatic fingerings and bowings for the music.

In his excellent biography of Brahms, Karl Geiringer reproduces a passage from the solo part as Brahms wrote it originally, then with the suggested alterations of Joachim, and finally as it appears in the finished version. Some of the elements of Joachim's emendation have assuredly been embraced by Brahms, but the musical treatment is entirely Brahms' own.

Because of its inordinate difficulty the concerto was regarded with some disdain early in its career. Hans von Bülow summed up this attitude most graphically by remarking that Max Bruch, the esteemed contemporary of Brahms, had written concertos *for* the violin; Brahms had written one *against* the violin. That this attitude was conditioned by the technical limitations of the violinists of the time seems rather obvious; today the concerto is one of the ultimate tests of the musical scope and vision of its performers.

In its original drafts, the concerto was to consist of four movements. Later, however, Brahms abandoned the thought of a Scherzo, and he subjected the *Adagio* movement to a good deal of reworking. "The middle movements have gone," he wrote, "and of course they were the best! But I have written a feeble Adagio." Brahms' friend and biographer, Max Kalbeck, speculates that the original Scherzo may have found its way into the Second Piano Concerto, where Brahms finally did succumb to the temptation of a four-movement symphonic design.

An astute analysis of the concerto was written by Lawrence Gilman for the concert bulletin of the New York Philharmonic:

The main theme of the first movement is announced at once by cellos, violas, bassoons and horns. This subject, and three contrasting song-like themes, together with an energetic dotted figure furnish the thematic material of the first movement. The violin is introduced, after almost a hundred measures for the orchestra alone, in an extended section, chiefly of passage-work, as preamble to the exposition of the chief theme. The caressing and delicate weaving of the solo instrument about the melodic outlines of the song themes in the orchestra is unforgettable.

This feature is even more pronounced in the second movement, where the solo violin, having made its compliments to the chief subject (the opening melody for oboe), announces a second theme, which it proceeds to embroider with captivating and tender beauty. Perhaps not since Chopin have the possibilities of decorative figuration developed so rich a yield of poetic loveliness as in this Concerto. Brahms is here ornamental without ornateness, florid without excess; these arabesques have the dignity and fervor of pure lyric speech.

The Finale is a virtuoso's paradise. The jocund chief theme, in thirds, is stated at once by the solo violin. There is many a hazard for the soloist: ticklish passage work, double-stopping, arpeggios. Also there is much spirited and fascinating music—music of rhythmical charm and gusto.

In general, there seem to be two distinct ways of approaching the Brahms Violin Concerto in performance. One might be called the philosophizing, Middle European way; the other, the uninhibited, extroverted style of virtuoso fiddling commonly associated with the Russian school. The concerto adapts itself to either approach, though it is an interesting commentary on performance values of our time that the razzle-dazzle, slam-bang virtuoso performance has largely yielded to the more probing, analytical one.

The most obvious illustration of this fact is the recording of the concerto by David Oistrakh with Otto Klemperer conducting (Angel S 35836). As the most illustrious of all current Russian violinists, Oistrakh might reasonably be expected to be a representative of the knock-'em-between-the-eyes school of Brahms Violin Concerto performances. On the contrary, his performance is a probing, deeply felt one. It has power, perception and (in the last movement) puckishness. Much of the credit, of course, belongs to Klemperer, but together Oistrakh and he have fashioned a performance of the concerto that I find extremely satisfying.

Also very satisfying is the performance Fritz Kreisler recorded in London during the 1930s with Sir John Barbirolli conducting the London Philharmonic Orchestra (Angel COLH 35, mono only, now withdrawn). Kreisler was already beyond the age of sixty at the time, but all the hallmarks of his style are still there: a thorough and absorbed identification with the emotional spirit of the music and a completely natural—I am tempted to say inevitable—expression of it. Furthermore, his technical security was still sufficient to the demands of the concerto. Here, then, is a performance which seems to have set the example for most of our present-day violinists. The sound of the reproduction is still quite acceptable.

Also in this same tradition is the performance by Henryk Szeryng with Pierre Monteux conducting the London Symphony Orchestra (RCA Victrola VICS 1028)—and it is on a budget label!

Those who want a no-holds-barred virtuoso treatment are referred to the recording by Heifetz, with Fritz Reiner and the Chicago Symphony Orchestra (RCA LSC 1903). Heifetz takes an emotionally detached, thoroughly objective view of the score and pursues this attitude relentlessly to the final double bar. The playing is astonishing in its perfection and brilliance, and Heifetz phrases much of the time with an elegance and poise beyond that of his colleagues in the field. Yet I am curiously unmoved by this essentially bloodless performance. The technical problems posed by the score are mastered beyond compare, but the musical values are served up in dehydrated, prepackaged fashion. The stereo sound is a product of the very early days of stereo technology, and there is a somewhat pinched, raspy sound to it all. Also, Heifetz has been placed very close to the solo microphone so that the aural spectrum is an unbalanced one.

The massive and measured Oistrakh-Klemperer collaboration impresses me more than Oistrakh's re-recording of the score with Szell and the Cleveland Orchestra (Angel S 36033), though the latter performance is a tighter, more elemental one—and it seems to be the only reel-to-reel performance currently available (Angel M 36033). The Oistrakh-Szell-Cleveland Orchestra recording is the preferred one of the two available in the cassette medium (Angel 4XS 36033).

SYMPHONY NO. 1 IN C MINOR, OP. 68

A sensational pronouncement appeared on October 23, 1853, in the pages of one of Germany's most respected musical periodicals, the *Neue Zeitschrift für Musik*. Robert Schumann was the author, and he was writing after ten years of virtual retirement from the literary arena. Under the heading *Neue Bahne*, "New Directions," Schumann wrote that a young composer had appeared "who should reveal his mastery, not by gradual development, but should spring, like Minerva, fully armed, from the head of Jove. And now he has come, the young creature over whose cradle the Graces and heroes have kept watch. His name is Johannes Brahms." Schumann went on to venture the hope that Brahms would soon "point his magic wand to where the might of mass, in chorus and orchestra, lends him his power."

Schumann's prophecy seems premature when one remembers that the Johannes Brahms of 1853 was a raw stripling barely into his twenty-first year. If the world of music was not prepared for Schumann's pronouncement, the object of his enthusiasm was appalled at the heavy responsibility thus placed on his inexperienced shoulders.

A corollary and altogether awesome responsibility for the twenty-year-old Brahms was the general, if tacit, acceptance of him as the heir apparent to the heroic symphonic mantle of Beethoven. Other composers, such as Schubert, Schumann and Mendelssohn, may have composed symphonies whose lyrical cast showed them to be unintimidated by the long shadow of Beethoven, but not Brahms. "You have no conception of how the likes of us feel when we hear the tramp of a giant like him behind us," he once confided to Hermann Levi, the conductor.

According to D. Millar Craig, the work we now know as Brahms' First Symphony was completed and ready "for about fourteen years" before it was heard. Craig says that "Professor Lipsius of Leipzig University, who knew Brahms well and often entertained him, told me that from 1862 onwards, Brahms almost literally carried the manuscript score about with him in his pocket, hesitating to have it made public." Friends urged Brahms over and over again to let it be heard, but not until 1876 could his diffidence about it be overcome.

When Brahms was finally ready to reveal his First Symphony to the world, the event took place not in one of the large and cosmopolitan music centers of Germany or Austria. Instead, Brahms chose the comparatively small town of Karlsruhe for the premiere—"a little town," he called it, "that holds a good friend, a good conductor, and a good orchestra." After the Karlsruhe premiere in November 1876, which was conducted by Otto Dessoff, Brahms himself conducted performances of the score in Mannheim, Vienna, Leipzig and Breslau. It cannot be said that the symphony was an immediate success. Its first audiences listened to it with respect, perhaps even admiration, but with no real love. Only years later, after the silly factional rivalry between the pro-Brahmsians and the neo-Germans (i.e., the Wagnerites) had subsided, did Brahms' First Symphony establish a firm hold upon the affections of the wide music-loving public.

The first movement begins with a majestic thirty-seven measure introduction which is one of the great exordiums in all music. The ascending chromatic phrases of the strings and the simultaneous descending phrases of the woodwinds set a scene of majestic inner struggle which permeates the entire movement. The *Allegro* which follows continues the dramatic tension and somber coloring of the introduction and there is a coda of calm yet unsettled repose.

The second movement is a meditative, lyrical outpouring of great poetic feeling. Near the end of the movement there is a duet for French horn and solo violin that can only be called sublime.

The third movement is a gentle zephyr, a graceful *Allegretto* that Sir George Grove characterized as "a sort of national tune or folk song of simple sweetness and grace." The opening subject appears first in the clarinet. In place of a Trio, there is a contrasting section of a sterner nature, but then the mood and thematic material of the opening of the movement returns and the conclusion is calm.

The last movement is, in the words of Lawrence Gilman, "the chief glory of the symphony." Again, as in the first movement, there is an elaborate introduction, this time tinged with mystery. Then, like the sun, there shines forth that broad, majestic melody which is one of the glories of symphonic music. In a movement dotted with highly dramatic episodes, two sections especially stand out: the melting song of the horn in the introduction, heard through a misty string tremolo against sustained chords in the trombones; and the triumphant declaration by the trumpets of the chorale-like melody near the end. The symphony ends in a blaze of glory and triumph, a jubilant affirmation of the heroic. That, after all, is what this symphony is all about.

Early in the art of electrical recording, in the late 1920s, there was a performance of Brahms' First Symphony by Leopold Stokowski and the Philadelphia Orchestra that was positively electrifying in its vitality and excitement; the performance has long been unavailable, however. A highly regarded performance of the past that is still to be found—though the sonics are now rather badly dated—is the version conducted by Toscanini (in RCA Victrola album VIC 6400, containing all the Brahms symphonies as well as the *Tragic* and *Academic Festival* Overtures and the Variations on a Theme by Haydn, all on four discs). It is on the shrill side and deficient in bass. The limited sonics, however, cannot hide the fact that nobody has quite matched the Toscanini performance in its high-strung, nervous intensity.

My own favorites among the contemporary recorded performances of the score are those by Klemperer (Angel S 35481), Ormandy (Columbia MS 6067) and Szell (Columbia D3S 758—a three-disc set devoted to Szell's performances of all four Brahms symphonies). One of Klemperer's most distinctive qualities is his ability to create a mood of rapt and exalted grandeur. His performance of Brahms' First Symphony is a rare spiritual communication. One comes away from it with a sense of absolute catharsis. Unfortunately, however, the recording now betrays its origin in the primitive stages of stereo technology; the sound is shallow and unfocused. Even so, this is a performance to be cherished. Ormandy, for his part, really identifies with the music and is absorbed in it. The playing of the Philadelphia Orchestra and Columbia's recording of it are absolutely luxurious. Szell's performance starts out with a rather mannered reading of the first movement but then it blossoms out into a truly noble and uniquely satisfying account of the score. Like Ormandy's, it is magnificently played and recorded.

In tape configurations, Karajan's labored account has a monopoly in the cassette department (DGG 923023) and a virtual monopoly in the reel-to-reel department (DGG K 8925).

SYMPHONY NO. 2 IN D MAJOR, OP. 73

As a symphonist, Johannes Brahms was late in developing—or, rather, he was late in committing himself with a work of full symphonic dimensions. But once he had been persuaded to risk that step he quickly followed it with another. The result was his Second Symphony in D Major, the sunniest, most cheerful of his four works in this form and one of the most popular compositions in the orchestral repertoire. The premiere of the work was given in December of 1877, just thirteen months after the premiere of the First.

The Second Symphony quickly made its way into the international concert repertoire. Two weeks after the first performance, Brahms himself conducted it in Leipzig; then Josef Joachim introduced it in Düsseldorf, and Brahms conducted a performance in Hamburg. Within a year of its first presentation, the symphony had reached London and New York.

From the very beginning, perceptive commentators have found a mood of sunny exuberance in the work. The composer himself, in a letter to the Viennese critic Eduard Hanslick, called the music "cheerful and likable," and C. F. Pohl, writing after the initial rehearsals, said: "It brims with life and strength, deep feeling and charm. Such things are made only in the country, in the midst of nature."

In his review of the symphony following its premiere, Hanslick wrote a perceptive and most interesting reaction and analysis:

> The character of this symphony may be described in short as peaceful, tender, but not effeminate . . . The first movement begins immediately with a mellow and dusky horn theme. It has something of the character of the serenade, and this impression is strengthened still further in the Scherzo and Finale. This first movement, an *Allegro moderato* in 3-4, immerses us in a clear wave of melody upon which we rest, swayed, refreshed by two slight Mendelssohnian reminiscences which emerge before us. The last fifty measures of this movement expire in flashes of new melodic beauty. A broad, singing *Adagio* in B follows, which, as it appears to me, is more conspicuous for the de-

velopment of the themes than for the worth of the themes themselves. For this reason, undoubtedly, it makes a less profound impression on the public than do the other movements. The Scherzo is thoroughly delightful in its graceful movement in minuet tempo. It is twice interrupted by a *Presto* in 2-4, which flashes, spark-like, for a moment. The Finale in D, 4-4, more vivacious but always agreeable in its golden sincerity, is widely removed from the stormy Finales of the modern school. Mozartean blood flows in its veins.

Except for the lack of sympathy with Brahms' noble slow movement, Hanslick's first impressions accord fully with our own contemporary view of this glorious work. The warm lyricism and sunny, romantic flavor of the music are lastingly engaging and the intensity and passion of the slow movement are now seen as the crowning glory of the whole.

Though the work has no official subtitle, it might well be called Brahms' "Pastoral" Symphony. The pervading feeling is one of idyllic serenity—despite the brooding melancholy of the slow movement —and the closing pages are among the most rousingly exuberant outpourings in all symphonic literature.

The symphony has been very well served by the conductors who have recorded it, for the most part. I would single out as most worthwhile the performances conducted by Klemperer (Angel S 35532), Kertesz (London CS 6435), Steinberg (Command 11002 SD) and Szell (included in Columbia D3S 758, a three-disc album devoted to Szell performances of the four Brahms symphonies).

Klemperer conveys a sense of mystery in the music, and he shapes the slow movement most affectionately. Space is left on the second side for a bold and vigorous performance of Brahms' *Tragic* Overture. The sound is generally good. Kertesz and Szell deliver performances that rather closely resemble one another: each radiates a healthy vitality, aided by splendid playing and vivid sound reproduction. Steinberg's performance is in the great tradition of Felix Weingartner's style; forthright and lucid, with the music proceeding from first to last in an inexorable flow. Beecham's mellow and genial account of this score with the Royal Philharmonic Orchestra now exists in Angel's budget-priced Seraphim line (S 60083).

This and the Kertesz-Vienna Philharmonic recording (London CS 6435) are my current favorites among all recorded performances of this vernal score.

The Karajan performance is for me even less felicitous than is his performance of the composer's First Symphony, but for those impressed by his calculated music-making the same reel that contains his performance of the First (DGG K 8925) also holds his reading of the Second Symphony. Cassette buyers have very little choice: Abbado's rigid performance with the Berlin Philharmonic (DGG 3300180) or nothing.

SYMPHONY NO. 3 IN F MAJOR, OP. 90

When Brahms produced his Second Symphony within a year of the long-delayed appearance of the First, the musical world settled back to the comfortable expectation of a steady flow of symphonies from his pen. But again Brahms confounded his audiences. Six more years passed after the premiere of the Second Symphony before he was ready to submit his Third to an impatient public. The year was 1883 and Brahms had just turned fifty. If the First Symphony is an intense emotional outpouring of heroic feelings, and the Second a radiant, lyrical effusion, the Third surely represents a more personal, intimate side of Brahms the symphonist: Brahms the philosopher and poet. Restraint and reflection predominate in the Third Symphony, along with a sophistication that only a mature artist at the very height of his powers can communicate. Through the confluence of these characteristics there emerges a symphony that bursts with vitality and towering strength.

When the Third Symphony was new, Eduard Hanslick immediately dubbed it Brahms' "Eroica" Symphony. Hanslick wrote: "Truly, if the First Symphony in C Minor is characterized as the *Pathetic* or the *Appassionata*, and the Second in D Major as the *Pastoral*, the new symphony in F Major may be appropriately called Brahms' *Eroica*." Hanslick pointed out, however, that the "heroic" designation could be applied only to the opening and closing movements

since there were passages in the score that quivered "with the romantic twilight of Schumann and Mendelssohn."

If the Third Symphony is today probably the least performed of
the composer's four, part of the reason, no doubt, stems from the
fact that it is the only one of them which does not have a rousing,
triumphant final climax to "bring down the house." But there are
other reasons, too: the Third Symphony presents special problems
in performance. The conductor is faced with the challenge of presenting to his audiences a ruminating, personal score which can
become tedious and unrewarding in the wrong hands. In the right
hands, however, Brahms' Third Symphony exerts an extraordinary
feeling of sober, autumnal fulfillment.

In his book *Brahms: His Life and Work* Karl Geiringer has written the following description of the symphony:

Like the first two symphonies, the Third is introduced by a motto;
this at once provides the bass for the grandiose principal subject of
the first movement, and dominates not only this movement, but the
whole Symphony. It assumes a particularly important role in the first
movement, before the beginning of the recapitulation. After the
passionate development the waves of excitement calm down, and the
horn announces the motto, in a mystic E Flat major, as a herald of
heavenly peace. Passionless, clear, almost objective serenity speaks to
us from the second movement. No *Andante* of such emotional tranquillity is to be found in the works of the youthful Brahms. Particularly
attractive is the first theme of the following *Poco Allegretto*, which
(in spite of its great simplicity) is stamped with a highly individual
character by its constant alternation of rhythms. Further, Brahms
contrived to make the concise three-fold form of the work more effective by orchestrating the da capo of the first part in quite a different
manner. Such a mixture of simplicity and refinement is characteristic
of Brahms in his later years. The Finale is a tremendous conflict of
elemental forces; it is only in the Coda that calm returns. Like a
rainbow after a thunderstorm, the motto, played by the flute, with
its message of hope and freedom, spans the turmoil of the other voices.

One of the most spectacular failures among the many recordings
of Brahms' Third Symphony is the performance by Arturo Toscanini

and the NBC Symphony Orchestra (included in RCA Victrola
VIC 6400; see the section on Brahms' First Symphony for details).
In his valuable book *Toscanini and the Art of Orchestral Performance* Robert C. Marsh reveals that before he consented to record
Brahms' Third Symphony, Toscanini had the NBC engineers put
together an "ideal" performance for him to study, made from sections
of performances he had conducted in 1938, 1946 and 1948. The
"ideal" performance, however, turned out to be tense and hard-driven
and out of keeping with the character of the music. When Toscanini finally came to record the score, he erred in exactly the
opposite direction. The recorded performance is surprisingly slack
and soporific, lacking forward motion, continuity and rhythmic pulse.

Four conductors whose recordings have all these qualities plus
a marvelous rapport with the spirit of Brahms' music are Otto
Klemperer (Angel S 35545), William Steinberg (Command 11015
SD), Carlo Maria Giulini (Seraphim S 60101) and George Szell
(Columbia MS 6685). Klemperer's is perhaps the most successful
of his generally superb recordings of the four Brahms symphonies,
and continues to be the version I prefer, even despite rather faded
sonics. Here is just the right easy, spontaneous flow so indispensable
to the natural expression of the music—and yet there is no relaxation
of tension or drive. Both Steinberg and Szell offer performances of
virile excitement, supported by a calm and relaxed response to the
poetic elements in the score. Giulini's account is also persuasive.

Where tape and cassette are concerned, no satisfactory recordings
are available, since the tape version of Steinberg's performance is
now no longer listed.

SYMPHONY NO. 4 IN E MINOR, OP. 98

One day in September of 1885 Johannes Brahms sat in a coffeehouse
in Vienna comparing notes with his friend Max Kalbeck on their
doings of the summer just past. When Kalbeck ventured to ask if
the composer had written any chamber music recently, Brahms replied, "God forbid! I have not been so ambitious. I have put together
only a few bits in the way of waltzes and polkas." Kalbeck's anten-

nae must have been set to quivering, for Brahms' friends had by then become accustomed to having him speak of imposing new scores in just such a depreciatory manner. A few years earlier, in a letter to Elisabeth von Herzogenberg, he had mentioned the completion of what he called "a tiny, tiny *pianoforte concerto* with a tiny, tiny wisp of a *scherzo*"; this trifle had turned out to be nothing less than his Second Piano Concerto.

A few days after their *Kaffeeklatsch*, Brahms invited Kalbeck and a few other friends to a private reading of the new "bits," which he and another associate, Ignaz Brüll, were to play in a reduction of the orchestral parts for two pianos. Actually, the composer's casualness about his music masked a real concern about the impression the work would make on its hearers, and his reference to what he had written as "a few . . . polkas and waltzes" had about it something of the same jittery overcasualness that a teen-ager might show when introducing her latest boy friend to her parents. For, in point of fact, the new score, which turned out to be his Symphony No. 4 in E Minor, was certainly no mere collection of dance tunes; it was a closely reasoned, austere, even somber work, with a most uncompromising passacaglia as its Finale, and Brahms' doubts as to its easy acceptance were well founded. The symphony took longer than any of his others to win popularity. The reaction of the friends he had invited to the private audition was respectful but cool and guarded, and the reaction to the early orchestral performances was not notably more enthusiastic.

The ripening forces of time and repetition, however, served to reveal to audiences the greatness of the music, and Brahms' Fourth Symphony is today one of the cornerstones of the symphonic repertoire. It is also, perhaps, Brahms' most intensely stimulating work in symphonic form. The opening movement builds to a highly dramatic, tension-packed climax out of a beginning that is one of the composer's most lyrical outpourings, and the slow movement has a nostalgic serenity of the sort that is characteristic of Brahms' art at its ripest. The Scherzo is an irresistible explosion of rollicking good spirits, and the passacaglia Finale, with its superb development of a Bach-derived theme, is of magnificent proportions.

A set of curious circumstances surrounded the American premiere of Brahms' Fourth Symphony. Wilhelm Gericke, who in 1884 had succeeded Sir George Henschel as conductor of the Boston Symphony Orchestra, scheduled the first American performance of the score for his public rehearsal and public concert of November 25 and 26, 1886—little more than a year after Brahms himself had conducted the world premiere in Meiningen. Gericke did duly conduct the symphony at the Friday afternoon public rehearsal, and—according to a contemporary newspaper account—conducted it without a pause. He was unhappy with the performance, however, and withdrew the score for further study, hurriedly substituting Schumann's "Spring" Symphony for it at the Saturday evening concert. Thus the honor of the *official* American premiere of Brahms' Fourth Symphony went to Walter Damrosch, who conducted it in a concert by the New York Symphony Society about two weeks later, on December 11, 1886.

Toscanini's performance of the Fourth Symphony (included in RCA Victrola VIC 6400) is as great a triumph as his recording of the Third is a failure. In this 1951 performance the Maestro's intensity of phrasing and his feeling for formal design found an ideal outlet. The smoldering drama that underlies the surface serenity of the first two movements is captured perfectly; the Scherzo is a tumult of explosive vigor and tension; and the concluding passacaglia, played in absolutely steady rhythm, is overwhelming in its power and passion. At the time the recording was made, RCA was having reasonable success in capturing the sound of Toscanini's orchestra; even though there is a certain amount of shrillness, the reproduction is quite serviceable even now. Furthermore, the discipline of the playing is something awesome to hear.

Also exceptionally satisfying are the performances conducted by Klemperer (Angel S 35546), Munch (RCA LSC 2297) and Szell (included in Columbia D3S 758). Klemperer's is, as usual with him; a heroic conception of the music, one with great cumulative power. Not every listener will be convinced by the exaggerated pauses Klemperer introduces just before the heavy string chords heralding each reappearance of the main theme in the Scherzo, and the recorded sound now seems excessively coarse in sound; but it cannot be denied that Klemperer delivers a powerful statement of the music. Munch conducts a performance that is exciting in its vitality and deeply satisfying in its introspection. The recorded sound is rich and embracing, with fine detail and nicely calculated balance. Szell succeeds in producing a performance as provocative as Klemperer's, yet as impetuous as Toscanini's. And he has the benefit of vivid and extremely life-like recorded sound.

None of the available reel-to-reel tape accounts is really satisfactory, now that the Szell reel is no longer to be had. Of the cassette versions, my selection would be the Giulini-Chicago Symphony recording (Angel 4XS 36040), though the performance has neither the propulsion nor the cumulative power that both Toscanini and Szell bring to the music.

Anton Bruckner

Born: Ansfelden, Upper Austria, September 4, 1824
Died: Vienna, October 11, 1896

Much of Bruckner's early training and education was at the hands of Augustine monks. The pious simplicity of the monastic life was a profound influence on the developing youth and throughout his lifetime he was much under its spell. He composed his first mass during his teens and for much of his mature lifetime he served as organist and choirmaster in churches, settling in Vienna in 1868. For the remaining twenty-eight years of his life he was court organist, professor of organ, harmony and counterpoint at the Vienna Conservatory and lecturer in theory at Vienna University.

Aside from his teaching activities, Bruckner devoted his life entirely to composition. Much of his creative activity was accomplished with no public knowledge of his work. Because he was an ardent follower of Wagner, he came under attack from the opposing camp, principally the critic Hanslick. None of this bothered Bruckner, however, and he continued to produce his masses and symphonies in Olympian detachment. Bruckner's final years were spent in relative serenity: the Emperor granted him a government pension and he lived in royal apartments. In the meantime his first eight symphonies, composed between 1865 and 1890, began slowly to make their way in public esteem, along with his Te Deum of 1883 and *Psalm 150* of 1892.

Bruckner worked on his Ninth Symphony for the last ten years of his life. Three movements were completed, and he labored over a fourth until the very end: indeed, on the very day of his death he made a few feeble notations in the music. The three completed movements of the symphony—as is true of the two completed movements of Schubert's so-called "Unfinished" Symphony—represent, nevertheless, a fully realized artistic whole: it is impossible to think of any music following the sublime third-movement *Adagio* of the Ninth Symphony. At one time it was not uncommon for conductors to attach the Te Deum as a choral fourth movement conclusion to the Ninth Symphony (in the manner of Beethoven's Ninth); this practice has been largely abandoned in recent years and the three completed movements are now generally allowed to stand by themselves.

The publication in 1936 of the original editions of many of the Bruckner symphonies sparked a lively controversy in musical circles that raged for about twenty years. The original editions showed that many of Bruckner's more audacious bits of instrumentation were "refined" and scrubbed clean by well-meaning but ill-advised friends and editors. There is now fairly general agreement that Bruckner's intentions are best served by the original texts of the symphonies and most conductors today perform them from the original editions.

The music of Bruckner has enjoyed an unprecedented popularity in the years following the Second World War and there are no signs of any lessening of this trend.

SYMPHONY NO. 7 IN E MAJOR

On December 30 of the year 1884, the conductor of the orchestra at the State Theater in Leipzig led the world premiere performance of a new symphony by a sixty-year-old composer from Vienna who was then known only to a very few devoted disciples. He was Anton Bruckner, the symphony was his Seventh, and the conductor was a twenty-nine-year-old firebrand named Arthur Nikisch, who was just beginning his career. For four decades to follow, Nikisch was probably the most influential of all active conductors, and he left his mark on the musical life of Hamburg, London, Leipzig and Berlin, as well as Boston, where he served as conductor of the Boston Symphony Orchestra for several seasons in the early 1890s.

That end-of-the-year performance of Bruckner's Seventh Symphony served to launch the careers of both the young conductor and the aging composer. For fifteen minutes after the music drew to a close, the audience assembled in the Leipzig State Theater applauded both men. A critic who was present wrote:

> One could see from the trembling of his lips and the sparkling moisture in his eyes how difficult it was for the elderly composer to suppress his deep emotion. His homely but honest countenance beamed with a warm inner happiness such as can appear only on the face of one who is too good-hearted to succumb to bitterness even under the pressure of most disheartening circumstances. Having heard his work and now seeing him in person, we asked ourselves in amazement, "How is it possible that he could remain so long unknown to us?"

Bruckner did not remain unknown for long. Ten weeks later the German conductor Hermann Levi presented the Seventh Symphony in Munich, calling it "the most significant symphonic work since 1827"—an obvious gibe at Brahms, who had already enjoyed considerable success with his first three symphonies. This choosing-up of sides, with Brahms in one camp and Bruckner and Wagner in the other, was to cost Bruckner dearly for years in terms of acceptance, especially while the arch-anti-Wagnerite critic, Eduard Hanslick, was on the scene in Vienna. Because of this, the Austrian premiere of the Seventh Symphony was given not in Vienna but in Graz, where Karl Muck conducted it on March 14, 1886. Bruckner, in fact, tried unsuccessfully to prevent the Vienna premiere scheduled for the following week, fearing that the hostility of Hanslick and a significant segment of the Viennese musical public would only cause him pain. This time, however, Hanslick was forced to concede that the performance, under Hans Richter's direction, caused Bruckner to be "called to the stage four or five times after each section of the symphony." Also present at the performance was Vienna's reigning musical hero, Johann Strauss, Jr., who afterward sent Bruckner a telegram: "Am much moved—it was the greatest impression of my life."

Bruckner's trials in Vienna were not completely over, however. Months later, Hanslick unleashed a blistering attack on the composer and his Seventh Symphony in the *Neue Freie Presse*:

I frankly admit that I can scarcely give a right judgment on Bruckner's symphony, so unnatural, overblown, wretched, and corrupt does it appear to me. As every greater work of Bruckner has inspired spots, interesting and even beautiful places—between these flashes are stretches of impenetrable darkness, leaden boredom and feverish agitation. One of the most unregenerate musicians of Germany writes me in a letter saying that Bruckner's symphony is like the bewildered dream of a player who has just survived twenty *Tristan* rehearsals. That I would call valid and to the point.

Also to the point is the fact that Hanslick's blind opposition to Wagner undoubtedly influenced his reaction to the music of Bruckner, who unashamedly adored Wagner. Indeed, Bruckner encouraged the association of the dirge-like *Adagio* of the Seventh Symphony with the death of Wagner, even though the movement was completed four months before Wagner died. Music historians have referred to this movement as "the *Adagio* of premonition," and in a letter to the conductor Felix Mottl in connection with an impending performance of the score in Karlsruhe in 1885, Bruckner wrote of the *Adagio* that "[It is] funeral music for tubas and horns. Please take a very slow and solemn tempo. At the close in the dirge (in memory of the death of the Master), think of our Ideal!"

The Seventh Symphony is dedicated "To His Majesty the King, Ludwig II of Bavaria, in deepest reverence." The first movement, marked *Allegro moderato*, opens with the principal theme stated immediately in the cellos, followed by a repeat in the violins and winds. The second theme is heard first in the oboe and clarinet. The second movement, *Adagio*, is probably the best known of all Bruckner's symphonic creations. After his death this sorrowful lamentation was played as a tribute to his memory all over Germany. Two main themes dominate the body of the Scherzo, the first having a hunting character, the second a tempestuous quality. The Trio affords a gentle, lyrical contrast, and then the Scherzo is repeated. The Finale is a massive structure that has a feeling of headlong propulsion. The end is a brilliant coda of enormous power.

Fine performances of the score have been recorded by Klemperer (Angel S 3626), Rosbaud (Turnabout 34083—two sides, and budget-priced, at that) and Solti (London CSA 2216). All except Rosbaud's space the symphony out over three record sides. Klemperer's disposition for massive musical architecture and sonority finds a perfect outlet in this score and the orchestral playing and recorded sound are both first-rate. Solti's recorded sound is probably the best of the lot, but he doesn't quite convince me that he has the measure of this score; spontaneity is notably absent in the performance and it ends up being only a series of rhetorical and emotional postures. Rosbaud's is a highly articulate, emotionally committed performance that merits serious consideration.

Best of them all for me is the recently released Karajan recording (Angel SC 3779, three discs that also contain the conductor's account of Bruckner's Fourth Symphony). Superb playing (by the Berlin Philharmonic) and expert recorded sound characterize Karajan's album, and the conductor mercifully refrains from disfiguring the score by superimposing his own (often misguided) ideas onto the music—a Karajan quality that makes most of his music-making intolerable to me. But here all is well ordered and organized and a really fine performance results. No satisfactory cassette edition of the score is available—unless, of course, the Karajan performance has appeared as a cassette release by the time these words appear in print. Of the available reel-to-reel tape performances, my preference is for the Jochum-Bavarian Radio Symphony recording (DGG K 9138).

SYMPHONY NO. 9 IN D MINOR

In the summer of 1887, during his sixty-second year, Anton Bruckner completed his Eighth Symphony, and immediately began to work on a ninth. Less than two years earlier Bruckner had at long last experienced a measure of success: his Seventh Symphony, conducted by Hans Richter, had served to introduce his music to the subscription audiences of the Vienna Philharmonic concerts. From that day (March 21, 1886), Bruckner's position in the heirarchy of nineteenth-century symphonists was assured. Yet it has taken most of the musical world the better part of a century to concede him his deserved place in the musical firmament.

Progress on the Ninth Symphony was uneven, and Bruckner set it aside several times in order to work on other projects, such as the revision of both the Eighth and the First Symphonies. He returned to the Ninth Symphony, to devote his full attention to it, in February 1891. By September 1894, when Bruckner had passed his seventieth birthday and was already desperately ill, only two movements of the Ninth Symphony were completed—the serene third-movement *Adagio* lay unfinished on his writing table. At this time Bruckner told a friend: "I have done my duty on earth. I have accomplished what I could, and my only wish is to be allowed to complete my Ninth Symphony. . . . There remains only the Finale. I trust Death will not deprive me of my pen." He prayed nightly to God to complete the symphony. "If He refuses, then He must take the responsibility for its incompleteness." Bruckner lived nearly two years longer, but at his death, on October 11, 1896, the last movement of the Ninth Symphony was still not finished.

The musical world, unaware that three movements of the Ninth were well-nigh complete, took it for granted that whatever work Bruckner had in progress had died with its creator. More than six years passed, and then came an incredible announcement: Ferdinand Loewe, a disciple of Bruckner, had constructed a playable edition of the first three movements of the Ninth Symphony; furthermore, Loewe would conduct his version in Vienna in February 1903. The premiere was a sensation. A year later Loewe's edited score of the Ninth Symphony was published, and this was the form in which the music was known to the world for years.

Yet knowledgeable listeners harbored doubts. Some began to suspect that wholesale changes had been made in Bruckner's original orchestration and noted disturbing evidences of highly un-Brucknerian transitions in the score. One writer put it this way: "Where are those abrupt, Bruckneresque transitions between the passages? Why do the various phrases end in gentle expirations? In short, whence comes this odd finesse, this smooth polish, into the work of a composer universally noted for his rugged individuality?" The publication of the ninth volume of a critical edition of Bruckner's works in the early 1930s provided the answers to such questions. The Loewe edition was revealed to be a sandpapered, wholly conventionalized version of a score that contained some of Bruckner's most audacious musical thought: the dynamic scheme had been altered unmercifully, tempo indications and whole patches of orchestration had been changed—even parts of the harmonic structure had been recast.

In April 1932, both the Loewe version and the Bruckner original version were played at a semi-private concert in Munich with Siegmund von Haussegger conducting the Munich Philharmonic Orchestra. This was probably the most influential performance of Bruckner's music in the twentieth century, for it clearly established the superiority of Bruckner's original manuscript and served to trigger the modern pursuit of the original versions of all his symphonies.

The fact that Bruckner's Ninth Symphony is in the key of D minor immediately established a relationship between it and another Ninth Symphony in D minor—Beethoven's—in the minds of some commentators. The analogy was drawn even further by a now-discarded practice of employing Bruckner's Te Deum as a choral Finale for the Ninth Symphony. The three extant movements of the Symphony are marked *Feierlich* (Solemnly), *Scherzo* and *Adagio*. Like the so-called "Unfinished" Symphony of Schubert, Bruckner's Ninth may contain fewer than the traditional four movements, but there is nothing unfinished about its fully realized conception and dynamic.

The structure of the first movement is quite unorthodox. There are four major theme groupings, each of which is built up to a climactic pitch of shattering power. The second main section of the movement is a free fantasia and review, and in the coda the principal musical material is the chief theme, with a reminiscence of a motive from the introduction.

The second movement, an expansive Scherzo, begins with its main theme pizzicato in the strings. After an extensive elaboration, the trio section takes over. It is comprised of two main theme groups, the first for strings, the second for strings and oboes. The movement ends with a return of the Scherzo proper.

The long concluding *Adagio* is the heart of the symphony. The first theme, in the violins, has been characterized by Lawrence Gilman as "characteristically Brucknerian, though the wraiths of Liszt and Wagner do unmistakably peer out at us through the bars." The second theme is also first sounded in the violins. Both are then expansively developed and there is a final crescendo, with the orchestra recalling the first theme fortissimo. The music suddenly subsides to a calm, sublime peace. Werner Wolff wrote: "The flickering violins and the dark-tinged tubas convey the picture of the deeply absorbed composer writing the last pages with a trembling hand. This time Bruckner tells us a story—the story of his end."

The first recording of the original version of the Ninth Symphony was made, appropriately enough, by the forces that first disclosed it to the public—the Munich Philharmonic conducted by Siegmund von Haussegger. As RCA Victor album 627, it was an imposing set of seven twelve-inch 78-rpm discs. The performance was a massive one, and it was splendidly recorded. Throughout the 1940s this was the only available recording of the score. Only in the early 1950s, not long after the beginning of the era of the long-playing record, did Bruckner's Ninth Symphony really come into its own on discs —and, to a large extent, in the concert hall.

The most individual among the current recordings of the score is the one taken from a German radio broadcast by the Berlin Philharmonic Orchestra conducted by Wilhelm Furtwängler. Those who experienced Furtwängler's music-making in either the concert hall or the opera house speak of the unique spell this conductor's art cast over performers and audiences alike. Much of this quality comes through in his performance of Bruckner's Ninth, which carries with it something of the aura of a religious rite. Fortunately, the Furtwängler performance is now available as a single disc, in an astonishingly successful electronic re-recording to simulate stereo effect (Heliodor 2548701). The inimitable character of Furtwängler's way with this score shines forth in rich and glowing sound. Clearly this disc is an absolute must for any collection.

Carl Schuricht's recording with the Vienna Philharmonic Orchestra (Seraphim S 60047—budget-priced) is a light-textured, if sometimes scaled-down approach, but it has its own particular conviction and dedication. It is also very well played and recorded.

Two other exceptionally worthy recordings are those conducted by two outstanding representatives of the younger generation of

conductors—Bernard Haitink (Philips 900162) and Zubin Mehta
(London CS 6462). Both deliver extremely moving performances and
each conveys a sense of inevitability about the unfolding of the
music. Each also has the benefit of vivid, massive recorded sound.

Mehta's is the only one of the first-class performances available
on tape (London L 80170). It is well worth having.

The only other performance in the reel-to-reel category is Karajan's, a perfect example of this conductor's inability to make difference work for its own sake. Unfortunately, though, Karajan's is
the only performance available on cassette (DGG 923078).

Frédéric Chopin

Born: Zelazowa-Wola, Poland, February 22, 1810
Died: Paris, October 17, 1849

Chopin, who was perhaps the most instinctive composer of music for the piano in the history of the art, was the son of a French father and a Polish mother. His first studies were at the Warsaw Gymnasium, where his father was a teacher. He was a child prodigy, appearing in public for the first time at the age of nine as a pianist. Before he was fifteen he had composed polonaises, mazurkas and waltzes for the piano. Before he was twenty he had composed his two concertos for piano and orchestra, along with a string of mazurkas, nocturnes and rondos. Following a concert he played in Vienna at the age of nineteen, a critic was moved to call him "one of the most remarkable meteors blazing on the musical horizon."

In 1831, following a concert in Paris, he decided to settle in that city permanently. In the same year Robert Schumann was moved by Chopin's Fantasy for Piano and Orchestra, Opus 2, to remark: "Hats off, gentlemen—a genius." Eight years later, reviewing certain Chopin preludes, mazurkas and waltzes, Schumann wrote further: "He is and remains the keenest and staunchest poet-soul of the time."

Between 1836 and 1844 Chopin was involved in a liaison with Madame Dudevant—the novelist "George Sand." In 1838 an attack of bronchitis drove him to the island of Majorca, where she seems to have been a devoted nurse. The affair was a stormy one, however —complicated by Chopin's peevishness and weakness as a result of developing tuberculosis. Their ultimate estrangement was an unpleasant one and Chopin is believed to be caricatured in her novel *Lucrezia Floriani*. Chopin's always precarious hold on life began to slip noticeably when the relationship with George Sand was dissolved. His health failed quickly and he completely lost all interest in composition. He spent the greater part of 1848 in England and Scotland, and was the center of devoted attention. Despite his desperately poor health, he nevertheless managed to do some teaching and to play some concerts. He returned to Paris in November 1848 and managed to survive for nearly a year more before he died, at the age of thirty-nine, on October 17, 1849. On the first anniversary of his death a monument to him was unveiled at the cemetery where he was buried; at the same time some Polish earth was strewn on his grave.

Into a very short lifetime Chopin managed to crowd a lot of living and a lot of composing. His works for piano—and they are very numerous—are at the very foundation of the literature for the instrument. He also composed a number of songs, a sonata for cello and piano, and a piano trio.

CONCERTO NO. 2 IN F MINOR FOR PIANO, OP. 21

At the age of nineteen, in 1829, Frédéric Chopin was a young man beginning to feel the strength of his powers. He had recently returned from Vienna, after his first important sojourn outside Poland, and was flushed with the success of two public recitals he had played there. There was another reason for his ebullience at the time, as he confessed in a letter to his friend, Titus Voytsyekhovski: "I have —perhaps to my misfortune—already found my ideal, whom I worship faithfully and sincerely. Six months have elapsed, and I have not yet exchanged a syllable with her of whom I dream every night. Whilst my thoughts were with her I composed the adagio of my concerto." The work Chopin refers to is the Piano Concerto No. 2 in F Minor, first performed by the composer himself on March 17, 1830, in Warsaw.

The "ideal" of whom Chopin wrote was a twenty-year-old student at the Warsaw Conservatory, an operatic aspirant named Constantia Gladkowska. Chopin's biographer Casimir Wierzynski writes of Constantia:

She had been studying voice at the Conservatory for four years and was considered to be one of Soliva's best pupils. She was also said to be one of the prettiest. Her regular, full face, framed in blond hair, was an epitome of youth, health and vigor, and her beauty was conspicuous in the Conservatory chorus, for all that it boasted numbers of beautiful women. The young lady, conscious of her charms, was distinguished by ambition and diligence in her studies. She dreamed of becoming an operatic singer. . . .

Chopin did not actually meet Constantia until April 1830, six months after he wrote of her to his friend Titus. In the meantime, his concealed passion may have inspired not only the *Adagio* of the F Minor Piano Concerto, but also the E Minor Concerto, some of the Opus 10 Etudes, and the *Andante spianato*. Another letter to his friend reveals that the mere mention of Constantia's name filled Chopin with awe: "Con—no, I cannot complete the name, my hand is too unworthy. Ah! I could tear out my hair when I think that I could be forgotten by her!" But as if to prove that he had not taken complete leave of his senses, Chopin then indulges in a bit of levity concerning the growing of his whiskers on the right side only: "On the left side they are not needed at all, for one sits always with the right side turned to the public."

In 1832, Constantia was married to a Warsaw merchant named Joseph Grabowski and "left the stage to the great regret of all connoisseurs." Chopin seems to have weathered the loss stoically. By the time he came to publish and dedicate the F Minor Concerto, in 1836, the memory of Constantia was far from his consciousness; the title page bore an inscription to Countess Delphine Potocka, one of the grand ladies of the Paris salons, a charmer of wealth and taste and a singer into the bargain.

The two Chopin piano concertos were composed within a year of each other. The F Minor Concerto was actually the first, but it bears the number two because it was published later than the E Minor. Liszt found the *Larghetto* slow movement of this concerto to be "of an almost ideal perfection, now radiant with light and anon full of tender pathos." James Gibbons Huneker, a distinguished American music critic of the early twentieth century, found that the first movement of the F Minor Concerto "far transcends that of the other Chopin Concerto in breadth, passion, and musical feeling. . . . The Mazurka-like Finale is very graceful and full of pure, sweet melody."

Over the years there has been considerable fussing with the orchestration of the Chopin concertos; some have found the orchestral parts weak and insufficiently realized. Sir Donald Francis Tovey, the great English writer and pianist, should by right have put a stop to this once and for all in his brilliant analysis of the reworking of the F Minor Concerto by Karl Klindworth in the late nineteenth century. In reorchestrating the concerto "in the style of a full-swell organ," Klindworth also found it necessary to alter the piano solo part so that the instrument could be heard above the inflated orchestral sonorities. In his preface, Klindworth warned prospective performers that if they preferred Chopin's original piano part, it was best to play it with the original accompaniment. "In other words," Tovey concludes, "Chopin's orchestration, except for a solitary and unnecessary trombone part (not a note of which requires replacing), and a few rectifiable slips, is an unpretentious and correct accompaniment to his pianoforte writing. We may be grateful to Klindworth for taking so much trouble to demonstrate this."

Chopin's biographer Frederick Niecks rhapsodizes over the qualities of this work:

This concerto opens with a tutti of about seventy bars. When after this, the piano interrupts the orchestra impatiently, and then takes up the first subject, it is as if we were transported into another world and breathed a purer atmosphere. First, there are some questions and expostulations, then the composer unfolds a tale full of sweet melancholy in a strain of lovely, tenderly-intwined melody. In the second subject he seems to protest the truthfulness and devotion of his heart, and concludes with a passage half-upbraiding, half-beseeching, which is quite captivating, nay more, even bewitching in its eloquent persuasiveness.

The development section of the movement follows strict formal precepts, and Niecks finds himself regretting this. "How charming if Chopin had allowed himself to drift on the current of his fancy, and had left rules and classifications to others!"

The affecting lyric inspiration of the slow movement prompted this remark from Schumann: "What are ten editorial crowns compared to one such adagio as that in the second concerto!" And again to quote Liszt:

Passages of surprising grandeur may be found in the Adagio of the Second Concerto, for which he evinced a decided preference, and which he liked to repeat frequently. The accessory designs are in his best manner, while the principal phrase is of an admirable breadth. It alternates with a Recitative, which assumes a minor key, and which seems to be its Antistrophe.

In describing the last movement, Niecks speaks of

its feminine softness and rounded contours, its graceful, gyrating, dance-like motions, its sprightliness and frolicsomeness. Unless I quote every part and particle, I feel I cannot do justice to it. The exquisite ease and grace, the subtle spirit that breathes through this movement, defy description, and, more, defy the attempts of most performers to reproduce the original.

If this last statement was true at the time Niecks wrote it, it now no longer is. The Chopin F Minor Concerto generally calls from its interpreters their most devoted care and attention; indeed, it is rarely essayed by any but the most sympathetic pianists. On records it has been remarkably well served by the artists who have recorded it. A performance no longer available is an absolutely stunning version by Clara Haskil with Igor Markevitch conducting the Lamoureux Orchestra of Paris (it used to be Philips PHS 900034, PHM 500034). Though one tends to associate the great Romanian pianist with the classical repertoire of Mozart and Beethoven, she proves in this performance that she was one of the most electrifying Chopin players we have ever had. Hers is a stylish, nobly conceived performance full of personality and vitality, and with an inner strength that immediately captures the imagination. Markevitch offers an orchestral performance of matching substance, and the whole is vividly recorded. Clearly, this version should be the number-one choice if and when it is ever re-released.

Other fine recordings of the score are those by Vladimir Ashkenazy (London CS 6440) Artur Rubinstein (RCA LSC 2265) and Tamas Vásary (Deutsche Grammophon 136452). Among them, the Rubinstein recording is perhaps the least successful, because of flabby orchestral support and indifferent sonics; Rubinstein himself, however, gives one of his most convincing performances. As for the others, any one will pay the listener repeated musical dividends. There is also available a private-subscription release of the concerto as played by the great Josef Hofmann. Anyone interested in hearing this legendary artist at the very peak of his powers should investigate this 1936 radio broadcast performance available through the International Piano Library at 331 West 71st Street, New York, N.Y. 10023.

Rubinstein's re-recording of the score with Ormandy and the Philadelphia Orchestra (RCA LSC 3055; tape TR3 1002, 3¾ ips; cassette RK 1110) lacks some of the impetuosity of his earlier version with Wallenstein and the Symphony of the Air (RCA LSC 2265). Too, the recorded sound leaves too much of the music shrouded in mists. But the Rubinstein-Ormandy performance is the only one available to the cassette collector. Disc and reel-to-reel fanciers have available to them the sensitive and committed performance by Ashkenazy—which also boasts of superlatively clear and well-focused sound (London CS 6440; tape L 80173).

WALTZES

The democratization of the existing social order in early-nineteenth-century Europe was accomplished in diverse ways—revolution, of course, being the prime mechanism. But there were other, more subtle, influences as well—the waltz, for example. The waltz, it now seems fairly certain, first made its appearance in the last third of the eighteenth century. It was probably German in origin. A Bavarian traveler toward the end of the eighteenth century wrote:

The people here are excessively fond of the pleasure of dancing; they need only hear the music of a waltz to begin to caper, no matter where they are. The public dance floors are visited by all classes; these are the places where ancestors and rank seem to be forgotten and aristocratic pride laid aside. Here we see artisans, artists, merchants, councilors, barons, counts and excellencies dancing together with waitresses, women of the middle class and ladies. Every stranger who stays here for a while is infected with this dance malady.

The waltz malady, moreover, proved to be contagious, for it soon spread across all of Europe, reaching Paris during the Napoleonic wars. At about the same time, the British Isles became afflicted with the disease, and Byron, with considerable venom, wrote of "this German article of importation to whom bow Irish Jig and ancient Rigadoon, Scotch reels and country dances." After earning for itself a reputation as "licentious," "obscene" and "suggestive," the waltz finally secured complete acceptance and respectability in the England of 1816, when it was included in a ball given by the Prince Regent.

Fourteen years later, in 1830, a twenty-year-old pianist and composer named Fryderyk Franciszek Chopin left his native Poland, never to return. (It was not until later, in Paris, that he became Frédéric François Chopin.) In Vienna he found the populace spinning furiously in three-quarter time. "Among the numerous pleasures of Vienna," he wrote home, "the hotel evenings are famous. During supper Strauss or Lanner play waltzes. . . . After every waltz they get huge applause; and if they play a Quodlibet, or jumble of opera, song and dance, the hearers are so overjoyed that they don't know what to do with themselves." In another Chopin letter of the period an unmistakable note of derision creeps in: "Here, waltzes are called works! And Strauss and Lanner, who play them for dancing, are called Kapellmeister! This does not mean that everyone thinks like that; indeed, nearly everybody laughs about it; but only waltzes get printed."

Despite these harsh words, Chopin had already fallen victim to the waltz. His waltzes in E-flat major (Opus 18) and A minor (Opus 34, No. 2) date from his days in Vienna. Stylistically, however, they are far removed from the Viennese waltzes he heard all about him.

They are more personal, more introspective—especially the thoroughly Slavic A minor waltz, which is sometimes called the *Valse mélancolique.*

But it was not until he settled in Paris in 1831 that Chopin began to compose the urbane, elegant waltzes that so mirror the kind of life he loved. Luxury, refinement, sophistication were the essence of life in Paris; he was invariably dressed in one of his ten dark-blue tailcoats, with a wide necktie and a diamond stickpin, white gloves, and a flowing cloak. He would give concerts in salons for the titled nobility and the aristocracy, and for these occasions he wrote more waltzes.

During Chopin's lifetime a total of eight of his waltzes saw publication, including the two from the Vienna period. At least seven more were published after his death, but several of these date from his student years, and he may have wanted them to be destroyed.

The waltz in A-flat major (Opus 34, No. 1) is the very spirit of grace and elegance, and is said to have been Paderewski's favorite among all the Chopin waltzes. The A-flat major waltz of Opus 42 is a brilliant virtuoso vehicle, and the three of Opus 64 are charming and chic: the D-flat major waltz of Opus 64 is the familiar "Minute" Waltz, and the C-sharp minor waltz from the same set is dedicated to one of Chopin's wealthy Parisian patronesses, the Baroness de Rothschild.

Two of the posthumous waltzes—the G-flat major (Opus 70, No. 1) and the A-flat major (Opus 69, No. 1)—are associated with Chopin's romantic life. The one in G-flat major, composed in 1829 before he left Poland, was written for the great love of his youth, Constantia Gladkowska (who is supposed also to have been the inspiration for the slow movement of the F Minor Concerto); and the one in A-flat major was a parting gift for Maria Wodzinska at Dresden in 1835.

While an integral concert of the Chopin Nocturnes, for example, or of the Etudes, would be unthinkable as an evening's program, the mood and atmosphere of the waltzes is so varied that they lend themselves readily to complete performance. One who regularly played them in this fashion was the Romanian pianist Dinu Lipatti, who died in December 1950 at the age of thirty-three. Two Lipatti recordings of the Chopin waltzes are available—one a studio recording dating from the late 1940s (now in electronically simulated stereo sound, Odyssey 32160058), the other taken from Lipatti's last public appearance in September 1950, at the Besançon Festival (Angel 3556, mono only—a two-record album of the entire concert). The playing in both cases is illuminated with a rare quality of personal identification and perception. Lipatti obviously loved this music, and he communicated his feeling with almost hypnotic intensity. A tragic element in the Besançon Festival performance is the absence of the *Valse brillante* in A-flat major (Opus 34, No. 1): racked with the pain of his terminal illness, Lipatti no longer had the strength to play it. The Odyssey disc presents the more fully realized performances, but the Angel has a peculiar excitement all its own.

Another superb integral recording of the collected waltzes is Rubinstein's (RCA LSC 2726)—performances that bristle with imagination, vitality and insight and that are beautifully recorded. The Rubinstein collection is also available in a 3¾ ips tape (RCA TR 3-5013) that contains in addition a miscellany of Chopin pieces played by Rubinstein, and in cassette (RK 1071).

Aaron Copland

Born: Brooklyn, New York, November 14, 1900

Copland's musical instruction began with piano lessons from his sister. After more formal study, and upon his graduation from high school, he entered into serious theoretical work with Rubin Goldmark. Three months at the Fontainebleau School of Music and three years with Nadia Boulanger completed his musical training and apprenticeship.

When Serge Koussevitzky became the conductor of the Boston Symphony Orchestra in 1924, he actively sought out Copland as one of the most promising of America's younger composers. He scheduled Copland's *Music for the Theater* for his concerts during 1925 and thereupon began a close association between Copland and Koussevitzky that lasted until the conductor's death in 1951. When Koussevitzky established the Berkshire Music Center as a summer school of music held in conjunction with the Boston Symphony Orchestra's Berkshire Festival concerts at Tanglewood, Copland became Chairman of the Faculty and Assistant Director—positions he continued to hold until the mid-1960s.

Between 1928 and 1931 he and Roger Sessions organized concerts of music by American composers that served as an important stimulus to native composition and its creators at a time when American composers of serious music were still fairly generally regarded as freaks. Ever since then, Copland has been in the forefront of champions in the cause of American music. He has lectured extensively over the length and breadth of the United States and in many foreign countries as well and he has written articles on contemporary American music for many leading musical and nonmusical publications. Two books by Aaron Copland, *What to Listen*

for in Music and *Our New Music,* have become standard text-
books on the respective subjects.

Since the 1950s he has become increasingly in demand as a con-
ductor—not only of his own music and not only in the United States.
During May and June 1960 he toured the Far East, Australia and
New Zealand as co-conductor of the Boston Symphony Orchestra.
He has conducted the New York Philharmonic, the Cleveland
Orchestra, the San Francisco Symphony and many other American
orchestras, and also the London Symphony and other major Euro-
pean orchestras. In addition to his own works and those by other
American composers, he has conducted symphonies by Haydn,
Schubert, Brahms and Tchaikovsky and he is one of a handful of
American musicians who champion the cause of the early-twentieth-
century German-Italian composer Ferruccio Busoni.

Copland's own music has entered into the bloodstream of international concert life. He has composed for many diverse media—
opera, ballet, the concert stage, films and television (the thirty-
second musical theme employed by the "CBS Playhouse" series was
composed by Copland on commission from the television network).
His *Connotations for Orchestra,* written for the New York Philharmonic on a commission for its first season at Philharmonic Hall in
the Lincoln Center for the Performing Arts, represents a significant
break with the "popular" Copland style of the 1930s and '40s—when
the "folksy" orientation of much of his output made an immediate
and direct contact with audiences everywhere. *Connotations,* however, is beginning to make its way in the repertoire and it is now
seen as a major, if not revolutionary, Copland creation. No such hard
struggle was faced by many of the composer's earlier creations, and
it is safe to predict that many of Copland's works will be played as
long as audiences turn to any music for pleasure, comfort and inspiration. Among these durable scores one would surely list *Appalachian Spring, Billy the Kid* and *Rodeo*—Copland's three great
ballets—along with *Quiet City, Music for the Theater, El Salón
México, A Lincoln Portrait* and his Third Symphony. What the
future will bring for *Connotations* and other Copland scores of the
1960s only time will tell. His role as one of the chief architects of

twentieth-century American musical history is, however, as secure as his own dedicated service to principle and progress.

BILLY THE KID AND RODEO

Bounded at the start by the orchestral version of *El Salón México* and at the finish by the Third Symphony, the decade between 1936 and 1946 has been the most productive in the composing life of Aaron Copland. To these years belong the ballets *Rodeo*, *Billy the Kid* and *Appalachian Spring*; *Quiet City*; *A Lincoln Portrait*; the Piano Sonata; and the scores for the films *Of Mice and Men* and *Our Town*.

It is no coincidence that the same decade also marked the high point of the quarter-century tenure of Serge Koussevitzky as conductor of the Boston Symphony Orchestra. For from the time in 1924 when Koussevitzky first sought out Copland and asked him to deliver a score for performance by the Boston Symphony, Copland could always count on a friendly hearing from Koussevitzky and the Boston public. Thus encouraged, Copland and other composers of his generation—Roy Harris, William Schuman and Walter Piston, to name just three—proceeded to enrich the symphonic literature of our country with a quantity and quality of music that will not soon be equaled.

During a five-week period in the summer of 1938, Copland composed the music for a ballet that had been commissioned by Lincoln Kirstein for performance by the Ballet Caravan, that extraordinary forerunner of the New York City Ballet Company. The ballet was to be about Billy the Kid, one of the most famous outlaws in the history of the American "Wild West." Kirstein himself suggested the story line, which deals with events leading up to the shooting of Billy the Kid by Sheriff Pat Garrett, a former friend of the Brooklyn-born desperado. History tells us that Garrett trailed Billy, caught up with him and ambushed him while he was asleep. Some license is taken in the ballet treatment, for here Garrett shoots Billy when the latter reveals his whereabouts by lighting a cigarette in the dark.

The familiar concert suite *Billy the Kid* comprises about two thirds of the complete ballet score. It is continuous, but falls into six sections: *The Open Prairie*, an introduction symbolizing the march to the frontier; *Street in a Frontier Town*; *Card Game at Night Under the Stars*; *Gun Battle*; *Celebration after Billy's Capture*; and *Epilogue*, again on the open prairie. During the course of the score Copland makes incidental use of some American cowboy songs, including *Great Granddad*; *Whoopee-Ti-Yi-Yo*, *Git Along, Little Dogies*; *The Old Chisholm Trail*; and *Old Paint*. But these are woven into the fabric of the score, and are made an integral part of Copland's musical expression. One of the most remarkable of Copland's inventions is the *Gun Battle*, an amazingly vivid scene scored for percussion alone in which one is almost moved to run for cover from the ricocheting bullets.

Four years after *Billy the Kid*, Copland produced another ballet score with a Wild West setting. This was *Rodeo*, with choreography by Agnes de Mille, who also danced the leading female role in the initial presentations of the work by the Ballet Russe de Monte Carlo in 1942. Later that same year Copland extracted a concert suite of four dance episodes from his *Rodeo* music, and the suite has become one of the best known of all American scores.

The story of *Rodeo* is a simple one about a cowgirl who is infatuated with the Head Wrangler and the Champion Roper and tries to attract their attention by showing off her own skill as a rider. They pay her no heed until she appears at the end of the ballet dressed in feminine frills and finery. Then, of course, she has to fight off the attentions of the competing males. She finally accepts the invitation of the Roper to dance and the two of them join the other cowboys and cowgirls in a wild hoedown.

The four dance episodes of the concert suite are: *Buckaroo Holiday*, *Corral Nocturne*, *Saturday Night Waltz* and *Hoedown*. Again Copland employs some cowboy songs in the score, but, as in *Billy the Kid*, they are part of a fabric that is unmistakably Copland's in its exuberance, vigor and healthy affirmation.

Because of their similar subject matter, the two scores have often been recorded together. Successful couplings of the two are the performances conducted by Bernstein (Columbia MS 6175), Johanos (Turnabout TV 34169) and Morton Gould (RCA LSC

2195). For my money Bernstein's is the finest of these; he has an
absolutely intuitive feeling for the Copland idiom and his performances have real zip and sparkle. Also, his recorded sound is the best
of the three, warmer and more resonant than Johanos', and with
more clearly delineated textures than Gould's (presumably a product
of the sometimes untamable echo of New York City's Manhattan
Center).

Fine as are Bernstein's performances of these two scores (also on
tape, Columbia MQ 397), the composer's own, with the London
Symphony Orchestra (Columbia M 30114; cassette MT 30114), are
even finer. Bernstein's rhythms still have greater snap, but Copland
achieves a greater unity in both works and he is even more atmospheric. The recorded sound given him is superb.

Claude Debussy

Born: Saint-Germain-en-Laye, near Paris,
August 22, 1862
Died: Paris, March 25, 1918

Debussy came from a family of tradespeople with no musical background. At the age of eleven he entered the Paris Conservatory where he was awarded several prizes for his piano playing. He won the Prix de Rome of the Conservatory with his cantata *L'Enfant Prodigue,* and in 1885 he left for Rome under the terms of the award. Though he did not stay in the Italian capital for the full period prescribed by the prize, he nevertheless completed two works during his Roman years that already pointed toward the individual direction he was to take throughout the remainder of his life as a composer. One was the orchestral suite *Printemps* that shocked the conservatives because of its harmonic audacities; the other was a score for two women vocalists, female chorus and orchestra, *La Damoiselle Elue.*

Upon his return to Paris in 1887 he became attracted to the circle of the progressive poets and writers. His early works were influenced by his older French contemporaries and also by Wagner, but he soon developed an original style that was labeled—over his violent protests—Impressionism. Debussy's harmonic palette—a combination of Wagnerian chromaticism with ecclesiastical modes and other ancient principles—is a unique and instantly recognizable language. His Prelude to *L'Après-midi d'un Faune,* inspired by the cryptic nature poem by Mallarmé, created a deep impression when it was completed in 1894, entirely revising the possibilities contained in orchestral tone color.

A long series of works in many different forms followed, each of them reinforcing Debussy's position as one of the most important and influential composers of recent times. Chief among those of the period between 1893 and 1910 are the String Quartet, the three Nocturnes for Orchestra (the third of which, *Sirènes*, also calls for a wordless female chorus), *La Mer*, the three *Images for Orchestra* and numerous songs and song cycles. Perhaps Debussy's masterpiece is his music drama *Pelléas et Mélisande*, a setting of the symbolic play by Maurice Maeterlinck. Debussy's opera was given a cool reception at its first performance at the Paris Opéra-Comique in 1902, and its fragile charms are even today something of an acquired taste. It operates in an atmosphere of half-lights, mystery and poetry, with harmonic dissonance taking the place of consonance; old church modes are used or suggested, along with the whole-tone scale and other exotic progressions. The voices employ a form of spoken song and the climaxes are all rigidly restrained. Yet few works in the literature exert the same kind of mystical spell.

In 1899 Debussy married an unassuming dressmaker named Rosalie (Lily) Texier. Though hardly a stimulating intellectual companion for him, Lily was supremely devoted to him and everyone knew it. It was therefore a crushing blow to her when Debussy abandoned her five years later to run off with Madame Emma Bardac, a woman of superior culture and breeding. Debussy and Emma were married the following year, after he and Lily were divorced, but public sympathy was always on the side of Lily and Debussy was vilified for years thereafter by both press and public.

In the last years of his life Debussy suffered from a debilitating and depressing cancer that sapped his energies as well as his strength. He drew more and more into himself and there was also a considerable amount of irresolution in his artistic plans. At various stages during his final years he considered and then rejected operas on the stories of Tristram and Yseult, *As You Like It* and Poe's *The Devil in the Belfry* and *The Fall of the House of Usher*. During the final seven years of his life Debussy produced incidental music for the D'Annunzio mystery play *The Martyrdom of Saint Sebastian*; the ballet *Jeux*, composed for the troupe of Diaghilev; and many works for chamber combinations. The three sonatas of his final productive outburst (1915–17) reveal a growing austerity in his style and attitude.

Debussy was unquestionably one of the most influential composers of the twentieth century. The fact that he has for long been regarded a classic in no way detracts from his stature as a true revolutionary. It is probably safe to say that every composer after him has in one way or another been influenced by him.

IBÉRIA (NO. 2 FROM IMAGES POUR ORCHESTRE)

Nikolai Rimsky-Korsakov, Maurice Ravel, Emmanuel Chabrier and Georges Bizet can hardly be regarded as castanet-clicking sombrero wearers; yet the best-known "Spanish" music in symphonic literature was composed by these thoroughly un-Spanish gentlemen and others like them. It bespeaks the virulent nature of Spanish folk-music tradition that the intoxicating rhythms and abandoned flamboyance of the idiom pollinated the musical cultures of nations all across the face of Europe. Nevertheless, the truth is that the "Spanish" elements in Rimsky's *Capriccio Espagnol* or Ravel's *Rapsodie Espagnole* are no more than superficial graftings upon a musical aesthetic which remains essentially the composer's own.

One non-Spaniard who did manage to capture truly the essence of a Spanish musical atmosphere when he set out to do so was Claude Debussy. *Ibéria*, the second of Debussy's three *Images for Orchestra*, is the most notable example. Debussy worked on the three *Images* for six years, between 1905 and 1911. A letter to his publisher, Durand, indicates that the *Images* were intended originally for two pianos. But as the material took shape and Debussy's imagination took wing, he realized that the two-piano medium would be inadequate. Then the *Images* gradually took orchestral form and Debussy flavored each of them with the popular music of three countries. *Gigues* and *Rondes de Printemps*, the first and third, evoke British and French folk song, while *Ibéria*, the centerpiece of the trilogy, is imbued with Spanish color and mood.

Describing his *Images* Debussy once wrote: "I am trying to achieve something *different*—an effect of *reality*—what some imbeciles call *impressionism*, a term that is utterly misapplied, especially

by the critics." If by *reality* Debussy meant an experience with
which he was familiar at first hand, then *Ibéria* would have been
completely without Iberian flavor, for Debussy had spent only a few
hours on Spanish soil some years before when he had crossed the
border into San Sebastián to attend a bullfight. No, the *reality*
of Spain as Debussy knew it came to him the same way it has
come to the rest of us who have never been there—from books, pictures and music. And yet no less an authority than Manuel de Falla,
Spain's most renowned composer, has written that Debussy's was
"better and truer" Spanish music than that of many Spanish contemporaries. *Ibéria*, in Falla's view, is a superlative example of a composer utilizing "the fundamental *elements* of popular music, instead
of following the usual method of employing authentic folk songs." It
is only when the *implications* of folk music are absorbed into a composer's bloodstream and permeate his own melodic expression that
he is ready to create artistic material of his own. It is this quality
which lends distinction to the Bohemian music of Dvořák and Smetana, the Russian music of Moussorgsky, the American music of
Copland—and the Spanish music of Debussy's *Ibéria*.

Falla was quite explicit in his description of what he found in
Debussy's score:

> Echoes from the villages, a kind of *sevillana*—the generic theme of
> the work—which seems to float in a clear atmosphere of scintillating
> light: the intoxicating spell of Andalusian nights, the festive gaiety of
> a people dancing to the joyous strains of a *banda* of guitars and
> *bandurrias* . . . all this whirls in the air, approaches and recedes,
> and our imagination is continually kept awake and dazzled by the
> power of an intensely expressive and richly varied music.

If Falla's enthusiasm for *Ibéria* was rhapsodic, it was by no means
an appreciation unanimously shared. Two of the leading French
critics of the time, Gaston Carraud and Pierre Lalo, both of whom
had ardently championed Debussy in the *Pelléas* days, found *Ibéria*
a thorough failure, and both critics did not hesitate to say so in
print. But another who rallied to the defense of *Ibéria* was Maurice
Ravel.

You were quite well able to understand [Ravel wrote], you who yielded yourself up without effort to the vivid charm and exquisite freshness of the *Rondes de Printemps*; you were moved to tears by that dazzling *Ibéria* and its intensely disturbing *Parfums de la nuit*, by all this novel, delicate harmonic beauty, this profound musical sensitiveness; you, who are only a writer or a painter. So too was I, and so were Messrs. Igor Stravinsky, Florent Schmitt, Roger Ducasse, Albert Roussel, and a host of young composers whose productions are not unworthy of notice. But the only musicians, the only people with real sensibility, are M. Gaston Carraud, to whom we owe three songs and a symphonic poem, M. Camille Mauclair, who has become known for his literary and pictorial works, and M. Pierre Lalo, who has not produced anything at all.

Time, of course, has been on the side of Debussy and his supporters for *Ibéria* is today regarded not only as a flavorful evocation of Spanish feeling, but also as a masterpiece of orchestral coloration. It is a tightly organized, brilliantly effective symphonic staple and —with *La Mer* and the Prelude to *The Afternoon of a Faun*—one of Debussy's greatest achievements in the realm of orchestral music.

The three sections of Debussy's score are titled *Par les rues et par les chemins* ("In the Streets and Byways"), *Les parfums de la nuit* ("The Fragrance of the Night") and *Le matin d'un jour de fête* ("The Morning of a Festival Day"). The first section begins with a carefree seven-measure introduction, which is followed by the first principal melody, given to the solo clarinet. This tune has about it an air of gay improvisation, and the clarinetist is directed to play it elegantly and to keep a good, secure rhythm. There are other brief melodic snatches but the clarinet tune is the predominant one and it is tossed from one instrument to another. The second major section of the movement begins with a melody for four unison horns, with an added trumpet fanfare. After a while the mood and the music of the opening returns and the movement ends wistfully. The second movement is a languorous, vague and dream-like section, with subtle shadings of orchestral color and an affecting misty character. Toward the end of the movement there is a quotation from the first part, and then the music plunges without pause into the raucous street noises of the Festival Day celebrations. The direction in the score calls for the music to be played "In the rhythm of a distant march." It is exuberant, colorful and infectious, and the end is a joyous whoop.

The *Ibéria* recordings exist in two contexts: (1) those that are part of an integral recording of all three of the orchestral *Images*; and (2) those that couple the score with other, non-related music.

I still remember the thrill with which I received in the early 1940s a two-record 78-rpm Victor recording by Pierre Monteux and the San Francisco Symphony Orchestra that presented the first recordings ever made of the other two Images—*Gigues* and *Rondes de Printemps*. The music was virtually unknown to all but specialists, and that recording well may have established the pieces in the orchestral repertoire. Today there are several excellent integral recordings of all three *Images*. No conductor clarifies and illuminates this work or its two companions in Debussy's *Images* quite the way Pierre Boulez does in his recording with the Cleveland Orchestra (Columbia MS 7362). The Argenta (London STS 15020) and Ansermet (London CS 6225; tape L 80085) recordings are both also first-class. Argenta's is a reading of surpassing rightness and penetration. The orchestra plays brilliantly for him and the recorded sound, though early stereo, is fine. Argenta's death in a freak auto mishap at the age of forty-four during the 1950s robbed us of a brilliant conductor.

The cassette collector has available the marginally less atmospheric performances of these works conducted by Michael Tilson Thomas with the Boston Symphony Orchestra (DGG 3300187; disc 2530145; tape L 3145). Of the available recordings of just *Ibéria* with miscellaneous other orchestral material, the reissued Stokowski performance (Seraphim S 60102) is noteworthy for its vivid dynamism and color.

LA MER

In any list of original music creators the name of Claude Debussy must surely rank near the top. Debussy found in music new colors, new harmonic structures and relationships, new procedures of symphonic development. The catalog of Debussy's music is comparatively small—he left us only a single opera, a single string quartet, and no symphonies as such—but its quality is on an extraordinarily high level. Some of it, like *La Mer*, has such universal appeal that the *musicien français*—as Debussy proudly signed himself—has become a musician who is admired and loved in every country.

From the days of his youth Debussy had a consuming passion for the sea. It was in Cannes, at the age of seven, that he discovered the manifold joys and beauties of the Mediterranean, and quite often in later years he would visit coast resorts to find comfort and relaxation.

For generations the sea has been a source of inspiration for French artists—one need only recall the seascapes of the Impressionist painters, the *Fanny* trilogy of Marcel Pagnol, or the haunting beauty of Charles Trenet's song *La Mer*—but probably no work of art has captured the sea's ebb and flow, its majesty and mystery, more successfully than Debussy's *La Mer, Three Symphonic Sketches*.

On September 12, 1903, Debussy wrote to Durand, his publisher, from Burgundy, where he was vacationing, to inform him that he was at work on a composition dealing with "my old friend, the sea, always innumerable and beautiful." The same day he also wrote to the composer André Messager: "You will say that the ocean does not exactly wash the Burgundian hillsides—and my seascapes might be studio landscapes; but I have an endless store of memories, and, to my mind, they are worth more than reality, whose beauty often deadens thought."

Two years later *La Mer* was completed. In everything but its title the score is a closely knit three-movement symphony, superbly evocative of its subject matter. Each of the movements has a descriptive title: "From Dawn to Noon On the Sea"; "Play of the Waves"; and "Dialogue of the Wind and the Sea." And near the end of the work Debussy achieves an effect of binding unity by repeating themes from the first movement.

The years 1903–5, when he was working on *La Mer*, were crucial ones for Debussy. It was during the summer of 1904 that he left his wife, Lily, for Emma Bardac, wife of a well-known financier and the former mistress of the composer Gabriel Fauré. Lily promptly

attempted suicide and aroused feelings of sympathy throughout
Parisian artistic circles. Debussy, they buzzed, had been bought by
a rich woman. The truth was, however, that Debussy had known
Emma intimately almost from the day of his marriage to Lily; the
dissolution of the marriage was no sudden caprice—Debussy had
considered it carefully over a period of time.

When *La Mer* was given its first performance at a concert of the
Lamoureux Orchestra in Paris in October 1905, the public resentment of Debussy's private life entered into the reception the new
score was accorded. "Prudish indignation had not yet been appeased," wrote one critic, "and on all sides people were ready to
make the artist pay dearly for the wrongs that were imputed to the
man." The controversy flourished for some time; when the score was
performed for the first time by the Colonne Orchestra in Paris, a
wild demonstration followed. It subsided for a while but then flared
up again during Jacques Thibaud's performance of the Bach Chaconne that followed *La Mer*. Thibaud was forced to stop in mid-
stream and wait for peace to be restored.

Seventeen months after the first performance of *La Mer* the music
was introduced to the United States at a concert by the Boston
Symphony Orchestra conducted by Karl Muck. Ever since then, the
music has been a particular specialty of the Boston Symphony,
and the orchestra has recorded the score under three of its permanent
conductors since 1920: Pierre Monteux, Serge Koussevitzky and
Charles Munch. (Erich Leinsdorf, who succeeded Munch, once recorded *La Mer* with the Los Angeles Philharmonic Orchestra).

The Koussevitzky recording originally appeared on RCA Victor
78-rpm discs in the late 1930s and is the performance by which a
whole generation of collectors came to know *La Mer*. It was reissued
for a brief time on an RCA Victor Camden disc (CAL 376) but it is
no longer available. This is a pity, for the performance is a superb
one, with a thrilling sense of controlled fury and absolutely awesome orchestral ensemble.

The Monteux-Boston Symphony recording (RCA LM 1939, mono
only) is also no longer available. It is a lucid, forthright account
of the music that generates convincing vitality.

Munch has been closely identified with *La Mer* for years, beginning with a recorded performance made with the Paris Conservatory Orchestra in the 1940s. Unfortunately, his recording with the Boston Symphony Orchestra (RCA Victrola VICS 1041) only dimly suggests the best of which he was capable with the music: too frequently the pervading mood is one of semi-hysteria. The sound, too, is less than first-rate, with harsh and glassy reproduction.

An overwhelming account of the music is the 1950 Toscanini recording with the NBC Symphony Orchestra, available on RCA Victrola VIC 1246 (along with the Toscanini performances of Debussy's *Ibéria* and an episode from Franck's *Psyché*). *La Mer* was a work Toscanini conducted again and again: during the twenty-nine-year period he made music in this country (1925–54), he conducted no fewer than fifty-three performances of *La Mer*. What is more, he edited the score in the most painstaking manner imaginable, adding doublings of instruments where he felt it necessary to establish the clarity of the scoring. And when he recorded the work in June of 1950 both he and the NBC Symphony were functioning at the height of their powers. Each strand in the orchestral fabric is revealed in the recording, and the interrelation of the strands is a joy to hear. There is an inexorable flow from first note to last and the recorded sound, happily, is still quite serviceable, with an especially fine dynamic range.

The Boulez-conducted performance (CBS 32110056)—highly regarded in some circles—I find overrefined and analyzed to the point of evisceration.

Other fine recordings of *La Mer* are the performances conducted by Ernest Ansermet (London CS 6437) and Carlo Maria Giulini (Angel S 35977). On tape my recommendation is Ansermet (London L 80178). To these versions must also be added the flamboyant but extraordinarily evocative account of the music by Stokowski and the London Symphony Orchestra (London SPC 21059; tape L 75059; cassette M 94059).

Antonín Dvořák

Born: Mühlhausen, Bohemia, September 8, 1941
Died: Prague, May 1, 1904

Dvořák was intended by his simple peasant parents to become the village butcher. They ruined their plans, however, by allowing their son to study the violin with the local schoolmaster. From that point on Dvořák was determined to pursue only one career—music. At the age of sixteen he entered the Prague Organ School where he received a thorough grounding in repertoire and theoretical studies. Upon his graduation from the school in 1862 he became a viola player at the National Theater in Prague. It was not until he was thirty-three that he produced his first important composition, a hymn for male chorus and orchestra that attracted such attention that in 1875 he was given a special government stipend that enabled him to devote himself to composition. The modest financial security also enabled him to marry Anna Čermáková, a contralto who was a member of the Prague National Opera Chorus. The marriage was apparently a very happy one, and produced six children.

A Bohemian nationalism was very much in the air during Dvořák's early maturity and he resolved to follow on the path boldly explored by his older colleague Smetana. The national element is predominant in much of Dvořák's output. Thus he composed two separate sets of *Slavonic Dances*; three *Slavonic Rhapsodies*; a *Czech Suite*; an overture titled *Husitská* written to celebrate the victory scored for religious freedom in the early fifteenth century by the national leader Jan Hus; and numerous operas utilizing as their story bases folk and national tales.

Early in his career Dvořák received valuable support from Brahms, who brought his music to the attention of the publisher Simrock. "Dvořák has written in all possible branches," wrote Brahms to

Simrock in 1877, when Dvořák was still little known outside of Prague. "Decidedly, he is a very talented man. Besides, he is poor. Please take this into consideration." The door thus opened by Brahms proved to be the beginning of a long and deep friendship between the two composers. They also had much in common in their art and each influenced the other. At Brahms' funeral more than twenty years later, Dvořák was one of the pallbearers.

Dvořák's fame spread far and wide during the 1880s and into the 1890s. He produced music in great profusion in all forms and was invited to visit many foreign lands, including England, Russia and Germany. In 1892, at the invitation of Mrs. Jeannette Thurber, who founded the National Conservatory of Music in New York, Dvořák came to the United States as director of that school. He became an active figure on the American musical scene during his three-year stay, provoking some controversy with his advice that American composers should find their inspiration in Indian, Negro and other folk sources. Dvořák himself composed several important works during his stay in this country, principal among them being his last symphony, "From the New World," and his F Major ("American") String Quartet. Like nearly all his other music, however, these scores pulsate with the national feeling and climate of his native Bohemia.

When he returned to Prague in 1895, he again took up his post as professor of composition at the Prague Conservatory and in 1901 he was appointed Director of the Conservatory. His sudden death three years later occasioned national mourning in Czechoslovakia and his funeral and burial were occasions of spontaneous demonstrations of the respect and love an entire people felt for him.

Sir Charles Stanford, that greatly influential figure on the British musical scene during the later nineteenth century, once said of Dvořák: "He is one of the phenomena of the nineteenth century—a child of nature, who did not stop to think, and said on paper anything which came into his head." This kind of tribute is, of course, a two-edged sword: at his best Dvořák produced some of the most divinely inspired music in the entire literature; it is also true that some of his music lacks a certain substance and nobility. It is time, however, to stop criticizing Dvořák for what he was not and to welcome him for what he was: an absolutely inspired melodist with an intuitive feeling for workmanship and technique. The nine Dvořák symphonies, taken together, stand as a unified body of creativity that is one of the chief glories of nineteenth-century symphonic thought.

CONCERTO IN B MINOR FOR CELLO, OP. 104

At least three distinguished cellists of the 1890s strongly influenced Antonín Dvořák during the period of the conception and composition of his Cello Concerto in B Minor. The first of these was Victor Herbert, who was later to win renown as the composer of some of the best-loved operettas of the early twentieth century. In the early 1890s, however, Herbert was a cellist—and a highly gifted one —in the orchestra of the Metropolitan Opera in New York. In 1894 he appeared as soloist with the New York Philharmonic Society Orchestra in the premiere of his own Second Cello Concerto. Dvořák, then the Director of the National Conservatory of Music in New York City, attended the Herbert performance and was deeply impressed with the musical potentialities that lay in the combination of cello and orchestra.

Next to enter the picture was Alwin Schroeder, first cellist of the Boston Symphony Orchestra. When it became known in musical circles that Dvořák was at work on a concerto that promised to be a notable addition to the scant literature for cello and orchestra Schroeder offered to assist the composer in writing the passagework for the solo instrument. It logically fell to Schroeder to introduce the concerto to Boston Symphony audiences, and he did so in December 1896, just a few months after the world premiere performance in London that Dvořák himself had conducted.

The third cellist to be associated with the concerto, and probably the most influential, was Professor Hanuš Wihan of Prague, a teacher at the Conservatorium there and founder of the Bohemian String Quartet. Indeed, there is strong evidence to support the contention that even before Dvořák heard the Victor Herbert concerto, Wihan had suggested to his countryman that he turn his attentions to a piece for solo cello and orchestra.

Dvořák began work on the concerto in November 1894, in his East Seventeenth Street apartment in New York City. The score was completed in Prague the following summer. Dvořák's correspondence with his publisher, Simrock, indicates the extent of Wihan's co-operation: "The principal part with fingering and bowing indictions has been made by Professor Wihan himself," the composer wrote. And there are clear signs that Wihan wanted to have a much more definitive voice in the final form of the score than Dvořák permitted him. In a letter to Simrock dated October 3, 1895, Dvořák forbade further editing of the music by the cellist:

> My friend Wihan and I have differed as to certain things. . . . I give you my work only if you will promise me that no one—not even my friend Wihan—shall make any alterations in it without my knowledge and permission—also no cadenza such as Wihan has made in the last movement—and that its form shall be as I have felt it and thought it out. The cadenza in the last movement is not to exist either in the orchestral or the piano score. . . . The finale closes gradually diminuendo—like a breath—with reminiscences of the first and second movements; the solo dies away to a pianissimo, then there is a crescendo, and the last measures are taken up by the orchestra, ending stormily. That was my idea, and from it I cannot recede.

A measure of the bitterness that seems to have developed between the two friends is the fact that, though Dvořák dutifully dedicated the concerto to Wihan, the cellist never performed the work in public.

Like much of the music that Dvořák composed or first conceived in the United States, the Cello Concerto has an unmistakable Slavic folk quality. In many of its pages there is a genuine nostalgia which can only be attributed to Dvořák's homesickness for the Bohemian countryside he loved so deeply.

The first movement of the concerto is a free-flowing *Allegro*. The movement begins with a long orchestral tutti that introduces the two principal themes—the first one at the very beginning in the clarinet, the second a little later in the solo horn. The entrance of the cello soloist is a magical moment: a commanding, imperial statement of the theme we first heard in the clarinet at the outset of the score. The balance of the movement is a dialogue between the solo cello and the orchestra. The slow movement, marked *Adagio ma non troppo*, has a feeling of subdued repose. There is a contemplative cadenza for the soloist and then the movement ends in an exhalation of serenity. The concluding movement is a march-like *Allegro moderato*. The most unusual feature of the movement is its "reminiscences of the first and second movements." Near the end, the solo cello and the principal violin in the orchestra engage in a sinuous duet and the concerto ends in a blaze of triumph.

A classic recording of the piece is the one made in Prague during the later 1930s by Pablo Casals, with George Szell conducting the Czech Philharmonic Orchestra. This was an occasion when everything conspired to bring about a performance as close to perfection as one is ever likely to hear. The recording sessions found Casals at the zenith of his powers; his playing is by turns hair-raising in its drama, eloquent in its serenity and ennobling in its poised lyrical command. Few who have heard it will forget the knife-like thrust of the solo cello's first entry in the first movement. Unfortunately, the Casals-Szell performance is currently no longer available. It is to be hoped that it is an early candidate for reissue in the Seraphim series of Great Recordings of the Century, for its special qualities of passion and commitment make it a unique document.

Other superlative performances are those by du Pré-Barenboim (Angel S 36046—be warned, however, that the engineers have given the solo instrument exaggerated prominence); Fournier-Szell (DGG 138755; cassette 923060); Gendron-Haitink (Philips 802892; cassette 18143CAA); Rose-Ormandy (Columbia MS 6714); Rostropovich-Boult (Seraphim S 60136); and Starker-Dorati (Mercury SR 90303; cassette MCR4-90303). My own favorite among them all is Leonard Rose's, with Eugene Ormandy and the Philadelphia Orchestra. Rose's consummate artistry and his supreme mastery of his instrument are heard against an orchestral realization that ranks among the finest of Ormandy's many recorded achievements over the years. The disc also offers a first-rate account of Tchaikovsky's Rococo Variations for Cello and Orchestra.

Tape collectors have only one choice: a rather quixotic performance by Rostropovich with Karajan conducting (DGG L 9044).

SYMPHONY NO. 7 IN D MINOR, OP. 70

Owing to Antonín Dvořák's highly self-critical nature and the scattering of the more than eight hundred musical manuscripts he turned out in his lifetime, there existed for many years a great deal of confusion concerning his output. But the thematic catalog of Dvořák's music published in 1917 by his biographer Otakar Šourek was revised and enlarged by Jarmil Burghauser and republished in Prague in 1960, and the most important effect of this musicological achievement has been a renumbering of the Dvořák symphonies. To the five Dvořák symphonies previously catalogued and numbered were added four earlier works, two that had been published posthumously and two that had not been published at all until very recently. Dvořák is now credited with nine symphonies, putting him on a par with such masters as Beethoven and Bruckner—not only quantitatively, but qualitatively as well, in my opinion. Antonín Dvořák may well have been the most underrated symphonic composer of the nineteenth century; the re-evaluation of his works is one of the most gratifying features of the contemporary musical scene.

Dvořák composed his Seventh Symphony in D Minor—formerly known as his Second—in Prague between mid-January and mid-March 1885. The score was commissioned by the London Philharmonic Society on the occasion of Dvořák's election to the Society as an honorary member. Inevitably a symphony in D minor suggested itself to Dvořák as homage to the great institution that more than sixty years earlier had commissioned a symphony from Beethoven, a symphony that turned out to be that composer's monumental Ninth (also in D minor). Šourek writes:

Dvořàk worked at the D Minor Symphony with passionate concentration and in the conscious endeavor to create a work of noble proportions and content, which should surpass not only all that he had so far produced in the field of symphonic composition, but which was also designed to occupy an important place in world music.

On the 25th of March, 1885, Dvořák wrote to his publisher, Fritz Simrock: "Whatever may happen to the symphony, it is, thank God, completed. It will be played in London for the first time on April 22, and I am curious as to the result." Dvořák himself conducted the premiere, on a program that was otherwise led by Sir Arthur Sullivan, and he was able afterward to report to Simrock, "It had an exceptionally brilliant success." About nine months later the score was introduced in the United States at concerts of the New York Philharmonic Orchestra; later, Hans Richter introduced it on the continent with the Vienna Philharmonic, and Hans von Bülow led the Berlin premiere.

In its orchestral textures and colors the symphony is very Brahmsian, but its spirit and character throughout are Dvořák's own. The first movement, an *Allegro maestoso*, starts quietly and mysteriously in the tympani, horns and low strings; a gently lyrical second theme contrasts with this primary material, and the movement then builds to an impassioned climax that subsides again into an aura of mystery. The slow movement, *Poco adagio*, established a mood of reverence at the beginning, and is especially noteworthy for the richness of its orchestration and for its melodic invention and ornamentation. The third movement is a driving Scherzo, full of slashing rhythms and contrasting themes, with a gentle Trio in G major. And the Finale is a vigorous *Allegro* built almost entirely upon the opening phrase of the first theme.

It is only in recent years that Dvořák's D Minor Symphony has taken firm hold in the orchestral repertoire, and it is safe to say that much of the score's present standing derives from the number of recorded performances it has received during the past quarter century. The pioneer recording was one released by RCA Victor about 1940 as a 78-rpm album (663), with Václav Talich conducting the Czech Philharmonic Orchestra. This performance had the field all to itself for about a decade, until London Records released a long-playing recording of the score with Hans Schmidt-Isserstedt conducting the North West German Radio Orchestra. Since then there have been perhaps ten other recordings of the symphony, originating from such diverse locales as Prague, London, Amsterdam and New York.

The splendid Monteux-London Symphony Orchestra performance is back in circulation, this time on the budget-priced London Stereo Treasury Series label (STS 15157). It is a pleasure to welcome it back to the company of select recordings of this score, along with the performances conducted by Kertesz (London CS 6402; tape K 80189), Mehta (London CS 6607; tape K 80217) and Szell (included in Columbia D3S 814, three discs also containing Szell-Cleveland Orchestra performances of the composer's Eighth and Ninth Symphonies). Kertesz, the young Hungarian-born conductor, has the benefit of the most vivid recorded sound, and the London Symphony Orchestra is marginally more responsive to him than it was a few years earlier when it recorded the score under the direction of Monteux. (Note, however, that the Monteux-London Symphony performance is available at a budget price.) The association of Monteux with this symphony goes back at least to the early 1920s, when he performed it with the Boston Symphony Orchestra; the maturity of his interpretation bespeaks a long-standing knowledge of the score. And Szell, who has this music in his blood, is at his most convincing here. Any one of these recordings will afford the listener a rich and rewarding musical experience.

There apparently is no currently available cassette performance of this symphony.

SYMPHONY NO. 8 IN G MAJOR, OP. 88

There is little question that the music of Antonín Dvořák is enjoying a renascence in our time. Much of his chamber music figures in the active performing repertoire of chamber groups around the world, superior recorded performances are available of Dvořák scores that at one time were known only to the cognoscenti, and many conductors in different parts of the world are suddenly discovering that the Bohemian master composed symphonies other than the ubiquitous E minor, the "New World" Symphony. This is certainly as it should be, for Dvořák the symphonist was unappreciated by the world at large until fairly recently. Dvořák's symphonic output spans a period of nearly three decades, and together the composer's total output of nine symphonies represent the peak of his creative impulse.

The G Major Symphony, his Eighth, is one of the loveliest, most spontaneous works in the repertoire. Its bucolic nature inevitably suggested the Bohemian countryside to commentators. After the London premiere, a critic remarked upon the symphony's "pastoral character. . . . All is fresh and charming." Dvořák composed the G Major Symphony in 1889 as a token of appreciation for his election to the Prague Academy. In the manuscript the score is dedicated "To the Bohemian Academy of Emperor Franz Josef for the Encouragement of Art and Literature, in thanks for my election." Its first performance was given in Prague in February 1890. Two months later Dvořák conducted it in London with the London Philharmonic Orchestra, and the score was eventually published by the English firm Novello—circumstances that led to the work's being known at one time as the composer's "English Symphony." This now-discarded title was actually no more irrelevant to the G Major Symphony than the nickname "New World Symphony" is to the following E Minor. Both symphonies—indeed, almost everything Dvořák wrote—have in abundance the folk spirit and atmosphere of Bohemia. If the G Major Symphony is to be called by any title, that title most assuredly should be "Bohemian Symphony."

The first movement, *Allegro con brio*, opens with a solemn, pensive theme in G minor played by the low strings. This soon gives way to a bird-like theme in the flute, now in the bright "home" key of G major, which becomes the principal musical material of the movement. The whole character of the movement is one of joyous exuberance. The slow movement, *Adagio*, has a pervading brooding quality, but the second section, with its staccato figures and singing theme in the violins, lightens the atmosphere considerably. The third movement, *Allegretto grazioso*, has as its principal theme one of the most haunting melodies Dvořák ever composed. There is a bittersweet quality to it which is quite enchanting and there is no mistaking its roots in the folk music of Bohemia. The Trio section offers a contrasting theme in slow waltz tempo with a pulsating rhythmical accompaniment. There is a return to the principal section and then the coda of the movement is in accelerated speed—it is marked *Molto vivace*—very much in the style and character of some of Dvořák's *Slavonic Dances*. The last movement, *Allegro ma non troppo*, opens with a trumpet fanfare followed by a theme of broad and ceremonial cast which is then subjected to a series of variations. The very end is in the nature of a Bohemian furiant, wildly proclamative and joyously bracing.

In the years before the long-playing record, the Václav Talich-Czech Philharmonic recordings of the later Dvořák symphonies were the classic performances of these scores. That they were for long the only recordings of all but the "New World" Symphony was of little consequence, for Talich delivered masterful readings of them all. Talich and Dvořák are as indivisible in the minds of long-time record collectors as Beecham and Delius or Koussevitzky and Tchaikovsky.

The choice versions among currently available performances are those by Kertesz (London CS 6358; tape K 80193), Kubelik (DGG 139181; tape L 9181; cassette 923030) and Szell (Angel S 36043; cassette 4XS 36043). This Szell performance is a more recent one than his previously recommended recording (still available in Columbia album D3S 814)—a product of the late 1950s. The Angel disc was made in the spring of 1970, just a few months before he died. It is a lyrical and eloquent account of this ever-fresh score. The Kertesz performance is one of the gems in that conductor's generally outstanding traversal of all the Dvořák Symphonies on discs. It has an easy and disarming charm about it that is quite marvelous, and the recorded sound is exceptionally clear and vibrant. Kubelik's has much the same quality, except that his orchestra (the Berlin Philharmonic) is less successful in negotiating the music's tricky passages than is Kertesz' orchestra (the London Symphony).

SYMPHONY NO. 9 IN E MINOR, OP. 95, "NEW WORLD"

In May 1891 one of the world's most esteemed composers, Peter Ilyitch Tchaikovsky, was in the United States for a tour which found him conducting six concerts of his own works: four in New York, including a program marking the dedication of the newly built Carnegie Hall, and one each in Baltimore and Philadelphia. Tchaikovsky was a huge success in the New World, and it was that success which undoubtedly emboldened Mrs. Jeannette M. Thurber to invite another prominent European musician to come to New York as the head of the music school which she had founded there six years earlier under the name National Conservatory. He was Antonín Dvořák of Bohemia.

Dvořák at the time had just turned fifty. He had four published symphonies to his credit and was universally respected both as a composer and teacher. Dvořák would have found it difficult to turn down the salary offered him by Mrs. Thurber, which was six times what he was receiving at the Prague Conservatory and which would enable him to compose comfortably for the rest of his days. So it was in October 1892 that Dvořák and his family arrived in the United States and settled in a five-room apartment in a brownstone house on East Seventeenth Street in Manhattan, just a few doors from the Conservatory.

American life bewildered him at first. In an article for *Harper's Magazine* he wrote that American "push" annoyed him terribly in the beginning, but "now I like it; for I have come to the conclusion that this youthful enthusiasm and eagerness to take up everything is the best promise for music in America." A scant three months after his arrival in America, Dvořák was at work upon a new symphony, and the sketches were completed during the winter and spring of 1893. During the summer holiday from his duties at the Conservatory, Dvořák packed his family up and journeyed with them to the small farm community of Spillville, Iowa, a settlement of a few hundred people, mostly Bohemians. This was perhaps the one spot in the New World where Dvořák could be among people of his own race and language and where he could almost imagine himself back home in the rolling Bohemian countryside. The Dvořáks took up modest quarters in Spillville, were immediately befriended by many of the townfolk, and in the midst of this friendly atmosphere Dvořák completed the orchestration of the new symphony and wrote, in addition, a string quartet—the "American" in F major— and a string quintet.

In the fall Dvořák and his family returned to New York and the new symphony was scheduled for its premiere in December, with Anton Seidl conducting the New York Philharmonic Society. Shortly before that first performance Dvořák made the following statement for publication:

I am satisfied that the future music of this country must be founded upon what are called the Negro melodies. These can be the foundation of a serious and original school of composition to be developed in the United States. When first I came here, I was impressed with this idea, and it has developed into a settled conviction. These beautiful and varied themes are the product of the soil. They are American. They are the folk songs of America, and your composers must turn to them. All the great musicians have borrowed from the songs of the common people.

Such a statement immediately prior to the first performance of a symphony titled "From the New World" naturally aroused tremendous curiosity, especially since Dvořák had been made very familiar with the music of the Negroes by three of his American friends: Henry T. Burleigh, the Negro baritone and arranger, and two critics, James Huneker and Henry E. Krehbiel. The curiosity was fanned into a bright flame after the symphony was heard and some commentators found in the second theme of the first movement a resemblance to the Negro spiritual "Swing Low, Sweet Chariot," while others detected what they thought were Indian themes. A tremendous swirl of supranational American pride was stimulated by the symphony, but after the initial hysteria had subsided, it became evident, even to many who would have wanted it otherwise, that whatever national elements there were in the music were primarily Bohemian. Dvořák himself clinched the case when he denied using any actual Negro or Indian melodies in the score. As to the familiar *Largo,* which to this day has Indian or Negro connotations to some listeners, the only tangible association seems to be that Dvořák once told Krehbiel that he had Longfellow's *Hiawatha* in mind when he composed it. But the music has no more special kinship with Indian music than do any of several of Dvořák's dumka movements with their Slavic folk song character and sudden shifts from melancholy to exuberance.

In a letter to an admirer who showered exaggerated praise upon him Dvořák once wrote: "You are not speaking to a demigod! I am a very simple person to whom such expressions . . . as yours are entirely inappropriate. I remain what I was: a plain and simple Bohemian *Musikant.*" It remains to be added that this "plain and simple Bohemian *Musikant*" wrote a chapter of significant importance in the musical history of a country which he touched for only a brief three-year period. By directing the attention of American musicians to the "songs of the common people" Dvořák set in motion the beginnings of exploration into the music of the American folk, which, even in its third generation, is still bearing creative fruit for the American composer.

The first movement begins with a slow introduction marked *Adagio.* The culminating dramatic measures of the introduction, with their punctuation from the tympani, foreshadow the principal theme of the main *Allegro molto*—a rising, pulsating theme that serves as the general motto for the entire symphony. The second theme, announced by the flute and then taken over by the violins, is the one that reminded certain early listeners of the spiritual "Swing Low, Sweet Chariot." The second movement, marked *Largo,* begins with a series of solemn chords before the celebrated English horn theme makes its first appearance. This melody is the one to which the words "Goin' Home" were set. There is an episode in which the oboe has a skipping rhythmic melody; Dvořák himself indicated that this melody was intended to suggest the gradual awakening of animal life on the prairie. Trills are tossed back and forth from one choir of the orchestra to another and finally the movement ends in the same mood of solemn dignity with which it began. The third movement, *Scherzo: molto vivace* has evoked American Indian connotations from some commentators, Czech abandon and gaiety from others. It is a vigorous, dance-like movement with two contrasting Trios. The last movement, *Allegro con fuoco*, begins with a surging, rising theme in the strings, followed by the principal theme of the movement trumpeted out by horns and trumpets against fortissimo chords for the full orchestra. The second theme is a contrasting gentler one, first heard from the clarinet against tremolo strings. Themes from the earlier movements then reappear, and at the end there is a burst of triumph.

The Toscanini recording of the "New World Symphony" (RCA Victrola VIC 1249) is one of the Maestro's most successful recordings ever. It was made in Carnegie Hall in February 1953 when RCA Victor was employing a single-microphone technique. The results produced a brilliance and clarity, as well as depth, that are quite extraordinary for Toscanini reproduction. And the performance is a marvel of coiled tension and vitality.

Among more recent performances there are several that are outstanding, including those by Fiedler (RCA LSC 3134; cassette RK 1160); Kertesz (London CS 6527; tape K 80193); Ormandy (Columbia MS 7089); and Szell (included in Columbia D3S 814). Fiedler's performance has an impassioned drama and momentum, leading one to regret his forty-years-plus type-casting as a "pops" conductor only; obviously, he has much to say in the standard "respectable" symphonic literature.

Edward Elgar

Born: Broadheath, near Worcester, England,
June 2, 1857
Died: Worcester, February 23, 1934

Edward Elgar's father was a successful music merchant in Worcester; he also was organist of St. George's Roman Catholic Church there and a fairly competent violinist. It was thus into an atmosphere of music that Edward Elgar was born. He himself studied the violin, bassoon and organ and often deputized for his father at the organ in St. George's Church. As part of his early professional career he served, between 1879 and 1884, as bandmaster at the County Asylum, with attendants as his musicians. Between 1882 and 1889 he conducted the Worcester Instrumental Society and from 1885 to 1889 he was the official organist at St. George's, succeeding his father. In 1889 he married the daughter of a major-general in the British Army, Caroline Alice Roberts, and her devotion and confidence in his art served as prime stimuli for the ultimate success that came to him.

Until his marriage, Elgar had composed a few trifling miniatures. From his marriage onward, he began to think in terms of the larger forms. After a two-year residence in London, Elgar and his wife took up residence in the small community of Malvern and it was there, during the next thirteeen years, that he produced many of his large-scale choral and orchestral works. In 1904 a three-day Elgar Festival was given at Covent Garden and in the same year Elgar was knighted for his services to Britian and British music. For the next thirty years, until his death, he was one of Britian's most honored and respected subjects. His death, of cancer, was the occasion for nationwide memorial services throughout Britain with impressive pomp and circumstance.

Elgar's music is in the richest Romantic tradition and through most of it there runs a healthy vigor and nobility that are inspirational in the finest sense of the word. His most important orchestral scores, in addition to the "Enigma" Variations, are two symphonies; a violin concerto; a cello concerto; the symphonic study *Falstaff*; five *Pomp and Circumstance Marches*; the *Serenade for Strings*; three concert overtures (*Froissart, In the South* and *Cockaigne*); and the *Introduction and Allegro* for String Quartet and String Orchestra. Chief among his large-scale works for chorus and orchestra are the oratorios *The Light of Life, The Dream of Gerontius, The Apostles* and *The Kingdom*; and several odes for solo voices, chorus and orchestra, including the *Coronation Ode, The Music Makers* and *The Spirit of England.*

"ENIGMA" VARIATIONS

"The variations have amused me because I've labelled 'em with the nicknames of my particular friends. That is to say, I've written the variations each one to represent the mood of the 'party.' It's a quaint idea and the result is amusing to those behind the scenes and won't affect the reader who 'nose nuffin.'"

The words are those of Sir Edward Elgar, and they were spoken about the Variations on an Original Theme for Orchestra, Opus 36, called the "Enigma" Variations. The year was 1899, and Elgar was then forty-two years old. He had already attained a certain fame in England as a composer, but he was not yet well known outside his homeland. The "Enigma" Variations changed all that. With a canny awareness of what we might call public relations, Elgar calculated his score to make the maximum effect. Above the theme, instead of *Tema* or some other form of the word, he wrote "Enigma," and above each of the variations he put the initials of a friend ("musical or otherwise"). The calculation was on the mark: today the piece is perhaps the most popular symphonic work by an English composer.

The musical community all over the world was quick to engage in the intrigue proposed by the "Enigma" Variations. Who were the various persons depicted by Elgar in the fourteen variations? And was the theme itself a musical anagram of some other familiar melody? Today the people portrayed have long since been identified—Sir Adrian Boult had in his possession since 1920 an autographed score of the music in which Elgar himself wrote the list of names. But the provenance of the theme has continued to baffle musical detectives right down to our own day. One remembers with amusement the contest run by one of our leading periodicals some years ago, coincidental with the release of a recording of the score by Arturo Toscanini and the NBC Symphony Orchestra, designed to discover the true origin of Elgar's "Enigma" theme. Some of the suggestions were wild indeed, ranging from nursery rhymes to late Beethoven quartets.

Recently there has been an inclination on the part of program annotators and critics to ignore the whole silly business of the "true meaning" of Elgar's "Enigma" and to concentrate instead on the musical values of the score. You get a lot to like when you approach the music in this fashion. In character, the work spans a wide range: from the gentle lyricism of the first variation (a portrait of the composer's wife) to the vigor of the fourth (descriptive of a Gloucestershire squire of abundant energy), from the elegant grace and charm of the eighth (portraying a lady of regal manner and bearing) to the rousing climactic vitality of the last. The "Enigma" Variations is a fully realized symphonic work quite apart from programmatic implications. It is brilliantly scored for the large orchestra employed by composers in the last years of the nineteenth century, and when it is heard in a devoted and perceptive performance, it comes across as unique.

The music begins with the "Enigma" theme, brief and eloquent, shifting in tonality from G minor to G major.

Variation I (C.A.E.)—A tender portrait of Elgar's wife, Caroline Alice.

Variation II (H.D.S.-P.)—The pianist Hew David Stuart-Powell, with whom Elgar often played in trios. Mrs. Richard Powell, the Dorabella of Variation X, said that this particular variation revolved around "finger-loosening exercise that occupied moments of preparation for trio playing, while stands were being put up and music found."

Variation III (R.B.T.)—Richard Baxter Townshend, who had a "strange, reedy voice" and who liked to produce low falsetto tones. Bassoon and high winds are prominent in this variation for obvious reasons.

Variation IV (W.M.B.)—William Meath Baker, called by the Elgars "The Squire." He was a very decisive man who liked to give orders and set up a day's activities for groups of his friends. The music is quick and energetic, punctuated with many accent marks.

Variation V (R.P.A.)—Richard Penrose Arnold, son of Matthew Arnold. He was a man of contrasting moods, pensive, charming, entertaining. All these are in the music that Elgar created to characterize him. Mrs. Powell recalls that he had a "funny little nervous laugh: HA-ha-ha, ha-ha-HA-ha-ha! (You can hear it plainly in the woodwinds)."

Variation VI (Isobel)—Miss Isobel Fitton was a violin pupil of Elgar's who later studied the viola, hence the prominence of the viola in this variation.

Variation VII (Troyte)—Arthur Troyte Griffith was an architect and a close friend of Elgar's. He was characterized by another member of the Elgar circle as "refreshing but highly argumentative." There is a repeated tympani figure throughout the variation that probably expresses this aspect of Griffith's character.

Variation VIII (W.N.)—Miss Winifred Norbury, a pianist who often accompanied Elgar in sonatas and excerpts from his own music.

Variation IX (Nimrod)—Elgar's beloved friend Arthur
Jaeger (Jaeger means hunter in German, hence the
"Nimrod" association) is portrayed in this variation.
Elgar himself described the variation in these words:
"It is a record of a long summer evening talk when my
friend Jaeger grew nobly eloquent—as only he could—
on the grandeur of Beethoven and especially of his
slow movements."

Variation X (Dorabella)—Miss Dora Penny (later
Mrs. Richard Powell) is the subject of this portrait, a
touching dialogue between the strings and the winds.

Variation XI (G.R.S.)—George Robertson Sinclair
and his bulldog, Dan, are portrayed in this variation
racing along the banks of a river. Actual barking of the
dog is portrayed in the brass instruments.

Variation XII (B.G.N.)—Basil Nevinson was the cellist in the Elgar-Stuart-Powell trio mentioned in Variation II. Here, quite logically, the principal musical
material is given to the cello.

Variation XIII (***)—Elgar had asked permission to
use the initials of Lady Mary Lygon in this variation.
His letter, however, arrived after Lady Mary had already embarked upon a sea journey to Australia. The
clarinet quotes one of the themes from the Mendelssohn overture, *Calm Sea and Prosperous Voyage*.

Variation XIV (E.D.U.)—"Edoo" was the nickname
coined by Mrs. Elgar for her husband. This final variation, then, is a self-portrait and it brings the music to a
rousing conclusion.

During the long years of his illustrious career, Arturo Toscanini
conducted the "Enigma" Variations many times. Unexpectedly, he

was an ideal interpreter of the music. The shifting patterns of the variations summoned from him the ultimate in imaginative sensitivity, and from his extraordinary impact upon the orchestras he led there emerged playing of great refinement and dynamic vitality. Toscanini recorded the "Enigma" Variations with the NBC Symphony Orchestra in 1951 and it is one of the most cherishable of his recordings. When it was new, the sound seemed uncommonly good; now it is beginning to show its age. I still direct all but the most finicky sound enthusiasts to it, however (RCA Victrola VICS 1344).

Shortly after Toscanini's death in 1957, an extraordinary memorial concert was given in Carnegie Hall by the Symphony of the Air, composed largely of former members of the Toscanini NBC Symphony Orchestra. Each of the three conductors—Bruno Walter, Charles Munch and Pierre Monteux—conducted a score that had been close to Toscanini's heart. Walter led Beethoven's "Eroica" Symphony, Munch conducted Debussy's *La Mer* and Monteux electrified the audience with a dazzling performance of the "Enigma" Variations. During the last decade of his lifetime, in fact, Monteux became as famed an interpreter of the score as Toscanini had been. Not long after that Carnegie Hall performance, Monteux recorded the music on its native soil with the London Symphony Orchestra. Monteux chose the same coupling as had Toscanini for his recording: Brahms' Variations on a Theme by Haydn. The Monteux performance is unfortunately no longer available. There are available two different performances of the music conducted by Sir John Barbirolli (Vanguard Everyman 184 SD, with the Hallé Orchestra; and Angel S 36120, with the Philharmonia Orchestra). I prefer the earlier one with the Hallé Orchestra; the later performance seems contrived and overrefined, with a good deal of the vitality drained from the music. The price of Vanguard's Everyman series is an added attraction.

Boult's recently released performance, in sumptuous sound and elegantly played (Angel S 36799), is a warmer, more affectionate treatment of the music. And Davis' (Philips 835317; cassette 18123-CAA) is a meticulously prepared, well played and recorded version. There no longer exists any reel-to-reel edition.

César Franck

Born: Liége, Belgium, December 10, 1822
Died: Paris, November 8, 1890

César Franck's father was determined that his two sons should pursue musical careers. Thus they were both enrolled at an early age at the Conservatory in Liége. By the time young César arrived at his eleventh birthday, he had absorbed all that could be taught to him there. The following year the father moved the family to Paris in order to give the two boys a wider field for the development of their gifts. César entered the Paris Conservatory when he was fifteen and upon his graduation he won the Grand Prix d'Honneur in piano and a second prize in composition.

The Franck family finances were extremely modest and Franck *père* was determined that his son César would become a traveling piano virtuoso who would earn vast sums of money. For his part, César had other plans. The final schism between father and son came with César's marriage in 1848 to an actress; such a "dishonorable" professional woman could not be tolerated by Franck senior within the tight family group. The younger Franck thereupon withdrew, set up a home for himself and his wife and settled down to the routine schedule of teaching and organ playing that was to be his lot for the rest of his days. For the last twenty years or so of his life he was professor of organ at the Paris Conservatory and organist at the Church of Sainte Clotilde. Most of his composing was accomplished in the early morning hours between 5:30 and 7:30 and during his summer holidays.

Franck's modesty and nobility of soul were allied with a unique individuality and originality. The sensuous and mystical in music were the elements that most strongly appealed to him. He revolutionized the pattern of French instrumental music by reviving the polyphony that had long since ceased to be a prominent factor in it, and his harmonic freedom was much more daring than had been the norm in French music before him. Through his pupil and disciple, Vincent D'Indy, he set in motion a whole school of "Franckists" who dominated French musical life until the inevitable counterreaction set in, triggered by Debussy and his musical thinking.

Franck is today remembered chiefly for his Symphony in D Minor, the Symphonic Variations for Piano and Orchestra and the Violin and Piano Sonata in A Major. There are also three symphonic poems for orchestra: *Ce qu'on entend sur la montagne* (after Victor Hugo; Liszt, a few years later, also composed a symphonic poem on the same subject), *Les Eolides* and *Le Chasseur Maudit*; a considerable body of church music and choral works; some solo piano music; a Piano Quintet and a String Quartet.

SONATA IN A MAJOR FOR VIOLIN AND PIANO

Born in Belgium, César Franck for years labored virtually unknown as an organist and teacher, composing unperformed operas and oratorios in his spare time. Not until he was fifty did his life take a forceful purpose and direction; until then, his generally docile nature provided neither the benefit of sharp self-criticism nor the will to reject others' misguided advice. According to Debussy, Franck was "a man without malice to whom the finding of a beautiful harmony was sufficient for a whole day of contentment."

The founding of the fiercely nationalistic *Société Nationale* by Saint-Saëns during the Franco-Prussian War was one of the turning points in Franck's life. Many of his friends and admirers flocked to affiliate with the aims of the group—among them Massenet, Fauré, Guiraud, Duparc and D'Indy—and the music of Franck soon became standard fare in the concerts of the *Société*. In 1879, when he was fifty-seven, Franck produced his Piano Quintet in F Minor, a work of unabashed Romantic fervor, and the image of the ascetic "Seraphic Father" was promptly and finally dispelled.

As popular and critical success came his way, there also came the inevitable jealousies. The fanatical devotion of certain of his follow-ers brought about a reaction: several of his colleagues at the Conservatory evinced their hostility by denying awards to some of Franck's pupils for no reason, apparently, other than spite. Franck maintained his beatific reserve in the face of the mounting backbiting, and only in the turbulent and impassioned music of his final four years do we encounter the voice of the self-assertive creator. In this period he produced two superbly vital and original chamber works that, with the quintet, a considerable body of informed opinion holds to be his most significant music: the String Quartet and the Violin and Piano Sonata.

Franck composed his A Major Violin and Piano Sonata in 1886 as a wedding present for his renowned compatriot, the Belgian violin virtuoso Eugène Ysaÿe. It is a work that reaches out and involves performers and listeners in the strength and beauty of its lyricism. Cyclic form—the quotation in later movements of musical material from earlier ones—was a favorite device of Franck's, and we find it operating in the sonata with tremendous effect: the first three notes played by the violin serve as a motif that recurs in all four movements. The crown of the work is its magnificent last movement, a soaring dialogue in canon that rises to heights of exultant fervor. The main theme of the movement bears a striking resemblance to the opening of Beethoven's "Archduke" Trio.

Vincent D'Indy attended the first performance of the sonata and left a vivid description of the event. The program, a long one, began at three o'clock in the afternoon in one of the rooms of the Museum of Modern Painting in Brussels. The Franck sonata closed the program, and by the time the first movement ended the room was quite dark. Regulations forbade the use of candles or gaslight in rooms that contained paintings. The musicians were almost unable to see the music on their stands, but they proceeded with the final three movements, playing from memory "with a fire and passion the more astounding to the listeners in that there was an absence of all externals which could enhance the performance. Music, wondrous and alone, held sovereign sway in the darkness of night."

The sonata is in four movements. The first, marked *Allegretto ben moderato*, is a sweeping section of expansive violin rumination. The second theme is first stated by the piano, and after the development there is a return to the opening material. The movement ends on a note of calm repose. The second movement, *Allegro*, is a restless, churning section with vivid accents and strong syncopation. There is a quieter middle section, *Quasi lento*, and then the passion of the beginning of the movement returns. The sequence of events is repeated and the movement ends in the fury of a blazing coda. The third movement, *Ben moderato*, is an improvisatory-like movement, with extended cadenzas for the violin. The concluding movement, *Allegretto poco mosso*, begins as an imitative canon, with phrases tossed from one instrument and echoed by the other. New material is then introduced, and episodes from earlier movements are brought back for reassessment. The conclusion is a mighty affirmation of victory.

Several fine recordings of the sonata are available, among which my own favorites are the performances by Erica Morini and Rudolf Firkusny (Decca DL 710038), and Isaac Stern and Alexander Zakin (Columbia MS 6139). The former is one of the gems of recorded literature, a unified collaboration by two superb artists who pool their considerable gifts and deliver a performance of total involvement and dedication. Stern and Zakin, for their part, do not have quite such an evenly matched conception of the score—Stern is sometimes more assertive than his pianist—but there is great conviction to the playing and Stern's big, robust tone is ideally suited to the music. Both performances are very well recorded.

To these admired versions by Morini-Firkusny and Stern-Zakin should now be added the newer performances by Oistrakh-Richter (Angel/Melodiya S 40121) and Perlman-Ashkenazy (London CS 6628; tape L 80219; cassette M 10219). Both new versions present fiery and impassioned performances; the Perlman-Ashkenazy team has the better recorded balance between the two instruments.

A smaller-scale but beautifully articulated performance is the one by David Nadien and David Hancock (Monitor S 2017), which is also distinguished by exceptionally clear and well-balanced sound.

SYMPHONY IN D MINOR

When the Symphony in D Minor by César Franck came to performance in Febuary 1889—a scant twenty months before the composer
died—it immediately became the rallying point for opposing forces:
those promoting the composer and his music, and those against both.
Franck's disciple Vincent D'Indy has left us a biography of the composer in which he portrays Franck as a neglected and maligned
genius who was misundertood by his contemporaries. In his description of the first performance of the symphony at the Conservatory,
for example, D'Indy comments about the official resistance within
the institution and quotes liberally from some of the vitriolic remarks
made by musicians who attended the first performance. Gounod is
quoted as calling Franck's symphony the "affirmation of incompe-
tence, pushed to dogmatic lengths."

Franck no doubt had his detractors, but the situation apparently
was not so completely one-sided as D'Indy's emotional account
would have us believe. Some years ago, the distinguished French
music critic Léon Vallas wrote a new biography of the composer in
which he pointed out that Franck was constantly being singled out
for performance and that encouraging attention was paid to him by
the press. Refuting the remarks attributed to Gounod, Vallas writes:

Both the opinion and the meaningless jargon in which it is couched
seem improbable in the last degree. According to another anecdote,
told by George Rodenbach in *Figaro* on December 24, 1896, Gounod
is reported as saying "It is the negation of music." That remark, too,
seems hardly credible. Whatever differences in outlook and taste
separated the two old friends, Gounod always recognized the mastery
of his fellow-musician. If at times he criticized certain of Franck's
tendencies—his excessive refinement and his lack of simplicity—he
never ceased to acclaim him as a great artist. One need attach no
importance to certain solemn pontifical utterances of the composer
of *Faust*, bandied about, distorted, and twisted out of recognition by
the malignancy of the public.

D'Indy's biography, reinforced by the familiar painting of Jeanne Rongier, has given to posterity the vivid picture of the Maître seated in his organ loft at the Sainte Clotilde Church in Paris improvising to the amazement of all hearers and for his own intellectual stimulation. For thirty-two years, from 1858 until his death in 1890, Franck served Sainte Clotilde as organist. The sanctuary and remoteness he felt there became an integral part of his being, and the sonorities of the organ are germane to all of his musical thinking. The symphony is as good an example as exists of this essential truth. Right at the beginning, after the two-part questioning phrase which opens the work, there is a swell at the woodwind entrance which calls to mind the sound of an organ. And throughout the music one can logically draw parallels between the orchestral sounds and organ sonorities.

Carrying this analogy a step further, it is possible to find in the symphony's interpreters differences of approach which would correspond to the different styles of organ composition and performance. Some conductors, for example, approach the score with a Baroque attitude: the textures are clear and clean, with distinct colors and shading. Others apply to it the thicker-textured conception of the nineteenth century, and their performances of the Franck symphony put heavy emphasis upon the lush sonorities and "interpretive" opportunities afforded by the structure and quasi-Wagnerian orchestration of the score.

The symphony opens with a somber three-note motive that bears a striking similarity to the opening of Liszt's *Les Préludes* and the "Muss es sein?" ("Must it be?") question with which Beethoven began the final movement of his last quartet. The main body of the movement is an energetic *Allegro* built upon rather traditional formal lines. The middle movement, *Allegro*, is actually two movements telescoped into one. The first, with the now-famous English horn solo, corresponds to the usual slow movement, after which a delicate wisp of a Scherzo is introduced by the muted strings. The last movement, *Allegro non troppo*, introduces two new themes: the first is a flowing melody for cellos and bassoons, the second a heroic theme for brass alone. Rather than developing these themes in the usual sonata-allegro fashion, however, Franck brings back material from the first two movements and the symphony ends in a triumphant brass affirmation of the mysterious three-note motto with which it began.

During the early 1950s two widely divergent approaches to the Franck symphony were recorded in Detroit and Vienna, respectively, by Paul Paray and Wilhelm Furtwängler. Both performances have now passed into the limbo of non-availability, but they illustrated the opposite poles of interpretative approach to the symphony. Paray was a respected organist in France before he decided to devote the major part of his musical activities to conducting. In essence, his approach to the Franck symphony in his recording was that of the Baroque organist par excellence. The athletic nature of the music was underlined and everything was forthright and dynamic, with inner balances carefully adjusted for the utmost clarity and with a healthy feeling of exuberance about it all. Furtwängler, on the other hand, sought the other element in the music: its mystical character. His tempi were a good deal slower, more introspective than Paray's, and his phrasing was much more elastic. His rhythmic pulse was more capricious than Paray's and one sometimes had the feeling that the whole thing might suddenly go out of control. It never did, of course, but there was that feeling of tension that was such a characteristic of Furtwängler's music-making. It was a very controversial reading and there was no middle-ground reaction to it: one was either overwhelmed or appalled.

Of the performances currently available, there is one that is reminiscent in some respects of Furtwängler's; this is the Bernstein recording (Columbia MS 6072) with the New York Philharmonic. Bernstein, like Furtwängler, tends to slower tempi and one has the feeling that the performance is generated from the deepest emotional recesses of the conductor's being. The music churns and heaves, but under Bernstein's ministrations it leaves one with a profound feeling of exaltation—and this, after all, was one of Franck's prime musical motivations.

A performance of a completely different character is the one by Munch with the Boston Symphony (RCA Victrola VICS 1034). Munch tends to the more vigorous, emotionally taut attitude of Paray. I well remember a particularly hair-raising account of the music which Munch conducted in Boston in 1947, a couple of years before he became the music director of the Boston Symphony. It was a performance of feverish intensity that left one limp at its conclusion. Not long afterward, London released a performance of the score with Munch conducting the Paris Conservatory Orchestra that was very much the same kind of driving, biting reading of the music. When Munch finally came to record the score in Boston, some of the headlong impetuosity of the earlier recorded performance was gone, but there remained enough dynamic brilliance and excitement to make the performance one of the finer ones in the catalog. At its current Victrola status it is, of course, an exceptional buy as well.

Two other, smaller-scaled performances are those conducted by Sir Thomas Beecham (Seraphim S 60012) and Carlo Maria Giulini (Angel S 35641). Both are elegant, tasteful performances, cleanly articulated and finely adjusted, and each yields much musical enjoyment. Beecham's has a special response to the mystical qualities of the music. Also superlative is the noble and somber recording by Klemperer (Angel S 36416).

My own favorite among all the recorded editions of the Franck symphony is the performance by Pierre Monteux and the Chicago Symphony Orchestra (RCA LSC 2514). Monteux, it seems to me, strikes exactly the proper balance between the drive of Munch and the mysticism of Bernstein-Furtwängler. The orchestra plays magnificently and the recorded sound is vibrant. Monteux truly recreates the symphony and it is as close to a definitive performance as anything in the current record catalogs.

In the tape and cassette fields the only apparently available performance is the one conducted by Karajan—Angel L 36729 and 4XS 36729 respectively. I can only say that for me Karajan's approach to this score is hopelessly pompous and ponderous.

George Gershwin

Born: Brooklyn, New York, September 26, 1898
Died: Hollywood, California, July 11, 1937

The salient biographical facts of Gershwin's life appear in the text pieces that follow this brief note. Gershwin was essentially an intuitive musician whose genius was somewhat circumscribed by traditional musical forms. Thus, *Grove's Dictionary of Music and Musicians* can remark condescendingly of *An American in Paris* that it "shocked the audience of the 1931 International Society of Contemporary Music Festival in London by its excessive commonness, though admittedly that audience was the wrong one for such music." The world has little noted nor long remembered some of the other works played at that Festival but it can never forget the exuberance, the flair and the audacity of Gershwin's "common" but masterful score.

In the thirteen years between the first performance of the *Rhapsody in Blue* and Gershwin's tragically early death from a brain tumor at the age of thirty-eight, the exhilaration of his music and his vibrant personality permeated every level of American musical life. Now, more than thirty years after his death, it is safe to say that he changed the course of American musical history in all its aspects.

The principal works in Gershwin's concert output, in addition to *An American in Paris*, the Piano Concerto and the *Rhapsody in Blue*, are the *Cuban Overture* (titled *Rumba* originally) and the Second Rhapsody for Piano and Orchestra (both 1932); the *Variations* for Piano and Orchestra on "I Got Rhythm" (1934); and the opera *Porgy and Bess* (1935). The long list of Broadway shows for which Gershwin composed the music (usually to lyrics by his brother Ira) includes such memorable landmarks as *Lady, Be Good* (1924); *Oh, Kay!* (1926); *Funny Face, Strike Up the Band* and

Rosalie (all 1927); *Girl Crazy* (1930); *Of Thee I Sing* (1931); and *Let 'Em Eat Cake* (1933).

Gershwin's final activity comprised music for three Hollywood films—*Shall We Dance* and *A Damsel in Distress* (both released by RKO in 1937) and *The Goldwyn Follies* (released by Goldwyn-United Artists in 1938). "Let's Call the Whole Thing Off" and "They Can't Take That Away from Me" were the hits of *Shall We Dance;* "A Foggy Day" and "Nice Work If You Can Get It" were in the score for *A Damsel in Distress;* and *The Goldwyn Follies* included "Love Is Here to Stay" and "Love Walked In."

In nineteenth-century German culture the song (or *Lied*) played a central role in musical creativity, Schumann, Mendelssohn, Brahms, Hugo Wolf all composed magnificent songs, but unquestionably the greatest of all nineteenth-century *Lieder* composers was Franz Schubert. Twentieth-century American life has produced a similar productive flowering of song composition and inspired composers—Jerome Kern, Cole Porter, Arthur Schwartz, Irving Berlin, Richard Rodgers—but the Franz Schubert of them all was the genius who walked among us so briefly named George Gershwin.

AN AMERICAN IN PARIS

On St. Valentine's Day, 1924, two days after the extraordinary concert in New York's Aeolian Hall at which Paul Whiteman and his orchestra introduced *Rhapsody in Blue*, George Gershwin received a letter from Carl Van Vechten, the novelist and writer about music. "The concert, quite as a matter of course," Van Vechten wrote, "was a riot; you crowned it with what I am forced to regard as the foremost serious effort by an American composer. Go straight on and you will knock all Europe silly." These words, addressed to a twenty-five-year-old composer whose career up to that time had been limited to Tin Pan Alley and Broadway successes, signaled a transition of major importance for Gershwin and for American music.

Gershwin may have had Van Vechten's advice in mind when, four years later, he went to Paris. During an earlier visit, he had conceived an idea for an orchestral score that would reflect an American tourist's impressions of the City of Light. Now, setting himself up in the Hotel Majestic, he went to work composing *An American in Paris*. In their invaluable words-and-pictures biography of Gershwin, called *The Gershwin Years*, Edward Jablonski and Lawrence Stewart wrote:

> George worked on *An American in Paris* and readily played it for the usual stream of callers, among them the young British composer William Walton, Vladimir Dukelsky (better known now as Vernon Duke), Dick Simon, the publisher, pianist Mario Braggiotti. One day Leopold Stokowski dropped by and became greatly interested in the work in progress, but this lasted only until he heard that the first performance had been promised to Damrosch.

While Gershwin worked on *An American in Paris*, he also sought out the many great composers who were then living in Paris, among them Milhaud, Ravel, Stravinsky, Poulenc and Prokofiev. His life in Paris was a continuous social whirl, yet he managed to complete the orchestration of his new work in three and a half months. About a month later, on December 13, 1928, Walter Damrosch conducted the world premiere performance of *An American in Paris* at a Carnegie Hall concert with the New York Philharmonic-Symphony Orchestra.

To an interviewer for *Musical America*, Gershwin had already described the work:

> This new piece, really a rhapsodic ballet, is written very freely and is the most modern music I've yet attempted. The opening part will be developed in typical French style, in the manner of Debussy and The Six, though the themes are all original. My purpose here is to portray the impression of an American visitor in Paris, as he strolls about the city, listens to the various street noises, and absorbs the French atmosphere.
>
> As in my other orchestral compositions I've not endeavored to represent any definite scenes in this music. The rhapsody is programmatic only in a general impressionistic way, so that the individual listener can read into the music such episodes as his imagination pictures for him. The opening gay section is followed by a rich blues

with a strong rhythmic undercurrent. Our American friend, perhaps after strolling into a café and having a couple of drinks, has suddenly succumbed to a spasm of homesickness. The harmony here is both more intense and simple than in the preceding pages. This blues rises to a climax followed by a coda in which the spirit of the music returns to the vivacity and bubbling exuberance of the opening part with its impression of Paris. Apparently the homesick American, having left the café and reached the open air, has disowned his spell of the blues and once again is an alert spectator of Parisian life. At the conclusion, the street noises and French atmosphere are triumphant.

When one examines the formal structure of *An American in Paris*, the bones of its design are all too apparent. But the melodic vitality and freshness of Gershwin's creative gift far transcend his naïveté and insecurity in the handling of traditional musical forms.

Some years ago RCA carried out an idea that in theory, at least, seemed to have considerable merit: Darius Milhaud was commissioned to write *An American in Paris* in reverse, as it were. The resulting score, titled *A Frenchman in New York*, unfortunately proved to be a tired collection of musical clichés. Arthur Fiedler and the Boston Pops Orchestra recorded both the Gershwin and Milhaud scores back-to-back (RCA LSC 2702)—but an indication of the failure of the Milhaud piece is the fact that the disc was withdrawn not too long after it was released. The performance of *An American in Paris* that it contained, however, was one of the best—flashy, exuberant and vital.

Another Fiedler performance of the score exists in a coupling with Gershwin's *Rhapsody in Blue* (RCA LSC 2367), and this, too, is a sympathetic exposition of the Gershwin flavor.

Among all the other recordings of the score, only Bernstein's, it seems to me, successfully comes to grips with the essential character of the music. Back in the late 1940s, when he was recording for RCA, Bernstein led a splendid version of *An American in Paris*—one full of sparkle, vitality and—the indispensable commodity for a performance of this work—brashness. His re-recording of the score with the New York Philharmonic for Columbia (MS 6091) duplicates his earlier success and the recorded sound is fine.

Newly entered into the Gershwin sweepstakes is a disc by André Previn and the London Symphony Orchestra devoted to *An American in Paris* and the two great scores for piano and orchestra, the Concerto in F and *Rhapsody in Blue* (with Previn as soloist). The performance of *An American in Paris* (Angel S FO 36810) is a finely manicured one, but it lacks the brashness of Bernstein's and the confident sophistication of Fiedler's.

Both Bernstein's and Fiedler's performances are available on tape (Columbia MQ 322, RCA FTC 2004, respectively). Either version is a worthy tape library choice: Fiedler's is perhaps the more vividly reproduced. Of the two versions available on cassette, my choice would go to the surprisingly idiomatic account conducted by Stanley Black (London M 94009). But Bernstein and Fiedler are still the most convincing of all the conductors who have recorded this music.

CONCERTO IN F MAJOR FOR PIANO

A chance hearing of a performance of Dvořák's *Humoresque* at a school assembly in New York in the early 1900s may well have changed the course of American musical history. Present in the auditorium that day was a schoolmate of the performer—a boy named George Gershwin. Right then and there young George decided to "look into this music stuff." Before long he was practicing the piano, without benefit of formal instruction, at the home of a friend. When a secondhand upright piano somehow found its way into the Gershwin household, George astounded the family with his expert performances of current popular songs.

Music lessons were now considered a must for him, and he was paraded from one teacher to another. The first great influence in Gershwin's life was Charles Hambitzer, a composer who was accomplished on many instruments. Hambitzer thought his new pupil a genius. "He wants to go in for this modern stuff, jazz and whatnot," the teacher said, "but I'm not going to let him for a while. I'll see that he gets a firm foundation in the standard music first." Gershwin, for his part, wrote later:

Under Hambitzer I first became familiar with Chopin, Liszt, and Debussy. . . . Harmony, up to this time, had been a secret to me. I've always had a sort of instinctive feeling for tone combinations, and many of the chords that sound so modern in my orchestral compositions were set down without any particular attention to their theoretical structure. When my critics tell me now and then I betray a structural weakness, they are not telling me anything I don't know.

It was very likely Hambitzer's influence that bore fruit years later in Gershwin's "theoretical" composition, the Concerto in F Major for Piano.

After Hambitzer died of tuberculosis, Gershwin took occasional lessons from Ernest Hutcheson, Edward Kilenyi and Rubin Goldmark, but for the most part he taught himself. When he was sixteen, Gershwin got a job as a "song plugger" with a music-publishing house. At the same time he began to invent tunes of his own. In 1916 the first Gershwin tune was published, a profound ditty called "When You Want 'Em You Can't Get 'Em, When You've Got 'Em You Don't Want 'Em." For this and another song published soon after, Gershwin collected the sum of twelve dollars. A job as rehearsal pianist for *Miss 1917*, a Dillingham-Ziegfeld production with music by Victor Herbert and Jerome Kern, gave him a steady income—$35 a week—and some much-needed encouragement.

In 1919 he composed his first score for a revue, *La, La Lucille*, and in the same year came the song "Swanee," which received on its own a fair degree of attention. But then it was incorporated into a show called *Sinbad*, with Al Jolson starring, and overnight all America was singing "Swanee," catapulting Gershwin into the front rank of popular tunesmiths. Then began the long string of scores for the Broadway stage, including *George White's Scandals, For Goodness Sake,* and *Our Nell.*

Early in 1924 Paul Whiteman, the "King of Jazz," was planning a concert in New York's Aeolian Hall. He invited Gershwin to compose a concert work for the occasion, and in three weeks the *Rhapsody in Blue* was created. From its first performance on Lincoln's birthday, 1924, with Gershwin himself at the piano, the *Rhapsody in Blue* has been one of the most loved American works.

Soon after the premiere of the *Rhapsody*, Gershwin was invited by Walter Damrosch, conductor of the Symphony Society of New York, to compose a piano concerto. Gershwin accepted the invitation eagerly. On December 3, 1925, Gershwin's Piano Concerto in F Major was played for the first time. Hailing the score at the time of the premiere, Damrosch said that Gershwin had made it possible for jazz to be received in respectable musical circles.

> He had done it boldly by dressing this extremely independent and up-to-date young lady in the classic garb of a concerto. Yet he has not detracted one whit from her fascinating personality. He is the Prince who has taken Cinderella by the hand and openly proclaimed her a princess to the astonished world, no doubt to the fury of her envious sisters.

In his own description of the concerto, Gershwin wrote that the first movement "is in sonata form—but." The second movement is a sustained *Andante* in three-part song form, and the Finale is a rondo that brings back melodic material from the first two movements. Formal deficiencies notwithstanding, the Gershwin Piano Concerto is a thoroughly unified, deeply satisfying artistic creation. Some years ago, indeed, the distinguished English conductor Albert Coates rated the score among the top fifty in the whole orchestral literature. With its brash swagger, athletic dynamism and uninhibited high spirits, it is certainly a work of unique and enduring attractions.

The concerto has been recorded many times over the years. At one time the patent on its performance was held by Gershwin's old crony Oscar Levant. A number of new performances have appeared in the recent past: Werner Haas with Edo de Waart and the Monte Carlo Opera Orchestra (Philips 6500118); Eugene List with Samuel Adler and the Berlin Symphony Orchestra (Turnabout 34457); Previn playing the piano and conducting the London Symphony Orchestra (Angel SFO 36810); and Roberto Szidon with Edward Downes and the London Philharmonic Orchestra (DGG 2530055; cassette 3300019). Previn's has the strongest claim to special attention: he coaxes a brilliantly evocative response from his London Symphony Orchestra colleagues, and he plays the piano part in thoroughly dedicated and idiomatic fashion. If the performance doesn't quite match the sparkle and vitality of his earlier collaboration as soloist with André Kostelanetz and his orchestra (Columbia CS 8286), the new one has superior sound and deserves a place near the very top of the list of available recordings of this score. My nomination for the very top spot goes to the Wild-Fiedler recording (RCA LSC 2586; tape TR3 5006, 3¾ ips), which has as its companions two rather more exotic Gershwin items—the *Cuban Overture* and the *Variations* on "I Got Rhythm" for Piano and Orchestra, with Wild as the pianist.

Among the other principal recordings of the concerto, I find the Entremont-Ormandy performance (Columbia MS 7013) heavy-handed, the Lowenthal-Abravanel (Vanguard Cardinal VCS 10017) rather earth-bound and four-square.

RHAPSODY IN BLUE

On New Year's Day, 1924, George Gershwin was hard at work putting the finishing touches on his score for the Broadway-bound musical, *Sweet Little Devil*, due to begin its out-of-town tryout in Boston within a few days. An interesting item appeared in the New York *Tribune* of January 4, 1924:

> Among the members of the committee of judges who will pass on "What is American Music?" at the Paul Whiteman concert to be given at Aeolian Hall, Tuesday afternoon, February 12, will be Sergei Rachmaninoff, Jascha Heifetz, Efrem Zimbalist and Alma Gluck. . . . This question of just what is American music has aroused a tremendous interest in musical circles and Mr. Whiteman is receiving every phase of manuscript, from blues to symphonies. George Gershwin is at work on a jazz concerto. . . .

When the item was read to George by his brother Ira, he was taken aback. George vaguely remembered discussing with Whiteman a projected jazz concert for which Gershwin would compose an ambitious piece using jazz rhythms and feeling; in the press of more immediate projects, Gershwin promptly dismissed the conversation from his active thinking. Now, suddenly, the scheduled concert was only five weeks away. Before he left for Boston and the run there of *Sweet Little Devil*, Gershwin met again with Whiteman. They agreed that since time was so short, Gershwin would be required only to provide a piano score for the new work; details of the orchestration of the piece would be handled by Whiteman's chief arranger and the best man in the business, Ferde Grofé.

On the train ride to Boston certain elements of the work began to take shape in Gershwin's mind. He wrote later:

> It was on the train, with its steely rhythms, its rattlety-bang that is so often stimulating to a composer (I frequently hear music in the very heart of noise), that I suddenly heard—even saw on paper—the complete construction of the *Rhapsody* from beginning to end. No new themes came to me, but I worked on the thematic material already in my mind, and tried to conceive the composition as a whole. I heard it as a sort of musical kaleidoscope of America—of our vast melting-pot, of our incomparable national pep, our blues, our metropolitan madness. By the time I reached Boston, I had the definite plot of the piece, as distinguished from its actual substance.

The *Rhapsody in Blue* was the next-to-last number on the Whiteman concert. Gershwin himself played the piano solo and since portions of the part were still not finished by concert time he improvised whole sections right on the spot, with Whiteman taking cues from Gershwin to bring the orchestra back in after solo passages. The audacity, the boldness and the rich melodic invention of the *Rhapsody in Blue* transformed what had been a dull, routine and stuffy concert into an event of historic importance in American music. At the age of twenty-five George Gershwin had burst upon the serious music scene. Olin Downes in the New York *Times* called him "a new talent finding its voice." Carl Van Vechten, the distinguished novelist and writer about music, wrote to Gershwin after the concert: "Quite as a matter of course the concert was a riot; you crowned it with what I am forced to regard as the foremost serious effort by an American composer."

The *Rhapsody* opens with a long glissando by the clarinet, written

—so it is told—because Ross Gorman, the clarinetist in the Paul Whiteman Orchestra, was capable of incredible glissando effects. There follow in rapid succession two more brief motives which form the germinal underpinning of the first half of the work. The first of them is the bass clarinet phrase that follows the opening, and the second is the repeated-note pattern played by the piano at its first entrance. A fourth pivotal theme is the one introduced a little later by the trumpets, who call attention to themselves first by a loud flutter-tongue trill. During the first part of the *Rhapsody*, the solo piano has several opportunities to play cadenzas of an improvisational nature. The last principal thematic element is the famous slow ascending and descending theme that served for so many years as the official theme of the Paul Whiteman Band. It is presented first by the orchestra, then by the piano, and then becomes the subject for a brilliant *Allegro* section. Finally, there is an inventive coda which introduces the three principal ideas of the very beginning, but in reverse order. The ending is a grandiose climax.

Structurally the work is naïve and transparently faulty—Gershwin was never really able to cope with traditional musical forms. But the great individuality and vitality of the music, its joyous outcry of unleashed temperament, has made it an American favorite from the day it was first performed.

The recordings of the music range from a piano solo version by Gershwin himself (taken from an old piano roll) to two-piano versions by Ferrante and Teicher and Rawicz and Landauer, to misguided jazz-oriented performances such as those by the orchestras of Ted Heath and Mantovani (with, respectively, Winifred Atwell and Julius Katchen as the pianists). Gershwin's own performance may be a historical document, but the playing sounds tired and lackluster and shows little of the brashness and superb technical control he is reliably reported to have exuded at the keyboard.

Two recordings, it seems to me, have more to offer in the way of fulfillment than any of the others: Leonard Bernstein conducting the Columbia Symphony Orchestra from the keyboard (Columbia MS 6091, MS 7518) and Earl Wild with Arthur Fiedler and the

Boston Pops Orchestra. Bernstein's is not immune from a charge of overinflection of both the orchestral and piano parts, but for me the characterful playing sweeps all criticism aside: for me the Bernstein recording is one of the glories of the literature and I hope it will be around for many years to come. The Wild-Fiedler collaboration (RCA LSC 2367 or LSC 2746) continues to be a thoroughly recommendable alternate version for those who prefer a straighter account of the music. Previn's recent re-recording of the score (Angel SFO 36810) has come out less well than the Gershwin concerto performance on the other side of the disc, and there are some gauche cuts in the *Rhapsody*.

Neither Bernstein's nor Wild's performance has been retained in the reel-to-reel catalog, though Bernstein's is available on cassette (Columbia 16 11 0130). Of the two that are listed for tape fanciers, I prefer the Katchen-Kertesz performance (London L 80225).

Edvard Grieg

Born: Bergen, Norway, June 15, 1843
Died: Bergen, September 4, 1907

The best-known composer yet to emerge from Norway, Grieg was
of Scottish extraction, his great-grandfather having emigrated from
Scotland in 1746 to enter the lobster-exporting business at the
Hanseatic port of Bergen. Grieg's first music teacher was his mother,
with whom he studied piano beginning at the age of six. The family
household was a very musical one and from his earliest years Edvard
was surrounded by the music of Mozart, Weber, Chopin and other
masters. The great Norwegian violinist Ole Bull was a friend of the
family and it was he who suggested that Edvard's musical talents
should be broadened by studies at the Leipzig Conservatory. Grieg
was fifteen when he was enrolled as a student at that institution,
but the formal and pedantic teaching methods left a lasting negative
impression upon the independent youth. More instructional than his
studies, however, were the opportunities in Leipzig to hear fine music well performed—especially at the Gewandhaus concerts. It was
here that Grieg heard Clara Schumann play her husband's Piano
Concerto—an experience that found its echo in Grieg's own Piano
Concerto of some years later.

An attack of pleurisy when he was seventeen forced him to with-
draw from the Conservatory temporarily and laid the foundation
for the respiratory difficulty that was to plague Grieg for the rest of
his life. He returned to Leipzig and the Conservatory after a summer's recuperation in Norway and completed his studies there before his nineteenth birthday. After a brief stay in his native city,
he went to Copenhagen, which was then the main center of Norwegian as well as Danish cultural life. The reigning musical figure
there was Niels Gade, and Gade gave Grieg encouragement and

advice. It was in Copenhagen also that Grieg met his cousin Nina Hagerup, a talented musician and singer, who had lived in Denmark from her earliest youth despite the fact that she, too, had been born in Bergen. The two became engaged in the summer of 1864.

At about this time a profound new influence entered Grieg's life: he met the young Norwegian composer Rikard Nordraak, who was immersed in the folk and peasant culture of Norway and was determined to develop a Norwegian national school of composition. Up to this time Grieg had lived in the Danish-oriented cultural environment of middle-class Norwegian life, with its predominantly Danish speech, heritage and attitudes. Grieg responded immediately to Nordraak's stimulation and declared that henceforth he would react "against the effeminate Mendelssohnian-Gade Scandinavianism, turning with enthusiasm into the new, well-defined path along which the Northern School is now traveling." He was one of the founders, along with Nordraak and several others, of the Euterpe Society for the promotion of Scandinavian music. A turning point in Grieg's life and in the life of music in Norway was the concert he arranged in Christiania in October 1866. It was made up entirely of music by Norwegian composers, with several of his own works included, and it was brilliantly successful.

In 1870 Grieg visited Italy a second time and in Rome he met Franz Liszt, who read over the score of Grieg's Piano Concerto and was most enthusiastic in his praise. When he returned to Norway Grieg threw himself with increasing intensity into the artistic ferment that was bubbling all around him. He was a leading figure in Norwegian theater circles and in 1872 he composed his first music for the stage, incidental pieces for Bjørnson's *Sigurd Jorsalfar*. The success of that venture prompted the two men to consider plans for an opera on a Norwegian subject, *Olav Trygvason*. Work on it was actually begun, but then there was a falling-out between Grieg and Bjørnson and the composer accepted the invitation of Ibsen that he compose incidental music for his play *Peer Gynt*. Grieg worked on the *Peer Gynt* music for nearly two years; its first performance, with Ibsen's revised stage version of the play, took place in February 1876.

The next few years were busy ones for Grieg. He traveled extensively throughout Europe, composed a good number of songs, piano pieces and his String Quartet in G Minor, and also conducted the concerts of the Bergen Symphony Orchestra from 1880 to 1882.

During the last twenty-five years of his life he was a universally honored and admired figure. He met Brahms, Tchaikovsky and Reger, contributed musical articles to many Norwegian and foreign journals and in general involved himself in the affairs of the world. He had, for example, very strong opinions concerning the shameful Dreyfus affair in France; when these opinions appeared in print, they caused a furore in Paris. His never vigorous health began to deteriorate in 1900 and though he was able to make several more trips abroad in the ensuing years, it was evident that he had not much longer to live. His sixtieth birthday in 1903 was the occasion for notable celebrations, with Bjørnson making a moving and impassioned speech to honor him. His death was a national calamity and his funeral brought world-wide expressions of bereavement. Grieg's body was cremated and the urn containing the ashes is in a rock-hewn recess overlooking the fjord in Bergen at Trollhaugen, the home of Edvard and Nina Grieg.

CONCERTO IN A MINOR FOR PIANO, OP. 16

Grieg composed more than 120 songs for solo voice and piano, and nearly double that amount of short pieces for piano solo. Nearly every one of them is touched with a particular poetic sensitivity and simplicity, for Grieg was essentially a lyrical composer and a miniaturist. Rather early in his career he discovered that his rhapsodic nature could not function freely within the structures of the bigger musical forms. As a consequence, Grieg left us very little sustained large-scaled expression: a single string quartet; three sonatas for violin and piano; a cello sonata; and the Piano Concerto in A Minor. It is paradoxical that the work by which Grieg is almost universally remembered today—his Piano Concerto—is one that only dimly reflects the essence of the composer's musical language.

Grieg composed his Piano Concerto in 1868, when he was twenty-five years old. Its musical viewpoint and aesthetic is typically nineteenth-century Romantic, with a good deal of Brahms and Schumann in it. And yet the Grieg concerto has been called "a typically Norwegian" score. It is difficult to justify this characterization, really, except that there does seem to be something of the North about this music, with its suggestion of vast distances and a certain gray bleakness.

While Grieg was working on his Piano Concerto, he received an entirely unsolicited letter of praise from the mighty Franz Liszt, who had seen Grieg's F Minor Violin and Piano Sonata, Opus 8. This letter was instrumental in Grieg's receiving a grant of money from the Norwegian government to enable him to accept Liszt's invitation to come visit him in his monastery home in Rome. In 1869, therefore, Grieg brought the newly completed manuscript of his Piano Concerto to Liszt in Rome and he waited for the Old Master's reaction with bated breath.

In a letter written to his parents, Grieg vividly describes the meeting:

I was very anxious to see if he would really play my Concerto at sight. I, for my part, considered it impossible; not so Liszt. "Will you play?" he asked, and I made haste to reply: "No, I cannot" (you know I have never practiced it). Then Liszt took the manuscript, went to the piano, and said to the assembled guests, with his characteristic smile, "Very well, then, I will show you that I also cannot." With that he began. I admit that he took the first part of the concerto too fast, and the beginning sounded helter-skelter, but later on, when I had a chance to indicate the tempo, he played as only he can play. It is significant that he played the cadenza, the most difficult part, best of all. His demeanor is worth any price to see. Not content with playing, he, at the same time, converses and makes comments, addressing a bright remark now to one, now to another of the assembled guests, nodding significantly to the right or left, particularly when something pleases him. In the Adagio, and still more in the Finale, he reached a climax, both as to his playing and the praise he had to bestow.

A really divine episode I must not forget. Toward the end of the Finale the second theme is, as you may remember, repeated in a mighty fortissimo. In the very last measures, when in the first triplets the first tone is changed in the orchestra from G-Sharp to G, while the piano part, in a mighty scale passage, rushes wildly through the whole reach of the keyboard, he suddenly stopped, rose up to his full height, left the piano, and with big, theatric strides and with arms uplifted walked across the large cloister hall, at the same time literally roaring the theme. When he got to the G in question he stretched out his arms imperiously and exclaimed "G, G, not G-sharp! Splendid! . . ." In conclusion, he handed me the manuscript, and said in a peculiarly cordial tone: "Keep steadily on; I tell you, you have the capability, and—do not let them intimidate you."

This final admonition was of tremendous importance to me; there was something in it that seemed to give it an air of sanctification. At times, when disappointment and bitterness are in store for me, I shall recall his words, and the remembrance of that hour will have a wonderful power to uphold me in days of adversity.

It has been said that Grieg modeled his concerto after the one by Schumann. Indeed, the two works have more in common than merely their A-minor tonality. Both open with a dramatic statement from the solo instrument and both have a fantasy, improvisatory nature. Structurally, the opening movement of Grieg's concerto, marked *Allegro molto moderato—Cadenza—Tempo I*, is in purest sonata form. The first theme is stated originally by the woodwinds and horns; it has a march-like character and is then taken up by the solo instrument. There are subsidiary themes and then the second principal theme is announced by the trumpet. It, too, is picked up by the piano, developed and embellished. There is an exact recapitulation of the exposition, the cadenza is a brilliant one, and then the movement ends vigorously.

The second movement, *Adagio*, is a lyrical gem. Muted strings announce the first subject, which is then echoed by the horn before the solo piano makes its first entrance. The theme is varied by ornamentation and embellishment, it wells up full-throated from both piano and orchestra, and then the movement ends in peace and serenity.

The third movement has a gay folk-music flavor. It is marked *Allegro moderato molto e marcato—Andante maestoso*, and it follows the *Adagio* movement without a break. Excitement is whipped up in fine shape and in the coda a triumphant theme surges up in the trumpets and trombones against the piano and orchestra.

Not too many years ago the Grieg Piano Concerto was ubiquitous in our concert halls, and its stirring melodies were heard season after season. When Tin Pan Alley was raiding the classics for melodic material during the 1940s, a Freddy Martin treatment of the opening theme even found its way onto the popular Hit Parade. Its melodies still do turn up in that summer musical theater favorite, *Song of Norway*. Fashions and tastes seem to have shifted away from the concerto in the concert hall in recent years, but its popularity on records continues unabated.

One pre-LP recording still deserves consideration, it seems to me. This is the performance recorded by the unique Romanian pianist, Dinu Lipatti, with Alceo Galliera conducting the Philharmonia Orchestra (Odyssey 32160141, mono only). The sound is now rather tubby and restricted, to be sure—much more so than in Lipatti's performance of the Schumann Concerto that is on the other side —but Lipatti had some extraordinary things to say in the Grieg and his combination of sensitive poetry and steely fingered brilliance still cast their spell.

Several more recent stereo performances are also exceptionally felicitous readings of the music, if without the special qualities of perceptive identification with the score that Lipatti brought to it; among them are the performances by Curzon-Fjeldstad (London CS 6157; tape L 80064); Anda-Kubelik (DGG 138888; tape L 8888; cassette 923016); Freire-Kempe (Columbia MS 7396); and Rubinstein-Wallenstein (RCA LSC 2566).

Rubinstein's is the pianist's fourth performance of the score for RCA Victor, his second in collaboration with Alfred Wallenstein as conductor (Eugene Ormandy and Antal Dorati were the two earlier conductors). The album cover boldly reproduces a statement by Rubinstein himself to the effect that he considers this performance of the Grieg Concerto one of the most nearly perfect recordings he has ever made. Strong words, indeed. In fact, Rubinstein plays with great dramatic strength and there is no question of his total involvement in the score. The sound is superb, with especially warm stereo.

Solomon (Pickwick S 4034) offers a sympathetically understated account of the music in which a gentle and pervading lyricism is the principal quality. The paralytic stroke that Solomon suffered not

many years after this performance was recorded removed from the
music scene an artist whose dignity and serenity we have sorely
missed. The recorded sound of his Grieg Concerto performance is
good, if lacking in the exceptional breadth and spaciousness of
Rubinstein's.

George Frideric Handel

Born: Halle, Germany, February 23, 1685
Died: London, England, April 14, 1759

Handel's father was a barber who later became the surgeon and valet to the Prince of Saxe-Magdeburg. He was destined by his parents for a life as a lawyer but as a very small child he learned secretly to play the spinet. At the age of seven, on a visit to his older stepbrother, who was valet at the court of Saxe-Weissenfels, young George was heard by the Duke playing on the chapel organ. It was the Duke himself who persuaded Handel's father to allow the boy to study music. Zachau, who was the organist at Halle, was the boy's first teacher in theory; he also studied the oboe, spinet, harpsichord and organ. He soon composed sonatas for two oboes and bass, became the assistant organist at the Halle Domkirche and for three years composed a motet for every Sunday.

In 1696, at the age of eleven, he visited Berlin and there, at the court of the Electress Sophia Charlotte, he first came into contact with Italian music and musicians. The Princess wished to send the lad to Italy for further musical studies but his father took him back to Halle to pursue a well-grounded general education. The father died the following year, and Handel, respecting his father's wishes, entered the University in February 1702 and finished the study of law. At the same time he served as organist at the cathedral at a salary of $50 a year. In 1703 he left the University, gave up his position as organist and forsook Halle for Hamburg.

In Hamburg he came to the attention of the director of the opera, Reinhard Keiser, who engaged him first as a violinist and then as a harpsichordist. There also Handel made the acquaintance of Mattheson, an influential musician who became his friend and biographer ultimately, but with whom he maintained rather stormy relations in the beginning. The two of them journeyed together to Lübeck to audition for the position of organist that was being relinquished by Buxtehude. They both qualified for the position on musical grounds, but neither one would have any part of one of the "fringe benefits" of the position—marriage to Buxtehude's daughter! Interestingly, the position was still open two years later and another young aspirant who could have had the job turned it down for the same reason; his name was Johann Sebastian Bach.

Handel almost was lost to posterity even before he had reached his full manhood. In 1704, when he was nineteen, he was playing harpsichord in a performance of Mattheson's *Cleopatra*. For reasons best known to him, the composer tried to replace Handel at the harpsichord. One thing led to another and the two of them engaged in a duel in back of the theater after the performance. Handel was saved, so the story goes, by a button on his waistcoat.

Handel's first opera, *Almira*, was produced at Hamburg in 1705 and later that year another opera, *Nero*, was given. The following year Handel completed two more operas, *Florindo* and *Dafne*, and then with virtually no money at all he left Hamburg and journeyed to Italy. In Italy he enjoyed a certain amount of success as a composer of Italian operas. He lived for a time in Florence, then Rome, then Naples. In addition to operas during that period he also produced a serenata titled *Aci, Galatea e Polifemo* that contains a bass aria with a compass of two octaves and a sixth. The year 1709 found him in Rome again, and then at the end of the year he journeyed to Venice where his opera *Agrippina* was being readied for performance. It was in Venice that Handel met Prince Ernst August, younger brother of the Elector of Hanover, and also the Duke of Manchester, who was the English ambassador to the Venetian court. Offers came to Handel to settle in Hanover and London and he accepted the offer of the Elector Georg of Hanover; first, however, he stipulated that he should be free to visit England on leave.

It was in January of 1710 that Handel took up his position as Kapellmeister to the court of Hanover and after only a few weeks there he took his leave and went to London. In two weeks' time he composed the opera *Rinaldo* and it was produced very successfully at the Haymarket Theatre. Handel remained in England for six months and then he returned to Hanover. The success he had tasted in London proved a powerful magnet, however, and in little more than a year's time he once again asked for and was granted a leave from Hanover to visit London a second time. A few weeks after he arrived, he produced another new opera, *Il Pastor Fido*. For the celebrations of the Peace of Utrecht he composed the Utrecht Te Deum. Queen Anne, for whom he had composed a birthday ode in February 1713, now settled a yearly pension of two hundred pounds on Handel. So fulfilling was Handel's life in London that he over-stayed his leave from Hanover and as more time passed, he became increasingly reluctant to consider a return to his position there. This rather irresponsible behavior irritated Handel's Hanover employer considerably but the composer serenely ignored the situation. It suddenly came to an unexpected and potentially dangerous situation for Handel: Queen Anne died in 1714 and she was succeeded to the British throne by none other than Handel's spurned employer, the Elector of Hanover, who became King George I of England. At first the strained relations between Handel and the new king caused the composer serious problems: he was pointedly ignored and thus deprived of his social recognition and principal opportunities for earning an income. The continued ostracism of Handel, however, was intolerable to the monarch also, who had an intense love of music and recognized in Handel a true genius. Whether or not the reconciliation between the two was brought about by the *Water Music* of 1717, or whether they had patched up their relationship some time earlier (as some scholars seem to have proven pretty well), is really beside the point. The important thing is that Handel returned to royal favor after a comparatively brief period of diffi-culty and he remained in England for the rest of his life.

In 1718 Handel became chapel master to the Duke of Chandos. To this period belong the Chandos Anthems (1719), the pastorale *Acis and Galatea* (1720), and the first form of the oratorio *Esther* (1720), which came into being originally as *Haman and Mordecai, A Masque*. Handel also taught the daughters of the Prince of Wales during this period and for Princess Anne he composed *Suites de Pièces* for harpsichord, among which is to be found "The Harmoni-ous Blacksmith."

In 1719 a new opera venture was begun in London with the support of the king. Called the Royal Academy of Music, its three directors were Giovanni Maria Bononcini, Attilio Ariosti and Handel. The first season was a brilliant success, both artistically and financially, but soon jealousies and feuds developed between the three directors, especially after one of Handel's operas, *Radamisto*, enjoyed a spectacular success. Thus embarked on an opera-producing career in London, however, Handel continued to compose in the medium for the next twenty-one years, producing one opera after another in breathless succession.

In 1726 Handel took out naturalization papers as a British subject. In June of the following year George I died, and for the coronation of George II Handel composed four Coronation Anthems, of which the most prominent is *Zadok the Priest*. Between 1729 and 1731 he was in partnership in a new opera-producing venture at the King's Theatre, but by this time public taste had begun to turn from Italian opera to more contemporary and idiomatic subjects—a trend hastened by the instant success of the Pepusch-Gay *The Beggar's Opera* in January 1728. For the King's Theatre venture Handel composed *Lotario* and four more operas, but none of them enjoyed the popular favor of some of his earlier efforts.

In March 1733 his oratorio *Deborah* was given for the first time. For most of the remainder of the decade he was still involved in opera production and management, but with constantly growing frustrations and irritations. Overexertion brought on a stroke and paralysis in one of his hands, and he left London in 1737 to seek relaxation and recuperation at Aix-la-Chapelle. He returned in 1738 much improved and with renewed determination to continue composing operas. Another steady stream of operas flowed from his pen, including *Faramondo*, *Serse* and *Deidamia*, but it became increasingly apparent to him that he was swimming against the tide. In 1739 he abandoned the stage and composed two oratorios, *Saul* and *Israel in Egypt*. In 1740 came *L'Allegro, il Penseroso e il Moderato*, a resetting by Charles Jennens of Milton's poem. In the following year Handel journeyed to Dublin and it was there, in April 1742, that the oratorio *Messiah* (with a text arranged by the same Jennens) was given for the first time. Not only did *Messiah* restore Handel to public favor, but it also raised him from bankruptcy. *Messiah* was followed in 1743 by *Samson*, the Dettingen Te Deum, *Semele* and *Joseph*, and in 1744 by *Belshazzar* and *Hercules*. Still there were intrigues aimed against him and in 1745 he was again bankrupt. For a year and a half he composed virtually nothing, and then there was another flaming of inspiration: *Judas Maccabaeus* appeared in 1746, followed by *Joshua* (1747), *Solomon* (1748), *Susannah* (1748), *Theodora* (1749), *The Choice of Hercules* (1750) and *Jephthah* (1752). During the composition of *Jephthah*, his last oratorio, he underwent three operations for eye cataracts. They were unsuccessful and he was nearly blind for the rest of his life; yet he continued to play organ concertos and to accompany his oratorios on the organ until 1759. On April 6 of that year he presided at the organ at a Covent Garden performance of *Messiah*. Eight days later he died in his house in Grosvenor Square. He was buried in Westminster Abbey with the full pomp and circumstance of a royal funeral ceremony.

For years the enormous popularity of *Messiah* tended to blot out the other major accomplishments of Handel as a composer. In recent years, however, Handel has been rediscovered as a composer of operas. Much of the impetus for this rediscovery began at the University of Göttingen, where German adaptations of such works as *Rodelinda, Ottone, Giulio Cesare* and so forth were staged in annual festivals during the 1920s. During the 1960s the movement gained momentum through the efforts of the New York-based Handel Society, which recorded and presented concert performances of several Handel operas, including *Rodelinda* and *Serse*, and through the brilliantly staged version of *Julius Caesar* presented by the New York City Opera Company (and also recorded).

MESSIAH

By 1741, Handel was firmly convinced that his future lay in the composition of oratorios rather than operas, and in that year he produced *Messiah*.

On Tuesday last Mr. Handel's Sacred Grand Oratorio, *Messiah*, was performed in the new Musick Hall in Fishamble Street; the best judges allowed it to be the most finished piece of Musick. Words are wanting to express the exquisite Delight it afforded to the admiring crowded Audience. The Sublime, the Grand and the Tender adapted to the most elevated, majestick, and moving Words, conspired to transport and charm the ravished Heart and Ear.

With these words, the first performance of *Messiah*, on April 13, 1742, in Dublin, was described in the pages of the monthly *Faulkner's Journal*. The score of *Messiah* had been composed the previous year between August 22 and September 14, a period of twenty-four days during which Handel shut himself up in his house and produced this masterpiece in a burst of inspiration. The first performance in London took place in 1743, and, after an initial coolness, the English too recognized *Messiah* as a work of unique distinction. From 1750 until his death in 1759, Handel conducted it yearly as a benefit for the Foundling Hospital in London.

Handel never hesitated to modify the *Messiah* score to suit the needs of the moment. Thus many of the best-known solo arias exist in several different versions, each of them apparently sanctioned by the composer himself. The distinguished Danish scholar and Handel authority Jens Peter Larsen reflects the musicologists' dismay at this state of affairs: "We must conclude that it will scarcely ever be possible to determine an absolutely standard form of *Messiah* as the one authentic version." But he goes on to point out that "in the case of nearly every number we can say which form is to be preferred for inclusion in a performance aiming at as close a reproduction as possible of Handel's own practice."

The "action" of *Messiah* deals with the Prophecy, Advent, Nativity, Mission, Sacrifice and Atonement, Ascension, Gospel Tidings and Resurrection of Jesus Christ. It is in three parts, with more than fifty individual numbers. Following a broad and typically French-style overture (slow-fast-slow), the first two solo vocal numbers are the tenor recitative and aria "Comfort ye" and "Ev'ry valley." The texts are from Isaiah XL, in which the prophet offers solace to a grief-stricken Jerusalem and then gives promise of the new life to come. This is followed by the first of the work's great choruses, "And the glory of the Lord," which continues the promise of the preceding aria. The following bass recitative, "Thus saith the Lord," and the aria "But who may abide" are imposing and fearful sections, with typical Baroque runs, shakes and other embellishments. The following chorus, "And He shall purify," is from the Book of Malachi, and it is followed by the recitative and aria with chorus "Behold a Virgin shall conceive" and "O thou that tellest," with texts from Isaiah and Matthew. These two sections have a gentle, almost dance-like cast to them. In the following bass recitative and aria, "For behold" and "The people that walked in darkness," the mood of solemn prophecy returns, to be dispelled with the light and hope of the promise of Salvation. The chorus, "For unto us a Child is born" is one of the most famous and dramatic of all the sections in *Messiah*; at the words "Wonderful, Counsellor, The Mighty God" a great shout goes up from the assembled voices, anticipating the arrival of the Messiah.

The next section is the familiar Pastoral Symphony, which sets the mood for Christmas Eve, a mood of peace and serenity. This is followed by a series of recitatives set to words from St. Luke's Gospel, with very imaginative and pictorial effects in the accompaniments. The great chorus "Glory to God" which follows is also set to a text from Luke and is one of the finest examples of Handel's eloquent harmonic and contrapuntal invention. There follows the highly florid aria "Rejoice greatly" and then the seraphic mood of the Pastoral Symphony returns in the recitative and aria "Then shall the eyes of the blind be opened" and "He shall feed His Flock." Part I of *Messiah* concludes with the chorus "His yoke is easy and His burden is light," set to words from Matthew.

The Second Part begins with the chorus "Behold the Lamb of God," set to a text from John, and this introduces the Passion. It is followed by the aria "He was despised," recalling the prophecy of Isaiah in mournful and somber tones, and then come three choruses, all to texts from Isaiah: "Surely He hath borne our griefs," "And with His stripes we are healed" and "All we like sheep have gone astray." The following tenor recitative, "All they that see Him," suggests in its accompaniment the mocking of the multitude, and then comes the chorus "He trusted in God," from Psalm 22. Two recitatives and arias for tenor follow, to texts from Psalms 69 and 16 and the Books of Lamentations and Isaiah. Then a choral setting for five parts (the only five-part writing in *Messiah*), "Lift up your heads," from Psalm 24, sounds the optimistic note once again. Three brief sections follow, the recitative "Unto which of the angels," the chorus "Let all the angels" and the aria "Thou art gone up on high." The next seven pieces, beginning with the chorus "The Lord gave the word," have about them the fierce zeal and protestation of the prophets of the Old Testament, with the exception of the pastoral quality of the aria "How beautiful are the feet." This is followed by the chorus "Their sound is gone out," and then the stormy bass aria "Why do the nations so furiously rage together." Next is another great chorus, "Let us break their bonds," followed by the tenor reci- tative and aria "He that dwelleth in heaven" and "Thou shalt break them with a rod of iron," which calls down savage justice and retri- bution. The second part of *Messiah* concludes with the familiar Hallelujah Chorus. Handel himself wrote that the whole host of Heaven stood before him when he wrote this chorus. And the mighty affirmation of the music caused George I to rise to his feet at an early performance of the oratorio, giving rise to the custom— observed ever since—of the entire audience rising to its feet for the performance of the Hallelujah.

Part Three opens with the exalted aria "I know that my Redeemer liveth," followed by the chorus "Since by man came death" and the bass recitative "Behold, I tell you a mystery." Another great florid aria follows—the bass aria "The trumpet shall sound," replete with trumpet embellishments high up in the stratosphere of the instru- ment's register. Four more sections of healthy affirmation follow, with texts from the Books of Corinthians and Romans: the recitative "Then shall be brought to pass," the duet "O death, where is thy sting?" the chorus "But thanks be to God," and the aria "If God be for us." Two great choruses, "Worthy is the Lamb" and "Amen," bring the work to a majestic conclusion. The "Amen," with its mag- nificent fugal treatment, is one of the glories of the entire work.

There was a time in the not-too-distant past when the standard *Messiah* performance enlisted as many participants as could be crowded onto a concert platform. Recent scholarship, however, has resulted in performances much closer in concept and numbers to those given in Handel's own time. Both these extremes, and various performing attitudes in between them, are represented in the several complete recordings of *Messiah* currently available. I have no hesitation in pointing to two among them as representing the finest of contemporary Baroque performance ideals—the recordings by Colin Davis and the London Symphony Orchestra (Philips C71AX 300) and Charles Mackerras and the English Chamber Orchestra (Angel S 3705). Both conductors have taken meticulous pains to ensure that their performances will not only be stylistically correct, but that they will also constitute vibrant re-creations of the drama and majesty inherent in the music. Both employ relatively small forces and both require their solo singers to embellish their arias in proper Baroque style. If I prefer the Mackerras recording, it is because this underrated American-born conductor seems to have a livelier imagination than his very worthy English colleague. Both performances are splendidly recorded and annotated and both amount to major restorations of Handel's intentions. Neither one, unfortunately, has yet had a tape release, though chances are that Mackerras' soon will. Tape addicts are advised to wait for it. Another valuable recording is the one conducted by Johannes Somary (Vanguard C 10090/1/2).

There remains one other recording of the score, now no longer available, that I should like to mention—the one made by Sir Thomas Beecham in the late 1950s for RCA's special Soria series (RCA LDS 6409). This was Beecham's third *Messiah* recording over a period of about a quarter of a century, and probably the most controversial recording he ever made. Employing a new orchestration made for the occasion by Sir Eugene Goossens at Beecham's request, this version of *Messiah* introduces such non-Handelian instruments as clarinet, triangle and cymbals, and in general clothes the score in the garments of late Romanticism. But if you can forget any preconceived ideas you may have about the way the music should sound—and in particular, thoroughly disassociate this version from either of the three mentioned above—this recording can be a lot of fun, particularly since the snap and *élan* typical of Beecham at his best are present in abundance.

Unfortunately, no cassette version of *any* performance exists. Of those available to the reel-to-reel collector, I'd say it is a toss-up between the more intimate Shaw-conducted performance (RCA TR3 8005, 3¾ ips) and the stylistically uneven Boult-conducted one (London R 80077).

WATER MUSIC

Under the date August 23, 1662, Samuel Pepys wrote the following in his diary, the most quoted of its kind in the English language:

> To the top of the new Banqueting House over the Thames, which was a most pleasant place as any I could have got; and all the show consisted chiefly in the number of boats and barges; and two pageants, one of a King, and another of a Queen. . . . Anon come the King and Queen in a barge under a canopy, with 1000 barges and boats I know, for we could see no water for them, nor discern the King nor Queen. And so they landed at White Hall Bridge, and the great guns on the other side went off.

Pepy's description of this grand pleasure fleet is evidence that the Thames played diverse roles in English life of the seventeenth and eighteenth centuries, for in addition to being one of London's main commercial highways, it was one of British royalty's favorite spots for a social gathering. It is in the latter role that it figures in the legend, now viewed as of doubtful authenticity, that has long surrounded the creation of that series of short instrumental pieces by George Frideric Handel known as the *Water Music*. True or apocryphal, the legend is now so much a part of our musical lore that it warrants retelling.

In 1712 Handel obtained leave to visit England from his employer, the Elector of Hanover, whom he was serving as Kapellmeister. So flattered was Handel by his treatment by Britain's Queen Anne that he overstayed his leave. Further complicating his situation was the fact there was little love lost between Queen Anne and Georg Ludwig, the Elector of Hanover. It was during this period that Handel composed his Ode for the Birthday of Queen

Anne, and his Te Deum and Jubilate for the Peace of Utrecht of 1713.

Queen Anne died in 1714, and because of the complicated intertwining of royal European blood lines, her successor on the British throne turned out to be Georg Ludwig, who was crowned as King George I of England. Notwithstanding Handel's honor and fame in England, the composer suddenly found himself in precarious circumstances. At first he was snubbed by his late employer, but his friends were ready to do whatever they tactfully could to bring about a reconciliation of the two. One such friend, we are told by Mainwaring, Handel's first biographer—he wrote in 1760, one year after Handel's death—was the Baron Kielmansegge, Royal Master of the King's Horse, According to Mainwaring, Kielmansegge took advantage of the opportunity offered by a Thames water-party for the king and his retinue in August of 1715, and without the king's knowledge arranged for Handel to compose and conduct the music for the occasion. This music was performed by instrumentalists gathered on a barge within the hearing but out of sight of the king. So pleased was George with the music that drifted to him across the water that he asked the name of the composer. When he was told, the king immediately summoned Handel from the nearby barge, and the reconciliation was effected on the spot.

The now more generally accepted account of the creation of the *Water Music* assigns it to the year 1717. The *Daily Courant* of July 17, 1717, carried a report of a royal barge party on the Thames. It read in part:

Many other barges with persons of quality attended, and so great a number of boats that the whole river in a manner was covered. A City Company's barge was employed for the music, wherein were fifty instruments of all sorts, who played . . . the finest symphonies, composed express for this occasion by Mr. Handel, which his majesty liked so well that he caused it to be played over three times in going and returning.

Herbert Weinstock, in his modern biography of Handel, attempts to resolve the conflict between the two stories by speculating that Handel may have composed a first suite in 1715, and then wrote fresh music two years later on the strength of his first success.

In 1785, Samuel Arnold began the first complete and authoritative edition of the works of Handel, and a suite of twenty movements was published bearing the title *Water Music*. Since Handel's original autograph and parts had been lost, Arnold had to make educated guesses about many aspects of the music, including its proper instrumentation, the correct order of the movements and so forth. So wisely did Arnold do his work that his edition has served as the model for modern realizations of the full score.

In format and layout, the twenty pieces of the complete *Water Music* comprise an enormous suite of dance tunes, airs and other movements, introduced by an overture. The prevailing texture of the sound is bright and clear, as befits music composed for outdoor performance. And since there still is conflicting scholarly opinion concerning the exact sequence of movements—indeed, it is questionable whether Handel really intended any specified order or not—we shall not here go into a movement-by-movement description of the score. Let it merely be said that for sheer entertainment and joy, the music that Handel composed for the king's pleasure on that hot summer evening has few rivals in the whole literature. During the 1920s, '30s and '40s the Suite of six movements from the complete *Water Music* that was selected and arranged by the distinguished Irish composer and conductor Sir Hamilton Harty was the only way one ever got to hear anything from Handel's score. Whatever quarrels one may have with Harty's arrangement of the music for a typical orchestra of post-Wagnerian proportions, it is nevertheless true that Harty's Suite undoubtedly laid the foundation for the present-day popularity of the entire score. Of the several available recordings of the Harty Suite, the performances conducted by Steinberg (Pickwick S 4003) and Szell (London CS 6236) seem to me to be the most successful; both are well played and recorded and both conductors make a joyous, exhilarating experience of it all. Leopold Stokowski has recorded a Suite of his own devising (RCA LSC 2612) that is overinflated and overinflected, and yet in its own way it is a uniquely satisfying experience.

Several excellent recordings of the complete score exist, among which the most immediately winning, in my opinion, are those by Thurston Dart and the Philomusica Orchestra of London (L'Oiseau Lyre (60010), Rafael Kubelik and the Berlin Philharmonic Orchestra (Deutsche Grammophon 138799), Yehudi Menuhin and the Bath Festival Orchestra (Angel S 36173) and Hermann Scherchen and the Vienna State Opera Orchestra (Westminster WST 8114). Scherchen and Kubelik use the Arnold edition of the score; Dart and Menuhin employ modern editions prepared, respectively, by Brian Priestman and N. D. Boyling, eminent Handel scholars both.

Though the Kubelik performance does not quite have the measure of inspired imagination the other three do, it is nevertheless a highly worthy account of the music. Of the other three, Menuhin's is perhaps the best combination of superb playing, excellent reproduction and stylistic rightness. But Dart's version has many distinctions, too, not the least of which is the improvised ornamentation. Scherchen's account has moments of inimitable joy and spontaneity.

Menuhin's performance is now also available on cassette (Angel 4XS 36173), and continues to impress me as a highly imaginative treatment of the complete score. Only Kubelik's slightly less imaginative account (DGG C 8799) is available to tape collectors. Of the recordings of the Suite arranged by Sir Hamilton Harty, Szell's account, which is the most vigorous, is available on tape (London L 80089) and cassette (London M 10089).

Franz Josef Haydn

Born: Rohrau, Lower Austria, March 31, 1732
Died: Vienna, May 31, 1809

Haydn's parents were poor peasant folk—his father was a wheelwright who also doubled as sexton and organist of the local village church, and his mother, who sang in the choir, had served as cook to Count Harrach. At the age of five Haydn was taken to the home of a cousin, Johann Mathias Franck, who taught him Latin, singing, and the violin and other instruments. At eight Haydn went to Vienna and there continued his studies, gravitating to composition very early in his life. By the time he was twenty he had composed six trios, sonatas, a mass and a comic opera titled *Der neue krumme Teufel.*

During his twenties the name and fame of Haydn traveled widely: he was a respected performer and teacher and there was a growing interest in his own music. In 1759 he was appointed conductor and court composer to the Count Ferdinand Maximilian Morzin, who employed a chamber orchestra that numbered some twelve to sixteen players. For these musicians Haydn composed a whole series of instrumental works, including a divertimento in six parts for strings and winds, and his first symphonies. His position in the Count's employ seemed to him sufficiently secure that he began to consider marriage. He fell in love with the younger daughter of a village wigmaker named Keller; the young lady in question, however, entered a convent and thus became permanently unavailable. Anxious to keep the budding musician in the family, Keller persuaded Haydn to marry instead his older daughter, Maria Anna. It was the biggest mistake of Haydn's lifetime. The marriage was a disaster from which the composer suffered for forty years—until Maria Anna died (she was three years Haydn's senior) in

March 1800. The miserable home life undoubtedly accounted for Haydn's wanderlust and his many romantic intrigues over the years.

Soon after the marriage the Count Morzin was compelled to dismiss his orchestra and its conductor, but Haydn was not long without work. He was quickly engaged as second Kapellmeister by Prince Anton Esterházy for the family country seat at Eisenstadt. Thus began, on May 1, 1761, Haydn's employment by the Esterházy family, in whose service he was distined to remain for the rest of his life. Prince Anton was succeeded in 1762 by his brother, Prince Nikolaus, and in the service of Nikolaus during the next three decades Haydn produced scores of symphonies, forty quartets, a concerto for French horn, many operas, and many other assorted works for various performing forces. In 1790 Prince Nikolaus was succeeded by his son Anton, who increased Haydn's annual stipend by nearly 50 per cent and who was proud to have Haydn as his principal musician.

In 1791 Haydn accepted an invitation from the London impresario Salomon to visit the British capital. The visit lasted eighteen months, during all of which time Haydn was the lion of the social season. He was given a Doctor of Music degree by Oxford and everywhere he was feted and celebrated. In the midst of all the partying he nevertheless found time to compose six symphonies during this visit—his Symphonies 93 through 98. On his return to Vienna he visited his native Rohrau to witness the unveiling of a monument erected in his honor by Count Harrach.

Back from London toward the end of 1792, Haydn welcomed a new pupil in Vienna, a young man in his early twenties whom he had met in Bonn a few months earlier: his name was Ludwig van Beethoven. Beethoven took lessons in theory and composition from Haydn from December 1792 until January 1794, when the older man left on a second visit to London at Salomon's invitation. The second stay in London was no less triumphant than the first one. Again Haydn composed six symphonies for Salomon (the Symphonies 99 through 104) and no less than the King of England invited Haydn to remain permanently in England. He declined the honor, however, maintaining his duty to respect his commitment to Prince Esterházy. Haydn left London a second time on August

15, 1795, and returned to Vienna—he now spent only a brief period each year at Esterháza. The two stays in the British capital had proven to be unusually stimulating for Haydn and he treasured the memories in all his remaining years; his diaries listing the works he composed during his London stays are voluminous and the works themselves cover more than seven hundred pages of music paper.

His two stays in England afforded Haydn an opportunity to hear and to learn at first hand the many oratorios of Handel. He was also mightily impressed by the loyalty to the British crown expressed in the anthem "God Save the King." Both experiences were to find their echoes in Haydn's output during the ensuing years. During January 1797 Haydn composed the music to the song "*Gott erhalte Franz den Kaiser*" ("God Save the Emperor Franz") and on the Kaiser's birthday, February 12, the song was sung simultaneously at the National Theater in Vienna and at all the principal theaters in the provinces. It became the National Anthem of Austria and it was Haydn's favorite among all his songs: variations on the theme form the musical basis for the slow movement of his "Emperor" Quartet, Opus 76, Number 3. During the remainder of 1797 Haydn worked on the composition of an oratorio with a text by Baron van Swieten based on sections from Milton's *Paradise Lost*. The mood of the composer at the time is best suggested by his own words: "Never was I so pious as when composing *The Creation*. I knelt down every day and prayed God to strengthen me for my work." *The Creation* produced an overwhelming impression right from the start and it is probably safe to say that in the oratorio literature its popularity is rivaled only by Handel's *Messiah*. Soon after *The Creation* was finished, van Swieten suggested to Haydn that they immediately collaborate on a second oratorio, suggesting as subject matter the seasons. Haydn protested that his strength and health were failing, but he was intrigued by certain passages and possibilities in van Swieten's text and soon *The Seasons* was completed. The effort had exhausted the composer, however, and he often remarked afterward, "*The Seasons* gave me the finishing stroke."

Haydn composed very little after 1801 and the exertion of *The Seasons*: some devotional vocal quartets; settings of Scottish, Welsh and Irish songs commissioned by George Thomson of Edinburgh;

and some string quartets. In his final years he made only one public appearance—at a performance of *The Creation* at the University of Vienna in March 1808. At the words "And there was light" Haydn's agitation became so great that he pointed upward and exclaimed "It came from thence." He was quite unable to sit through the entire performance and had to be taken home after the first half. As he was carried out, people thronged around him to bid him farewell, and Beethoven, who was in the audience, knelt and kissed his hand and forehead. At the door Haydn paused, turned around, and lifted his hands in blessing.

The occupation of Vienna by French troops in 1804 and again in 1809 was a severe shock to Haydn's national loyalties. The 1809 occupation was preceded by bombardment and some shells fell not far from Haydn's home. Undoubtedly the trauma hastened Haydn's death, even though the French occupation troops showed him great kindness and consideration. Indeed, one of the last visitors he received on his deathbed was a French soldier who moved him deeply by singing an aria from *The Creation*. On May 26, 1809, he called his servants together for the last time and asked to be brought to the piano; there he played the "Emperor's Hymn" three times. Five days later, at one o'clock in the morning on May 31, Haydn died.

Haydn's funeral was a solemn national event and he was buried in a churchyard outside the city. Eleven years later his remains were exhumed and reburied at Eisenstadt—but it was discovered that the skull had been stolen. It subsequently came into the possession of the Gesellschaft der Musikfreunde in Vienna and there remained for many years. Not until June 6, 1954, did the Society surrender Haydn's skull for burial with his other remains at Eisenstadt.

SYMPHONY NO. 94 IN G MAJOR, "SURPRISE"

In the twelve symphonies he composed for his two visits to London in the 1790s, Franz Josef Haydn crystallized his symphonic thought and development and presented to the world a dozen scores of boundless richness and invention. To the G Major Symphony of the first "London" series the nickname "Surprise" has come to be attached; with equal justification the title might have been applied to nearly any one of the other symphonies in the group—to the D Major, No. 93, for example, with its hilarious low C belch from the bassoon near the end of the slow movement; or to the No. 97, in C Major, with its unexpected full-bodied string pizzicatos in the last movement. As it is, however, the surprise in Haydn's "Surprise" Symphony refers to the sudden loud chord that intrudes in the sixteenth bar of the slow movement, following the pianissimo restatement of the main theme. Haydn himself is purported to have said that the loud chord "will make the women jump," and in those days of marathon concert lengths, it probably was not at all uncommon for some ladies in the audience to be lulled to sleep by the entertainment!

The London impresario Salomon, who brought Haydn to England for his two visits, placed at the composer's disposal an orchestra of strings and two each of flutes, oboes, bassoons, horns, trumpets and tympani. This was the orchestra for which Haydn composed the six symphonies of his first "London" series, Nos. 93 through 98. Clarinets were added to the orchestra for Haydn's second visit to the English capital, in 1794, and we find these instruments appearing in the second set of "London" symphonies.

The symphony begins with a slow introduction, *Adagio cantabile*, just sixteen measures long. The main body of the first movement is marked *Vivace assai* and is ushered in by a perky theme in the violins. The movement is full of sprightly melodic invention and is a delight from beginning to end. The slow movement, *Andante*, is made up of four variations on a shapely little tune that bears a striking resemblance to the old French air "Ah, *vous dirais-je, maman*" (or "Twinkle, Twinkle, Little Star" in this country). It is in the sixteenth bar of this movement that Haydn springs his little joke: the fortissimo chord is loudly asserted by the strings, winds, horns, trumpets and tympani. Haydn later used the basic theme of the movement in his oratorio *The Seasons*, as the accompaniment to an aria describing the plowman tilling his field and gaily whistling. The third movement is a Menuetto but in the robust style of an Austrian peasant dance rather than the refined court dance. The first theme is stated by the flutes, bassoons and first violins. The main theme of the contrasting Trio section is given to the bassoons and first violins in unison. The last movement, *Allegro di molto,* is a rollicking rondo with two main themes.

Thanks largely to the efforts of H. C. Robbins Landon and other Haydn scholars in recent years, many of the original Haydn manuscripts of the symphonies have been uncovered. They reveal that the printed scores that have been staples of international concert life for many generations contain glaring textual inaccuracies, particularly in the trumpet and drum parts. In the late 1950s Vanguard recorded the final six of the "London" symphonies in the authentic Robbins Landon texts (Mogens Wöldike conducting the Vienna State Opera Orchestra), and it is probably safe to conjecture that Denis Vaughan will record all twelve of the "London" symphonies in the newly authenticated texts with the Orchestra of Naples. By and large, however, our "star" conductors—whether through indolence or ignorance—have continued to perform the Haydn symphonies from texts that are known to be corrupt. Thus, though the "Surprise" Symphony has been recorded in recent years by such distinguished conductors as Beecham, Dorati, Giulini, Krips, Monteux and Steinberg, not a single one of them has bothered to use the corrected text. Hence, nearly every available recording of the "Surprise" Symphony utilizes a tympani part that has errors in the first movement and a wrong note in the flute, bassoon and first violin parts in the seventh measure of the Minuet.

At one time Beecham-conducted performances of the twelve "London" symphonies by Haydn were available on both disc and reel-to-reel tape from Angel. Now those performances have been withdrawn (though Everest has announced its intention of releasing the disc version). In the absence of the Beecham performance of the "Surprise" Symphony, the Szell performance, lithe, sprightly and inventive (Columbia MS 7006), stands out.

Another fine recording of the symphony is Giulini's with the Philharmonia Orchestra of London (Angel S 35712). It is a bright, good-sounding recording with some especially fine orchestral playing. On the overside is an overture and a symphony by Boccherini, both well served also.

Amazingly, *no* reel-to-reel tape version is currently available, and

only the rather strait-laced Karl Richter-conducted performance
(DGG 923033) exists in a cassette version.

SYMPHONY NO. 101 IN D MAJOR, "CLOCK"

What we of the mid-twentieth century are accustomed to thinking
of as the musical *dernier cri*, music produced by electronic tone
generators, is really only the latest link in a chain that goes back
hundreds of years. Composers have always experimented with extra-
musical sounds and noises in their works. A generation ago the *Ballet
mécanique* of George Antheil introduced the sound of airplane pro-
pellers into the texture of its instrumentation; a generation before
that, the scoring of Richard Strauss' symphonic poem *Don Quixote*
incorporated the sound of a wind machine. Toward the end of the
eighteenth century Benjamin Franklin's invention of the glass har-
monica stimulated the imagination of Mozart, and at the turn of that
century the automatic music-makers of Johann Maelzel captured
the fancy of Beethoven. It was for Maelzel's panharmonicon that
Beethoven originally scored his Battle Symphony, and the third-
movement *Allegretto scherzando* of this composer's Eighth Symphony was once thought to owe its inspiration to another of Maelzel's automatic contrivances, the metronome.

In 1794, during the second of his two extended sojourns in London under the sponsorship of the impresario Johann Peter Salomon,
Franz Josef Haydn produced a symphony, No. 101 in D Major,
that borrowed for the principal theme of its Minuet a tune that
Haydn had contrived the year before for another such exotic device,
the musical clock. In his book on Haydn, Karl Geiringer writes that
the composer's interest in musical clocks came from his friendship
with Pater Primitivus Niemecz, the librarian to Prince Esterházy at
Eisenstadt and a cellist in the orchestra Haydn conducted there.
Geiringer writes:

Niemecz built three clocks equipped with tiny mechanical organs,
the first in 1772, the other two in 1792 and 1793. In these he used
only music composed by his friend and teacher, Joseph Haydn. . . .

The clock of 1792 was built for Prince Liechtenstein. This tiny instrument with its sweet, weak tone plays twelve pieces, one every hour. Twelve numbers also form the repertory of the clock of 1793 which Haydn gave to Prince Esterházy before leaving on his second trip to England.

The Minuet of the D Major Symphony is not the only one of Haydn's major works to draw upon his compositions for musical clocks. In the compilation of such pieces made by Ernst Fritz Schmid, the fifth bears a relationship to the Trio of the Minuet from the Symphony No. 85; number twenty-eight is a simplified version of the Finale of the String Quartet, Opus 71, Number 1; number thirty is an arrangement of the *Perpetuum mobile* from the Quartet, Opus 64, Number 5; and number thirty-two is a sketch for the Finale of the Symphony No. 99 in E-flat Major. Quite obviously, the influence of the mechanical clocks of Niemecz was a pervading one in Haydn's music at the time.

But the fact that the Symphony No. 101 in D Major has come to be known as the "Clock" Symphony is not, oddly enough, because it incorporates one of Haydn's musical-clock compositions. Rather, the nickname comes from the "tick-tocking" accompaniment in the staccato strings and bassoon that pulsates under the main melodic line of the slow movement.

The first movement begins with a slow introduction of twenty-three measures marked *Adagio*. The main section is a *Presto* with a vivacious first theme that is rattled off in a staccato ascending scale by the first violins. The second theme is also first stated by the first violins, and the development section of the movement has great contrapuntal workings. The slow movement, *Andante*, is for the most part a series of elaborations upon the simple melody heard at the very outset. It is stated by the first violins, with the tick-tock accompaniment of second violins and basses pizzicato, and bassoons staccato. The Minuet presents a jolly first theme stated by the whole orchestra, forte, with a gentle answering theme by the strings and flute. In the Trio, Haydn introduces a drone bass by having the strings maintain a D-major chord through the first ten bars of the section. The Minuet is repeated and the movement comes to a happy end. The last movement, *Vivace*, begins with a chorale-like theme for the strings, which later serves Haydn as the subject for an animated fugue, first for strings alone and then for the entire orchestra.

Along with Haydn's "Surprise" Symphony, the "Clock" is the most-recorded of all his symphonies, though the list of currently available performances has shrunk, unaccountably, to only five. Of them, Wöldike's is my preferred choice (Vanguard S 187) because of its solid stylistic virtues. Again, no reel-to-reel tape performance of the score exists and the only existing cassette performance is Richter's (DGG 923033—the other sequence on the cassette being the conductor's strait-laced account of Haydn's "Surprise" Symphony).

SYMPHONY NO. 104 IN D MAJOR, "LONDON"

During Haydn's first visit to London, the impresario Salomon kept him constantly busy with social engagements and musical responsibilities. Early in 1792, after Haydn had been in the British capital for about a year, he wrote:

In order to keep my word and support poor Salomon, I must be the victim, and work incessantly. I really feel it. My eyes suffer the most. My mind is very weary, and it is only the help of God that will supply what is wanting in my power. I daily pray to Him, for without his assistance I am but a poor creature.

But the six symphonies of the first "Salomon" set (Nos. 93 through 98) betray no sign of strain; on the contrary, they are among the most spontaneous and vital works in all of orchestral music.

Haydn left London at the end of June 1792, after spending about a year and a half there. Salomon assured him that a return visit would be welcome at any time, and in January 1794 Haydn bowed to the impresario's repeated requests and once more traveled to London. The first experience had taught him well, however; this time he arrived in London with some new symphonies already composed and ready for performance. The second visit lasted even longer than the first—until the end of August 1795.

On top of the enormous social and artistic successes he enjoyed in London, Haydn also took substantial sums of money with him each time he departed. It is estimated that he grossed approximately 24,000 gulden in London—the equivalent of about $12,000 in contemporary currency. And from Haydn's point of view there was still another benefit to be derived from his long sojourns in London: relief from his shrewish wife in Vienna. An indication of the lady's character is contained in a letter she sent him during his first London visit, in which she asked for money to buy a house in which to spend her "widowhood." When he returned to Vienna, Haydn duly inspected and purchased the house. As fate would have it, he lived in it himself as a widower, for he survived his wife by nine years.

Six of the twelve "Salomon" symphonies bear identifying nicknames, most of which have to do with their musical characteristics: the loud and unexpected chord in the slow movement of the Symphony No. 94, for example, earned the symphony the nickname "Surprise," and the martial qualities in the second and fourth movements of the Symphony No. 100 resulted in its being dubbed the "Military." The last of the twelve is known as the "London" Symphony, for no apparent reason. As a matter of fact, of all the symphonies this one has perhaps the least justification for being so called, for the principal theme of the last movement is an undisguised Austrian peasant dance, linked to a song—"Oh, Jelena"—that Haydn may have heard at Eisenstadt.

This last bit of information sparked a lively controversy some years ago. W. H. Hadow, in an interesting study titled *A Croatian Composer—Notes Toward the Study of Joseph Haydn*, stated that "variants of this melody are found in Croatia proper, Servia and Carniola." A countertheory was advanced in 1926 by Michel Brenet, who wrote:

During the time Haydn lived at Eisenstadt or Esterháza, when his music resounded day and night in the castle and gardens of his prince, why should not his own airs or scraps at least of his own melodies have stolen through the open windows and remained in the memories first of the people whose duty it was to interpret them, or who were obliged to hear them, and then of the scattered population of the surrounding country?

To this question Hadow replied:

> Which is more likely—that these [tunes] were orally transmitted like all early folk songs and that Haydn found them and used them, or that the peasants "heard them through the windows," memorized them at a single hearing, fitted them to secular words, and carried them through the taverns and merrymakings of their native villages? Three of the melodies, for example, appear in the Symphony No. 104 which was written for London after the Esterházy Kapelle had been disbanded. Where and how could the villagers have come across them?

Logic would certainly seem to reside with Hadow, but in any case —whether the themes in Haydn's last symphony are folk-derived or are truly original—the symphony is a masterpiece, full of the master's unique invention and sparkle.

The first movement of Haydn's last symphony has been described as follows by the Haydn expert, H. C. Robbins Landon:

> The opening *Adagio* is actually a three-section form in miniature, modulating from the opening D Minor to F Major and back to D Minor, where the "main subject" (if one can call it that) returns with terrific power, *fortissimo*, to be followed by a *pianissimo* deceptive answer. The theme of the *Allegro* seems a happy release from the doomed, fateful weight of the D Minor introduction. In this *Allegro*, the dramatic tension of the development is the result of tremendous concentration on one tiny motive drawn from the main subject. It is a studied piece of ever-increasing excitement, brilliantly orchestrated. With unswerving singleness of purpose, Haydn builds a climax of great intensity, after which the recapitulation is a wonderful, lyrical contrast.

Another Haydn scholar, Karl Geiringer, has speculated that the profoundly moving slow movement, *Andante*, of this last symphony of Haydn's may have been meant as a farewell to Mozart, whose premature passing Haydn mourned deeply. In any event, the entire movement is one of the most poignant in Haydn's entire output; its coda prompted Landon to write "it reaches a profundity of emotion seldom encountered even in late Haydn, first in the remotely peaceful woodwind passage . . . then in the ethereal flute solo which rises out of the nearly motionless *decrescendo* . . . and finally in the simple, moving blessing which the master gives the movement." The third movement is a rollicking and vigorous Minuet; a particularly Haydnesque touch is the last-beat accent and the general pause near the end, followed by a trill for woodwind and string instruments. The Trio is in the contrasting key of B flat. The Finale, marked *Allegro spiritoso*, is a carefree romp with two main subjects. Accompanying the main theme is a bagpipe-like drone created by a sustained pedal note on D held by the horns and cellos, thus giving the music the character of a rustic peasant dance.

Three recordings of the score seem most successfully to communicate the essence of the music: those by Beecham (Angel S 36256, now withdrawn), Klemperer (Angel S 36346) and Wöldike (Vanguard Everyman 166SD), the last a budget-priced recording. Beecham's performance is full of the pointed rhythms, vital phrasing and interpretive charm that characterized this conductor at his best. Klemperer's is more stolid, but quite effective on its own terms. Both are well played by the respective orchestras, but Klemperer has the benefit of airier, more sharply defined recorded sound.

And so to the performance recorded in Vienna in the late 1950s under the direction of the Danish conductor, Mogens Wöldike. Quite simply, I find this one of the finest of all Haydn symphony recordings. Utilizing a corrected score, Wöldike gives us a robust, invigorating account of the work that is positively bracing in effect. Especially clearly etched are the all-important tympani and trumpet parts, and the sound in general is as clearly focused as anything being recorded today.

At the present time, not only is there no available reel-to-reel tape edition of the symphony, but no cassette version as well.

Franz Liszt

Born: Raiding, near Oedenburg, Hungary, October 22, 1811
Died: Bayreuth, Germany, July 31, 1886

Son and pupil of a musical amateur, Franz Liszt made his first appearance in public as a pianist at the age of nine in his native town. A group of Hungarian counts subscribed an annual annuity to the young virtuoso and he and his family were thus enabled to move to Vienna. He studied with the greatest teachers of the day, including Czerny (piano) and Salieri (theory). On one occasion he was the pianist in a performance of Beethoven's "Archduke" Trio, played in the presence of the composer; when it was finished, Beethoven embraced him warmly.

At the age of twelve Liszt played a series of very successful concerts in Vienna, whereupon his father took him to Paris to repeat the triumph. But Cherubini, the director of the Paris Conservatory and the arbiter of Parisian musical life at the time, refused permission on the grounds that Paris was not interested in the exploits of "infant phenomena." Liszt and his family settled in Paris for some years, however, and he paid two visits to England in 1824 and 1825, astounding the British public with his ability as a pianist. His one-act operetta, *Don Sanche*, was produced at the Académie Royale in Paris in October 1825 and received a total of five performances. In 1827 the responsibility of supporting himself and his mother was suddenly thrust upon the sixteen-year-old youth with the death of his father. He undertook a heavy teaching schedule and soon was delighting audiences in the most elegant salons with his derring-do as a keyboard virtuoso. He quickly became the darling of the aristocracy and hobnobbed with the leading literary figures of the time, including Victor Hugo, Lamartine and George Sand. He also came into contact with Chopin and Berlioz, both of whom exerted a profound influence upon him.

It was not long before he had embarked upon a spectacular career as a ladies' man, beginning with the Countess d'Agoult ("Daniel Stern"), with whom he lived in Geneva for four years, from 1835 to 1839, and who bore him a son and three daughters. Cosima, the youngest, became the wife of the pianist and conductor Hans von Bülow, and later left von Bülow to settle down with Wagner and eventually marry him. During the period of Liszt's residence in Switzerland and Italy with the Countess d'Agoult, he composed his *Années de pèlerinage* pieces for solo piano.

In 1839 Liszt undertook a series of concerts to raise enough money for the completion of the Beethoven monument in Bonn, and from then until 1847 he crisscrossed the continent of Europe dozens of times as a traveling, dazzling virtuoso of the piano. In 1848 Liszt settled in Weimar and he remained there for thirteen years. His constant companion during this period was the Princess Carolyne von Sayn-Wittgenstein, and their house at Weimar was for many years a center of artistic influence. In 1849 Liszt accepted an appointment as conductor of the Court Theater at Weimar, with the distinct purpose of becoming the advocate and champion of the rising generation of composers. During Liszt's years in Weimar, the small provincial town became a true headquarters of musical activity. He produced operas by Wagner, Berlioz and Schumann and generally made himself available, both as teacher and adviser, to all young "revolutionaries" who cared to seek him out. He remained in Weimar until 1861, though he resigned from his official position at the Weimar Opera in 1858 because of a squabble over a production of the opera *The Barber of Bagdad* by Cornelius.

Between 1859 and 1870 Liszt lived chiefly in Rome, where he was made an abbé by Pope Pius IX in 1866. In 1871 he was made a Royal Hungarian Councilor by the government of Hungary in order to ensure that he would be in Budapest during part of each year. And in 1875 he became President of the new Academy of Music at Pesth. The next decade Liszt spent at Weimar, Pesth and Rome, followed by a large retinue of disciples and pupils whom he taught free of charge.

On July 3, 1886, Liszt's granddaughter Daniela von Bülow was married at Bayreuth. Liszt traveled to Bayreuth for the occasion and he returned again three weeks later for the performance of Wagner's *Parsifal* on July 23 (Wagner was by this time his son-in-law). He caught a bronchial cold, but was sufficiently recovered a day or two later to attend another performance in the Bayreuth Festspielhaus— a production of *Tristan und Isolde* that made his face glow with pride and vitality. His strength was rapidly ebbing away, however, and upon his return from the performance he went to bed immediately. His generally prostrate condition was more the result of the ravages of time than the direct consequence of his bronchitis. His death during the night of July 31, 1886, was quiet and painless.

If we are to believe the testimony of those who heard him play and studied with him, Liszt may well have been the greatest pianist who ever lived. As a composer, some of his works that are the most popular really do not deserve this distinction, while his more solid accomplishments are not granted the credit and honor due them. In a long and colorful lifetime Liszt captured the imagination of his contemporaries in a manner such as has been achieved by few musicians in history.

CONCERTO NO. 1 IN E-FLAT MAJOR FOR PIANO

The E-flat Major Piano Concerto occupied Franz Liszt for some considerable time during the 1840s before he finally committed it to paper in 1849. Two years later he revised it and in 1857 the score was published. The year of the first fruition of Liszt's thoughts concerning the score, 1849, was a crucial one for the composer. It marked his withdrawal from the life of a touring piano virtuoso and his acceptance of the post as permanent conductor at the Court Theater in Weimar.

Extroverted to the point of exhibitionism and frankly virtuosic, the E-flat Major Piano Concerto is a perfect mirror of the flame-throwing pianist around whom all the Liszt legends have been created. A contemporary admirer of Liszt's performing style has left us this fanciful account of his mastery:

He treats his mistress—his piano—now tenderly, now tyrannically, devours her with kisses, lacerates her with lustful bites, embraces her, caresses her, sulks with her, scolds her, rebukes her, grabs her by the hair, then clasps her all the more delicately, more affectionately, more passionately, more volatilely, more meltingly, exults with her to the heavens, soars with her through the skies and finally settles down with her in a vale of flowers covered by a canopy of stars.

Hans Christian Andersen wrote a less flamboyant but no less evocative description of Liszt the pianist after he attended a concert by the twenty-nine-year-old virtuoso in 1840.

An electric shock seemed to thrill the hall as Liszt entered. Most of the women rose. A sunbeam flashed across each face, as though every eye were seeing a beloved friend. . . . As he played . . . I saw the pale face assume a nobler, more beautiful expression . . . he grew handsome—handsome as vitality and inspiration can make one. . . . It did not sound like the strings of a piano. . . . The instrument appeared to be changed into a whole orchestra. . . . When Liszt had done playing, the flowers rained down on him.

From these and other written accounts of Liszt's public performances, there can be no doubt that his playing exerted a magnetic influence upon his audiences. And though both his piano concertos are uninhibited flights of virtuosic abandon, they also reveal the true innovative side of Liszt the creator. Formally they are closer to the symphonic poem than the standard concerto. Though they naturally subdivide into sections, both works are in a single continuous movement with the sections merging freely and lacking the customary development. While the piano commands the center of attention, the orchestral parts are of considerable importance also. Liszt assigns a good many solos to the instruments of the orchestra, of which the most famous is the triangle solo in the Scherzo section of the First Concerto. This bit of inventive instrumentation caused that demon critic of the nineteenth century, Eduard Hanslick, to dub the score, in derision, the "Triangle Concerto." In the words of Lawrence Gilman, former critic of the New York *Herald Tribune* and program annotator for the New York Philharmonic and Philadelphia Orchestras, the fact that good Papa Haydn had used a triangle (likewise cymbals and a bass drum) in his G Major Symphony [No. 100, the "Military"], and that Beethoven and Schumann also used the triangle symphonically seems not to have appealed to the implacable Hanslick as constituting sufficiently respectable precedents. So he drew aside the skirts of his unsullied dressing-gown and turned this erring concerto out into the snowy night.

The First Piano Concerto is in four major sections that correspond in their broad outlines to four symphonic movements. The first of them is the proclamative phrase given at the very beginning by the strings, with interjections from the winds and brasses (*Allegro maestoso, tempo giusto*). An elaborate cadenza for the solo piano follows, with runs up and down the keyboard. The second theme, *Quasi adagio*, is first announced by the muted cellos and basses. The solo piano then takes it over and muses on it in almost improvisatory fashion. The third theme is the Scherzo section, *Allegretto vivace*, first announced by a long trill on the piano and then begun by the strings with the triangle tinkles. Concerning those triangle strokes, Liszt himself directed that they should be made with the utmost precision. The piano again develops the theme in free fantasia fashion, *Capriccioso scherzando*, and another cadenza brings the conclusion of that section. The fourth section is the bustling conclusion of the piece, *Allegro marziale animato*, which brings back the music of the very opening of the concerto, and then also recalls other themes heard earlier. The concerto comes to a breathless, headlong conclusion.

The first performance of the score was given at Weimar in February 1855, during a week-long series of concerts devoted to the music of Berlioz. The Liszt concerto was the only non-Berlioz work performed, but it was conducted by Berlioz, and Liszt himself was the piano soloist. How the rafters must have shaken!

Among several excellent recorded performances of the score, I have no hesitation in stating that the Richter-Kondrashin collaboration with the London Symphony Orchestra (Philips 835474) is one of the great recordings of the century. I am not an unqualified admirer of Richter; indeed, I sometimes find his playing precious and overly calculated. In the Liszt First Piano Concerto, however, he delivers a performance full of boundless energy and passion; at the same time, he invests the quieter, more poetic sections with his special brand of introspection and tonal coloration. Kondrashin has the orchestra musicians performing at top form and the Philips recording team has reproduced it all in superb detail and clarity.

Of the other recordings, Entremont (Columbia MS 6071) goes all out for flashing fireworks; Vasáry (Deutsche Grammophon 138055) is more intimate in approach, emphasizing the lyricism rather than the thunder; and Pennario (RCA VICS 1426) and Rubinstein (RCA LSC 2068) steer a middle course between these two attitudes. The Rubinstein version, dating from the mid-1950s, is now rather outdated sonically—he should re-record the concerto at the first opportunity, and now that Ormandy and the Philadelphia Orchestra are once again recording for RCA, they would make the ideal collaborators with Rubinstein. The recording by André Watts with Leonard Bernstein and the New York Philharmonic (Columbia MS 6955) is dynamic if somewhat overblown.

Richter's performance also dominates the field in tape and cassette format (Philips tape L 5474; cassette PCR4-900000). Of recordings more recently released, Martha Argerich's (DGG 139383; tape L 9383; cassette 923083) is superbly played, brilliantly recorded and viscerally exciting.

Gustav Mahler

Born: Kalischt, Bohemia, July 7, 1860
Died: Vienna, May 18, 1911

Gustav Mahler was the second of twelve children born to a penniless Jewish coachman and his wife. The sounds of the local military bands with their bugle calls fascinated the boy and he haunted the local barracks for hours on end listening to the noisy din. He would also follow the local organ-grinders around and then would return home to bang out their tunes on an old piano. The sounds of nature—birds twittering, a brook bubbling, violent thunderstorms—exerted a powerful stimulus upon his impressionable nature. All these sounds were later to echo through much of Mahler's own composition.

After some rather tentative piano lessons, Mahler was heard by a famous teacher who arranged for his admission to the Vienna Conservatory—no small accomplishment in light of the virulent anti-Semitism that poisoned the Viennese air even then. Mahler studied at the Conservatory until he was eighteen. Then he took some courses at the University of Vienna and at the age of twenty he went out into the world to seek his fortune. His first job was as Kapellmeister at a provincial theater in Hall during the summer season of 1880. The same year also saw the composition of his first important score, *Das klagende Lied,* for vocal soloists, chorus and orchestra. Then started a parade from one small town to another in Austria and Germany with Mahler in charge of provincial opera companies. During the summer of 1883 he made a pilgrimage to Bayreuth and was deeply moved by a performance of Wagner's *Parsifal.* In the same year he finished his *Songs of a Wayfarer* and took up a new post—his most important thus far—as conductor at

Cassel. After two years at Cassel he was invited to fill a similar post in Prague, and in 1886 came an invitation from Leipzig.

In 1888 the twenty-eight-year-old Mahler was called to one of the most prestigious opera houses in all Europe—the Royal Opera at Budapest. Here he remained for three years, galvanizing his excellent musical forces into an ensemble of unique cohesiveness. His fame now spread far and wide and Budapest became the meeting place for many of the day's greatest musicians. One of those who came to witness at first hand the musical miracles being wrought by the young Artistic Director of the Royal Opera was Johannes Brahms; after a Mahler-conducted performance of Mozart's *Don Giovanni*, Brahms was won over completely. All was not well in the internal functioning of the company, however; Mahler's often autocratic behavior provoked great frictions and jealousies among his staff, one of whom ultimately challenged him to a duel. It was never fought, however. When attempts were made to curb his authority at the Budapest Opera, Mahler resigned and he was promptly engaged by the Hamburg Opera.

The conductor of the symphony concerts in Hamburg at the time was the great Hans von Bülow, and the two of them became great friends—the younger man awed by the power and authority of von Bülow's conducting, and von Bülow quite overwhelmed by the demonic drive and dedication of Mahler's art. Mahler remained in Hamburg from 1891 until 1897, in the meantime succeeding von Bülow as conductor of the symphony concerts in 1893 when the failing health of the older man forced him to relinquish them.

In 1895 Mahler was converted to the Roman Catholic faith and in 1897 came a call from the music capital of the world at the time —Vienna, the scene of some of his most important earlier years. Remembering the impact of the *Don Giovanni* performance in Budapest some years earlier, Brahms, who was then very near his end, strongly recommended Mahler to the Vienna Court Opera as a conductor. For three years Mahler was the chief conductor at the opera, then in 1900 he was made Artistic Director of the company and given full control over its destinies. He was not one to shirk a responsibility and he ruled the affairs of the company with an iron fist. No detail of production went unexamined by him. He was totally consumed by his dedication to the finest possible musical presentation and he demanded the same kind of total commitment from all who came under his supervision. The period of Mahler's directorship of the Vienna Opera produced artistic results beyond compare and he was lionized by a large and loyal following. It was inevitable, however, that his uncompromising standards and his graceless dealings with people should cause him difficulty. And always polluting the air was the thinly disguised odor of Vienna's traditional anti-Semitism, which Mahler's conversion had dispelled not at all. By 1907 matters had become intolerable for Mahler in Vienna—and for Vienna with Mahler in her midst. He wrote out a letter of resignation, a sensitive and generous document, and had it posted on the opera house's bulletin board. The next day it was found ripped from the board and torn to shreds.

Mahler's personal life during the previous five years was anything but placid. In 1902 he had married Alma Maria Schindler, who by her own admission was a ravishing beauty who had captured the hearts of countless men: her career as a femme fatale was indeed one of the more distinguished ones in history—after Mahler's death she became at one time or another either mistress to or wife of the painter Oskar Kokoschka, the architect Walter Gropius and the writer Franz Werfel. By 1907 Alma had borne Mahler two daughters, whom he adored. Two days after the family arrived at their summer vacation retreat that year, the older child became ill with scarlet fever. During two agonizing weeks, when her condition lapsed from serious to grave to hopeless, Mahler existed in a trance. He locked himself in a room as if to shut out the dread march of events; a desperate last-resort laryngotomy was performed on the child but it was to no avail. She died and Mahler was inconsolable: the composer who two years earlier had completed a song cycle to poems by Friedrich Rückert titled *Kindertotenlieder* (*Songs on the Death of Children*) was now himself lamenting the loss of his own daughter. But Fate was not yet finished. A few days after the death of the child, Mahler's wife suffered some heart palpitations and a doctor was summoned to examine her. In the course of the examination the doctor also looked at Mahler—and discovered that he was suffering from a serious and incurable heart condition.

Now Mahler became driven by only one thought—to provide adequately for his family in the event of his early death. When the news of his resignation from the Vienna Opera was made known, he received an attractive offer from the Metropolitan Opera in New York to conduct several productions, including the first American performances of Smetana's *The Bartered Bride* and Tchaikovsky's *Queen of Spades*. The performances were revelations to New York operagoers. In 1909 Mahler also became conductor of the New York Philharmonic, at what was then the highest salary ever paid a conductor in this country—$30,000 a year. Mahler completely rebuilt the Philharmonic and his accomplishments caused the New York *Post* to exclaim in 1910: "Mahler has worked a miracle! No wonder the Mahlerites are growing fast in number."

His health was by now failing rapidly, however, and a streptococcus infection brought about a general collapse. Despite the resentments he felt toward Vienna, it was to that city that he wished to return to die. He arrived on a stretcher and a few days later, two months short of his fifty-first birthday, Gustav Mahler died.

Mahler composed nine symphonies and left a tenth incomplete (in recent years the Tenth Symphony has been completed from Mahler's sketches by several different Mahler scholars; the version by Deryck Cooke is now the one most commonly performed); he also composed two song cycles, various other song collections, and the song-symphony *Das Lied von der Erde* (*The Song of the Earth*). He once remarked, "A symphony is like the world. It must embrace everything." To this end Mahler chose subjects of vast scope, with programs drawn from literature for the most part. Many of his symphonies employ the human voice as an adjunct and the most colossal performing apparatus is sometimes required by his music—his Eighth Symphony, for example, is dubbed the "Symphony of a Thousand" because it is scored for enormous orchestra, several large choruses and a multitude of vocal soloists. There have been those who have been repelled by the vulgarity of some of Mahler's music as well as by the pretentiousness of some of its thought. Ever since the centenary celebrations in 1960 of Mahler's birth, however, his music has gained enormously in public esteem and popularity—and there appear to be no signs of any diminishing in this popularity. Mahler once remarked, "My time will come." The words now have about them the ring of prophetic truth.

SYMPHONY NO. 1 IN D MAJOR

In the 1880s a young musician was moving from one provincial German opera house to another as the conductor of the "second-string" repertoire of operas—Marschner, Lortzing and the like. When he was given an opportunity in Olmütz to conduct operas by Wagner and Mozart, he could not bring himself to "profane" these works with the inferior forces at his command. The flaming young musical idealist was Gustav Mahler. He had already composed a considerable amount of music himself, but it still lay, unperformed, in manuscript.

During the years 1883 and 1884, the twenty-three-year-old Mahler was the second conductor in the city of Cassel, and it was probably during that period that he began work on his First Symphony. He was best known to his contemporaries as a conductor, but Mahler's major significance in his own eyes was as a composer, and one of the remarkable aspects of the musical life of the mid-twentieth century is the extent to which we have come to agree with Mahler's own assessment of his importance.

Early in his second season at Budapest, in 1889, Mahler conducted the initial performance of his First Symphony. The audience had grown to respect the conductor in the highest degree, but that performance aroused conflicting emotions, perplexity perhaps chief among them. And small wonder, for Mahler had prepared a "Program Outline" of awesome proportions, calling the work a "Symphonic Poem in two parts" and giving it the title "The Titan," after the novel of the same name by the German Romantic writer Jean Paul. The various movements were described by Mahler as follows:

Part I. Days of Youth. Youth, flowers and thorns.
    1. Spring without end. The introduction represents the awakening of nature at early dawn.

2. A Chapter of Flowers. [This movement, an *Andante*, was with-drawn by Mahler after a Weimar performance of the score. He never reinstated it.]

3. Full sail! (Scherzo)

Part II. *Commedia umana.*

4. Stranded. A funeral march à la Callot [Jacques Callot, the seventeenth-century French engraver]. The following remarks may serve as an explanation, if necessary. The author received the external incitement to this piece from a pictorial parody well known to all children in South Germany, "The Hunter's Funeral Procession." The forest animals accompany the dead forester's coffin to the grave. The hares carry flags; in front is a band of gypsy musicians and music-making cats, frogs, crows, etc.; and deer, stags, foxes, and other four-footed and feathered denizens of the forest accompany the procession in comic postures. In the present piece the imagined expression is partly ironically gay, partly gloomily brooding, and is immediately followed by

5. *Dall'Inferno al Paradiso* (*allegro furioso*), the sudden outbreak of a profoundly wounded heart.

I have quoted Mahler's own vivid word picture of the First Sym-phony in full because it gives a fanciful and undeniably accurate indication of what was in the composer's mind at the time of the work's creation. Mahler later disavowed this program—and indeed all programmatic descriptions of his music—but the fact remains that the spirit of romantic fancy so directly conveyed by these words is integral to an understanding of the music. One could in fact wish that more conductors would take the trouble to read and ponder Mahler's words before conducting the symphony.

The first movement is marked in the score *Langsam, schleppend wie ein Naturlaut* (Slowly, and drawn out like a sound of nature). The long introduction truly evokes the sounds of nature: against a long-held A in the strings, various woodwind instruments gurgle out snatches of a theme, with clarinets and trumpets chiming in, but from afar. The call of the cuckoo is heard from the clarinet and then the main section of the movement is ushered in by an upward-rising theme in the basses. The melody is the same one Mahler used some years earlier in the second song from his cycle *Lieder eines fahrenden Gesellen* (*Songs of a Wayfarer*)—"Ging heut' Mor-

gen über's Feld" ("Across the field I took my way"). The second
theme is introduced softly in the horns and then taken up by the
cellos. There is an elaborate development of the material and the
end of the movement is an animated romp with punctuations of
dramatic silences. The second movement, *Kräftig bewegt, doch nicht
zu schnell* (Busily agitated, but not too fast), begins with a heavy-
footed passage in the low strings, with the woodwinds immediately
stating the peasant-dance Ländler that forms the principal basis of
the musical discourse. The Trio is a delicate, dream-like section
whose chief melodic material is first stated by the violins, pianissimo. *Feierlich und gemessen, ohne zu schleppen* (Solemn and
measured, without dragging) is the marking over the third movement, a macabre section that begins with alternating tympani
strokes pianissimo and then introduces a double bass solo that is a
parody burlesque on the old French nursery tune *"Frère Jacques,"*
in the minor. The second subject moves the music into the major
mode, and in the words of Mahler's biographer, Paul Stefan, "an
oboe bleats and squeaks in the upper register; the shrill E Flat
clarinet quacks; over a quiet counterpoint in the trumpets, the
oboes are tootling a vulgar street-song." It is all part of Mahler's
parodistic nature, even to his inclusion of another of the songs from
the *Fahrenden Gesellen* cycle—this time from the fourth of them,
"Die zwei blauen Augen" ("Your sweet eyes of blue"). The *"Frère
Jacques"* theme returns again at the end and the movement dies
out into nothingness. The brief silence is shattered by the erup-
tion of the turbulent final movement, marked *Stürmisch bewegt*
(Stormily agitated). Themes from the first movement are repeated
and the entire grandiose conception recalls what Mahler's friend
and disciple Bruno Walter called the "raging vehemence" of Mahler's
nature. The music rises to an enormous climax, as if to burst its own
bonds, and then it falls back exhausted to regain its strength for
the final peroration. Mahler directs that at the end seven horns must
cut through the heaving orchestra in a "chorale of salvation from
paradise after the waves of hell." In his monograph on Mahler and
his music, Walter writes that the demonic conclusion of this extraordinary symphony is a "triumphant victory over life."

After he conducted the New York premiere of the First Sym-

phony with the New York Philharmonic in December 1909,
Mahler wrote to Walter to describe his reactions to this youthful
colossus that he had created more than twenty years earlier: "A
burning and painful sensation is crystallized. What a world this is
that casts up such reflections of sounds and figures! Things like the
Funeral March and the bursting of the storm which follows it seem
to me a flaming indictment of the Creator. . . ."

It remains only to be added that the *Blumine* movement, the
original second movement of the five-movement format that Mahler
first laid out for the symphony, has recently been resurrected and
performed both in England and in this country. The pioneer Frank
Brieff-New Haven Symphony recording of the five-movement symphony (Odyssey 32160286), while a valuable document, convinces me
that Mahler was right in ultimately dropping the *Blumine* movement.
But of the two available recordings incorporating the movement, Ormandy's is the more polished (RCA LSC 3107; tape TR3 1007,
3¾ ips; cassette RK 1133).

Among the several available recordings of the four-movement
format, there are a couple—by otherwise highly expert Mahler conductors—that are just plain failures. The most spectacular failure
is the performance conducted by Leonard Bernstein (Columbia MS
7069), who is arguably the finest Mahler conductor of our time.
But his recording of the First Symphony is an overwrought, exaggerated performance that pulls the music all out of shape. Similarly,
the recording conducted by Paul Kletzki (Angel S 35913) is a blot
on that conductor's reputation as a dedicated Mahler conductor.
He brings little imagination to his performance, and Angel's reproduction is on the shallow side. But the performance is removed
from any serious consideration above all else by a huge and inexpli-
cable cut in the last movement. The movement rambles, to be sure,
but a conscienceless excision is no way to solve the problem.

A disappointment, too, is the performance by Erich Leinsdorf and
the Boston Symphony Orchestra (RCA LSC 2642). Early in his
first season as the Boston Symphony's music director Leinsdorf
scored a great personal triumph with exciting performances of the
Mahler First. The recording, unfortunately, does not capture the
brilliance and dash of the concert performances; it is too carefully

polished and overrefined. Another recording that does not pack the wallop that I have heard the same forces deliver in person is the performance by Bernard Haitink and the Amsterdam Concertgebouw Orchestra (Philips PHS 900017). Haitink has some individual ideas about the symphony, which have grown to maturity since this recording was made. If he should have an opportunity to record the music again during the next several years, his second chance at it should be very good indeed.

For three movements, Bruno Walter's second recording of the score (Odyssey 430047) is nearly ideal. A lifetime of devotion to the Mahler ethos is evident everywhere, and Walter infuses these movements with a deep and pervading personal meaning. But curiously, his performance of the last movement falls completely flat: the tempo seems to be deliberately held back and the thrust and cumulative impact of the score are stunted in their growth.

A completely successful performance of the symphony is the one conducted by Jascha Horenstein and recorded in the early 1950s (Turnabout 34355). Horenstein is assuredly one of the most underrated conductors of our time and his recordings, especially of Mahler, reveal a superb intellect and a highly communicative art. Horenstein has been given an opportunity to re-record his matchless interpretation of this score, and while the resulting disc (Nonesuch H 71240) is somewhat disappointing by virtue of sound that is not really up to the best of contemporary standards, it is nevertheless good enough to confirm Horenstein's mastery of the architecture of this score. His recording of Mahler's First Symphony reveals an instinctive response to the many shadings of Mahler's personality, especially in the last movement, which Horenstein succeeds in making more convincing than any other conductor who has recorded the score.

Perhaps the most successful all-round recording and performance (aside from Horenstein's, whose sonic qualities do not reflect the advances of the stereo era) is the one conducted by Georg Solti (London CS 6401). The music is shaped lovingly, yet the conductor succeeds in keeping the loose structure of the score under firm control. The playing by the London Symphony is superb in its dynamism and brilliance, and the engineers have produced a tour de force of contemporary sound technology. Solti's performance is also the preferred tape version (London L 80150). Kubelik's smaller scaled approach to the symphony offers a very good alternative choice (DGG 139331; tape L 9331; cassette 923070).

SYMPHONY NO. 4 IN G MAJOR

The renascence of interest in Mahler in the past few decades may have received its greatest impetus from the recording of the Fourth Symphony Bruno Walter and the New York Philharmonic made for Columbia in the early 1940s. A broad musical public was suddenly made aware of the manifold beauties of a symphony hitherto known and admired only be devotees. Once Bruno Walter had firmly demonstrated that the Mahler Fourth was not for the cognoscenti alone, the ice was broken, and other Mahler works began to be performed all over the world.

Whatever else may have happened to men's minds since the early 1940s, it is clear that the complexities of Mahler's character are now more widely understood than ever before, and with this understanding has come an empathic identification with the aesthetic of Mahler's music.

Next to his First Symphony, Mahler's Fourth is today the best known and most frequently performed. The reasons for this are not hard to discover: the last movement, with its child-like vocal fantasy of the heavenly life—the text is from a collection of German folk poetry, *Des Knaben Wunderhorn*—is the work in a nutshell. Here is a symphony of disarming poignancy and beauty, prodigious in its melodic invention, transparent in its orchestration—an example of perfect fulfillment as an artistic entity.

Bruno Walter, in his book on Mahler, has eloquently assessed the composer's first four symphonies:

In [them] an important part of the history of Mahler's soul is unfolded. The force of spiritual events is matched by the power of musical language. The correlation of the world of sound and that of imagination, thoughts, and emotions is thus common to them. While, however, in the First the subjective experience with its tempest of emotions is exerting its influence upon the music, metaphysical questions strive to find an answer and deliverance in music in the Second and in subsequent symphonies. Three times he gives the answer and every time from a different point of view. In the Second he asks the reason for the tragedy of human existence and is sure its justification is to be found in immortality. In the Third, with a feeling of reassurance, he looks out upon nature, runs the rounds of its circles, and finishes in the happy awareness that it is "almighty love that forms all things and preserves all things." In the Fourth, he assures himself and us of a sheltered security in the sublime and serene dream of a heavenly life.

In its dimensions of instrumentation and length, the Fourth is perhaps the most modest in scope. Though it runs nearly an hour, it is still the shortest of all Mahler's symphonies; and its orchestration is the lightest of them all, with trombones and tuba not called for at all, with the trumpets used only moderately, and with the number of horns normal compared to the six called for in the Second Symphony and the eight in the Third. The last movement of the Fourth Symphony was planned originally by Mahler to be a part of his Third Symphony. In this earlier score, he had attached a series of fanciful titles to the concluding movements: "What the Flowers of the Field Tell Me," "What the Animals of the Forest Tell Me," "What Night Tells Me," "What the Morning Bells Tell Me," "What Love Tells Me." Mahler intended to call the section that became the Finale of the Fourth Symphony "What the Child Tells Me." Thematically the movement recalls the "Morning Bells" section of the Third Symphony and it sustains much the same mood: "child-like peace symbolic of heavenly bliss."

The first movement bears the markings *Heiter, Bedächtig* and *Recht gemächlich* (Gay, Deliberate and Leisurely). It begins with the soft tinkling of sleigh bells followed immediately by a gentle, ingratiating melody in the violins. The lower strings have another theme, and then the second principal theme of the movement is introduced by the cellos. Other themes or theme fragments are introduced but they are merely transitory in nature. There are combinations and interweaving along the way, and the music rises at one point to an impassioned climax, but the basic sense of naïve simplicity pervades the entire movement.

The second movement, *In gemächlicher Bewegung* (With leisurely motion), begins with a gentle horn motive but almost immediately the solo violin takes over. The instrument is tuned one tone higher than normally, giving the sound a shrill quality, especially since Mahler directs the concertmaster to play *"wie ein Fidel,"* in the old-fashioned, vulgar style of a country fiddler. Mahler's friend and biographer, Paul Stefan, speculates: "Only one being can play thus: Death. He is very good-natured and lets the others go on dancing, but they must not try to overtake him; they are in major, but even that sounds creepy enough. Then the piece becomes somewhat livelier [the Trio], but the ghostly theme returns and remains." The general character of the movement is not sinister, however; rather, the quality is one of bittersweetness.

The third movement, *Poco adagio*, is marked *Ruhevoll* (Peacefully). It is a long series of variations on the opening simple theme in the strings. Along the way several new counterthemes are introduced, one by the oboe, another by the clarinets, and there is a considerable contrapuntal involvement. The music rises to a pitch of great intensity and there is a very loud climax punctuated by drumbeats and cymbal crashes. But the storm subsides and the music returns to its mood of calm and seraphic peace.

The last movement, *Sehr behaglich* (Comfortably), introduces verses from an old Bavarian folk song, *"Der Himmel hängt voll Geigen"* ("Many fiddles hang in Heaven"), taken from the collection of German folk poetry that Mahler loved so well. There are interludes after each verse that recall the jingling sleigh bell theme of the very opening of the symphony. The text is an enchantingly naïve description of a perfect peasant paradise of the Middle Ages: a joyful life of easy merrymaking, where game, fish, vegetables, wine and fruit are available for the asking, where rabbits and deer cavort effortlessly, and bread is baked by angels. St. John gives up his little lamb, St. Luke his ox. Herod is the butcher and St. Martha the cook. Eleven thousand virgins dance without teasing while St. Cecilia and all her kind form the excellent court orchestra, with St. Ursula smiling benignly on the entire scene. Above the soprano part in his score Mahler wrote: "With child-like, bright expression, always without parody." The whole could have been conceived only by an artist of genuine simplicity and child-like in nature.

Several very fine accounts of the music exist on recordings. One of the very best, as far as I am concerned, is Leonard Bernstein's highly personal reading of the music (Columbia MS 6152). The high point of the performance is the slow movement, a superb realization of the pensive reverie characteristic of the music. I do not think the climax of the movement has to be as violent as Bernstein shapes it, but in all other respects he wins me over completely. His soprano soloist in the last movement is Reri Grist and she sings the verses most beautifully and unaffectedly. Another excellent recording is George Szell's with the Cleveland Orchestra (Columbia MS 6833) and Judith Raskin as the soprano. Here it is perhaps the last movement that is the high point, despite a tempo that is rather on the slow side. But Miss Raskin sings it superbly, and everywhere else the tender beauty of Mahler's score is most sensitively conveyed by Szell.

A surprisingly successful performance is the one conducted by Solti (London CS 6217). The qualities of gentle and genial persuasiveness in this performance are not those one generally associates with this conductor's music-making. But Solti quite obviously loves Mahler's Fourth Symphony and he is able to feel comfortable with it without whipping up things to a frenzy. The Amsterdam Concertgebouw Orchestra plays magnificently for him, London's engineers have produced recorded sound of great clarity and depth, and the soprano soloist, Sylvia Stahlman, admirably communicates the fantasy and wonder of the music.

Reiner's performance (RCA LSC 2364) seems to me too matter-of-fact and bloodless and his soprano soloist, the usually fine Lisa Della Casa, makes no attempt to characterize the verses. Even more disappointing is the performance led by Klemperer (Angel S 35829). A pompous, almost menacing attitude pervades the opening movement, and there is no hint of humor and precious little grace. In the slow movement, surprisingly, Klemperer adopts a tempo that is considerably faster than normal—a miscalculation, to my mind, that compromises the dimensions of the movement. In the Finale, Klemperer's soprano, Elisabeth Schwarzkopf, is irritatingly affected and her careful projection cannot hide a disfiguring wobble. Completing an unhappy picture is recorded sound that is cavernous.

Paul Kletzki's account (Seraphim S 60105) is highly sensitive to the various moods of the music, and his soprano soloist, Emmy Loose, is superb.

That leaves the Bruno Walter recording that started off our discussion of this score (Odyssey 32160026). One of the projects unfinished at the time of Walter's death was the conductor's plan to re-record the Mahler Fourth for Columbia; it is doubtful that he could have improved upon the magical performance engraved on the Odyssey disc. Though the sound is faded, and Desi Halban, the soprano, is hardly an ideal exponent of the text, no other recorded performance matches Walter's in spontaneity and musical rightness.

The Szell-Raskin performance (Columbia MQ 783) and the Solti-Stahlman (London L 80075) version are fine alternate choices for the tape fan, though the Solti performance continues to be my favorite. And Haitink's cassette (Philips 18230CAA) is the more satisfying, for me, of the two available cassette performances— the other being the less personally involved Kubelik performance.

SYMPHONY NO. 9 IN D MAJOR

Throughout the last works of Gustav Mahler—*Das Lied von der Erde* (1908), the Ninth Symphony (1909) and the unfinished Tenth Symphony—a preoccupation with death is manifest. By nature Mahler was given to melancholia, and yet many pages of his earlier music reflect a naïve, almost child-like infatuation with life and its joys. Probably his surrender to a fixation in death was precipitated by the loss of his five-year-old daughter in October 1907, and by his discovery that he was himself suffering from chronic heart disease.

According to Bruno Walter and other intimate friends of the composer, Mahler was very reluctant to assign the number nine to a symphony, recalling that Beethoven had completed only nine symphonies and Bruckner had not lived to complete his ninth. Though Mahler called *Das Lied von der Erde,* which followed his Eighth Symphony, a "song-symphony," he would not attach a number to it, and a few years later, when he had completed the score of a new symphony, he hesitated before showing it to anyone. Bruno Walter, in his book *Gustav Mahler* (1941), wrote:

He probably brought it [the manuscript of the Ninth Symphony] back to Vienna in the spring of 1910, but I cannot recall having seen it at the time and it is likely that it came to me only after his death. Perhaps, too, he was prevented by superstitious awe from telling me of the fact that after all a ninth had come into existence. Up to that time, I had never noticed even a trace of superstition in his clear, strong spirit, and even on that occasion it turned out to be not that but an only-too-well-founded foreboding of the terrible consistency of the Parcae [the Fates].

The prevailing mood of the Ninth Symphony is one of liberation and profound release. In spirit it is linked to the "*Abschied*" movement of *Das Lied von der Erde:* its opening *Andante* and concluding *Adagio* are imbued with the feeling of peace found in the mystery of eternity that characterizes the "*Abschied.*" Contrast is provided by the two middle movements: the second is a vigorous Austrian Ländler and the third a mocking Rondo-Burleske.

Just before the American premiere of the Ninth Symphony, Alfred H. Meyer wrote a perceptive and penetrating description of it for the Boston *Transcript:*

It has been said that the music of "The Song of the Earth" and of the Ninth Symphony is music such as old men might be expected to write—in spite of the fact that Mahler was only at the end of his forties when he composed both. But death was soon to come; and this music is full of the feeling that life is complete. . . . Now in the Ninth Symphony he writes an opening *Andante commodo* of peace and of passion in which death itself finds place; a *Scherzo* (Im Tempo eines gemächlichen Ländlers—In the tempo of a leisurely Ländler) which looks back at life with irony and as a mockery and fantastic orgy; a third movement which continues the derision of this world in a *Rondo Burleske* that mounts to a tremendous climax; that is in many respects a larger counterpart of the "Drinking Song of Earthly Woes" from "The Song of the Earth," but that contains also a melody of transfiguring prophetic vision. This *Rondo Burleske* finally exhausts itself in its own fury. (Many a composer has deemed a similar content sufficient for a whole symphony.) A final *Adagio* ensues trying to pierce the veil, singing into the heart the message that Death is Godly Love.

The orchestra of the Ninth Symphony is modest—for Mahler. Woodwinds in threes, except that there are four flutes; four horns, three trumpets and the usual trombone-tuba quartet; the quintet of strings; for percussion, only two kettledrums, triangle, glockenspiel. None of the four movements is in the traditional sonata form. In all the preceding eight symphonies, whatever his structural experiments, Mahler had never abandoned this form. The first movement of the Ninth presents the duality of themes which lies at the basis of sonata form. But, the two themes presented, he places them in opposition to each other and works them with improvisatory freedom. The first theme occurs in the sixth measure, D Major; calm resignation, a dream-like peace or hope. The opposing theme is heard about twenty measures later, D Minor intense with passion, which comes to its highest point in sharp chords for trumpets.

Mahler soon reminds us of the significance of this Symphony, when he introduces reminiscences of the "Death-Dance" scherzo of his Fourth Symphony. The original title of this scherzo was "Freund Hein spielt auf" and we are told that "Freund Hein" is not an "evil, terrifying god, but a friendly leader, fiddling his flock into the hereafter." No reference could be more suggestive of the mood of this first movement, indeed of the whole Symphony. After much conflict in which the two opposing themes seem at times to devour each other Mahler introduces a solemn march-like music over which he writes the direction, "Wie ein schwerer Kondukt." These words take on especial meaning when one recalls that "Kondukt" is the Austrian circumlocution for funeral procession. After more interplay of the two principal themes, the movement ends on a new note, more quiet, more peaceful even than that of the principal theme, a note somehow prophetic of the final *Adagio*.

Introducing the *Scherzo* [Paul] Bekker writes: "As friend and redeemer, as gently lulling comforter, Death came in the first movement. As demon he rules over the two middle movements, Scherzo and Rondo. Not now as in the Fourth Symphony, in the mediaevally mummified form of 'Freund Hein' with his Death's-fiddle. This time he exercises the powers of darkness, bids them dance to his tune. The dance-pictures of earlier works return . . . clothed in a gruesome irony." After such illuminating remarks, detailed analysis of the themes is superfluous. Suffice it to say that the principal theme is gawky and awkward, that the secondary themes cover a wide range of effect. The introduction of a motif from the first theme of the first movement in one of the waltzes must not be overlooked.

Well does Mahler name his Rondo a Burlesque. Having found the pleasures of past life a mockery, he turns to more serious things to find them no better. The mood of irony continues, then rises as dance-music gives way to tones of more weighty character. . . . Near the middle of the movement a chorale is token of the seriousness of the artist amid all these sarcasms. Toward the end, before the final self-consuming play of the initial mocking theme, comes a melody gently expressive, yet more prophetic of the final *Adagio* than the close of the first movement.

Two measures of reminiscent agony introduce the final movement. Then that wondrous *Adagio* which is solemn revelation of worlds to come. One need not write more. One dare not analyze where such a spell is wrought.

And yet one unusual feature of the structure of the final *Adagio* must be mentioned: in its second part it builds to a gradual heightening of intensity which becomes almost unbearable. Then there is a gradual subsiding as instruments drop out of the argument successively, until the cellos are left all by themselves in a pianissimo passage that fades into complete silence. The concluding coda returns material heard earlier in the movement and the end "reaches the most profound and heart-searching degree of poignance."

It was Bruno Walter who conducted the first performance of the Ninth Symphony, in Vienna in June 1912, about a year after Mahler died. But nearly twenty years were to elapse before the symphony was heard in the United States. Serge Koussevitzky conducted the American premiere of the Ninth in October 1931, with the Boston Symphony Orchestra. Koussevitzky became an ardent champion of the work, and repeated it in Boston three times during the next ten seasons, long before Mahler had begun to attain popularity in this country. His last performances of the symphony were given in February 1941, and this writer remembers them as burning acts of faith. Along with his many other extraordinary accomplishments, Koussevitzky was an unusually persuasive Mahler conductor. It is a pity that he was never given an opportunity to record any of the Mahler symphonies.

The first recording of the Mahler Ninth, appropriately enough, was a concert performance by Bruno Walter and the Vienna Philharmonic Orchestra in Vienna on January 16, 1938. The recording was released in this country by RCA Victor, first as a bulging album of ten 78-rpm discs, then as one of the early issues in the company's long-playing catalog. The sound was never very good, but the performance was a marvel of emotional communication. In his last series of recording sessions, in 1961, Walter returned to the Mahler Ninth Symphony. This time the place was Hollywood and the orchestra was the Columbia Symphony, the remarkable group of Los Angeles and Hollywood musicians with whom Walter recorded so much of his repertoire during his final years. The recording of the Mahler Ninth Symphony made then (Odyssey Y2 30308) is surely one of the glories of recorded music. The lucidity and directness of the performance are extraordinary, the playing of the orchestra is pure poetry, and Columbia's engineers captured it all in magnificent sound. The album was released as a memorial tribute to Bruno Walter; he could have wished for none more fitting.

Another vitally compelling recording of the score is the one by Sir John Barbirolli with the Berlin Philharmonic Orchestra (Angel S 3652). Generally, Barbirolli's reading is even more passionate than Walter's; where intense feeling is required, as in the final movement, Barbirolli makes his biggest impact. Elsewhere, the performance is not on such a lofty plane, but the over-all impact is deep, and it is increased by fine playing and sound.

The performance by Leonard Bernstein and the New York Philharmonic (included in Columbia M3S 776) is one of that conductor's most persuasive and deeply moving Mahler performances. Bernstein's identification with the idiom is total, the orchestra plays the score magnificently and the whole thing is a profound and cathartic experience. Undoubtedly the performance will be released independently of its deluxe packaging; it deserves the most wide-spread circulation Columbia can give it.

The performances conducted by Klemperer (Angel S 3708), Horenstein (Turnabout 34332/3), Solti (London CSA 2220) and Kubelik (Deutsche Grammophon 139345/6) all have their good points, but for me they are outclassed by Walter, Bernstein and Barbirolli.

The Walter performance is also available as a tape release (M2Q 516); technically as well as musically it is an impressive achievement. As yet, no performance has been made available in the cassette configuration.

Felix Mendelssohn

Born: Hamburg, February 3, 1809
Died: Leipzig, November 4, 1847

Mendelssohn was the grandson of the great Talmudic philosopher Moses Mendelssohn, and the son of a successful banker named Abraham Mendelssohn who later used to identify himself as follows: "In my early years I was known as my father's son; now I am known as my son's father." The family life of the Mendelssohns is almost unique in musical history for its happiness and mutual devotion. When Felix was a youngster he studied music privately with his mother and other teachers. His father's business brought the family to Berlin and young Felix was enrolled at the age of ten in the Berlin Singakademie. Already the lad was composing music and his works were performed by the small string orchestra that gathered at the home of his father every Sunday. By the time he was twelve he had become a notable improviser and he already had a large number of compositions to his credit, including a cantata, a musical comedy, a piano trio, two piano sonatas, a violin sonata and many songs.

It was when he was seventeen that Mendelssohn composed his thoroughly remarkable overture to Shakespeare's *A Midsummer Night's Dream*, capturing to perfection the elfin and wispy quality of the play. In the same year he also composed his marvelous Octet for Strings and enrolled as a student at the Berlin University. He also became a passable painter and was proficient in gymnastics and billiards. In 1829, when he was twenty years old, he brought into being (at the Singakademie) and conducted the first performance since the composer's death of Bach's *Passion According to St. Matthew*. This was the first step in the continuing crusade he waged to take Bach out of obsolescence and to restore him to active repertoire status. That performance of the *Passion*, which was repeated ten days later, was the beginning of the great Bach revival of the nineteenth and twentieth centuries. In the words of the author Percy M. Young, writing in *Grove's Dictionary of Music and Musicians*, "it may well be that this was Mendelssohn's greatest single achievement."

In 1829 Mendelssohn made the first of nine separate voyages to England, where he came to stand second only to Handel in influence and popularity. He was invited to compose a hymn celebrating the anniversary of the emancipation of the natives of Ceylon but he declined; this did not deter him from referring to himself in letters of the period as "Composer to the Island of Ceylon." Further travels in Scotland, Switzerland and elsewhere served to reinforce his growing fame and popularity, and his next return to England was a triumphant one. His first six *Songs Without Words*, composed in Venice in 1830, were published in England, and he captivated the British public by conducting his *Hebrides* Overture and playing the solo parts in his G Minor Piano Concerto and *Capriccio Brilliant* for Piano and Orchestra. In November 1832 he was commissioned by the London Philharmonic Society to compose "a symphony, an overture and a vocal piece." The symphony, despite its source of origination, turned out to be the "Italian" Symphony, inspired by Mendelssohn's stay in various Italian cities during 1830 and 1831.

In 1835 Mendelssohn became the conductor of the Gewandhaus concerts in Leipzig, and together with his concertmaster, Ferdinand David, the two of them elevated the Gewandhaus Orchestra to a position of high prominence. It was for David that Mendelssohn later composed his Violin Concerto. A more immediate compositional concern in 1835 was the completion of the oratorio *St. Paul*, which had occupied Mendelssohn off and on for the two preceding years. Mendelssohn did complete the score before the end of the year but his joy was nullified by the profound sense of loss he suffered when his father, who had been beset by poor health and blindness in his later years, died on November 19, 1835. Only the presence of his sister Fanny saved Mendelssohn from falling into a deep abyss of depression.

In 1837 Mendelssohn married Cécile Charlotte Sophie Jeanrenaud, daughter of a French Protestant clergyman from Frankfort. She was an ordinary, pleasant girl who matured into a good wife and mother. They had five children, three sons and two daughters, but otherwise Mendelssohn was apparently unchanged by marriage: he continued his constant round of traveling and concert-giving, and everywhere he went, except in Berlin, he was regarded as an extraordinary personality. Much of the resentment against him in Berlin was occasioned by the same virulent abomination that a century later engulfed six million lives in its madness: anti-Semitism. Even though Mendelssohn adopted the Christian faith, his Jewish origin had been the principal deterrent to his being appointed conductor at the Singakademie in 1833. Toward the end of 1840 he was sounded out by none less than Friedrich Wilhelm IV to return to Berlin to take charge of the orchestral and choral concerts and to be in charge of the music department of a newly organized Academy of Arts. Negotiations for this latter position got bogged down in politics and evasions, but in the following year Mendelssohn agreed to take over the concert activities for a year. During this period he organized the famous Domchor (Cathedral Choir) in Berlin. When matters concerning the proposed Academy of Arts in Berlin showed little sign of progress, Mendelssohn decided, reluctantly, to concentrate on Leipzig as his main center of operations. He proceeded to organize the Leipzig Conservatory of Music, which became one of the most important institutions of its kind in the world, with a faculty that included some of the greatest figures of the time.

During 1845 and 1846 Mendelssohn was also busy at work on his oratorio *Elijah*. Despite the generally buoyant quality of much of Mendelssohn's music, the man himself was given to moodiness. The various machinations of the Berliners coupled with a series of illnesses in his immediate family left their mark upon him. The crushing blow came in May 1847 with the sudden death of Mendelssohn's beloved sister Fanny. Mendelssohn fell into a state of complete collapse; during the ensuing six months there were periods when he would occasionally speak hopefully of the future, but in general he lost all zest for living and within six months of the death of Fanny, he too was dead.

The funeral services in Leipzig were the kind given to a great statesman. Participating were the Gewandhaus Orchestra, two choirs and pupils from the Conservatory, one of whom carried a silver laurel wreath on a white satin cushion. The mourners at the service included clergy; representatives of civil and military authority; university, law and other friends. At the service, chorales by Bach and Mendelssohn himself were sung, as well as music from Bach's *St. Matthew Passion*. That night the coffin was placed on a train for the journey to Berlin. At every stop it was met by silent crowds and when it arrived in Berlin the following morning Mendelssohn was accorded in death what was denied to him in life—a respectful tribute from all segments of society.

CONCERTO IN E MINOR FOR VIOLIN, OP. 64

One tends to think of Mendelssohn's Violin Concerto in E Minor in the same terms as one thinks of the violin concertos of Beethoven, Brahms and Tchaikovsky—as a solitary sally into the violin concerto form by a composer who seems to have reserved some of his most inspired lyrical flights for the occasion. In fact, however, the E Minor Concerto is the third such score that Mendelssohn produced: the first two, products of his fifteenth year, were never published, although Yehudi Menuhin edited the D Minor Concerto some years ago and revived it for performance and recording (on a long-since-withdrawn RCA disc).

But Mendelssohn's E Minor Concerto *is* like Brahms' Violin Concerto in that it was the musical result of the composer's long and close friendship with a particular violinist—Ferdinand David, in Mendelssohn's case. By coincidence, Mendelssohn and David were born in the same house in Hamburg, Germany, but they did not meet until they were sixteen and fifteen, respectively. When Mendelssohn became the conductor of the Gewandhaus concerts in Leipzig in 1835, he chose David as his concertmaster. Because of Mendelssohn's precarious health, David was often obliged to take over much of the Leipzig routine; it was David who, stepping in when Mendelssohn was stricken with measles, conducted the premiere of his friend's oratorio *St. Paul*.

In July 1838, three years after Mendelssohn and David had settled in Leipzig, Mendelssohn, then thirty, again turned his thoughts to the composition of a violin concerto. In a letter written while he was vacationing away from Leipzig, Mendelssohn told the violinist, "I should like to write a violin concerto for you next winter. One in E minor runs through my head, the beginning of which gives me no peace." David apparently responded immediately and with enthusiasm, but nearly a year passed without further mention of the concerto. In July 1839, in another letter to David, Mendelssohn wrote: "Now that is very nice of you to press me for a violin concerto! I have the liveliest desire to write one for you, and if I have a few propitious days here I shall bring you something of the sort. But it is not an easy task. You want it to be brilliant, and how is such a one as I to manage that?"

During the next five years there was constant consultation between Mendelssohn and David on the evolving violin concerto. David gave Mendelssohn counsel on the writing of the solo part— apparently most of the first-movement cadenza as we know it was devised by David. But although Mendelssohn yielded to David's advice in matters of practical craftsmanship, his own sense of form and expression determined the over-all shape and content of the score.

David played the premiere of the work in Leipzig in March 1845, to a wildly enthusiastic audience. Since then the concerto has been a constant favorite with audiences the world over; it has been called "as perfect as can be" by one of Mendelssohn's biographers, and another finds in it "the charm of eternal youth."

The three movements of the concerto are linked together and should be played without pause. The first movement, *Allegro molto appassionato*, begins with a one-measure undulating figure and then the solo instrument enters immediately, singing a long-breathed and passionate melody. The violin develops this theme at length and then a transition theme is introduced by the orchestra and taken over by the violin. The second principal theme of the movement is stated first by clarinets and flutes in harmony over a long-sustained single note in the solo violin. The development section deals principally with the first theme and then there is a long and difficult cadenza for the solo instrument which ends with a series of arpeggios; underneath the arpeggios, Mendelssohn sneaks in the first principal theme in the strings and winds. The recapitulation and coda are brilliant. From the tempestuous ending of the first movement a lone note on the bassoon is sustained as an unbroken transition to the second movement, an *Andante*. Here again, the principal theme, which is announced almost immediately by the solo violin, is a broad, free-flowing melody. The middle section of the movement is a contrasting theme, restless and agitated. The movement ends with a return of the theme and mood of the opening, with the violin again singing the soaring melody but with the accompaniment changed somewhat from the opening of the movement. A brief connecting movement, *Allegretto non troppo*, again assigns the melodic bridge to the solo instrument, and then suddenly the Finale, *Allegro molto vivace*, bubbles out of the orchestra with calls of trumpets, horns, bassoons and drums, answered by arpeggios in the solo violin before it begins the principal theme of this rondo last movement. This theme has an elfin, puckish quality that is perhaps typically Mendelssohnian. The second theme is announced by the orchestra fortissimo and the movement comes to a joyous conclusion in an inspired flight of solo violin and orchestra rhapsodizing together over the principal rondo theme.

Over the past half century the Mendelssohn concerto has been recorded by nearly every important violinist who has appeared on the concert stage. Of the many performances currently available, most share a disc with either the Tchaikovsky Violin Concerto or the Bruch G Minor Violin Concerto. In the first category there are outstanding recordings of the score by Zino Francescatti (Columbia MS 6758) and Isaac Stern (Columbia MS 6062, or MS 7053—in a newer Stern performance recorded at the historic concert atop Mount Scopus in June 1967, shortly after the end of the Six-Day War between the Arab states and Israel). Supporting Francescatti's suave account of the solo part is a finely honed performance of the orchestral score by members of the Cleveland Orchestra led by George Szell. Everything about this performance reveals a loving care and tenderness. Both Francescatti and Stern bring an irresistible quality of soaring abandon to their performances.

Of the discs that couple the Mendelssohn concerto with the Bruch G Minor Concerto, especially winning are the versions by Laredo (RCA Victrola VICS 1033) and Milstein (Angel S 35730). Laredo's is a sweet-toned gentle performance that is one of the finest things this young artist has recorded. Milstein's is an imperious statement of the music, with some especially ravishing treatment of the double-stop passages.

Two other performances of the Mendelssohn concerto deserve consideration: that by Jascha Heifetz (RCA LSC 2314, which has Prokofiev's Second Violin Concerto as disc-mate) and that by Henryk Szeryng (Mercury SR 90406, with the infrequently performed and unjustly maligned Violin Concerto by Robert Schumann as its backing). The Heifetz performance is a dazzling display of pyrotechnics; the tempos are extremely fast, and there is an air of glibness about it all. But there is no denying the visceral excitement of the playing. Szeryng's is a much more relaxed and genial performance, with an easy flow. Both violinists are closely microphoned, resulting in a larger-than-life sound for the solo instrument. The conductors, Charles Munch and Antal Dorati respectively, contribute appropriate readings of the score, Munch with the Boston Symphony Orchestra and Dorati with the London Symphony Orchestra.

Of the most recent recorded performances of the score, Zukerman's (Columbia MS 7313; tape MQ 1197; cassette 16 11 0162) is a bit more on the reserved side but it is nevertheless very impressive.

The Francescatti performance also exists as a fine reel-to-reel tape (Columbia MQ 742).

SYMPHONY NO. 3 IN A MINOR, OP. 56, "SCOTCH"

As with Dvořák and Schumann, the commonly accepted number-ing of the symphonies of Felix Mendelssohn bears no relationship to the order in which they were written. Furthermore, Mendelssohn composed no fewer than twelve symphonies during his early teens, eleven of them for strings alone and one for full orchestra. These juvenilia have never been counted in the catalog of Mendelssohn's symphonic output, although at least one of them—the so-called String Symphony No. 9—has been recorded a couple of times and contains some delightful music. But officially there are only five Mendelssohn symphonies, and the last of them to be composed, the "Scotch" Symphony, is called the Third on most concert programs today. For the record, I list here the five in their order of composition, with dates:

Symphony No. 1 in C Minor (1824)
Symphony No. 5 in D Minor, "Reformation" (1832)
Symphony No. 4 in A Major, "Italian" (1833)
Symphony No. 2, "*Lobgesang*" (1840)
Symphony No. 3 in A Minor, "Scotch" (1842)

In the spring and summer of 1829 Mendelssohn visited England and Scotland with his friend Karl Klingemann, the secretary of the Hanover Legation in London. Mendelssohn was then a promising composer and pianist of twenty, and in the English capital he appeared with the London Philharmonic Orchestra as pianist and conductor. Both in his music and in his personality he was an instantaneous success.

After his professional appearances were over, Mendelssohn eagerly embarked on a tour of Britain. Scotland seems to have moved him particularly. From Edinburgh he wrote:

Everything here looks so stern and robust, half enveloped in a haze of smoke or fog. Many Highlanders came in costume from church victoriously leading their sweethearts in their Sunday attire and casting magnificent and important looks over the world; with long, red beards, tartan plaids, bonnets and feathers and naked knees and their bagpipes in their hands, they passed quietly along by the half-ruined gray castle on the meadow where Mary Stuart lived in splendor. . . . What further shall I tell you? Time and space are coming to an end, and everything must end in the refrain: How kind the people are in Edinburgh and how generous is the good God.

A trip to Abbotsford to visit the aging Sir Walter Scott proved to be a disappointment, for all Mendelssohn and Klingemann got for their trouble was "at best one half-hour of superficial conversation." From Abbotsford the two continued their journey, visiting the Hebrides, the Cave of Fingal and the Palace of Holyrood. A letter written late in the night after seeing Holyrood, the royal residence in Edinburgh, reveals Mendelssohn's excitement:

> In the evening twilight we went today to the palace where Queen Mary lived and loved. A little room is shown there with a winding staircase leading up to the door. The chapel close to it is now roofless, grass and ivy grow there, and at that broken altar Mary was crowned Queen of Scotland. Everything around is broken and mouldering, and the bright sky shines in. I believe I found today in that old chapel the beginning of my Scottish symphony.

There follow several bars of music that later became the introduction to the first movement of the symphony.

Early in the concert life of the "Scotch" Symphony there occurred an amusing incident that demonstrates the folly of ascribing the landscape painter's gifts to the composer. No less an "expert" than Robert Schumann, listening to the score under the mistaken impression that it was Mendelssohn's "Italian" Symphony, waxed eloquent about the Italian landscape he found mirrored so perfectly in the music: "It is so beautiful as to compensate a hearer who had never been to Italy." And this about a symphony whose last movement is thought by some to picture the gathering of the Scottish clans!

According to instructions printed in the original edition of the score, "The several movements of this symphony must follow each other immediately and not be separated by the usual pauses"—but each of the movements comes to a cadence on its own tonic chord. The first movement begins with a slow introduction marked *Andante con moto* that presents a flowing theme that finally ends suspended in mid-air until the main part of the movement begins, *Allegro un poco agitato*. The principal theme is stated first by the strings and oboes pianissimo. After a transitional passage, the clarinet introduces the second theme while the first violins combine the new theme with the first one. Following the standard sonata-form procedure of development, recapitulation and coda, there is, at the very end of the movement, a restatement of a few measures from the introduction. The second movement, *Vivace non troppo*, is in effect a Scherzo, with a running, Highland-type theme as its principal material and a contrasting subject that is only briefly developed. This movement is one of the finest of Mendelssohn's wispy Scherzos and its feathery lightness is a thorough joy from first to last. The third movement, *Adagio*, presents an exalted lyrical theme in the violins near the beginning. Then the woodwinds introduce a march-like subject before the second theme is introduced by the first violins with pizzicato accompaniment. The Finale, *Allegro vivacissimo*, returns the symphony to its basic tonality of A minor. The violins introduce the first subject of the last movement immediately, with violas, bassoons and horns supplying orchestral color. Following a transitional section for the full orchestra, the second theme of the movement is introduced by oboes and clarinets. Again there is an extended development and recapitulation. At the end there is a majestic section marked *Allegro maestoso assai*, in A major, that brings the symphony to a triumphant conclusion.

Peter Maag's absolutely electrifying performance (London STS 15091; tape L 80083) was unavailable on disc for several years after its initial release. It has now been brought back to currency, and at a budget price to boot. Clearly, it is the leader of the entire field. Maag, who is otherwise known chiefly in this country for his Mozart recordings, turns in a performance of extraordinary sensitivity and power. To the poetic pages of the introduction and slow movement he brings a tenderness and warmth that go right to the heart of the music. He delivers a most delicate and fanciful Scherzo and the last movement is alive with the vigor and joy of the dance. His handling of the final peroration is a lesson in inspired exuberance and elegance. The playing of the orchestra is superlative and the London recording engineers have captured all the colors of the performance brilliantly. Included on the disc is a similarly first-class performance of Mendelssohn's overture *The Hebrides*.

Also meritorious are the recordings of the symphony by Bernstein (Columbia MS 6976) and Klemperer (Vox 11840, mono only) —but in the final analysis both are outclassed by Maag. Klemperer's, incidentally, is an early recording dating from around 1950. He re-recorded the symphony more than a decade later for Angel (S

35880), but the older performance is more impetuous and more exuberant; it throbs with vitality and excitement and is obviously the product of a musician thoroughly committed to the music.

Maag's performance is also pre-eminent among the tape versions. For cassette collectors, the DGG performance conducted by Karajan (3300181) is unusually good—free of the usually annoying Karajan affectations.

SYMPHONY NO. 4 IN A MAJOR, OP. 90, "ITALIAN"

It was in 1831, when he was twenty-one years old, that Felix Mendelssohn visited Italy on a holiday. Mendelssohn the tourist would have delighted the modern travel agent: he had an insatiable curiosity about the places he visited and he threw himself wholeheartedly into exploring all the fascinating tourist attractions. Rome, Naples, Amalfi, Sorrento, Capri—Mendelssohn journeyed to all of them and drank in the local color and pageantry. "I work hard," he wrote in one of his letters from Rome, "and lead a pleasant, happy life; my mirror is stuck full of Italian, German and English visiting cards, and I spend every evening with one of my acquaintances."

That all was not holiday sight-seeing for Mendelssohn is immediately apparent from this letter written in Rome in February 1831 and addressed to his beloved sister Fanny: "I have once more begun to compose with fresh vigor, and the Italian Symphony makes rapid progress; it will be the most sportive piece I have yet composed, especially the last movement. I have not yet decided on the *Adagio*, and think I shall reserve it for Naples."

Despite the obvious enthusiasm which gripped Mendelssohn when he wrote these words, the symphony proved to be an elusive, worrisome project. Eleven months later, this time from Paris, Mendelssohn again wrote to Fanny, informing her that the symphony was proving troublesome and that he had put it aside temporarily. Finally in March of 1833, in Berlin, the score was completed. The Royal Philharmonic Society of London played the premiere of the symphony the following May, led by the composer.

But still Mendelssohn was not satisfied with the piece, and he set about revising it. From Düsseldorf in June 1834 Mendelssohn wrote to his friends, Ignaz and Charlotte Moscheles:

> The other day, Dr. Frank, whom you know, came to Düsseldorf, and I wished to show him something of my A Major Symphony. Not having it here, I began writing out the *Andante* again, and in so doing I came across so many errata that I got interested and wrote out the *Minuet* and *Finale*, too, but with many necessary alterations. . . . The first Movement I have not written down, because if once I begin with that, I am afriad I shall have to alter the entire subject, beginning with the fourth bar—and that means pretty nearly the whole first part—and I have no time for that just now.

Years passed and still Mendelssohn did not submit the symphony to his publisher. It was not until 1849, two years after Mendelssohn's death, that the revised version of the score was performed for the first time; and two years after that it was finally published. The great English musicologist, pianist and teacher, Sir Donald Francis Tovey, made a careful study of the symphony in an attempt to discover wherein lay Mendelssohn's dissatisfaction with it. Tovey came away convinced that nowhere could Mendelssohn have improved upon it. In common with the other first-rate works by this composer—the Violin Concerto, the music for A *Midsummer Night's Dream*, or the *Introduction and Rondo Capriccioso* for piano solo—there is about the "Italian" Symphony a feeling of inevitability, as though it had existed in some time capsule which Mendelssohn merely came upon and opened up.

The first movement is marked *Allegro vivace* and the opening is quite stunning: a loud string pizzicato followed by a throbbing rhythm in the woodwinds and then immediately the joyous first theme erupting out of the violins. The second subject, of a more gentle nature, is given to the clarinets. The development section is introduced by yet a third principal theme which is then treated fugally. The second movement, *Andante con moto*, is introduced by a brief and melancholy figure and then the principal theme makes its first appearance in the upper strings and the winds. The lower strings have a "walking bass" figure that throbs underneath the main melodic material throughout the movement, giving it the character of a slow march. Indeed, the movement has been likened to a Pilgrims' March. The third movement, *Con moto moderato*, is in everything but name a Minuet. Especially enchanting is the Trio section, which has the horns blowing an elfin call. The Finale, *Presto*, is a rollicking saltarello which has three main themes, the last of them suggestive of another Italian dance, the tarantella. The prevailing mood is one of exuberant good spirits.

The performance of the symphony that Columbia recorded at an actual concert at the summertime Marlboro Festival in Marlboro, Vermont, with Pablo Casals conducting the Marlboro Festival Orchestra (Columbia MS 6931) is one of the gems in recorded literature. Casals invests the music with a sparkling vitality and *élan* that are quite unique. The recorded sound is not of the very best, but it cannot detract from the glories of the performance. Also recommendable are the performances conducted by Bernstein (Columbia MS 6050), Munch (RCA LSC 2221), Steinberg (Pickwick S 4027), Szell (Columbia MS 6975) and Toscanini (RCA VICS 1341).

Of the versions available in multiple format, Maazel's is perhaps the better all-round recommendation (DGG 138684; tape L 8684; cassette 923013).

Modest Moussorgsky

Born: Karevo, Ukraine, March 21, 1839
Died: St. Petersburg, March 28, 1881

Moussorgsky was the youngest son of a formerly well-to-do land-owner who had fallen upon bad times. In an autobiographical sketch dictated to a nurse during the course of his final illness, Moussorgsky related that it was the Russian fairy tales that he learned as a very young boy that impelled him to improvise music even before he had learned the rudimentary elements of piano playing. His first formal piano teacher was his mother, but in composition he was largely self-taught. Before he was twenty he had already composed a sub-stantial number of songs. He came to know the composer Dargo-mizhsky and as a young officer in the Russian army he was intro-duced by another composer, César Cui, to the founding father of the Russian nationalist school of composition, Balakirev.

Moussorgsky lived in St. Petersburg as a minor State official, his life a constant struggle with poverty, depression and drink. One of the brighter spots in an otherwise rather grim existence was a tour he made to southern Russia in 1879 as piano accompanist to a singer. He died, at the age of forty-two, in the Nikolai Military Hospital at St. Petersburg.

Moussorgsky was largely unappreciated by his contemporaries, but his fame increased steadily after his death. He was perhaps the most original of the Russian nationalist composers and the father of the movement for anti-formalism and expression by means of folk idioms. Expression and character portrayal are vividly delin-eated in Moussorgsky's music, especially in his many songs, most of them grim and somewhat mordant. His two principal works are the stupendous operas *Boris Godounov* and *Khovantchina*. *Boris Godounov* was produced originally in St. Petersburg in 1874 but it was withdrawn after a few performances. Fifteen years after Moussorgsky's death the opera was revised by Rimsky-Korsakov, who added to it his brilliant orchestration and smoothed down what he considered were "uncouth" qualities. In the Rimsky-Korsakov edition *Boris Godounov* made its way over the opera stages of the world and made a profound impression. The opera is most originally conceived, with the people as the main protagonists and the chorus the featured performers; the title role, though a tour de force for a powerful singing-actor, is a relatively brief part. Not until 1925 was the original Moussorgsky orchestration and conception of the folk drama published and eagerly performed in Europe and the United States. In more recent years there have been adaptations of the Moussorgsky original by various musicians, including Karol Rathaus and Dmitri Shostakovich.

Other smaller operatic works by Moussorgsky are *The Marriage* (1868)—a one-act score based on the comedy by Gogol; and *The Fair at Sorotchinski*, which Moussorgsky only partially completed and which was finished by Tcherepnine. Moussorgsky's best-known orchestral piece is the symphonic poem A *Night on Bald Mountain*, much revised by Rimsky-Korsakov.

PICTURES AT AN EXHIBITION

Russian intellectual circles were shocked in 1873 when the painter and architect Victor Hartmann died suddenly at the age of thirty-nine. Hartmann was a member of the group whose mentor was the composer Mily Balakirev; others in the group were the writer Vladimir Stassov and the thirty-five-year-old composer Modest Moussorgsky. Soon after Hartmann's death, Stassov organized a showing of his watercolors and sketches, and this was the exhibition, these the pictures, that stimulated Moussorgsky to write the suite of piano pieces called *Pictures at an Exhibition*, whose orchestral transcription by Maurice Ravel has become so familiar a part of the symphonic repertoire.

Although the score, dedicated to Stassov, was dated 1874, the work was not published until 1886, some five years after one last indiscretion with a bottle of brandy in his hospital bed had ended Moussorgsky's life. Since then, various transcriptions have been made—by Sir Henry Wood, Lucien Cailliet and Leopold Stokowski, among others. As an English critic wrote, many years ago, *Pictures at an Exhibition* "almost asks for orchestration, for implicit in the original are coloristic and dramatic effects that transcend the capacities of the pianoforte." But during recent years, the one orchestral version that has gained precedence over all the others, and that has come to be regarded as truly inspired, is the transcription made by Maurice Ravel, on commission from Serge Koussevitzky, who gave it its premiere in May 1923 in Paris. This is the version with which we are concerned for the purpose of this evaluation.

There are, in all, ten sections, or pictures, in the suite, framed and related to each other by a theme called "Promenade." In the permutations of this theme, according to Stassov, "the composer . . . portrays himself walking, now right, now left, now as an idle looker, now urged to go close to a picture; at times his joyous appearance is shadowed, and he thinks in sadness of his dead friend. . . ." Here is the order of the sections, along with brief notes on the fanciful pictures to which they relate:

Promenade—Moussorgsky himself wrote that his "own physiognomy peeps out through all the intermezzos." The "Promenade" theme, in a characteristically Russian rhythm, makes its first appearance at the very beginning in a confident and assertive manner.

Gnomus—A grotesque dwarf shaped like a nutcracker drags himself along on his twisted legs and utters little shrieks. The awkward jumps in the music and the clumsy, crawling movements with which these are interspersed are forcefully suggested. (This is followed by the "Promenade" theme again, this time meditative.)

The Old Castle—A minstrel sings in front of an old castle. Moussorgsky seems to linger over this particular picture in a dream-like fascination. Ravel, in his orchestration, calls upon the saxophone to speak the nostalgic melody. (The "Promenade" theme which returns again at the end of this picture comes in boldly at first and then subsides.)

Tuileries—An alley in the famous French gardens, with nurses and children chattering. Moussorgsky has caught a plaintive quality in the children's voices; Ravel orchestrates them for high woodwinds.

Bydlo—A Polish oxcart lumbers past on its huge wheels. There is a huge crescendo as the wagon approaches, and a long decrescendo as it disappears off in the distance. Departing from the expected, Ravel scores the music with a prominent tuba solo depicting the approach and disappearance of the cart. (The following "Promenade" theme is again meditative.)

Ballet of the Unhatched Chicks—Hartmann had made sketches for the sets and costumes of the ballet *Trilbi*, which was performed at the St. Petersburg Bolshoi Theater in 1871. The sketches described in the catalog for the Hartmann exhibition show canaries "enclosed in eggs as in suits of armor. Instead of a head-dress, canary heads, put on like helmets, down to the neck." Also included in the stage personages was a "canary-notary-public, in a cap of straight feathers" and "cockatoos: gray and green."

Samuel Goldenberg and Schmuyle—In 1868 Hartmann spent a month in the Polish community of Sandomierz sketching inhabitants in the Jewish section. This is the only movement in Moussorgsky's original piano score that does not bear a title; rather, it was the composer's friend, the critic and historian Stassov, who put the two names on this character portrait. Hartmann, apparently, had called the two sketches that inspired this movement simply "A rich Jew wearing a fur hat: Sandomierz" and "A poor Sandomierz Jew." The Russo-German writer and critic Oscar von Risemann, called this number "one of the most amusing caricatures in all music—the two Jews, one rich and comfortable and correspondingly close-fisted, laconic in talk, and slow in movement, the other poor and hungry, restlessly and fussily fidgeting and chatting, but without making the slightest impression on his partner, are musically depicted with a keen eye for characteristic and comic effect. These two types of the Warsaw Ghetto stand plainly before you—you seem to hear the caftan of one of them blown out by the wind, and the flap of the other's ragged fur coat. Moussorgsky's musical power of observation scores a triumph with this unique musical joke; he proves that he can 'reproduce the intonations of human speech' not only for the voice, but also on the piano." Ravel, for his part, casts the words of the prosperous Jew in the low strings in unison, while his whining neighbor is characterized by the muted trumpet.

Limoges—The market place at Limoges, with women haggling furiously. The catalog of the Hartmann exhibition lists no fewer than seventy-five different sketches of the Limoges locale—obviously, it exerted a strong fascination upon the painter. Moussorgsky perfectly paints a picture in sound of a bustling hot spot, and Ravel's orchestration, with its pulsating horns and throbbing strings, complements the scene superbly.

Catacombs—The ancient burial vaults, their mystery and associations with death. Above one section in the original score Moussorgsky had written: "The creative spirit of the dead Hartmann leads me towards skulls, apostrophizes them—the skulls are illuminated gently from within." The "Promenade" theme returns once more after this portrait; it begins in a melancholy mood, but ends rather hopefully in the major.

The Hut on Fowl's Legs—The catalog lists this Hartmann drawing as "Baba Yaga's hut on hens' legs. Clock, Russian style of the 14th century. Bronze and enamel." Baba Yaga was the witch of Russian folklore and the subject of the Hartmann drawing suggested to Moussorgsky Baba Yaga herself, flying along in a pestle, propelling herself by a mortar. The music is angular and colorful, especially in Ravel's rich churnings of woodwinds, brass and strings.

The Great Gate at Kiev—The concluding section grows immediately out of *The Hut on Fowl's Legs* without pause. Hartmann had created six sketches for a projected new massive set of gates for the city of Kiev. The archway rests on granite pillars sunk into the ground. The head is decorated with a huge piece of Russian carved design, with the Russian imperial eagle high above the peak. To the right is a three-story-high belfry, with a cupola in the shape of a Russian helmet. Moussorgsky has contrived a final movement of overpowering majesty, and Ravel meets him on equal ground with a tour de force of brilliant orchestral sound. At the very end, the "Promenade" theme rings out grandly for the last time.

Ever since the early 1950s, the Ravel transcription of *Pictures at an Exhibition* has served as a muscle-flexing exercise for conductors and recording engineers. The recording that started it all was Mercury's initial entry into the field of modern high fidelity recording of symphonic music; that historic performance was played by the Chicago Symphony Orchestra conducted by Rafael Kubelik (Mercury 18028, 14028) and its success was striking: the performance had a thrilling combination of poetic sensitivity and crackling drama.

The next great recording of the score to come along was the one by Arturo Toscanini and the NBC Symphony Orchestra (RCA Victrola VIC 1273, mono only). In one of his very best recorded performances, the Maestro left us a *Pictures* of enormous vitality and color. At one time there was also an electronically processed stereo version of the performance available (RCA LME 2410), but it is just as well that it has been withdrawn: an illusion of stereo separation was created, but the acoustics were harsher than in the original monophonic release, and there were obtrusive spots of overloading distortion. It has since been reissued (RCA LSC 3278) in improved electronic stereo sound.

Among the very many more recent recorded performances of the score, my own two favorites are those by Ansermet (London CS 6177) and Ozawa (RCA LSC 2977; tape TR3 5043, 3¾ ips). Both conductors apply fertile musical imaginations to their performances and both are stunningly recorded. Ansermet's is actually his third try at *Pictures at an Exhibition* in a relatively short period of time. His two earlier efforts were rather small-scale and inhibited, but all is corrected in this last version with all the fire and vigor one could wish, mated to a fine sense of dignity and genuine sensitivity. Ansermet's is also an excellent tape release of the music (London K 800054).

Recent exercises in stereo wizardry offer vivid recordings by Bernstein (Columbia MS 6080; tape MQ 538) and Baudo (Angel 5 36683; cassette 4XS 36683).

It also should be mentioned that a heady performance of Leopold Stokowski's orchestration of the Moussorgsky piano original has been recorded by the New Philharmonia Orchestra under Stokowski's direction (London SPC-21006, cassette M 94006). This performance will give much enjoyment as a supplementary recording of the music after you have secured either Ansermet's or Ozawa's performance of the Ravel transcription; Stokowski's transcription is more garish in places than Ravel's, but it has a validity all its own—if you can forgive Stokowski his sin of omitting the *Tuileries*, and *Limoges* sections from the gallery of pictures. The playing and recording are both extraordinary and a fine taped version of the release is also available (London L 75006).

Wolfgang Amadeus Mozart

Born: Salzburg, January 27, 1756
Died: Vienna, December 5, 1791

Wolfgang Amadeus Mozart is one of the principal divinities of
music. At the age of three his precocity piqued the curiosity of his
father, who began to teach him the fundamentals of music. At once
he began to compose little minuets which his father and later he
himself noted down. When he was barely six, he and his sister
Maria Anna (called "Nannerl"), who was five years his senior, made
a joint debut in Munich. Later that same year he also appeared in
Vienna and taught himself the violin and organ. When he was seven,
he spent some time in Paris and it was there that his first pieces
were published (a series of sonatas for clavier). The next year he
was in London and he proceeded to delight the royal family, astound
musicians and overwhelm the public with his remarkable ability as
a sight reader and improviser. His father became seriously ill during
this London sojourn and while silence was required to ease the
recuperation, young Mozart composed his first symphony. Other
works followed, he became friendly with Johann Christian Bach and
he took singing lessons. Before leaving England he wrote a motet to
English words in commemoration of a visit to the British Museum.

On the way back from England the family stopped at various
cities en route and the children performed at royal courts to great
success. One such performance was given in Amsterdam in 1766,
at which all the instrumental music was Mozart's. Back home at
Salzburg, in 1767, he composed an oratorio and in the following year
an opera, *La Finta Semplice*, at the request of the Emperor. Production of the opera was postponed for a year, however, because of
rising jealousies among the musicians of the court. In the meantime,
another opera—this one in German—*Bastien und Bastienne*, had

been performed and Mozart had made his conducting debut in 1768 at the age of twelve.

In his early teens Mozart spent some time studying and giving concerts in Italy. He was a sensation; the Pope gave him the Order of the Golden Spur, an honor that carried with it the title Signor Cavaliere Amadeo. At his father's behest Mozart even signed some of his compositions with this new title, but he soon dropped it. After tests he was elected a member of the Accademia Filarmonica of Bologna. At the age of fourteen he gave a concert at Mantua in which the program promised that he would play

a Symphony of his own composition; a Clavichord Concerto, which will be handed to him and which he will immediately play at sight; a Sonata handed him in like manner, which he will provide with variations and afterwards repeat in another key; an Aria, the words for which will be handed to him and which he will immediately set to music and sing himself, accompanying himself on the clavichord; a Sonata for clavichord on a subject given him by the leader of the violins; a Strict Fugue on a theme to be selected, which he will improvise on the clavichord; a trio, in which he will execute a violin part *all' improvviso*; and finally, the latest Symphony composed by himself.

In Rome, after twice hearing the long-suppressed Miserere by the seventeenth-century composer Allegri, he correctly wrote out the entire score from memory. At Milan in 1770 he produced his opera *Mitridate, re di Ponto*, which had twenty consecutive performances under his direction.

In 1772 there was a sudden wrench in the direction of Mozart's life. His beneficent protector, the Archbishop of Salzburg, died and he was succeeded by Hieronymous, Count of Colloredo, who was despotic and tyrannical in his attitude toward Mozart; though the crowned heads of Europe competed with one another in their wish to extend every possible courtesy to the young genius, at home Mozart was treated with the greatest disdain and compelled by the new Archbishop to sit with the servants. Works from this period include his first piano concerto; music for a heroic drama, *Thamos, King of Egypt*; several masses; a bassoon concerto; and three stage works: *Il Sogno di Scipione* (1775), *Lucio Silla* (1772) and *La Finta Giardiniera* (1775).

Mozart and his mother journeyed to Paris in 1778 by way of Mannheim and other cities. In Mannheim he became enchanted with the superb orchestra that was resident there and he composed an astonishing number of works during a brief few months' stay, including a number of soprano arias; two flute concertos; several violin and piano sonatas; and two piano sonatas. In Mannheim also he met and fell in love with Aloysia Weber, a gifted soprano. The affair was apparently a profound one, and Mozart even considered taking Aloysia to Italy and composing a new opera for her debut there. Alarmed by the seriousness of his son's attachment, Leopold Mozart wrote to him from Salzburg: "Off with you to Paris, and that immediately! Take up your position among those who are really great. . . . From Paris the name and fame of a man of talent spread throughout the world." Mozart reluctantly acceded to his father's wish and left Aloysia behind in Mannheim.

Paris at that time was gripped in a struggle between the opposing forces of Gluck and Piccini and in this environment Mozart was able to make little impact. He gave lessons, composed a few works, including the Concerto for Flute and Harp and a sinfonia concertante for four solo woodwind instruments and orchestra, but in general the Paris sojourn was not a happy time for Mozart. It ended in disaster—his mother died in his arms and he was left desolate. There was nothing to do but return to Salzburg. He made his way back slowly, however, and stopped again at Mannheim on the return trip and also at Munich, where the Webers were now staying. If he had entertained hopes of rekindling the romance with Aloysia, they were quickly dashed, for she now paid him little attention.

It was therefore a thoroughly dejected Mozart who returned to Salzburg in the middle of January 1779. He was welcomed by his friends and colleagues with open arms but the life imposed upon him by the hated Archbishop soon made his situation there intolerable. Despite this, however, he continued to produce one masterpiece after another, including masses and other music for the church; his Symphonies 33 and 34; the *Sinfonia Concertante* for Violin, Viola and Orchestra; and a concerto for two pianos and orchestra. When he demanded in 1781 that he be released from his obligations to Salzburg, the Archbishop had him kicked out (literally!) by a servant.

A new opera, *Idomeneo, Re di Creta,* was produced in Munich later that year for the Carnival. Then in March he traveled to Vienna. Except for a few brief excursions here and there, Vienna was to remain Mozart's home for the rest of his life. In July of 1781 his opera *The Abduction from the Seraglio* was produced. During this period he also composed his "Haffner" Symphony and C Minor Serenade for wind instruments. Before the year was out, Mozart was married to Constanze Weber, the sister of Aloysia. The marriage produced six children, four sons and two daughters.

Marriage presented all kinds of problems. As neither Mozart nor Constanze were particularly good money managers, they were constantly plagued by financial crises. To the end of his days Mozart was constantly borrowing money from one friend or another and there were times when he was literally penniless despite a life crowded with composition and performance. In 1786 his little musical comedy *Der Schauspieldirektor* (*The Impresario*) was produced at Schönbrunn and a few months later his great opera buffa *The Marriage of Figaro* was given in Vienna. In the following year came *Don Giovanni,* first produced at Prague and a success from the very beginning. At about this time Gluck died and Mozart had hopes that he would receive an important court appointment as successor to Gluck—one that would free him of his constant money worries. Mozart did receive the designation "court composer," but at a salary that he considered little more than a beggar's dole. He wrote bitterly that he was being paid "too much for what I produce" —(dance music for court balls, etc.)—"and too little for what I could produce."

In 1789 Mozart accompanied Prince Karl Lichnowski to Berlin, playing at the Dresden court and at the Thomaskirche in Leipzig where Bach had served for so many years. King Friedrich Wilhelm II heard him at Potsdam and offered him the position as First Royal Conductor with a rather handsome annual salary. Mozart would not abandon his "good Kaiser" but he did compose three string quartets for Friedrich Wilhelm for which he was well paid. Hearing this,

Mozart's Emperor commissioned a new opera from him and the result, *Così Fan Tutte*, was produced in Vienna in 1790. The Emperor died soon afterward and his successor, Leopold II, had little feeling for music and none at all for Mozart. When Leopold II was to be crowned as King of Bohemia, however, Mozart was commissioned to write the festival opera. *La Clemenza di Tito* thus came into being and it was first performed on the night of the coronation, September 6, 1791.

Returning to Vienna, Mozart hurriedly completed another opera, *The Magic Flute*, that had been occupying his time for some months. During the previous few years Mozart had become a dedicated Freemason and some of the allegories of Masonry figure prominently in the opera. Its first performance in Vienna at the end of September was a triumph, but Mozart's health was now failing. He suffered from fainting fits and a generally weakened condition and he himself claimed that he had been poisoned and his life was slowly ebbing away. The situation was not helped any by the appearance, a few months earlier, of a mysterious stranger who insisted on anonymity and who commissioned Mozart to compose a Requiem. Mozart accepted the commission but he brooded that the messenger had come from the other world to announce his death. Mozart worked on the Requiem in the late months of 1791 but he was unable to complete it before he fell desperately ill with malignant typhus fever. His mind was constantly on the Requiem and when he realized that he would die before finishing it, he burst into tears and put the score away. On the evening of December 4, 1791, he was visited by his pupil Süssmayer, whom he gave some directions about the Requiem, and then he dozed off. Toward midnight he suddenly sat erect in bed with his eyes fixed straight ahead; then he turned his head to one side and lay back. Within an hour he was dead, seven weeks short of his thirty-sixth birthday.

The mysterious stranger who came to Mozart to commission the Requiem from him was subsequently unmasked as Leutgeb, the steward of Count Walsegg. The Count, it seems, was anxious to be considered a great composer and he commissioned the Requiem from Mozart with the intention of submitting it to the world as his own creation. This he in fact did do but he neglected to destroy the manuscript and so the whole unsavory business became common knowledge. The portions that Mozart did not live to complete were filled in by Süssmayer.

In the midst of Mozart's funeral a violent rainstorm engulfed the proceedings and the funeral party fled for shelter, leaving the coffin to be buried, unaccompanied, in a common pauper's grave in the churchyard of St. Marx. Mozart's actual burial site has never been discovered.

During his lifetime Mozart produced an astonishing abundance of music—more than six hundred works embracing all musical forms: symphony, opera, concerto, chamber, song, sonatas and incidental pieces. The cataloguing of all this music presented a nightmare to musical scholars until the nineteenth-century writer, botanist and mineralogist, Ludwig Köchel, devoted years to compiling a chrono-logical-thematic catalog of all Mozart's music. The letter K., used to identify any given Mozart piece, refers to its numerical place in Köchel's catalog.

CONCERTO NO. 20 IN D MINOR FOR PIANO, K. 466

During the last half of the eighteenth century the city of Vienna had already asserted her primacy as the world capital of the per-forming arts—a position she was to hold for a century and a half. Vienna hummed throughout the year with concert, operatic and theatrical activity, drawing to the city the leading figures from all those spheres of endeavor.

As rich and varied as Vienna's normal concert life was, it was intensified during the Lenten season because the theaters remained closed. Enterprising concert managers and performers saved their biggest and most important attractions for the Lenten period, when sizable audiences could be counted on for patronage. One of the busiest of Vienna's Lenten-time musicians during the early 1780s was Mozart. It was not unusual for Mozart to give a concert every week, at which at least one new work of his would be performed. It was at one such concert, in February 1785, that he played the first performance of his Piano Concerto No. 20 in D Minor.

The composer's father, Leopold, was spending some time in Vienna during that period visiting his son and daughter-in-law. After the first performance of the concerto, Leopold wrote glowingly to his daughter Maria Anna:

A great number of persons of rank were assembled. The concert was incomparable, the orchestra most excellent. In addition to the symphonies, a female singer from the Italian theater sang two arias, and then came the magnificent new clavier concerto by Wolfgang.

Leopold Mozart had additional reasons for parental pride during that sojourn. One evening none other than the great Franz Josef Haydn came to the Mozart residence on the Schulerstrasse to play first violin in three new string quartets Mozart had recently completed and dedicated to Haydn. After the session Haydn turned to the elder Mozart and said: "I tell you before God, and as an honest man, that your son is the greatest composer I know, either personally or by name. He has taste and apart from that the greatest science in composition."

Had Haydn been present in Vienna at the time of the first performance of Mozart's D Minor Piano Concerto, his admiration for the younger man would doubtless have been increased. The *Sturm und Drang* of the concerto is to be found in much of Haydn's own work, and it certainly points the way toward the storm-tossed, impassioned music of the nineteenth century.

Only two of Mozart's concertos for solo piano are in a minor key: the D Minor (K. 466) and the C Minor (K. 491). The key of D minor called forth from Mozart some of his most anguished and deeply felt music—witness this concerto, the String Quartet in D Minor (K. 421) and the opera *Don Giovanni*. As was to happen a couple of years later in *Don Giovanni*, the piano concerto ends in the sunshine blaze of D major, thus capping the whole in a transcendental burst of radiant joy.

The D Minor is one of no fewer than fifteen piano concertos that Mozart composed between the years 1782 and 1786. The half dozen that were ushered in by the D Minor Concerto are among the sovereign creations of Western civilization. In the words of C. M.

Girdlestone in his authoritative and exhaustive labor of love, *Mozart and His Piano Concertos*, the concertos of 1785–86 belong

at the summit of Mozart's concertos. One cannot make a selection, even a small one, of what is most valuable and most characteristic in his production, of what is most living and most his own, without bringing in every concerto of these two years. With as much right as his three great symphonies, his finest quartets and quintets, his best operas, his C Minor and *Requiem* Masses, the Concerto in D Minor and the five that follow it may claim to represent him at his highest point of creative power.

In accordance with established tradition of the period, the first movement, *Allegro*, begins with a long presentation of essential musical materials by the orchestra alone. The Mozart scholar Eric Blom described the opening as a "shudder" and further stated that the movement "is full of unhappy commotion." The brief brightness of the second theme, starting in F major but then moving back to the "home" key of D minor, is characterized by Blom "as though a false promise of relief were mockingly revealing itself as a tragic delusion." When the piano enters, it takes up the first theme and then the second and there is a lengthy treatment of both and a considerable development of the material. Before the cadenza occurs, there is an impassioned orchestral climax, and after the cadenza the movement ends restlessly but quietly.

The slow movement, the *Romanze*, begins with a simple, liquid theme stated at the outset by the solo piano. This melody will recur throughout the movement. It is echoed by the orchestra and before long a second theme is introduced, again first in the piano and then repeated by the orchestra. After a return to the first theme, there is a tempestuous outburst in both piano and orchestra that Blom called "a sudden fit of raving despair." Following this "wild episode," the peace and serenity of the first theme returns and the movement subsides into a gentle, lyrical conclusion.

The last movement is a rondo Finale marked *Allegro assai*. Again, as in the second movement, the first theme is stated by the unaccompanied piano, then the orchestra takes it over. A sunny second theme in F major is introduced, but then the darker color of D minor returns, only for the movement to erupt into the cheerful tonality of D major at the end, with trumpet flourishes to punctuate the conclusion. "After all," wrote Blom, "Mozart remembered this was a concerto, a piece meant to entertain. Feeling that he had done enough to startle his polite hearers with his most impassioned music, he relieved them at the end and let them go away emotionally relaxed."

There was a time, not too many years ago, when the D Minor Concerto was not just *a* Mozart piano concerto but *the* Mozart piano concerto, which is to say that it alone among the composer's prodigious output in the form had made a place for itself in the active concert repertoire. The D Minor has now been joined by at least half a dozen of its companions as contemporary pianists have expanded the boundaries of the "basic repertoire." It remains, however, the most-recorded of the Mozart piano concertos and is represented in current catalogs by several excellent recordings.

The recording with Barenboim conducting the English Chamber Orchestra from the keyboard (Angel S 36430) conveys to me more of the intensity and drama of this concerto than any other version available—this despite some less than perfect ensemble between piano and orchestra. Barenboim's is a superbly committed performance, with meticulous attention to phrasing and dynamics and a broad sweep to the entire conception. Conducting the English Chamber Orchestra from the keyboard, Barenboim proves once and for all that he is one of the leading musical performers of our time, regardless of age (he was still in his early twenties when this recording was made). Helping no little is the crystal-clear recorded sound provided by the recording engineers. Clearly this is a triumph for all concerned. Rubinstein's (RCA LSC 2635)— in the absence of the now withdrawn Clara Haskil recordings—would be my second choice. Just below these two I would place the Ashkenazy performance, available in all three configurations (London CS 6579; tape L 80214; cassette M 10214). The cassette version of Ashkenazy's performance should be checked carefully prior to purchase, however: an entire production run of this cassette came

out with the Mehta-Los Angeles Philharmonic performance of
Stravinsky's *Petrouchka* on tape that was supposed to contain the
Ashkenazy performances of Mozart's Piano Concertos No. 6 and
No. 20! Denis Matthews (Vanguard Everyman S 142), one of the
most underrated pianists of our time, performs the D Minor Concerto in a bold and forthright manner, with a broad line and
careful dynamic balance. Rudolf Serkin (Columbia MS 6534) delivers an unusually satisfying account of the score; gone is the
hysteria that marked an earlier recording he made of the music with
Eugene Ormandy and the Philadelphia Orchestra; it is replaced
by a polished poise that gives his performance a new dimension of
subtlety, particularly in the slow movement.

QUINTET IN A MAJOR FOR CLARINET AND STRINGS, K. 581

During the last third of the eighteenth century, musical activities at
the court of Mannheim were the envy of the whole continent. Carl
Theodor, Duke of Mannheim, was himself a trained musician and
brought to his service an impressive array of outstanding composers,
conductors and performers. Indeed, the orchestra at Mannheim
may be said to have laid the foundation for our contemporary
virtuoso symphony orchestras: in 1772 the English musicologist
Charles Burney referred to the Mannheim group as "an army of
generals."

In 1777 the twenty-one-year-old Mozart visited Mannheim during
the course of a concert tour. Not unexpectedly, he was bowled over
by the quality of the orchestra, especially by the exotic sound of
the two clarinets. "Oh, if only we had clarinets," Mozart wrote to his
father. "You cannot guess the lordly effect of a symphony with
flutes, oboes, and clarinets."

Mozart lost little time in employing just such a "lordly effect" in
composition. On a visit to Paris the following year he was invited
to provide a symphony for the season's opening of the brilliant
orchestra of the Concerts Spirituels, which prided itself on the excel-

lence of its wind players. Finding clarinets at hand, Mozart eagerly included them in the scoring of his new Symphony in D Major (K. 297), the "Paris" Symphony.

From its dawning in this charming work, the romance between Mozart and the clarinet persisted throughout the composer's life. Whenever he was afforded an opportunity to score for clarinet, he invariably did so. But the clarinet was still so new during Mozart's time that its availability was the exception rather than the rule. Sometimes, as in the great G Minor Symphony of 1788, he produced two versions of a work, one with and one without clarinets.

From 1781 to 1791, the last decade of his life, Mozart lived in Vienna. The court orchestra had a superb first clarinetist named Anton Stadler, with whom Mozart soon developed a close friendship. From Stadler Mozart learned the capacities and the limitations of the instrument and for him he composed a series of works that explored the clarinet's resources with wondrous perception and penetration. Among them are the Trio in E-flat Major for Clarinet, Viola and Piano (K. 498), the Clarinet Concerto in A Major (K. 622) and the Quintet in A Major for Clarinet and String Quartet (K. 581).

Alfred Einstein, the late Mozart scholar, in his study of the composer, *Mozart*, writes that the Clarinet Quintet is "a chamber music work of the finest kind, even though the clarinet predominates as *primus inter pares*. . . . There is no dualism here between solo and accompaniment, only fraternal rivalry." I have long felt that the Clarinet Quintet, with its clarity, long-breathed melodies, pages of hushed pathos and final rollicking good spirits, is the ideal introduction to the rarefied atmosphere of the chamber-music literature. Few can help but love this work, and from it relatively simple steps lead to Mozart's other chamber music, to the quartets of Haydn, to the early Beethoven quartets, and so *per ardua ad astra*.

The Clarinet Quintet is in four movements: an opening *Allegro* that emphasizes the general agility of the clarinet; a *Larghetto* of sustained, soaring melodic invention; a Minuet and Trio that actually has two trios, the first written for the strings alone, the second for the clarinet, with the strings accompanying; and a concluding Theme and Variations that is a kaleidoscope of shifting moods ending in a playful romp.

For years during the 1930s and 1940s the standard recorded performance of the quintet was Benny Goodman's with the Budapest String Quartet, an RCA Victor 78-rpm album. The recording was made at the height of his fame as the "King of Swing," but nowhere did Goodman permit himself the freewheeling geniality and warmth that made great experiences of such swing classics as "Don't Be That Way," "One O'Clock Jump," or "Sing, Sing, Sing." Rather, perhaps cowed by the "serious" milieu, Goodman adopted a deadpan performing demeanor that resulted in ennui. Goodman has twice recorded the score for LP, once with the American Art Quartet from California (Columbia ML 4483), and, later still, with the Boston Symphony String Quartet (RCA VICS 1402). Unhappily, both reveal the same inhibitions as the oldest one; only the RCA disc is still available.

Another clarinetist who has recorded the quintet three times is the distinguished English musician Reginald Kell. His first performance, with the Philharmonia String Quartet, had a brief currency in this country on Columbia toward the end of the 78-rpm era. It was an alert, sensitive performance, deeply felt and beautifully recorded. Kell's two subsequent performances of the music on LP—with the Fine Arts String Quartet (Decca DL 9600, and a later performance, Concert-Disc 203)—are noticeably more superficial. His playing is technically superb, however, and the stereo version of the Concert-Disc performance offers remarkably transparent sound.

Of the remaining performances currently available, my own favorites are the recordings by Alfred Boskovsky and members of the Vienna Octet (London CS 6379) and Gervase dePeyer and the Melos Ensemble of England (Angel S 36241). Both are warm, sensitive readings that leave something to be desired by way of spontaneity, but they both are expertly played and recorded and either will give lasting pleasure.

Apparently the Boskovsky-Vienna Octet version is the only one available on tape (London L 80145). It is worth having. There is no cassette version of any performance listed.

SINFONIA CONCERTANTE IN E-FLAT MAJOR
FOR VIOLIN AND VIOLA, K. 364

Mozart spent nearly all of his thirty-five years of life wandering over the face of Europe—first as an exploited child prodigy of the piano and violin, later as the composer of some of the most popular musical "hits" of the day. In September 1777, less than four months before his twenty-second birthday, Mozart and his mother set out on a journey that was to be perhaps the most important in his life. For even though he was to return two years later to Salzburg, the city of his birth, this journey represented the real dissolution of the ties that bound Mozart to the city and society that he hated.

The departure of mother and son was an unhappy one. The original plan was that the whole Mozart family would travel together. At the last moment, however, the despotic Archbishop Hierony-mus insisted that Wolfgang's father, Leopold, remain in Salzburg to fulfill his duties as court composer and Vice Kapellmeister. The son's ebulliency at "escaping" from an intolerable environment was tempered by having to leave his father and sister behind.

The travelers went first to Munich, where Mozart immediately became much in demand as a performer. His attempts to obtain a permanent appointment in the city failed, however, and so the two moved on to Mannheim, intending to stay there only a brief time. But because of the attractions of the city, social as well as musical, Mozart and his mother remained there much longer than they had anticipated. The seat of the Court of the Elector Palatine Karl Theodor, Mannheim had the most advanced orchestra in all Europe, one that was famous for its virtuoso wind players. The Mannheim orchestra was capable of a wide dynamic range, and the "Mannheim crescendo" was one of the musical wonders of the day. Mozart quickly became a member of Mannheim's inner musical circle and spent many a pleasant hour with the city's musicians. In Mannheim, too, Mozart fell in love with the young and talented soprano Aloysia Weber, and considered journeying with her to Italy to compose a new opera for her debut appearance. When Leopold, back in Salzburg, heard about this, he quickly dispatched a letter to his son urging him to forget such romantic nonsense and to set out immediately for Paris, where fame and fortune might await him.

Reluctantly, Mozart heeded the advice of his father, and on March 23, 1778, he and his mother arrived in Paris. The next months were busy with composition: among the works he produced were the Flute and Harp Concerto (K. 299); the ballet *Les Petits Riens* (K. Anh. 10): the *Sinfonia Concertante* for Flute, Oboe, Horn and Bassoon (K. Anh. 9); and the "Paris" Symphony (K. 297). Then suddenly Mozart's mother, who had been ailing ever since they had arrived in Paris, became desperately ill, and on the third of July she died in her son's arms. With her death one phase of Mozart's life came to an end; grieving over her loss, he knew that he would have to return to Salzburg. He took his time about it, however, and did not leave Paris until the end of September. He retraced some of the route that had brought him to Paris from Salzburg, stopping off in Mannheim, and then in Munich to visit Aloysia. Alas, since he had seen her the year before, she had married "a jealous fool"— Mozart's words—and now seemed quite indifferent to him. So Mozart returned to the home of his childhood in January 1779, mourning the loss of his mother, disappointed in love and with bleak prospects for the future.

Such misfortunes would be more than enough to sap the creative energies of the ordinary man. But Mozart was not ordinary. Shortly after he returned home, he composed his *Sinfonia Concertante* for Violin, Viola and Orchestra (K. 364), one of his most divinely inspired creations. The eminent musicologist Alfred Einstein called the score "Mozart's crowning achievement in the field of the violin concerto." In it, he continued,

Mozart summed up what he had accomplished in the concertante portions of his serenades, adding what he had learned of the monumental style in Mannheim and Paris, and, most important of all, treating all his materials with the personal and artistic maturity which he had by this time reached. . . . The living unity of each of the three movements, organic in every detail, and the complete vitality of the whole orchestra, in which every instrument speaks its own language:

the oboes, the horns, and all the strings, with the divided violas enhancing the richness and warmth of the texture—all this is truly Mozartean. So is the intimate conversation of the two soloists, rising in the Andante to the level of eloquent dialogue.

The first movement, *Allegro maestoso*, begins with an orchestral statement notably eloquent and dignified. There is a full-blown development of various musical ideas, and then the orchestra suddenly evaporates and the two soloists are left alone to make their initial entry in octaves, together. For the balance of the movement this equal sharing of the musical material is maintained as the two solo instruments partner one another lovingly. The movement is full of the most inspired melodic writing, and trills, both in the solo instruments and in the orchestra, play an important part in the over-all fabric. The cadenza was written out by Mozart himself. The slow movement, *Andante,* is one of the miracles in all music— a C-minor threnody of such profound passion that it has been suggested that Mozart composed it as a memorial to his mother. The solo instruments amplify and embellish the elegiac mood with great eloquence. In place of a development section, the subject matter is repeated with even more elaborate ornamentation and against a harmonic background of richer textures. The concluding movement, *Presto*, is a lighter, brighter release. In rondo form, the first two sections begin with the same theme stated in the first instance by the solo violin, in the second by the solo viola. The work concludes with a brilliant flourish.

That the *Sinfonia Concertante* has attracted the devoted attentions of many of the leading string players of our day is small wonder. Many recordings of the work are available. As luck would have it, my own favorite recording of the score is now apparently no longer available: a performance by Isaac Stern and William Primrose recorded at one of the first Casals Festivals in the early 1950s with Casals himself conducting (Columbia ML 4564, mono only). This was one of those rare collaborations when all the elements coalesced to produce a reading of the most dedicated and selfless artistry. If this recording is ever reissued by Columbia in its budget-priced Odyssey series, get it!

Stern's re-recording of the score with the London Symphony Orchestra, with Walter Trampler playing the viola part, is now available in two alternate couplings (on Columbia MS 7062, with Mozart's G Major Violin Concerto, and on Columbia MS 7251 with Brahms' Double Concerto—Leonard Rose playing the cello part). There is still a third Stern recording of this score in the offing, with Pinchas Zukerman playing the viola part and Daniel Barenboim conducting the English Chamber Orchestra. If the finished product lives up to the promise of the personalities involved, it well may be the logical successor to the Stern-Primrose-Casals version.

Among the other versions currently available, those that I favor most are the performances by Druian-Skernick-Szell (Columbia MS 6625), Joseph and Lillian Fuchs with Frederic Waldman (Decca 710037), Grumiaux-Pelliccia-Davis (Philips 835256), Heifetz-Primrose-Solomon (RCA Victor LSC 2734) and Menuhin-Barshai with Menuhin leading the Bath Festival Orchestra (Angel S 36190). Each of these is a deeply felt, communicative interpretation, very well played and recorded. The Heifetz-Primrose one may strike some listeners as being a shade too business-like and efficient; on its own terms, however, it is a splendid accomplishment. Similarly, some may find the recorded sound in the Menuhin-Barshai performance a bit too plush for the music. A clear-cut number-one recommendation is difficult to make, but if I were backed to the wall and forced to choose, I would probably nominate the performance conducted by George Szell. The two soloists, the principals of their respective sections in the Cleveland Orchestra at the time the recording was made, are distinguished performers indeed, and yield nothing to their more celebrated recorded rivals; also, as an old orchestral second violinist, I am delighted that Szell and the recording engineers have taken such pains to bring out clearly the all-important second-violin part in this score!

No version is available on cassette, and in the reel-to-reel format, the only currently available performance is the Romantically-inclined version by Igor and David Oistrakh, with Kondrashin leading the Moscow Philharmonic (London K. 80139).

SYMPHONY NO. 35 IN D MAJOR, K. 385, "HAFFNER"

One of the more prominent citizens in the town of Salzburg, Austria, during the latter half of the eighteenth century was Sigmund Haffner, son of a wealthy former burgomaster. In the spring of 1782, Haffner (some authorities have said it was his father, but recent research seems to show that the elder Haffner died in 1772) wanted a serenade for a special festivity, perhaps a celebration of his ennoblement that year, and he apparently asked Leopold Mozart to provide him the music. Leopold, in turn, promptly wrote to his son Wolfgang in Vienna, urging him to compose the score. But the younger Mozart was very busy at the time. He was working on an arrangement for wind band of music from his recently produced opera *The Abduction from the Seraglio*, he was putting the C Minor Serenade for Wind Octet (K. 388) into final form, and his head was full of other plans. Nevertheless, a commission from Haffner was not to be taken lightly. Six years earlier Mozart had composed a large-scale work for the marriage of Haffner's sister Elisabeth; this—the "Haffner" Serenade—had turned out to be a very ambitious project for which the composer was presumably generously paid. Money was a constant problem with Mozart, and never more so than in 1782, the year of his marriage. And so, during two weeks in July, he produced a serenade in six movements for Haffner, and then forgot about the piece.

Six months later Mozart was faced with the need to produce a new symphony for a concert he was to conduct in Vienna. As time was short, he wondered whether there might not be material in the serenade of half a year earlier that he could turn to good use for the new work. In a hastily dispatched letter to his father in Salzburg, Mozart urgently requested the score of the serenade. Another letter to Leopold, written after the score arrived in Vienna, reveals just how casual and offhand Mozart was in the creation of much of his most sublime music. "The new Haffner Symphony has astonished me," he wrote, "for I no longer remembered a word of

it; it must be very effective." He took four of the six original movements of the serenade, added clarinet and flute parts to the existing
scoring for oboes, bassoons, horns, trumpets, tympani and strings,
and came up with the Symphony No. 35 in D Major, one of the
enduring masterpieces of the literature. Because of its origin, the
score has been known as the "Haffner" Symphony almost from its
inception.

At the first performance, on March 22, 1783, the symphony
was loudly applauded and had to be repeated.

The Mozart scholar De Saint-Foix finds in the first movement a
real dramatic impact, "a thematic and harmonic hardness." The
movement, marked *Allegro con spirito*, continuously treats the opening energetic theme for the entire course of the movement. The
gentle charm of the following song-like *Andante* slow movement is
further enhanced by the simple instrumentation: only oboes, bassoons and horns, along with the strings, are allowed to handle
the fragile material. In the Menuetto third movement the trumpets
and drums return to the orchestral fabric and brighten the texture.
The Trio deals with an undulating melody for most of its length.
The Finale, a bright *Presto*, is in a jocular, lighthearted vein. The
constant recurrence of the opening theme of the movement lends
it the feeling of a rondo, but it is in reality in sonata form. In
a letter to his father Mozart wrote that "the first *Allegro* [of the
"Haffner" Symphony] must be fiery ['Recht feurig'], and the last as
quick as possible."

I must begin this discussion of the "Haffner" Symphony recordings with a brief mention of a performance that is no longer available and yet is one of the great landmarks in the history of musical
art—the "Haffner" Symphony recording made in 1929 by Arturo
Toscanini and the New York Philharmonic-Symphony Orchestra.
After countless hearings, this performance still amazes me. Its spirit
is one of exuberant vitality and freshness, the orchestral playing is
sheer perfection (there is one point in the slow movement when
the entire first-violin section phrases in unison like sixteen Fritz
Kreislers), and Toscanini's supreme dedication to the beauty of the
music is apparent everywhere. This recording, originally on 78s, of

course, was reissued on LP for a brief while on the RCA Camden label. Clearly it should be made available again.

Barenboim's absolutely poised and polished performance (Angel S 36512) now carries the day, with Klemperer's more massive approach (Angel S 36128) a stimulating alternative. The tender and caressing Walter performance (Columbia MS 6255) is recommended to those who cherish this conductor's style.

Barenboim's couples two other Mozart symphonies along with the "Haffner"—the No. 32 in G Major and the "Prague," No. 38. As in his conducted-from-the-keyboard performance of the Piano Concerto in D Minor, Barenboim here stands revealed as a Mozart conductor of the front rank. This "Haffner" Symphony performance has elegance, charm and wit. It is played superbly by the English Chamber Orchestra and extremely well recorded by the engineers.

The Klemperer performance may not be to everyone's liking. As is his wont, the conductor endows the music with a larger-than-life monumentality. I find it a stimulating approach, the more so because the playing and the recording are both first-rate.

By now it is certainly a commonplace to remark that Walter injected into his music-making qualities of geniality and serenity that seem all the more treasurable because they are generally absent in the performances of standard concert and operatic fare today. Walter's "Haffner" Symphony recording is a perfect example of the conductor's unique musical personality. He did not hesitate to caress a phrase or to point up an inner voice when it is turning a meaningful phrase. As few conductors have done, Walter made us acutely aware of the love he felt for the music he was conducting. Some may find his way excessively "romantic," but I do not. The great works of the symphonic literature should be dynamic and vital shared human experiences; Walter's "Haffner" Symphony recording assuredly is. The playing of the Columbia Symphony and the reproduction are both fine.

Apparently the only available tape performance is the one included in the DGG set devoted to Böhm-conducted performances of Mozart's Symphonies Nos. 25–41 (Y 9179, 3¾ ips). And absolutely nothing is available to the "Haffner" devotee on cassette.

SYMPHONY NO. 39 IN E-FLAT MAJOR, K. 543

What prompted the thirty-two-year-old Mozart to turn out three symphonies in a six-week period during the summer of 1788? No one is certain. There is nothing in the composer's papers to suggest that the scores were written to order—indeed, opera being all the rage in the 1780s, it is hardly likely that a patron would have commissioned Mozart to write a symphony. Thus, with no extra-musical stimuli to account for their composition, we must conclude that the three—the Symphony No. 39 in E-flat Major, the Symphony No. 40 in G Minor and the Symphony No. 41 in C Major, the "Jupiter"—were the fruits of an inner compulsion to create. Mozart seems to have had some time on his hands during the summer, and to have returned, for reasons of his own, to the form of the symphony—a form he had developed and ennobled over the previous two decades. The resulting trio of works, his last symphonies, excite wonder even for a composer whose whole musical output is a creative miracle.

Mozart apparently took a casual attitude toward the three scores: he barely mentions them anywhere except in his personal catalog, and he does not seem to have tried to arrange performances of the works during the three years of life that remained to him. But we must remember that up to his time a symphony was generally considered to be a diverting musical exercise of no great consequence. Only with the work of Mozart and Haydn did it become the outlet for the most deeply felt personal emotions. Haydn pointed the way fairly early in his symphonies. By 1773, when Mozart produced his first really penetrating and intense piece of music in this form—Symphony No. 25, the "Little G Minor"—Haydn had already provided such noble and passionate models as "The Philosopher" (1764), the "*Lamentatione*" (1765), and the six "*Sturm und Drang*" symphonies (1772). But once Mozart committed himself to the idea of a symphony as a vehicle for profound musical thinking, he never deviated from it.

The Symphony No. 39 in E-flat Major, the first of the great final trio, is for the most part a lighthearted score, full of abundant joy and ebullience. But the composer was anything but lighthearted at the time of its creation. On June 27, 1788, the day after Mozart finished the work, he wrote a letter to his friend and fellow Mason, the amateur musician Michael Puchberg, asking for money. In it he said, "I have worked more during the ten days I have lived here than in two months in my former apartment; and if dismal thoughts did not so often intrude (which I strive forcibly to dismiss), I should be very well off here, for I live agreeably, comfortably, and above all, cheaply."

The scoring of the E-flat Major Symphony represents something of a departure for Mozart. He had been growing increasingly interested in the clarinet (the great Clarinet Quintet was to be written the following year, and the Clarinet Concerto three years later, in 1791) and in place of the usual oboes, two clarinets are called for by the score of the E-flat Symphony. The characteristically liquid sound of the clarinet is heard throughout the work but to special effect in the trio of the minuet, in which the main melodic material is carried by the first clarinet while the second clarinet embellishes the line with arpeggios lying in its lower register.

The first movement begins with a slow introduction marked *Adagio*. The mood is meditative and somber and the tympani add their solemnity to the generally dark instrumental color as the wind and brass instruments intone fanfare-like calls against descending scales in the strings. The main body of the movement, *Allegro*, sneaks in gently with an arching theme, but soon trumpets and drums add their sonority and the vigorous nature of the movement becomes predominant. The short development section avoids manipulation of the principal musical material so that it is all the more powerful when we hear it again in the recapitulation. The second movement, *Andante con moto*, begins with a simple, folk-like melody but the second subject is at once more passionate and intense. The movement ends with a further statement of the first theme, shortened but with heightened intensity. The Menuetto third movement is marked *Allegretto*. The main section of the Minuet is a rustic dance. The contrasting Trio, with its clarinet duet, has a ring of nostalgia to it. The last movement, *Allegro*, is made up en-

tirely of the one nine-note theme heard right at the beginning. The
first five notes of the theme form the basis for the development
section, which becomes quite furious, and then the movement ends
dramatically and abruptly with the orchestra intoning the first seven
notes of the theme.

Among the available recordings of the symphony, four are particularly noteworthy: the performances by Klemperer and the Philharmonia Orchestra (Angel S 36129), Szell and the Cleveland
Orchestra (included in Columbia MG 30368), Bernstein and the
New York Philharmonic (Columbia MS 7029) and Walter and
the Columbia Symphony Orchestra (Columbia MS 6493). Klemperer's is an imposing reading of the score; this conductor sees
the slow and solemn orchestral introduction as the key to the work
and he invests the whole symphony with a solidity and an epic
character. The playing and recorded sound are both first-rate. Szell
is more concerned than Klemperer with capturing the shifting
kaleidoscopic qualities of the music. A special feature of Szell's performance is the marvelous articulation of the string passages. Bernstein's reading is a vigorous, dramatic one, with particular dash in
the last movement. Walter's performance is more personal than the
other three: he does not hesitate to linger over a passage that he
finds especially beautiful or meaningful.

All four of these performances share a disc with another Mozart
symphony, but no two couplings are identical. Klemperer's performance has Mozart's "Prague" Symphony, No. 38, on the reverse side;
Szell's, the "Haffner," No. 35, the G Minor and the "Jupiter" symphonies; Bernstein's, the G Minor, No. 40; and Walter's, the C
Major, No. 36, the "Linz." Any one of the four discs will give
lasting pleasure.

The only available tape performance seems to be in the Böhm
omnibus collection of Mozart's Symphonies Nos. 25–41 (DGG Y
9179 3¾ ips); and Böhm's is likewise the only available cassette
performance (DGG 923009).

SYMPHONY NO. 40 IN G MINOR, K. 550

One of the more astonishing things about the creative work of Mozart is that so much of it was written to order: instrumental concerti for his own use, or that of his pupils, or for certain virtuosi of the day; operas for specific occasions and for specific opera houses; serenades, divertimenti and cassations for outdoor performance at gala functions; minuets, waltzes and country dances for the regular Imperial masked balls which were highlights of every winter social season; and symphonies for performance at important concerts along his travel routes. That so much of the music which came into being in this manner is nevertheless so divinely inspired is perhaps the greatest tribute of all to the composer's genius.

In the last four years of his life Mozart was much occupied with the composition of operas: *Don Giovanni* in 1787, *Così fan tutte* in 1790, *The Magic Flute* and *La Clemenza di Tito* in 1791. Not called upon to produce symphonies, Mozart nevertheless did turn to the form once during these years—in the summer of 1788. A magical seven-week period between June 26 and August 10 produced a trilogy of symphonies which were to be his final and finest: No. 39 in E-flat Major (K. 543), No. 40 in G Minor (K. 550) and No. 41 in C Major (K. 551), the "Jupiter."

It is reasonable to wonder what prompted Mozart to compose three symphonies when none were asked or expected of him from an outside quarter. The most logical explanation would seem to be that he wrote them—like the six string quartets dedicated to Haydn —simply to please himself; the form of the symphony was dear to his heart and he must have rejoiced at the opportunity to exercise his fully matured powers in three distinct styles. The late great musicologist, Sir Donald Francis Tovey, characterized the symphonies as "expressing the healthiest reactions on each other—the E-flat Symphony has always been known as the *locus classicus* for euphony; the G Minor accurately defines the range of passion comprehended in the terms of Mozart's art; and the C Major (*Jupiter*) ends his symphonic career with the youthful majesty of a Greek god." Mozart's contemporaries were hardly aware of the existence of these three new symphonies, let alone their greatness.

The G Minor—one of Mozart's two symphonies not in a major key—is a remarkable example of sustained and concentrated orchestral power through deftness rather than through the employment of massive forces. It is scored for a modest orchestra (woodwinds in pairs, save for a single flute, and strings). There are no trumpets or tympani. And yet Mozart has created for this symphony a special timbre and color uniquely its own. Franz Liszt once boasted that the piano could produce the essential effects of an orchestra. Felix Mendelssohn is supposed to have replied to this: "Well, if he can play the beginning of Mozart's G Minor Symphony as it sounds in the orchestra, I will believe him." Mendelssohn, of course, was right: nothing can suggest the poignant passion of the pulsating violas at the opening of the symphony as they throb behind the gentle yet intense song of the violins. Richard Wagner, after a performance of the score in Munich, found it a work of "indestructible beauty." He wrote that the *Andante* was "exuberant with rapture and audacity" and the "beatitude of its last measures" conjured up for him one of his favorite concepts, that of "death through love." The Minuet, with its cross-play from section to section within the string body and from strings to winds, was considered by Arturo Toscanini to be one of the most darkly tragic pieces of music ever writtten. In the Paris *Revue Musicale* of May 11, 1828, there appeared a most sensitive appraisal of the G Minor Symphony; the writer, F. J. Fétis, said:

> Although Mozart has not used formidable orchestral forces in his G Minor Symphony, none of the sweeping and massive effects one meets in a symphony of Beethoven, the invention which flames in this work, the accents of passion and energy that pervade and the melancholy color that dominates it result in one of the most beautiful manifestations of the human spirit.

The first movement, *Allegro molto*, begins at once with the restless and poignant first theme given out by the first and second violins in octaves while the other strings are busy with a pulsating accompaniment. The second theme is more wistful and is cast in the major mode. The movement is dominated, however, by the character of the first theme and the pervading atmosphere is one of urgent, passionate intensity. The slow movement, *Andante*, is begun by the violas, who also started the first movement off with their pulsating figure; here they play repeated notes that fuse into chords. This movement reminded one commentator of a passage from a letter Mozart wrote to his father in 1787: "As death, rightly considered, is the true purpose of our life, I have for a year or two made myself so thoroughly acquainted with this true and best friend of man that his picture no longer frightens me; it brings much that is reassuring and comforting." The mood of unrest returns in the Minuet, *Allegretto*, but the Trio section offers complete contrast by way of smooth and melodic phrases from the woodwinds. The last movement continues the mood of agitated urgency. It begins with an eight-note ascending figure, whose intervals are identical with those that begin the Scherzo movement of Beethoven's Fifth Symphony. A bridge passage leads to a gentler, almost wistful second subject but the air of turmoil returns and the development section is shot through with trauma and tension. The end is in the same vein: dark and tortured.

Perhaps the most consistently satisfying conductor of this symphony where intensity is concerned is Otto Klemperer. His recording of the score with the Philharmonia Orchestra (Angel S 36183) is an epic reading of immense power, one that proves conclusively that the G Minor Symphony of Mozart is the first of the great heroic symphonies in the literature. A performance that focused on another element in this score—its tragedy—was the mono-only recording conducted by Sir Thomas Beecham (Columbia ML 5194—no longer available). Basically, this is the same approach that Beecham took many years ago in a 78-rpm recording of the score with the London Philharmonic Orchestra (Columbia album 316) that served as the *sine qua non* for many of us where this symphony was concerned. Beecham's Columbia LP recording of it with the Royal Philharmonic Orchestra reveals the same searching care and devotion. Bruno Walter's recording of the symphony with the Columbia Symphony Orchestra (Columbia MS 6494) emphasizes the more lyrical qualities in the music, and Leonard Bernstein's with the New York Philharmonic (Columbia MS 7029), the more passionate ones. Performances of pulsating vitality are also turned in by Britten (London CS 6598) and Casals (Columbia MS 7262). Britten's highly personal approach may not be to everyone's liking; it is to mine. Among his predilections is the observance of every repeat in the score—an extravagance not indulged in by either Klemperer or Casals.

Both the Klemperer and Walter performances are available on tape (Angel Y3S 3662, 3¾ ips—with the Klemperer performances of the other five of Mozart's last six symphonies—and Columbia MQ 611 respectively). Among the several performances available on cassette, I would select the passionate Barenboim performance (Angel 4XS 36814).

SYMPHONY NO. 41 IN C MAJOR, K. 551, "JUPITER"

At the beginning of 1788, Mozart had just been appointed court composer by Joseph II, Emperor of Austria. Gluck, his predecessor in that position, had died in November of 1787 and had been receiving an annual salary of two thousand florins. Mozart, however, was offered only eight hundred—the equivalent of about $224. Because he was in desperate financial straits, he was forced to accept, and he turned his attention to composing the inconsequential minuets, waltzes and court dances expected of him. Later he was reported to have made the complaint that his meager salary was "too much for what I produce—and too little for what I could produce."

Mozart's fame throughout Europe had brought him little financial return, and, to maintain himself and his family, he was obliged to perform in public and to teach. This busy life left him no time to concern himself with household bookkeeping, and his wife Constanze was as cavalier as he about money matters—and regularly pregnant besides. Don Giovanni had been an instantaneous triumph at its 1787 premiere in Prague, but when it was produced in Vienna for the first time in May of 1788, it was greeted with indifference. Lorenzo da Ponte, librettist of both Don Giovanni and The Marriage of Figaro, reported the Emperor's verdict: "The opera is divine, finer perhaps than *Figaro,* but it is not the meat for my Viennese." When Mozart heard this he is supposed to have replied: "We must give them time to chew it."

Meanwhile, Mozart was concerned about where his next meal would be coming from. On the twenty-seventh of June 1788 he wrote to his loyal friend (and fellow Mason) Michael Puchberg, begging for a loan. "My landlord in the Landstrasse was so pressing," he related, "that I was obliged to pay him on the spot (in order to avoid any unpleasantness), which caused me great embarrassment." He also spoke in this letter of gloomy thoughts that were oppressing him. But none of this seems to have dimmed his creative fire. The day before he wrote this letter he had completed the first of his three final symphonies, and within seven weeks, by August 10, 1788, he finished the last of them, the mighty "Jupiter," one of the cornerstones of the symphonic literature.

A London music publisher named J. B. Cramer is generally held responsible for the sobriquet "Jupiter," bestowing this title on it because of what he called the work's "loftiness of ideas and nobility of treatment." (Parenthetically, some years ago when the sleuths of the Haydn Society discovered a manuscript of Haydn's Symphony No. 13 in D Major, H. C. Robbins Landon, the chief musical detective, noticed that the first theme of Haydn's last movement was identical with that of the same movement of the Mozart symphony, and promptly dubbed the Haydn symphony that composer's "Jupiter.")

The first movement, *Allegro vivace,* contrasts strongly martial elements with more gentle ones. Right at the start, the character is clearly established with four bars that first announce a virile, stentorian quality but immediately present a softer, more feminine answer in the strings. The movement takes wing and the martial aspect is the predominating mood but it never really puts the softer element completely out of the picture. The third theme of the movement is taken from a buffa aria that Mozart had written shortly before he started to work on the symphony; the aria, *Un bacio di mano,* was written for bass voice and the lyrics direct a dense character named Pompeo to go and study the ways of the world. The movement's development is quite elaborate, encompassing nearly a hundred measures that combine the military, the tender and the gay aspects of the music. The slow movement, *Andante cantabile*, begins with a phrase in the muted violins which is followed immediately by a loud chord. The movement has about it the quality of a lamentation. The second theme has an increased emotional tension and the development increases the feeling of deep and abiding passion. In the third movement Minuet, *Allegretto*, the alternation between forcefulness and ease is exactly balanced in alternating eight-bar phrases. The movement begins with a lyrical descending phrase in the strings, which is then answered by a vigorous and proclamative section with punctuation from the drums. The Trio section is likewise delicately balanced between the gentler and the more assertive elements. The Finale, *Allegro molto*, is Mozart's supreme achievement in counterpoint. The movement is in sonata form with a fugato development and an enlarged coda that is a massive and heroic fugue. Eric Blom wrote of this last movement:

There is a mystery in this music not to be solved by analysis or criticism, and perhaps only just to be apprehended by the imagination. We can understand the utter simplicity; we can also, with an effort, comprehend the immense technical skill with which its elaborate fabric is woven; what remains forever a riddle is how any human being could manage to combine these two opposites into such a perfectly balanced work of art.

In years gone by, the outstanding recorded performance of Mozart's "Jupiter" Symphony was one by the London Philharmonic Orchestra under the direction of Sir Thomas Beecham. For vigor and forcefulness, that original Beecham recording, once available in this country in a Columbia 78-rpm album, may well have established the standard for our time. Beecham subsequently re-recorded the "Jupiter" Symphony twice more, both times with the Royal Philharmonic Orchestra. The first remake is still listed in the catalog (Odyssey 32160023), but unfortunately it does not match the power of his first version.

Another conductor from the past who was a great "Jupiter" conductor was Arturo Toscanini. Though I find almost all of Toscanini's other Mozart recordings hectic and frenzied, his "Jupiter" is in a class by itself (RCA LM 1030)—a stupendous performance full of the white heat of passion and drama. His heroic account still leads the pack for me, but its sound is now quite dated. Those looking for a stereo recommendation are directed to the noble and patrician performance conducted by Casals (Columbia MS 7066).

Among the other available "Jupiter" Symphony recordings, Klemperer's (Angel S 36183) is surprisingly lackluster, Leinsdorf's (RCA LSC 2694) plods and Karajan's (London CS 6369) is slick and uncommitted. Giulini (London CS 6479) and Szell (Columbia MS 6969) represent the opposite extremes of performance attitude: Giulini emphasizes the lyrical grace of the music, Szell its grandeur and vigor. My own favorite among the contemporary recordings of the symphony is Bruno Walter's (Columbia MS 6255)—a highly personal account of the music that rhapsodizes and brings out many inner voices; assuredly, the reading will not be to everyone's liking, but then that is what makes music such a vital and self-renewing artistic experience.

Walter's performance also exists as an excellent reel-to-reel tape (Columbia MQ 436). Klemperer's (Angel L 36183) is an alternate tape choice, and on cassette Böhm has the field to himself (DGG 923056).

Serge Prokofiev

Born: Ekaterinoslav, Russia, April 23, 1891
Died: Near Moscow, March 4, 1953

By the time he was six Prokofiev showed extraordinary musical gifts. He was already a pretty fair pianist and he began some elementary composition. At ten he began studies with Taneiev in Moscow and later won the Rubinstein Prize at the St. Petersburg Conservatory where he studied with Rimsky-Korsakov, Liadov and Tcherepnine. During his student years he composed many works, including two operas and numerous piano pieces; all went unpublished. In 1909 a concert made up entirely of his works was given by the St. Petersburg Society for Contemporary Music. His first big splash as a composer came with his *Scythian Suite* of 1916, a wild and barbaric score taken from a ballet he had composed the previous year for Diaghilev. Two years later came his "Classical" symphony in D Major, a work that is the complete antithesis of the *Scythian Suite*; the symphony is a lightly scored reminiscence of the period of Haydn and Mozart, but it is a distinctly individual work spiced with a fair amount of thoroughly unclassical dissonance.

In 1918, after visits to Paris, London and Japan, Prokofiev settled in the United States for a time and it was in Chicago that his opera *The Love for Three Oranges* received its first performance (in December 1921). Earlier that same year his ballet *The Buffoon* had been produced in Paris by the Diaghilev Ballet and in 1922 Prokofiev left the United States to settle in Paris for a time. Another *émigré* Russian was providing Paris with some of her most exciting concerts during that period—the conductor Serge Koussevitzky. He and Prokofiev became fast friends, with the conductor introducing many of the composer's works. The Koussevitzky advocacy of Prokofiev's music continued when the conductor left Paris to become the music director of the Boston Symphony Orchestra in the autumn of 1924. For the ensuing quarter of a century, Boston may well have heard more of Prokofiev's music than any other city in the world.

Prokofiev himself, in the meantime, had decided to return to Russia in 1927 after about a decade of nomadic wandering. Until the outbreak of World War II he was allowed to return to the West for concert tours and other appearances, and during the 1930s he appeared fairly frequently as conductor and pianist in many of his own works with the principal orchestras in the United States.

Prokofiev's early scores were characterized for the most part by a brash and cynical satirical vein, with an original rhythmic style and an adventurous experimentation. From the mid-30s onward, however, his style underwent a great simplification, a circumstance forced upon him by the prevailing dictates of Soviet musical culture. The works by which he is today generally represented in our concert halls are nearly all from this period—the *Lieutenant Kije Suite* (taken from his music for a Russian film); the Second Violin Concerto; the Fifth and Sixth Symphonies; the ballets *Romeo and Juliet* and *Cinderella*; and the orchestral fairy tale *Peter and the Wolf*. During and after World War II he composed a good number of empty patriotic works, including such titles as *Toasts to Stalin, The Ballad of the Unknown Boy, Ode to the End of the War, Cantata for the Thirtieth Anniversary of the October Revolution* and *Guarding the Peace*. This did not prevent Prokofiev from coming under attack in 1948 by the Central Committee of the Russian Communist Party, who branded him with the label "bourgeois formalist." Also attacked at the same time were the other two best-known Soviet composers, Shostakovich and Khachaturian.

From that point onward Prokofiev suffered from failing health, and his death on March 4, 1953, went unreported for nearly a week while the world was convulsed with the news of another Russian who died on the same date—Joseph Stalin. The irony is that in June 1958 the charges leveled against Prokofiev ten years earlier were withdrawn by the same Central Committee and directed instead against the 1948 rulers of the Communist Party: Stalin, Molotov, Beria et al. Sic transit . . . and so forth.

PETER AND THE WOLF, OP. 67

During Serge Koussevitzky's quarter century as music director of
the Boston Symphony Orchestra (1924–49), he made the Massachusetts capital a Prokofiev stronghold: many of the composer's
scores were given their first American performances in Boston. During those years, too, Prokofiev himself appeared frequently as a
guest conductor and pianist in Boston. In March of 1938 he made
what was destined to be his last Boston Symphony Orchestra appearance, conducting a program of his own music in which he also
was the soloist in this First Piano Concerto. The second half of the
concert consisted entirely of music new to this country: the second
suite from his recently completed ballet *Romeo and Juliet* and the
first performance outside Russia of something different and special
—an orchestral fairy tale, with narrator, called *Peter and the Wolf.*

I was not quite twelve at the time, but I distinctly recall my absorption in the story spun out by the best of *Peter and the Wolf*
narrators, Richard Hale, and the thunderous applause that erupted
in Symphony Hall when the performance was over. About a year
later RCA Victor released a performance of the work with Koussevitzky and the Boston Symphony Orchestra, and with Hale repeating his superb narration. It was even issued in long-playing disc
format for a brief while (RCA Camden CAL 101) but it has long
since passed into the never-never land of catalog withdrawal.

More than a quarter century has now passed since *Peter and the
Wolf* first burst upon the American musical scene; in that time the
work has become one of the best-loved "fun" pieces in the literature
—a staple of concerts for young people. The reasons are not hard
to find: Prokofiev created some unforgettable melodies to accompany the animal adventures, and the marriage of narrative text and
music is masterful. Even more important, however, are the universal
truths of the plot, making the work appropriate to many levels of
human experience. Who among us has not taken part in a quarrel
like the one between the duck and the bird over the respective
merits of swimming without flying or flying without swimming? For

that matter, the crafty cat who stealthily seeks his own gain from the distracted bickerings of others is a common character in our human society.

This explanatory preface appears in the printed score:

> Each character of this Tale is represented by a corresponding instrument in the orchestra: the bird by a flute, the duck by an oboe, the cat by a clarinet in a low register, the grandfather by a bassoon, the wolf by three horns, Peter by the string quartet, the shooting of the hunters by the kettledrums and the bass drum. Before an orchestral performance it is desirable to show these instruments to the children and to play on them the corresponding *leitmotivs*. Thereby the children learn to distinguish the sonorities of the instruments during the performance of this Tale.

The story begins as one fine day Peter goes out into the big, green meadow. He meets first the bird, then the duck, and as he greets them the melodies associated with each are heard. First the bird and duck themes are heard in combination with Peter's string melody, then the strings fade and the two animal themes are heard in duet. Soon the cat creeps into the picture. Peter warns the bird to fly up high to a treetop, the duck quacks away at the cat and in the meantime a big bad wolf comes out of the forest. In her excitement, the duck jumps out of the water and the wolf races after her, catches her and with one gulp devours her. By clever machinations Peter proceeds to outwit and catch the wolf, to the delight of his animal friends and the grudging admiration of his grandfather, who is disturbed, nevertheless, that Peter disobeyed the rule never to venture out into the meadow alone. At the end there is a triumphal procession in which all the representative instruments voice their themes as Peter and his friends lead the captured wolf to the zoo. And, the tale concludes, if you listen carefully you can hear the duck quacking away inside the wolf's belly, for in his haste the wolf had swallowed the duck whole.

The marvelous pomposity and disingenuous wonder that Hale brought to his narration with Koussevitzky are only intermittently present in his later recording with Arthur Fiedler and the Boston

Pops Orchestra (RCA LM 1803—mono only). Among the very many available recordings of the score, one which is especially successful, in my opinion, is the flamboyantly ostentatious version conducted by Skitch Henderson, with Beatrice Lillie as the narrator (London CS 6187, tape L 80061). The text has been specially adapted for Miss Lillie by someone who here goes under the name of "Bidrum Vabish," and some of the Lillie-isms are quite charming. Henderson conducts a meticulous performance and some of his effects—the slow, lumbering gait for the first appearance of the cat, for example —are marvelously appropriate. Those in search of a "straighter" version are directed either to the performances that enlist the narrative services of Michael Flanders (Seraphim S 60172) or Sean Connery (London SPC 21007; tape L 75007; cassette M 94007).

Another fine tape account in addition to the recordings available on tape mentioned above is the one conducted by Sir Malcolm Sargent with Lorne Greene as a straightforward and sane narrator (RCA FTC 2204).

SYMPHONY NO. 5, OP. 100

"It is a symphony about the spirit of man." The words are those of Serge Prokofiev, spoken in March 1945 to Robert Magidoff, then serving as the Moscow correspondent of an American radio network. Magidoff and Prokofiev were discussing the composer's latest score, his Fifth Symphony, which had been played for the first time just a few weeks earlier in Moscow with Prokofiev himself conducting. In a dispatch to the New York *Times,* Magidoff wrote: "The Fifth Symphony, unlike Prokofiev's first four, makes one recall Mahler's words: 'To write a symphony means to me to create a whole world.' Although the Fifth is pure music and Prokofiev insists it is without program, he himself said, 'It is a symphony about the spirit of man.'"

Fourteen years had elapsed between the composition of Prokofiev's Fourth Symphony and his Fifth Symphony. The Fourth Symphony was one of ten works commissioned for the 1930–31 season of the Boston Symphony Orchestra to celebrate that organization's fiftieth anniversary. Among the others were Stravinsky's *Symphony of Psalms,* Hindemith's Concert Music for Strings and Brass, Albert Roussel's Third Symphony and Howard Hanson's "Romantic" Symphony.

When Serge Koussevitzky gave the Fourth Symphony its premiere, in November 1930, the reaction of the Boston press and public was rather icy. Seven years later, still smarting from that reception, Prokofiev tartly let it be known that his most recent work, an orchestral fairy tale called *Peter and the Wolf,* would not offend the sensibilities or tax the musical intelligence of even Boston audiences.

Prokofiev was right, to be sure, but the bitterness of his observation just as surely represented an overstatement of fact, for by 1937 the Boston Symphony audiences had been thoroughly exposed to the orchestral music of Prokofiev by Koussevitzky. It was only fitting, therefore, that in another decade the American premiere of the composer's Fifth Symphony should have been entrusted to Koussevitzky.

I, for one, can never forget the occasion of that first American performance, on November 9, 1945. In those days, hard on the end of World War II, the phrase "a symphony about the spirit of man" had a special meaning for us. The world had just emerged from its darkest hour, and as we sat in Symphony Hall in Boston and listened to this latest symphony by Prokofiev, many of us felt that it reflected the torture of our times, much as Beethoven's "Eroica" Symphony reflects the torture of his times.

In fact, it may be said, with a good deal of truth, that Prokofiev's Fifth Symphony is his "Eroica." Like Beethoven's masterpiece of a century and a half earlier, also composed with the sounds of war ringing in its composer's ears, this work is an eloquent response to the struggles and aspirations of the human spirit.

The first movement is an *Andante* of churning turmoil and drama. There are two principal themes, an extensive development with much rhythmic contrast, and a concluding coda that is at once anguished and dramatic. The second movement, *Allegro marcato,* has an intense irony and sardonic bite. A steady rhythmic beat serves as the accompaniment for the main melody, which is tossed from one woodwind instrument to another. A middle section resembling a trio offers some relief from the constantly reiterated rhythm of the first part, but in this middle section, too, the rhythmic element is dominant. The return of the first part brings a slightly different treatment and then the movement ends in a frenzy. The third movement, *Adagio*, is a long, brooding lament. The principal theme appears first in the woodwinds and then is taken up by the strings. The tension and tragedy build to a climax, the tension is relieved somewhat by a livelier section and then the movement ends on a somewhat more optimistic note.

The last movement, *Allegro giocoso*, has an air of veiled buoyancy but beneath it the ominous threat of brutal warfare always seems to be lurking. The movement begins with a questioning phrase in the winds, followed by the divided cellos and basses intoning briefly a variant on the theme that was heard at the very beginning of the symphony. The first main theme appears in the clarinet over a pulsating rhythm in the winds and brass. The second theme is first stated by the flute, and then both themes are developed. The conclusion—brilliant and heroic—is interrupted briefly by a recollection of one of the ominous themes from the first movement. In the end, however, it is nobility and grandeur that triumph.

In Koussevitzky, its first spokesman in this country, the Fifth Symphony found an ideal interpreter. The "spirit of man" and its well-being was an abiding and lifelong concern of the conductor, and in conducting Prokofiev's Fifth Symphony he used to become possessed by the human implications of the music. The heartbreak of the score has never been more profoundly moving than it was under his baton. At the same time, the pages of affirmation have never rung out more proudly and triumphantly than they did when a red-faced and totally consumed Koussevitzky held his torch to the Boston Symphony Orchestra and set aflame in that superb body of players an intensity of dedication unequaled in my experience.

Shortly after conducting the American premiere of the symphony, Koussevitzky recorded it with the Boston Symphony Orchestra for RCA Victor. The recorded performance—originally released as a 78-rpm set and later transferred to the LP catalog as LM 1045—does not have quite the searing intensity I remember from some of the other Koussevitzky recordings—many of them matchless, as is this one—it is now no longer available. Clearly, RCA must be made to feel duty-bound to restore it to currency, perhaps even in an electronic stereo reprocessing of the type applied to some of the Toscanini recordings.

Of the recordings currently listed, three find particular favor with me: Rozhdestvensky's Angel/Melodiya S 40126; tape M 40126; cassette 4XS 40126), for its dynamism; Ansermet's (London CS 6406) for its straightforwardness; and Bernstein's (Columbia MS 7005)— considerably more personal (with a very measured first movement tempo) but for me superbly communicative of the powerful drama and tragedy of the score. In all fairness I should add that Karajan's account (DGG 139040; tape L 9040; cassette 923084) has found much favor with many reviewers; for my part, I find it superficial and glib.

Sergei Rachmaninoff

Born: Novgorod, April 1, 1873
Died: Beverly Hills, California, March 28, 1943

Born into an old Russian aristocratic family, Rachmaninoff began his musical studies at the age of nine at the St. Petersburg Conservatory. After three years he transferred to the Moscow Conservatory and there studied with Siloti and Arensky. In 1892 he was awarded the Conservatory's gold medal for composition and upon his graduation he began a long concert tour throughout Russia as a pianist. In 1893 he became professor of piano at the Maryinsky Institute for Girls in Moscow and in that same year he composed his one-act opera *Aleko*. Before the turn of the century he had completed his First Symphony. The failure of that score with the critics plunged Rachmaninoff into a state of abject despair.

Rachmaninoff visited the United States for the first time in 1909, conducting several of our principal orchestras and also appearing as piano soloist. He was offered the musical directorship of the Boston Symphony Orchestra, along with several other inducements to remain in this country, but he refused them all and returned to Russia. But the Revolution of 1917 drove him from his native land and he never again set foot there. For the remainder of his life he spent most of his time alternately in the United States and Switzerland. Until the very end he toured widely each season as one of the most celebrated and one of the most convincing pianists before the public.

It has been fashionable in some circles to denigrate Rachmaninoff the composer as a severely limited craftsman who was out of touch with the musical currents of his time. The other side of the coin is the undeniable revival of interest in some of Rachmaninoff's works, fostered by some of our younger performing artists, including Van Cliburn, Gary Graffman, Vladimir Ashkenazy and André Previn. What cannot be denied is the direct and enduring emotional impact of such works as the Second and Third Symphonies, the two Suites for Two Pianos, the Second and Third Piano Concertos and the Rhapsody for Piano and Orchestra on a Theme by Paganini.

CONCERTO NO. 2 IN C MINOR FOR PIANO, OP. 18

A symphony by a twenty-four-year-old composer named Sergei Rachmaninoff was given its world premiere performance in St. Petersburg in 1897. The occasion turned out to be one of the genuine fiascos in the history of music. Rachmaninoff himself later described how he sat rapt with horror through part of the performance and then fled from the concert hall. A post-concert party had been arranged in his honor, and Rachmaninoff went through the motions in a daze. The newspaper reviews were the crowning blow. In the *News* César Cui wrote: "If there were a conservatory in hell, Rachmaninoff would get the first prize for his Symphony, so devilish are the discords he places before us."

The whole affair proved to be traumatic for the sensitive Rachmaninoff. He was plunged into a fit of depression and despair that lasted for two long, desperate years. Finally, friends persuaded him to see one of the pioneers in the field of autosuggestion, a Dr. Dahl.

In his memoirs (*Rachmaninoff's Recollections*, as told to Oskar von Riesemann), Rachmaninoff tells the story:

My relations had told Dr. Dahl that he must at all costs cure me of my apathetic condition and achieve such results that I would again begin to compose. Dahl had asked what manner of composition they desired and had received the answer. "A Concerto for pianoforte," for this I had promised to the people in London and had given up in despair. In consequence I heard repeated, day after day, the same hypnotic formula, as I lay half asleep in an armchair in Dr. Dahl's consulting room. "You will start to compose a concerto—You will work with the greatest of ease—The composition will be of excellent quality." Always it was the same without interruption.

Although it may seem impossible to believe, this treatment really helped me. I began to compose at the beginning of the summer. The material grew in volume, and new musical ideas began to well up within me, many more than I needed for my concerto. By autumn I had completed two movements of the Concerto—the Andante and the Finale. These I played during the same autumn at a charity benefit concert conducted by Siloti. The two movements resulted in a gratifying success. This heightened my confidence to such an extent that I began once more to compose with great ardor. By the spring I had already completed the first movement of the concerto and the Suite for two pianos. I felt that Dr. Dahl's treatment had strengthened my nervous system to a degree almost miraculous. Out of gratitude I dedicated my Second Concerto to him.

Rachmaninoff himself was the soloist when the Second Concerto was given its official premiere at a Moscow Philharmonic concert in October 1901. The score was an instant success—for rather obvious reasons: the concerto is one long rhapsodic flight of soaring melodic inspiration. It served immediately to rehabilitate Rachmaninoff, professionally as well as personally. He became conductor of opera at the Moscow Grand Theater, he was in constant demand as a piano recitalist and he was again able to compose many pieces for piano. As a matter of fact, so steadily did the demands upon his time and energies grow that within a few years he was obliged to leave Moscow in search of peace and solitude. He settled in Dresden with his family and during the next decade he returned only intermittently to Russia. In 1918, following the Revolution, he determined that he must make a new home elsewhere, and for most of the last twenty-five years of his life he lived in the United States.

The emotional appeal of the Second Concerto was long ago exploited by music popularizers. It has figured in innumerable motion pictures (including Noël Coward's memorable *Brief Encounter*), and the principal theme of the last movement was adapted some years ago by Tin Pan Alley and titled "Full Moon and Empty Arms."

The opening movement, *Moderato*, begins with a series of chords for the piano that gain in intensity and volume. Finally the solo instrument plays a series of arpeggios and the orchestral strings announce the first principal subject. After an orchestral interlude the piano declares the second subject, a typical Slavic melody. The slow movement, *Adagio sostenuto*, begins with sustained harmonies in the muted strings. The woodwind instruments enter soon, and then the flute and clarinet state the principal melody that is to form the basis for the movement. In the coda Rachmaninoff introduces some new material. The last movement, marked *Allegro scherzando*, has a brief orchestral introduction followed by the initial statement of the first theme in the solo piano. The second theme is given first to the oboe and cellos, then it is taken up by the piano. A section marked *Allegro scherzando, moto primo* deals skittishly with the material of the first theme; there is a fugato working out and then the second theme, Tin Pan Alley's "Full Moon and Empty Arms," bursts forth in radiant splendor and the concerto ends in a brilliant coda.

The first recording ever made of the concerto (in 1929) appropriately featured Rachmaninoff himself at the piano, with the Philadelphia Orchestra under the direction of Leopold Stokowski. (Despite the fact that on two separate occasions Rachmaninoff was invited to become conductor of the Boston Symphony Orchestra, it was with the Philadelphia Orchestra that the composer maintained his closest American ties.) The Rachmaninoff-Stokowski collaboration was an extraordinary one, producing a reading of great strength and beauty, and the glowing sound that Rachmaninoff drew from the piano was captured on the early electrical recording with amazing fidelity. The performance, fortunately, was early transferred to the long-playing medium, and is still available in a three-disc album that also contains the composer's other three piano concertos along with his Rhapsody on a Theme by Paganini—all in collaboration with the Philadelphia Orchestra (RCA LM 6123). Sonically, of course, the more recent recordings are more satisfying, but Rachmaninoff's own performance is the one against which all others must be measured. The recording should be snatched up immediately by every serious collector, for Rachmaninoff set the standard where his own works were concerned. In England, as a matter of fact, the set is available on RCA's budget-priced Victrola label, so it may be that a Victrola reissue is in the works for this country as well.

Of individually available performances of the Second Concerto, several are outstanding: Cliburn, Reiner and the Chicago Symphony Orchestra (RCA LSC 2601; tape TR3 1018, 3¾ ips; cassette RK 1128) adopt a massive approach to this score in an attempt to emphasize its power and breadth; the team of Graffman and Bernstein (Columbia MS 6634; tape MQ 1108; cassette 16 11 0110) is painstakingly scrupulous in its attention to detail and they produce a reading of mounting tension and excitement; the Rubinstein-Reiner collaboration (RCA LSC 2068) continues to be a fine blend of extrovert dynamism and poetic sensitivity; and the Ivan Davis-Henry Lewis account of the music (London SPC 21057; cassette 94057) is a richly mellow, exuberantly Romantic approach. A new Rubinstein recording, with Ormandy and the Philadelphia Orchestra, awaits release on the RCA label.

CONCERTO NO. 3 IN D MINOR FOR PIANO, OP. 30

Sergei Rachmaninoff was invited to make his first tour of the United States, as both pianist and conductor, during the 1909–10 concert season. The tour was to consist of about twenty concerts, including appearances with the New York and the Boston Symphony Orchestras. Rachmaninoff looked forward to his American visit with great anticipation, and the excitement seems to have stimulated some musical ideas that were taking shape in his mind. The result of these ideas was the Third Piano Concerto, regarded by many as his finest large-scale work.

Considering the source of the work's inspiration, it was fitting that the first performance of the new concerto should take place in the United States during one of Rachmaninoff's appearances as soloist with the New York Symphony. The date was November 28, 1909, and Walter Damrosch conducted. The work's second performance was with the same soloist and orchestra, this time led by Gustav Mahler, then conductor of the New York Philharmonic Society.

When the concerto was new, it was analyzed brilliantly by Dr.

Otto Kinkleday, who wrote the notes for the New York performances:

Russian throughout—Russian in its melodic conception, in its rhythms, and in the robust, virile qualities even of its gentler passages. In several passages we may clearly discern the composer's place in the lineage of Tchaikovsky.

In form the concerto is more or less conventional, with lengthy working out of episodic material and free use of remodeled motives or melodies to secure unity throughout the whole work. The first theme of the first movement, a typical Slavic chant, is played very simply by the piano to a rhythmic accompaniment of muted strings and pizzicato basses. Horns and violas repeat the theme. The whole section has a subdued character which has something mysterious in it. The second theme, which is anticipated by horns and trumpets before it really appears in its full form after the first orchestra forte, is short and has a throbbing rhythm, played pianissimo and staccato by the strings and answered by the piano. From it is derived a beautifully warm and expressive episode for the solo instrument. Reminiscences of this theme and this episode will be heard in the second movement and will play a large part in the development of the last.

The second movement begins with another typical Russian theme, tender and melancholy, and yet not tearful. It is relieved by a section in 3-8 time, with a pizzicato waltz accompaniment in the strings, to which the reeds sing sweetly a melody, which is nothing but the first theme of the concerto in another guise.

The last movement (*Alla breve*) follows the second without interruption. Its general character is that of ceaseless, driving activity. The first theme at times takes on a martial sound. Several subsidiary themes are heard. One of them appears first as a long succession of syncopated chords in the piano, followed immediately by a smooth, flowing statement of the same melody, also by the piano. A Scherzando, 4-4, and a Lento are based largely upon reminiscences of themes in the first movement. After the Lento the restless *Alla breve* is resumed.

The first recording of the Third ever made was that of a performance in London in the early 1930s by a pianist still in his twenties—Vladimir Horowitz. On hearing this recording, Rachmaninoff himself pronounced the soloist "the only player in the world for this piece." That collaboration of many years ago between Horowitz and Albert Coates, who conducted the London Symphony Orchestra, bore the RCA Victor label in the 78-rpm days. The master was a product of EMI, however, and this fact makes it a possibility for future reissue in Angel's Great Recordings of the Century series. That it is a great recording is indisputable: the young Horowitz was a keyboard poet whose like we have yet to hear—unless we count Horowitz himself, back with us after a twelve-year absence from the concert hall. Speculation about such things is risky, but I would imagine that a Horowitz performance of the concerto now would be closer in spirit to the Romantic effulgence of the early recording than to the more rigid approach that marks the Horowitz-Reiner performance of the early 1950s (RCA LM 1178). Let us hope that in time Horowitz can be persuaded to record the concerto again.

A quarter century after that first Horowitz recording, another pianist in his twenties became closely identified with the Rachmaninoff Third Concerto. In 1958, Van Cliburn won the International Tchaikovsky Competition in Moscow on the strength of his performances of this work and the Tchaikovsky B-flat Minor Concerto, among others. It was to be expected that both of these concertos would figure in his subsequent Carnegie Hall concert of May 1958, with Kyril Kondrashin conducting the Symphony of the Air. Shortly afterward, Cliburn and Kondrashin recorded the Tchaikovsky concerto in New York's Manhattan Center, but sessions to record the Rachmaninoff Third were postponed. Finally, about a year later, the concert performance of the Third, taped in Carnegie Hall on that memorable evening, was released. However, the sonics of this concert-hall recording are now beginning to show their age. Is it now time for Cliburn to re-record this work with Ormandy and the Philadelphia Orchestra?

The Cliburn-Kondrashin performance (RCA LSC 2355) is in many ways an ideal account of the concerto. The electric quality of the occasion can be heard in the playing, and although the recorded sound is not as expansive as it might have been under controlled studio conditions, it is nevertheless perfectly acceptable. The important thing is that Cliburn and Kondrashin had worked out between them a perfectly unified conception of the music, and the performance builds in momentum and excitement from beginning to end.

Another pianist with a special affinity for this Romantic and effulgent Concerto is Alexis Weissenberg, whose recording of the score with Georges Prêtre and the Chicago Symphony Orchestra (RCA LSC 3040) crackles with the excitement of a vibrant, tension-laden communication. Too, it is superlatively well recorded by the engineers.

Other stereo-mono recordings of the concerto are by Vladimir Ashkenazy with the London Symphony Orchestra under Anatole Fistoulari (London CS 6359), Byron Janis with Antal Dorati conducting the London Symphony Orchestra (Mercury SR 90283), and another Janis recording, made earlier than the foregoing, with Charles Munch and the Boston Symphony Orchestra (RCA Victrola VICS 1032). The more recent Janis recording has about it a frenzy that threatens at times to become uncontrolled, and the recorded sound has a harsh, abrasive quality. Yet there is no denying the vitality of the performance. It is the earlier Janis reading with Munch, however, that is the more satisfying of the two for me —the excitement is less hysterical here, and the sound warmer and more full-bodied. Ashkenazy seems to combine the approaches of Cliburn and Janis. He brings to his performance a full measure of lyrical poetry, and he completely masters the technical difficulties presented by this work—and they are considerable. Furthermore, Ashkenazy has the advantage of the finest recorded sound given any of these pianists—the balance between piano and orchestra is exemplary. He has, incidentally, re-recorded the score—along with the other three Rachmaninoff concertos and the Paganini Rhapsody—with André Previn and the London Symphony Orchestra; they await release on the London label.

Still available is the performance of the concerto by the composer himself, with Eugene Ormandy and the Philadelphia Orchestra, in the three-disc RCA LM 6123. Curiously, Rachmaninoff's playing of the concerto is rather matter-of-fact and tired. Notwithstanding the documentary importance of this recording, it is outclassed in almost every respect by those of Ashkenazy, Janis and especially Cliburn.

The Ashkenazy and Cliburn performances are also available on 7½ ips four-track stereo tape. Ashkenazy's is on an Ampex release (London K 80125) that includes the same pianist's performance of the Tchaikovsky B-flat Minor Concerto, and Cliburn's is on a conventional-length tape from RCA (FTC 2001). The basic sound characteristics of each recording are heightened in the tape versions: London's is even more brilliant and bright-hued than the corresponding disc release, and RCA's is more lacking in resonance.

Maurice Ravel

Born: Ciboure, Basses-Pyrénées, March 7, 1875
Died: Paris, December 28, 1937

Ravel's birthplace was in the Pyrenees, and childhood impressions
of Spanish music are evident in some of his works. The bulk of his
musical studies was accomplished at the Paris Conservatory where
he was especially interested in contemporary creativity and the music of some of the earlier French composers. These, along with
Liszt and various Russians, exerted a profound influence on his own
style. In 1901 he won second-place in the Prix de Rome competition, but in the next two years he was refused the first prize and
in 1905 he was declared ineligible for the competition altogether
after the preliminary examination. This affront to a composer who
had already written some of his early piano works, along with his
brilliant String Quartet and the *Shéhérazade* song cycle! This sum-
mary action caused a furore in French musical circles and brought
about the resignation of Théodore Dubois as head of the Conservatory. Another controversy raged about Ravel's head in 1907
when his *Histoires Naturelles* for voice and piano divided listeners
into two camps on the question whether or not Ravel was an
imitator of Debussy.

Ravel's music gained steadily in public favor, however, with the
publication of his brilliant *Rapsodie Espagnole* for Orchestra, the
piano suite *Gaspard de la Nuit* and the buoyant one-act opera
L'Heure Espagnole with its satirical elements. The ballet *Daphnis
and Chloé*, considered by many to be Ravel's masterpiece, was
produced by Diaghilev in 1912. Perhaps the two outstanding productions of his later years are *La Valse* (1920) and *Boléro* (1928).
La Valse is an "apotheosis" of the dance that uses all the modern
wizardry of instrumentation to create a brilliant and frightening

picture of the collapse of an era; *Boléro* develops a monotonous dance theme by a process of repetition until the effect on the listener is almost hypnotic—Ravel himself once described the score, created to be danced by Ida Rubinstein, as "orchestral effects without music."

During 1931 and 1932 he composed two piano concertos, one of them for the left hand alone, commissioned by the one-armed Austrian pianist Paul Wittgenstein. He was also commissioned by a French film company to compose the score for a movie on Cervantes' *Don Quichotte*, which starred the great Russian basso Feodor Chaliapin. Some kind of falling out between Ravel and the film producers caused the composer to suspend work on the project and to threaten a legal suit. The score for the movie was ultimately composed by Jacques Ibert, but Ravel was able to convert the effort he had already expended upon the project into three songs for baritone and orchestra titled *Don Quichotte à Dulcinée*.

This was Ravel's last score. Toward the end of 1932 he was involved in an auto accident that triggered a nervous breakdown from which he never recovered. His friends rallied around him but his condition deteriorated slowly. Five years later it was decided to perform a brain operation as a last resort. He underwent the surgery in Paris on December 10, 1937; two and a half weeks later he died without ever having regained consciousness.

In addition to the works already mentioned, his principal scores include the charming series of richly colored nursery pictures for orchestra titled *Ma Mère L'Oye* (*Mother Goose*); his brilliant orchestration of Moussorgsky's *Pictures at an Exhibition*; a nursery opera, *L'Enfant et les Sortilèges* (*The Child and the Sorcerers*), in which a naughty child is punished when his toys come to life; his *Introduction and Allegro* for Harp, Flute, Clarinet and String Quartet; a trio and a septet; and a large number of piano pieces.

DAPHNIS AND CHLOÉ

During the two decades before and after World War I the most vital performing organization in the world of musical theater was undoubtedly the fabled Ballets Russes of Serge Diaghilev. Diaghilev had a positive genius for recruiting the collaborate efforts of the leading graphic, musical and dancing artists of the day. The resulting confluence of creative endeavor produced a series of twentieth-century masterpieces that are still unparalleled in their utilization of talents from the various fields of art. For example, the following artists were responsible for the world-premiere presentation (in London in July 1919) of the ballet *The Three-Cornered Hat*, based on the Spanish folk novel by Alarcón: Manuel de Falla, who composed the score; Pablo Picasso, who designed the scenery and costumes; Leonide Massine and Tamara Karsavina, who danced the leading roles; and Ernest Ansermet, who conducted the performance.

Seven years earlier, an equally distinguished group of artists created for Diaghilev a ballet on the *Daphnis and Chloé* story by the fifth-century Greek author Longus. Maurice Ravel composed the music; Michel Fokine did the choreography; Leon Bakst created the sets; Nijinsky and Karsavina danced the leading roles; and Pierre Monteux conducted the performance. Another distinguished composer for Diaghilev, Igor Stravinsky, once wrote of *Daphnis and Chloé*: "It is not only Ravel's best work, but also one of the most beautiful products of all French music."

Ravel, being a classicist, was strongly drawn to the story of the Greek pastoral and its tale of the instinctive and uninhibited love between Daphnis, the shepherd, and Chloé, the shepherdess. And yet there is little of classical remoteness in the music; rather, there is mirrored in its pages the essence of Ravel's art: elegant, polished and sophisticated. John N. Burk has pointed out that this is not ancient Greece, but France, the France of Versailles, where simplicity was achieved in the most studied, elegant and sophisticated manner possible.

The opening measures of the score immediately establish the tonal atmosphere: against soft, muted strings we hear a harp arpeggio, gentle chords from the chorus, a ravishing flute solo and horn calls. The dream-like, ancient mood is delineated to perfection and the scene is set for the action that follows. The ballet's first scene is laid in a meadow on the borders of a sacred grove. Young men and ladies appear, carrying baskets with gifts for the nymphs.

Daphnis is a handsome shepherd and he is surrounded by dancing shepherdesses. Chloé makes her entrance and she is drawn into the dance. Dorcon, a country bumpkin, is the rival of Daphnis for the love of Chloé, and, just to complicate matters further, another shepherdess named Lyceion contests with Chloé for the love of Daphnis. Three ancient statues of nymphs are at the entrance to the grove and off in the distance a large rock bears a likeness to the form of Pan, the special patron of the shepherds. Pirates burst in and carry off Chloé. Daphnis finds a sandal that she has dropped and he prays to the nymphs for her safety. The sculptured nymphs come to life and all pay homage at the altar of Pan.

In the second scene we are at the pirates' camp by the sea. Chloé, her hands tied, is brought in and she performs a dance of supplication. When she tries to escape, the pirates intercept her but then satyrs, the emissaries of Pan, surround the pirates, and Pan himself appears. The pirates flee in terror and Chloé is left alone.

The third and last part of the ballet returns the action to the scene of the very beginning. Daphnis, having lost Chloé, is prostrate with grief before the grove. The nymphs rouse him and lead him slowly toward the large rock, which then becomes transformed, and Pan himself is seen once again. Chloé arrives and there is general rejoicing as the lovers are reunited. The pantomime is concluded by a sacrifice at the altar of Pan, and then a wild "General Dance" begins. Chloé falls into the arms of Daphnis and the ballet ends in a joyous tumult.

Ravel, in an autobiographical sketch written in 1928, said of *Daphnis and Chloé:* "The work is constructed symphonically according to a strict tonal plan by the method of a few motifs, the development of which achieves a symphonic homogeneity of style." These words are especially pertinent in discussing the complete ballet score (as distinguished from the two concert suites that Ravel himself extracted from the larger work). The two suites, especially the second, have long been favorites of the repertoire, but in recent seasons conductors have been turning with increasing frequency to the complete score of the work for their concert performances.

Of the available recordings of the complete ballet, there are several that are quite unusually successful: Ansermet's (London CS

6456) and the two conducted by Charles Munch (especially the second one, RCA LSC 2568). Ansermet's is a beautifully refined, exquisitely shaped performance that is ravishingly played and recorded. The definition of instrumental and choral timbres is carefully calculated and the whole enterprise is one of the finest accomplishments of Ansermet's long and distinguished career. The Munch recording is the culmination of an interpretation that has constantly grown in authority and sensitivity ever since he first recorded the two suites from the complete ballet for English Decca in the late 1940s. *Daphnis and Chloé*, with its violent contrasts, its shifting colors and languorous atmosphere, is a perfect score for the mercurial art of Charles Munch. The quality of sound is mellow, owing to rather distant microphone placement. But there is great refinement and mystery in this Munch recording.

A rather more detached view of the score is taken by Pierre Monteux in this recording of the complete ballet (London STS 15090). There is a quality of austerity here that underlines the classical directness of the music. For those to whom understatement is the preferred ideal, the Monteux version will prove eminently satisfactory. The sound is slightly more forward than in the Munch recording. Munch, incidentally, takes over fifty-five minutes for his performance; Monteux takes just over fifty-one.

A performance of the score conducted by Leonard Bernstein (Columbia MS 6260) draws much broader effects than do either Munch or Monteux, and the Bernstein recorded sound has more presence than that of the two rival versions. There is no denying the vigor and excitement of the Bernstein recording—and a special word of praise must be directed to the enthusiastic collaboration of the Schola Cantorum of New York—but the atmosphere and aesthetic of *Daphnis and Chloé* are more authentically communicated by Ansermet, Munch and Monteux. Like Monteux, Bernstein also takes about fifty-one minutes for the performance, yet his tempos seem considerably more rushed.

No tape or cassette exists at all of any performance of the complete ballet.

Many recordings are available of the Second Suite alone—which encompasses the entire third scene of the ballet. Most of the Second

Suite recordings omit the brief part for the wordless chorus in the "General Dance," but there are a few that do include it. Of several recent recordings of the Suite, two are outstanding: the one by Boulez with the Cleveland Orchestra (Columbia M 30651; cassette MT 30651)—an extraordinarily clear and finely detailed performance; and the one by Stokowski with the London Symphony Orchestra (London SPC 20159; tape L 75059; cassette M 94059)—a richly sensuous and extraordinarily beautiful account of the score, provided you can forgive Stokowski his indulgence of prolonging the final choral chord beyond the point indicated by Ravel. Both Boulez and Stokowski employ chorus in their performances. Of the performances without the choral portions, Martinon's (RCA LSC/LM 2806) is the most striking.

Nikolai Rimsky-Korsakov

Born: Tikhvin, Novgorod, March 18, 1844
Died: St. Petersburg, June 21, 1908

Rimsky-Korsakov came from an aristocratic family of landowners who employed a small band of Jewish musicians on the family estate. The lad's first musical impressions came from the colorful music played by these instrumentalists. He began to be taught the piano at the age of six and attempted his earliest composition at the age of nine. A career as a musician was beneath the consideration of one of his station in Czarist society, however, and so young Rimsky-Korsakov was prepared for a life in the Russian Navy. Between 1856 and 1862 he was a student at the Naval College in St. Petersburg, but he managed on Sundays to take lessons on the cello and piano. A meeting with Balakirev in 1861 eventually served as the trigger to his decision to fly in the face of the wishes of his family and to pursue an active career as a musician. During the course of a three-year tour of duty as a naval officer at sea, he managed to complete his First Symphony, which was performed in December 1865 at one of the concerts of the Free School of Music in St. Petersburg with Balakirev conducting.

During the next eight years Rimsky-Korsakov devoted himself increasingly to composition, producing the symphonic poem *Sadko* in 1867 and the opera *The Maid of Pskov* in the period 1868–72. In 1871 he became professor of composition and instrumentation at the St. Petersburg Conservatory and in 1873 he resigned from the Navy. At the request of the Grand Duke Konstantin Nicholaye-vich, however, he was appointed to the position of inspector of naval bands, which he held until 1884 when the post was abolished. The rest of his life was centered in St. Petersburg, where he was active as a conductor in various capacities. Several times he also conducted outside of Russia, earning much favor wherever he went. He was several times offered the directorship of the Moscow Conservatory but he turned it down each time.

In March 1905 he was dismissed from his professorship at the St. Petersburg Conservatory because of a letter he wrote advocating the autonomy of the institution (which previously had been under the management of the Imperial Russian Musical Society) and complaining against the use of armed force in the Conservatory to suppress students' political expression. In response to Rimsky-Korsakov's dismissal the Conservatory was hit by a whole series of resignations by prominent faculty members, including Glazounov and Liadov. Later he was reinstated, and Glazounov was named the director. His opera *The Invisible City of Kitezh* was produced in the same year but another opera, *Le Coq d'Or*, was held up by censorship because it was a thinly veiled criticism of Imperial Russia during his time.

Rimsky-Korsakov orchestrated Dargomizhsky's *The Stone Guest*, Moussorgsky's *Boris Godounov* and *Khovantchina* and Borodin's *Prince Igor*. He composed three symphonies, including one titled "Antar"; more than a dozen operas; a piano concerto; and *Scheherazade*. His treatise on instrumentation has been the classic work of its kind ever since it first appeared posthumously in 1913. A master of orchestration, he carried on the Liszt tradition of the tone poem but he added his own brilliant finesse of instrumental coloring.

SCHEHERAZADE, OP. 35

When the Academy of Motion Picture Arts and Sciences awarded an Oscar some years ago to Dmitri Tiomkin for his score for the film *High Noon*, the composer proceeded to deliver a Thank You speech to end all Thank You speeches. In the hoary tradition of the Academy Award dinners, Tiomkin began to name all the people to whom he was indebted, and to thank them for their assistance. The names he called off were Peter Ilyitch Tchaikovsky, Nikolai Andreyevich Rimsky-Korsakov, Sergei Vassilievich Rachmaninoff, etc., etc. The speech brought down the house, naturally, and injected a note of genuine and unexpected humor into an otherwise dreary occasion.

If some of the laughter in the audience sounded self-consciously forced and embarrassed, it was only because Tiomkin had assuredly acknowledged not only his own debt to the Romantic Russian composers, but also the debt of most of the assembled Hollywood composers. The colorfully orchestrated and highly evocative scores of Rimsky-Korsakov and Company have proven a rich treasure-trove of inspiration for movie music ever since sound was added to the sights on the screen. The dazzle and brilliance of *Capriccio Espagnol* and the *Russian Easter* Overture, the richly flavored exoticism of "Antar" and *Scheherazade* are the fountainheads from which have sprung innumerable adventure and quasi-oriental film scores.

Rimsky-Korsakov and his colleagues came naturally by their feeling for the exotic music of the East. The Caucasian and Asiatic provinces of Russia have had their own musical culture and traditions since antiquity. The ancient sculpture of the region, indeed, shows instruments almost exactly like those still in use there today —with a heavy emphasis upon flute, tambourine, cymbals and drums. Soviet musicologists of the present day are devoting much serious study and research to the music of these far-flung areas and the music of the Asian republics is assuming a great importance in the development of the musical life of the contemporary Soviet Union.

Yet as long ago as the middle of the eighteenth century composers in Western Europe had come under the influence of the so-called "Turkish" music with its lavish and colorful use of the exotic percussion instruments. Mozart, for example, called upon the triangle to create an Eastern flavor in *The Abduction From the Seraglio* of 1782 and Beethoven scored prominent parts for triangle, bass drum and cymbals in the Turkish March from *The Ruins of Athens* of 1811. With both composers, however, one has the feeling that the exoticism is a superficial graft upon music which is no more Eastern in feeling than any other music we have from them.

Rimsky-Korsakov's development as an orchestral painter reached a summit of brilliance during the years 1887 and 1888. In an eighteen-month period culminating in the summer of 1888, he produced his *Capriccio Espagnol, Scheherazade* and *Russian Easter* Overture. In the composer's own words in his autobiography, these works

> close this period of my activity, at the end of which my orchestration had reached a considerable degree of virtuosity and bright sonority without Wagner's influence, and within the limits of the usual make-up of Glinka's orchestra. These three compositions also show a considerable falling off in the use of contrapuntal devices, which is noticeable after *Snegourochka*. The place of the disappearing counterpoint is taken by a strong and virtuoso development of every kind of figuration which sustains the technical interest of my compositions.

Carl van Vechten has written of Rimsky-Korsakov that "he was always seduced by the picturesque and the exotic. He might be called, indeed, a musical Eurasian." Surely no more fitting subject could have existed for a composer of this natural bent than the *Arabian Nights* or *Thousand and One Nights* stories. The autograph score of *Scheherazade* indicates that the entire work was composed within the single month of July 1888.

Rimsky-Korsakov himself attached this note to the score:

> The Sultan Schahriar, persuaded of the falseness and the faithlessness of women, has sworn to put to death each one of his wives after the first night. But the Sultana Scheherazade saved her life by interesting him in tales which she told him during one thousand and one nights. Pricked by curiosity, the Sultan put off his wife's execution from day to day, and at last gave up entirely his bloody plan.
>
> Many marvels were told Schahriar by the Sultana Scheherazade. For her stories the Sultana borrowed from poets their verses, from folk songs their words; and she strung together tales and adventures.

Two themes recur throughout the music like an *idée fixe:* the one is bold and imperious, obviously characterizing the stern Sultan; the other, given to the solo violin, is warm and seductive, a cadenza of virtuoso flavor which just as obviously is intended to portray

Scheherazade as she spins her tales. The composer's early fascination with percussion instruments finds its mature fulfillment in the
Scheherazade orchestration: tympani, snare drum, bass drum, cymbals, tambourine, triangle and tam-tam, in addition to the usual
strings, winds and brass.

The four sections of *Scheherazade* proceed as follows:

I—*The Sea and Sinbad's Ship*. Right at the very start, *Largo e
maestoso*, is the theme depicting the Sultan. It is belched forth in
unison by the trombones, tuba, strings and low woodwinds. Afterward, in a violin solo with harp chords, comes the motive of
Scheherazade herself. The movement proper begins immediately afterward. It is an *Allegro non troppo* dominated by an undulating
figure that has been called the Wave motive, and another theme, first
sung by the flute accompanied by arpeggios on a solo cello, that has
been called the Ship motive. There is a full orchestral climax on the
Sultan's theme and the movement subsides into a calm ending.

II—*The Story of the Kalendar Prince*. Scheherazade's theme is
again heard on the solo violin with harp accompaniment (*Lento*) and
then the bassoon sings a mournful, mock-heroic theme that ushers in
the main body of the movement, *Andantino*. The pace quickens,
there are flourishes and fanfares from the brass instruments, and the
whole now has the character of a brilliant and colorful pageant. A
long and fanciful elaboration on this material ensues and the movement ends in a flash of orchestral brilliance.

III—*The Young Prince and the Young Princess*. A languorous and
richly rhapsodic theme is played by the strings at their lushest to
open the movement, *Andantino quasi allegretto*. This undoubtedly
characterizes the Prince. The Princess enters as a graceful, somewhat
saucy clarinet solo, *Pochissimo piu mosso*, and the orchestration
grows increasingly more colorful as snare drum, tambourine, cymbals
and triangle add their voices. Toward the end of the movement, after
extensive manipulation of the two main themes, the voice of Scheherazade is heard once again in the solo violin spinning out her tale.

IV—*Festival at Bagdad—The Sea—The Ship Goes to Pieces on a
Rock Surmounted by the Bronze Statue of a Warrior—Conclusion*.
As at the start of the work, the Sultan's theme once again roars out
at the beginning of this last movement, and once again the storytell-
ing Sultana is heard in the solo violin. Then the *Festival at Bagdad*

begins, *Allegro molto e frenetico*, later *Vivo*. The hustle and bustle of crowds is portrayed vividly, with percussion punctuation from the tambourine and cymbals. But then suddenly the mood changes and we are on board ship, inexorably heading for the magnetic rock. The Sultan's theme, which now apparently has become the motive of the Sea, is proclaimed by menacing trombones. The music writhes and surges spectacularly and the ship is dashed against the cliff into a thousand pieces. Out of the debris the song of Scheherazade emerges once again as, triumphantly, she has spun her tales of adventure. The ending is one of beatific peace and resolution.

From all the foregoing it should be obvious that *Scheherazade* is a virtuoso score which demands of its performers the ultimate in technical polish along with an absorption in the persuasive exoticism of the music.

The ability to coax these qualities out of an orchestra is a trait which is by no means in abundant supply among conductors, and though *Scheherazade* is one of the most-duplicated works in the record catalogs, many are the distinguished practitioners of the art of conducting who never recorded the score. I'll never understand why Koussevitzky was not given an opportunity to record his dazzling account of the music, which, with the Boston Symphony, was one of the great performances of our time—but *Scheherazade* is but one of a number of sovereign Koussevitzky readings now lost to posterity due to RCA Victor's negligence during the 1940s.

Which brings us to the version which I consider to be the finest recorded performance *Scheherazade* has ever had—Beecham's Angel recording with the Royal Philharmonic Orchestra (S 35505; cassette 4XS 35505). Sir Thomas many times in his recording career acted as a human Pulmotor in breathing fresh, new life into exhausted war-horses of the repertoire. In *Scheherazade* his ministrations are positively magical: here is Rimsky-Korsakov's score in all its spontaneous color and varied orchestral moods, played as though for the first time, and with vigor, conviction and uninhibited abandon. The orchestral ensemble work crackles with excitement, while Beecham's first-chair players—Steven Staryk, violin; Jack Brymer, clarinet; and Gwydion Brooke, bassoon, to mention only the three most prominent—give the performances of their lives in their important solo parts. Angel's recorded sound is luscious and detailed in mono; the stereo, one of Angel's earliest efforts in the two-channel medium, adds little to the over-all aural perspective and sounds suspiciously like a good mono recording fed equally through two channels. But no matter, Beecham reigns supreme, and his performance is also available on tape (Angel ZS 35505).

Among the other available performances, those by Ansermet (London CS 6212; tape L 80076; cassette M 10076) and Previn (RCA LSC 3042) are my current alternate choices. These is also an Ormandy-Phildelphia Orchestra performance in the RCA "ice-box" awaiting release.

Charles Camille Saint-Saëns

Born: Paris, October 9, 1835
Died: Algiers, December 16, 1921

Like so many of the other composers included in this volume, Saint-Saëns began his musical studies at a very tender age with his mother as his first teacher. He then went on to study with others and at the age of eleven he played his first piano recital in the Salle Pleyel in Paris. At thirteen he became a student at the Paris Conservatory and three years later won the first prize in organ. It was during this period that he first met Franz Liszt, a man who was to have a profound influence upon him and to whom he later dedicated his Third Symphony.

During the 1850s Saint-Saëns served as organist first at the church of Saint-Merry, then at the Madeleine. In 1851 he produced his First Symphony; his Second followed in 1856, composed for a competition opened in Bordeaux. Between 1861 and 1865 he was professor of piano at the Ecole Niedermeyer—the only teaching he did during his long lifetime. For the next half century Saint-Saëns was one of the most honored and respected musicians on the international scene. He composed music in all forms and was renowned far and wide as a pianist of elegance and taste. His own music shows refinement, spirit, genial melody and a fine sense of form. He was one of the principal influences in restoring French composers into the mainstream of symphonic thought and creation. He also traveled widely and lived a full and fulfilled life.

His most notable works, in addition to *Carnival of the Animals* and the Third Symphony, are the symphonic poems *Danse Macabre* and *Omphale's Spinning Wheel;* five piano concertos; the Third Violin Concerto; the *Introduction and Rondo Capriccioso* and the

Havanaise, both for violin and orchestra; and a host of works for the stage, of which *Samson et Dalila* is the best known.

CARNIVAL OF THE ANIMALS

In a lifetime that began eight years after the death of Beethoven (1835) and ended eight years after the premiere of Stravinsky's *Scare du Printemps* (1921), Charles Camille Saint-Saëns managed to remain throughout his entire career the very archetype of the cultivated, urbane cosmopolitan. An honored and respected musician for nearly sixty years, Saint-Saëns was also a brilliantly literate writer of poems, plays and books. In his later years he did much traveling, showing a predilection for faraway, exotic places, including Algiers—he ultimately produced a *Suite Algérienne*—French Indochina and South America. He also visited the United States twice—in 1906, when he appeared with a number of our leading orchestras conducting programs of his own music, and again ten years later, when he journeyed to San Francisco as the French representative at the Panama-Pacific Exposition.

Saint-Saëns composed prolifically in many musical forms and media—his output includes ten concertos, five symphonies, many works for smaller instrumental combinations, and thirteen operas. Where Saint-Saëns was at one time one of the most performed of composers, much of his music has now fallen into neglect. Conversely, however, a score that seems to be growing in public favor is his "Grand Zoological Fantasy" titled *Carnival of the Animals*. Composed in 1886—the same year as the composer's Third Symphony—*Carnival of the Animals* reveals Saint-Saëns' gift for parody and humor in music.

Carnival of the Animals was composed as a private joke for a group of Saint-Saëns' friends and colleagues for performance at a Mardi Gras concert. It was scored originally for two pianos and small instrumental ensemble, and though Saint-Saëns later orchestrated it for a larger instrumental group, he refused to allow it to be performed in public or published during his lifetime. The first public

performance took place two months after Saint-Saëns' death, with
Gabriel Pierné conducting the Colonne Orchestra in Paris. The
music was published in the same year, 1922.

Walter Damrosch conducted the score in New York for the first
time in October 1822 and speculated at that time that Saint-Saëns
had suppressed the score for so long because he had little faith in
the sense of humor of the average concert audience. Lawrence Gilman wrote: "No doubt Saint-Saëns was bored by the anticipated
necessity of reminding pious academic souls that a good jest, tersely
and pointedly told, is a welcome thing even in the haunts of the
Ninth Symphony and the *Liebestod*. So he probably smiled sourly
to himself, boarded up his Zoo, and hid the key."

There are fourteen sections, during the course of which Saint-
Saëns quotes freely from other composers. A note at the beginning
details the interpolations:

In No. 4, *Tortoises*, the composer has utilized two tunes from
Orpheus in the Underworld by Offenbach, which he has re-har-
monized. He has chosen an excerpt from the final ballet and several
measures from the finale of the first act. In No. 5, *The Elephant*,
the composer interpolates several measures of the Ballet of the
Sylphs from *The Damnation of Faust* by Berlioz with a passing
souvenir from *A Midsummer Night's Dream* by Mendelssohn. In
No. 12, *Fossils*, there are introductions of motifs from *J'ai du bon
Tabac*; *Ah! Vous dirai-je Maman*; *Danse Macabre*; *The Departure
for Syria*; and the Air of Rosina from *The Barber of Seville*.

Here are capsule descriptions of the sections in the music:

I. *Introduction and Royal March of the Lion* (*Andante maestoso*;
Allegro non troppo). There is an anticipatory build-up before the
strings, in unison, declare a majestic theme. The roar of the lion is
heard in chromatic scales for the two pianos and the low strings.

II. *Hens and Roosters* (*Allegro moderato*). Unmistakable cackling
is heard from the two pianos, the strings and clarinet.

III. *Wild Asses* (*Presto furioso*). Mad racing up and down the two
piano keyboards is Saint-Saëns' way of characterizing these animals.

IV. *Tortoises* (*Andante maestoso*). The strings and the first piano
lumber along in this section, quoting from Offenbach's *Orpheus*.

V. *The Elephant* (*Allegretto pomposo*). The double basses, as elephants, disport themselves to the tune of Berlioz' "Dance of the Sylphs." Enlarging upon the parodistic aspect is a quotation from Mendelssohn's A *Midsummer Night's Dream* music.

VI. *Kangaroos* (*Moderato*). Like No. 3, this section is for the two pianos only and the music depicts the grotesque hopping and skipping of these beasts.

VII. *Aquarium* (*Andantino*). Muted strings and liquid piano arpeggios paint the picture of a watery scene. Flecks of color are added by flute and clarinet, and the celesta glissandos are meant to depict darting fish.

VIII. *Persons with Long Ears* (*Tempo ad lib*). The violins are given the task of making like braying donkeys. They succeed admirably!

IX. *The Cuckoo in the Woods* (*Andante*). Meditative chords in the two pianos conjure up a forest scene, while an offstage clarinet intones the call of the cuckoo.

X. *Birds* (*Moderato grazioso*). Against a constant fluttering in the strings, the flute scampers and twitters, aided and abetted by the pianos.

XI. *Pianists* (*Allegro moderato*). What these nearly human creatures are doing in a gallery of zoo animals is unexplained by the composer—but is an explanation really necessary? In his program notes for the New York premiere of the score, Ernest La Prade wondered whether Saint-Saëns "meant to imply that pianists—beginners, at least—are dangerous beasts that ought to be kept behind bars; or does he suggest that they would be better seen than heard? The hearer may decide after listening to this delightful parody of a Czerny exercise (piano and strings)."

XII. *Fossils* (*Allegro ridicolo*). Among other themes parodied in this section is one from the composer's own *Danse Macabre*. Xylophone, strings, clarinet and pianos are the instruments employed.

XIII. *The Swan* (*Andantino grazioso*). This is the only section from the score that Saint-Saëns allowed to be published during his lifetime. It is familiar in a variety of diverse settings; here it is scored for cello solo with a rippling accompaniment from the two pianos.

XIV. *Finale* (*Molto allegro*). Themes from various earlier sections are recalled in this Grand Finale, scored for the entire orchestra. The principal theme of the movement is a headlong romp, and the last word is had by the donkeys.

In the late 1940s Columbia Records commissioned a set of verses for *Carnival of the Animals* from Ogden Nash, and then the music was recorded with André Kostelanetz and his Orchestra, the two-piano team of Leonid Hambro and Jascha Zayde, and the verses of Nash spoken by Noël Coward. Until recently the performance was still carried in the Columbia catalog with two alternate couplings (ML 4355, with Ravel's *Mother Goose Suite,* and CL-720, with Prokofiev's *Peter and the Wolf,* narrated by Arthur Godfrey). There is a decided air of disingenuous cleverness about it all, and yet I continue to find it disarmingly amusing. Of all the various recordings of *Carnival of the Animals* that employ verses of one kind or another (most of them employ the Nash verses), the original Coward-Kostelanetz performance is my recommended recording, even though it exists in monophonic sound only, and even though locating a copy of the disc may prove to be as difficult as penetrating Fort Knox in search of souvenirs. A notable failure is the recording with Beatrice Lillie reading thoroughly self-consciously (London CS 6187). In addition the whole thing is overproduced, with all manner of animal noises at the beginning, and with trick microphone techniques, echo chambers and the like cluttering up the enterprise.

A totally different kind of narration is included in Leonard Bernstein's recording of the music—a "Music Appreciation" guide to the score, delivered by Mr. Bernstein himself in the manner of his famous Young People's Concerts on television. What worked exceedingly well on the home screen becomes increasingly irritating on the home hi-fi set as Mr. Bernstein, in his role of animated guide throughout the score, constantly interrupts the flow from one piece to the next with his didactic tutoring. Chalk this up to a miscalculation where repeated listening is concerned.

In the absence of the Coward-Kostelanetz performance of the version with the Nash lyrics, and the withdrawal of my previously favored Kurtz-conducted performance of the musical score sans lyrics (once available as Capitol SG 7211), my choice goes—by default—to the Downs-Fiedler recording for music-with-lyrics (RCA LSC 2596), and to the Prêtre-conducted Angel release (S 36421) for music alone.

Tape or cassette? No really satisfactory performance exists in either medium.

SYMPHONY NO. 3 IN C MINOR, OP. 78, "ORGAN"

Saint-Saëns once wrote: "The artist who does not feel completely satisfied by elegant lines, by harmonious colors and by a beautiful succession of chords does not understand the art of music." Content mattered little to him; the successful composition was the one which combined formal perfection with purity of style. With this as his basic musical philosophy Saint-Saëns had little trouble producing an enormous output in all forms. "In doing my work," he wrote, "and fulfilling the functions of my nature, as an apple tree produces apples, I have no need to trouble myself with other people's views." Though this attitude may seem excessively simplistic in our complicated society, the best of Saint-Saëns' works reveal the composer's keen sense of proportion, clarity and form.

Saint-Saëns composed his Third Symphony—frequently called the "Organ" Symphony because of the extensive and brilliant scoring for the instrument—on commission from the London Philharmonic Orchestra. The composer himself conducted the premiere of the symphony with that orchestra in St. James' Hall, London, on May 19, 1886, in a program otherwise conducted by Sir Arthur Sullivan. (On the same evening Saint-Saëns was the soloist in Beethoven's Fourth Piano Concerto.)

The score bears a dedication to Franz Liszt, whom Saint-Saëns had befriended in the 1850s. Indeed, some commentators have found in the solemn and devotional pages of the music an implied "memorial" to Liszt. In point of fact, however, Liszt died two months *after* the symphony was first performed and he had heard the greater part of the score in a piano transcription that Saint-Saëns himself had played for him. Thus, as with the *Adagio* from the Seventh Symphony of Bruckner, in which some have found grief over the death of Wagner (even though Wagner died some months after the movement was completed), Saint-Saëns' dedication of his

Third Symphony to Liszt must be regarded as a posthumous tribute.

One of this country's most distinguished music critics, Philip Hale,
wrote after an early Boston performance of the Third Symphony:

> Saint-Saëns' Symphony in C Minor has the finest and most character-
> istic qualities of the best French music: logical construction, lucidity,
> frankness, euphony. The workmanship is masterly. There is no hesita-
> tion. The composer knew exactly what he wanted and how to express
> himself. A few of the themes, that when first exposed might seem to
> some insignificant, assume importance and even grandeur in the de-
> velopment. The chief theme of the *Adagio*, the theme for strings, is
> very French in its sustained suavity, in a gentle, emotional quality
> that never loses elegance, and the preparation for the entrance of this
> *Adagio* is worthy of the greatest masters.

The importance of Saint-Saëns' Third Symphony in the development of French symphonic music cannot be overstated. Its success
prompted other French composers to essay the symphonic form,
and the symphonies of D'Indy ("On a French Mountain Air"),
Franck and Chausson followed hard upon it.

For the first performance of the score Saint-Saëns prepared a detailed analysis of the symphony, which read in part:

> This symphony is divided into parts, after the manner of Saint-
> Saëns' Fourth Concerto for Piano and Orchestra and Sonata for
> Piano and Violin. Nevertheless, it includes practically the traditional
> four movements: the first, checked in development, serves as the
> introduction of the *Adagio*, and the Scherzo (*Presto*) is connected,
> after the same manner, with the Finale. The composer has thus
> sought to shun in a certain measure the interminable repetitions
> which are more and more disappearing from instrumental music.

The slow introduction has reminded some commentators of the
first- and third-act preludes from Wagner's *Tristan und Isolde*. The
Allegro moderato section of the movement begins with a whirring
violin figure that is not unlike the opening of Schubert's "Unfinished" Symphony. This section develops considerable momentum,

there is a contrasting second theme of a calm and tranquil nature, and then both themes are subjected to a considerable development. The music then subsides to a *Poco adagio*, a virtually independent slow movement which introduces the sounds of the organ into the texture of the scoring. This section is meditative and peaceful, almost ecclesiastic in mood. The movement ends with a coda of mystical character and ambiguous tonality with alternating chords in D-flat major and E minor.

The second movement begins with a vigorous section marked *Allegro moderato*, with a bold string theme echoed by the woodwinds and tympani. In a *Presto* section that follows there are flashing arpeggios and scales for the piano while the rest of the orchestra has a syncopated rhythm. There is a repetition of the *Allegro moderato* and then of the *Presto* but then a new and solemn theme appears in the trombone, tuba and double basses. This episode ends in a phrase that "rises to orchestral heights, and rests there as in the blue of a clear sky." (The words are Saint-Saëns' own description.) There follows a majestic *Maestoso* section in C major, with brilliant organ chords and four-hand piano rippling arpeggios. After much interplay between the various tonal and thematic elements, there is a coda that brings a triumphant conclusion with brass proclamations, thundering organ sonorities and booming drums.

A renewed interest in this country in Saint-Saëns' Third Symphony was kindled on December 26, 1946. It was on that date that Charles Munch made his debut appearance in the United States as a guest conductor with the Boston Symphony Orchestra. The Saint-Saëns' Third Symphony was the *pièce de résistance*, and it brought down the house. A few weeks later Munch appeared with the New York Philharmonic and he again included the symphony on his programs. Immediately afterward he and the Philharmonic recorded it for Columbia Records. The performance first was released as a set of four 78-rpm discs and then it was one of the first transfers to the new LP medium. It was a bold, vigorous performance, superbly recorded for its time, and it held its place in the Columbia catalog (as ML 4120) for many years. In the late 1950s, after he had been the music director of the Boston Symphony Orchestra for nearly a decade, Munch undertook to re-record the symphony, this time in Symphony Hall with the Boston Symphony. The resulting performance (RCA LSC 2341) is a triumph. Here is the same searing passion and irresistible vitality that galvanized the Symphony Hall audience at Munch's Boston debut. Berj Zamkochian, who plays the organ solos in the recording, is a virtuoso performer and he and the orchestra together send off sparks of dynamic excitement—abetted by some truly Herculean recorded sound captured by the RCA engineering crew. This, in toto, is one of the most memorable of Munch's achievements during his thirteen Boston years.

The tape version of the Munch recording has now been withdrawn for some unfathomable reason. A respectable second choice, though it lacks by a good measure the sheer panache of the Munch performance, is the account by Zubin Mehta and the Los Angeles Philharmonic (London CS 6680; tape L 80241; cassette M 10241).

Respectable performances are also available conducted by Ormandy (Columbia MS 6469) and Prêtre (Angel S 35924) with E. Power Biggs and Maurice Duruflé, respectively, as the organists. Both are overshadowed by the Munch recording, however.

Franz Schubert

Born: Lichtenthal, near Vienna, January 31, 1797
Died: Vienna, November 19, 1828

Schubert was one of the fourteen children of a schoolmaster at Lichtenthal, a suburb of Vienna. His father was his first music teacher and at the age of ten he became first soprano in the church choir. About this time he also began to compose songs and short instrumental pieces. The following year, 1808, he became a singer in the Vienna court choir and also in the Konvict, the training school for court singers. He played violin in the school orchestra, rising ultimately to the position of first violinist. His first extant score is a fantasy in twelve movements for four-hand piano duet, composed when he was thirteen. By the time he was sixteen he had composed his First Symphony and much else besides.

A profound crisis was precipitated in Schubert's life in 1813: his voice broke and he was obliged to leave the Konvict choir, though he remained as a student at the seminary school for about another year. On his music for a mass by Winter he scribbled, "Schubert, Franz, crowed for the last time, 26 July 1812." In order to escape military conscription he studied for a few months at a training school for elementary teachers and by the autumn of 1814 he was teaching at his father's school. He taught there for two years and spent his leisure time in studying and composing, particularly songs; as many as eight songs in one day flowed out of him and in 1815, his eighteenth year, he composed more than a hundred songs including such a masterpiece as *Der Erlkönig*. Between 1814 and 1816 he composed a whole series of works, including operettas, *Singspiele*, stage pieces and masses. In 1816 he was an unsuccessful applicant for the position of Director of a new State Music School.

From 1817 Schubert lived in Vienna, except for the summers of

1818 and 1824 when he served as music teacher to the family of Count Esterházy at Zelész, Hungary. How Schubert was able to exist on a no-income basis is something of a mystery but it is known that his friends were extremely generous and helpful. By 1821 Schubert had written over six hundred compositions and he was coming to be recognized as one of Vienna's most important creative artists. An 1821 performance of *Der Erlkönig* at a concert by the Vienna Musikverein attracted wide attention. In the following year Schubert declined what may have been the one genuine opportunity he ever had to hold a salaried job—the position as organist at the court chapel.

For most of his mature years Schubert was strongly attracted by the theater and he wanted desperately to compose for the stage. Though the catalog of his output lists more than half a dozen completed "operas," not one of them has survived the test of time. Whether better librettos might have changed the picture is open to conjecture; one wonders if Schubert wasn't really striving after an area that was not truly congenial to his nature and talent. Whatever the reasons, however, only a few overtures and the Incidental Music to the Play *Rosamunde* seem worthy of performance today.

Toward the end of 1822 a catastrophe befell Schubert that was to cut his life mercilessly short. He contracted syphilis, a disease then rampant in Vienna for which there was no cure in those pre-penicillin days. By the spring of 1823 he was desperately ill but then he seemed to recover. It has been suggested that the syphilis was the reason for Schubert's leaving the "Unfinished" Symphony incomplete: he was working on the score at the time he contracted the disease; he had to put it aside, naturally, when he became so ill, and upon his improvement from the ravages of the illness he may simply have avoided returning to the score which surely would have been associated in his own mind with the onset of the sickness.

Despite his pushing aside the "Unfinished" Symphony, Schubert continued to produce music at a feverish pace—sonatas and other works for solo piano; his greatest string quartets; the song cycles *Die Schöne Müllerin* and *Die Winterreise*; the two piano trios; the "Great" C Major Symphony; and the C Major Quintet for Strings. The feverish creative activity of 1828 along with Schubert's generally debilitated condition left him an easy prey to typhoid fever. On the last day of October 1828 Schubert tried to eat fish at the Red Cross Tavern and was nauseated by it. He went home and got into bed. On the twelfth of November he wrote to a friend: "I am ill. I have eaten nothing for eleven days and drunk nothing, and I totter feebly and shakily from my chair to bed and back again." On the sixteenth of November two doctors conferred at Schubert's bedside and presumably typhoid was diagnosed. Between periods of delirium Schubert was able to recognize and converse with friends who kept vigil over him continuously. At three o'clock on the afternoon of November 19 Schubert turned from his brother Ferdinand with the words, "Here, here, is my end," and he died.

Two days later Schubert's body was borne by students to the Währing Cemetery and there he was buried, only two graves away from where Beethoven had been laid to rest twenty months earlier.

QUINTET IN A MAJOR, OP. 114, D. 667, "TROUT"

Franz Schubert was a ripe old twenty-two at the time he wrote his "Trout" Quintet, but he had already composed six symphonies, eleven string quartets, four masses and nearly four hundred songs. What gives the "Trout" Quintet pride of place in the composer's instrumental output up to that time is its wonderfully effective blending of the qualities that together add up to the magic of Schubert's early art. It gives off an irresistible lyric glow; its instrumentation is transparent and pure; its thematic development is masterful. To this I might also add that this combination of sheer melodiousness, together with the instrumentation that calls for piano with strings, makes the "Trout" Quintet an ideal introduction to chamber music. It has always seemed to me that one should tackle the string-quartet literature only after becoming acquainted with some of the masterpieces for piano and strings, or clarinet, oboe, or flute and strings.

The circumstances that produced the "Trout" Quintet were extremely casual. Schubert was spending the summer of 1819 on a

walking tour of Upper Austria with his friend Johann Vogl, the renowned baritone of Vienna's Imperial Opera. Only once before
had the composer been out of Vienna, during the previous year,
when he spent some dreary time as music teacher to the Esterházys.
Now he was enchanted by everything—the beauty of the countryside, the congeniality of the people, the excitement of discovery.

The two friends spent some time in the little town of Steyr, the
birthplace of Vogl, and they soon became the leading participants
in the town's intellectual life. Regular musical evenings were held at
the home of Sylvester Paumgartner, an amateur cellist and the assistant manager of the local mines. Paumgartner conceived the idea
to commission a work from Schubert, specifying that one of the
movements should be a set of variations on *"Die Forelle"* ("The
Trout"), a charming song Schubert had composed about two years
earlier.

Schubert set to work on the piece soon after his return to Vienna
in the early autumn. He was filled with the pleasant memories of his
delightful summer, and the music he produced was the perfect mirror of his warm, amiable experiences. It is quite likely that he composed the work with specific performers from the Steyr circle in
mind, which probably explains the unusual instrumentation: piano,
violin, viola, cello and double bass. Only one other work for the
same combination is readily recalled, a quintet by Schubert's contemporary Johann Nepomuk Hummel. An earlier theory had held
that Schubert was acquainted with the quintet by Hummel, that in
fact the score might have been one of those played in Paumgartner's
house. Recent research shows, however, that Hummel's quintet
was not published until 1821, in Vienna, and the likelihood of a
performance from manuscript two years earlier is extremely slim.
It is more probable that Hummel took Schubert's quintet as a
model, rather than vice versa.

The first movement of the quintet, *Allegro vivace*, opens with a
single chord, followed by an upturning arpeggio in the piano that
firmly establishes the A-major tonality. After about two dozen measures of introductory material, the real first principal theme occurs
in the violin. The cello introduces the second theme, and the piano
the third. Following this prodigiously melodious exposition, the de-

velopment section is comparatively sparse, with the greatest emphasis on the material from the introductory measures. The recapitulation, though, treats us once again to all the melodic delights we heard in the exposition. The second movement, *Andante*, has three principal themes, the first in the piano, the second in the viola and cello, the third once again the piano. After all three are stated, they are then repeated in sequence to form the second part of the movement. The third movement is a Scherzo, marked *Presto*. It is a vigorous movement, with sharp accents, until the Trio section reduces the tension and introduces music of an almost folk-like quality. The fourth movement, marked *Andantino-Allegretto*, is a Theme and Variations treatment of Schubert's song "*Die Forelle.*" There are five variations in all, and a coda. For the most part the technique of embellishment and decoration is used by Schubert, as one instrument after another participates in the series of variations. In the coda the melody of the song is given to the strings while the piano plays the same rippling accompaniment assigned to the instrument in the version for voice and piano. There is also a fifth movement, *Allegro giusto*, in rollicking rhythm. Like the second movement, it is in two parts, with the second repeating sequentially the melodic material from the first.

Over the years the "Trout" Quintet has been well served by its performers on records. The first great recording of the music came in the mid-1930s, with Artur Schnabel, members of the Pro Arte Quartet and Claude Hobday, double bass. It is now available once more in Angel's Great Recordings of the Century series (COLH 40), with astonishingly good sonics (the bite of the double bass is particularly well defined) and in a smooth-surfaced LP transfer. One must occasionally raise an eyebrow at the out-of-tune playing from the violinist, Alphonse Onnou, but the performance has great good spirits and a contagious *élan*. Unless you must have stereo, the Schnabel-Pro Arte version is definitely a serious contender for top honors in the "Trout" fishing contest.

Stereo collectors have available to them a superb performance by Peter Serkin, with a quartet of string players headed by Alexander Schneider, violin (Vanguard VSD 71145). The playing is responsive in the finest sense of chamber-music ensemble: every one of the five instrumentalists is a vital thread in a beautifully adjusted fabric, and the performance has a fresh vitality and invention that are extraordinary. There are other perceptive accounts of the score available on discs—including one with Serkin's celebrated father, Rudolf, as the pianist—but none has the special qualities of joyous abandon that distinguish the Schnabel and Serkin *fils* recordings. The tape edition of the Serkin performance is now no longer available, hence I would direct tape collectors to the more traditional performance by members of England's Melos Ensemble, with Lamar Crowson as pianist (Angel G 3770).

QUINTET IN C MAJOR, OP. 163, D. 959

Franz Schubert composed his C Major Quintet for Strings during 1828, the final year of his incredibly short, thirty-one-year life span. The quintet is considered by many to be Schubert's finest work. Indeed, all his preceding chamber music seems to be but a preparation for this masterpiece, the final summation of Schubert's emotional range and formal perfection.

Schubert grew up with the sound of ensemble chamber music in his ears. His father was a cellist, his two brothers violinists, and he himself played the viola. The four played together regularly as a family string quartet. It was for the family group that Schubert composed his early chamber scores, which were often played before gatherings of friends.

In addition, Schubert was also one of the busiest free-lance musicians in the Vienna of the 1820s. A directory of musicians of the time lists him as a pianist and violinist attached to the Philharmonic Society. He was often a member of groups that entertained at local celebrations and official functions. During this period he managed to produce a large and masterly body of chamber music.

The year before Schubert composed his C Major String Quintet he wrote two superb piano trios, one in B-flat major, Opus 99, the other in E-flat major, Opus 100. They are as different as day and night: the one in B-flat major is an inspired work from first note to last, tender and exuberant; the E-flat major is generally less spontaneous but bolder and more heroic than its companion. In the two works Schubert thoroughly explored the color possibilities of the piano-violin-cello combination. Impelled to return to music for strings alone, he passed over the quartet form—he had, after all, composed many quartets—in favor of the quintet.

Mozart and Beethoven before him, pouring some of their noblest thoughts into the string quintet, scored their works for two violins, two violas and cello. For his model, Schubert turned to the quintets of an earlier composer, Luigi Boccherini, and scored his C Major Quintet for two violins, a single viola and two cellos. Undoubtedly it was the brighter, more conspicuous tonal color of the cello as against the viola that attracted Schubert, and very early in the work we realize how absolutely right this combination of instruments is: the second theme is announced by the two cellos in a soaring melody of surpassing beauty, and immediately the rich, full, almost orchestral sound-palette envelops us.

The C-major tonality generally creates an atmosphere of triumphant, life-giving vitality, as witness Mozart's "Jupiter" Symphony, the Finale of Beethoven's Fifth, or Schubert's own "Great" C Major Symphony. The mood and message of the C Major Quintet, however, are something quite different. The opening establishes a feeling of intensity and resigned struggle, and the development of the initial movement conveys a sense of anguish. The crown of the work is probably the slow movement, an *Adagio* in E major, of transcendent poignancy and passion. The middle section is a stormy, agitated outburst, of which a fleeting recollection returns near the end. The movement subsides in the seraphic beauty of the opening E major. The Scherzo is demonic, propulsive, seething with energy. In the Trio, however, dark thoughts again intrude—some have found in this section the shadow of impending death. The last movement, for the most part, is a release of tension, but near the end the music is suddenly driven into the despair of F minor, and the shadows again take over.

Two recordings of the score may be termed all-star performances: the RCA recording (LSC 2737) with Jascha Heifetz and Israel

Baker, violins; William Primrose, viola; Gregor Piatigorsky and Gabor Rejto, cellos; and Columbia's recording (included in M5 30069, a five-disc package of outstanding recordings involving Pablo Casals) made at one of the European Casals Festivals with Isaac Stern and Alexander Schneider, violins; Milton Katims, viola; and Casals and Paul Tortelier, cellos. Two more widely diverse views of an established repertoire favorite would be difficult to imagine. The RCA virtuosos deliver a streamlined, chromium-plated performance, all glitter and very little substance. The tempos, by and large, are hectic and frenzied, and the glorious, expansive music is given very little room to breathe. Too, the recorded sound is cramped and wiry. On the other hand, the Casals-oriented performance on Columbia is extremely broad and easygoing—too much so, to my taste, for the music's passion and intensity. But if a performance is extreme in one direction, I would rather that direction were the one taken by Casals and Company. There are moments of less than ideal ensemble unity, and some patches of questionable intonation, but one does come away from the recording with a sense of fulfillment.

The Budapest String Quartet and Benar Heifetz, second cello, held the patent on recorded performance of this score for more than twenty years by virtue of their early Columbia recording (ML 4437 —now no longer available). These same artists re-recorded the score a few years ago, and their second version (Columbia MS 6536) is equally successful—except that I find myself even more impressed with the recording made by members of the Vienna Philharmonic Orchestra (London CS 6441). The rich lyrical flow of this great work is communicated most movingly by the five players and the recorded sound is crystal-clear. It is also available in a magnificently processed tape version (London L 80183). Apparently there is no currently available cassette issue of this score.

SYMPHONY NO. 8 IN B MINOR, D. 759, "UNFINISHED"

On April 10, 1823, the name of Franz Schubert was proposed for honorary membership in the Styrian Music Society at Graz in Austria. His qualifications were presented as follows in the nomination papers: "Although still young, he has already proved by his compositions that he will someday rank high as a composer."

When the governing body of the Society voted to elect Schubert to membership, the twenty-six-year-old composer gratefully accepted the honor and wrote: "May it be the reward for my devotion to the art of music that I shall one day be fully worthy of this signal honor. In order that I may also express in musical terms my lively sense of gratitude, I shall take the liberty, at the earliest opportunity, of presenting your honorable Society with one of my symphonies in full score."

The late Alfred Einstein, in his masterful book *Schubert: A Musical Portrait*, surmises that soon thereafter Schubert presented the score and parts of a two-movement symphony he had recently completed to the director of the Society, Anselm Hüttenbrenner. Hüttenbrenner apparently stuck the symphony away in a drawer and promptly forgot about it—and so, too, did Schubert! It was not until 1865, thirty-seven years after the composer's death, that the symphony finally came to performance. And thereby hangs a tale.

In 1860 Hüttenbrenner's brother, Joseph, had written to the conductor of the Gesellschaft der Musikfreunde concerts in Vienna, Johann Herbeck, that Anselm had in his possession a "treasure in Schubert's B Minor Symphony." For five years Herbeck ignored this information, fearing perhaps that part of any deal to pry the Schubert symphony loose from the Hüttenbrenners would involve a commitment for the simultaneous performance of one of Anselm's dreary overtures. Finally, in 1865, Herbeck had occasion to stop at Graz. He sought out the aging and eccentric Anselm and is supposed to have said to him: "I am here to ask your permission to produce one of your works in Vienna." According to the account of Herbeck's son, Ludwig, Anselm's response was instantaneous and uninhibited: he threw his arms around Herbeck in an embrace and then proceeded to parade before the weary conductor manuscript after worthless manuscript of his own music. Finally, Herbeck decided upon one of the overtures and informed Hüttenbrenner that he intended to give a concert of music by three contemporaries, Schubert, Hüttenbrenner and Lachner. "It would naturally be very appropriate to represent Schubert by a new work." "Oh, I have still a lot of things by Schubert," came Hüttenbrenner's reply, and he pulled a pile of manuscript paper out of an old chest. On the cover of one of the manuscripts Herbeck saw the words "*Sinfonie in H Moll*" in Schubert's own handwriting. Casually, he evidenced interest in the score and Hüttenbrenner promptly obliged by giving it to him for performance. On December 17, 1865, the music was finally heard for the first time. Since then Schubert's "*Sinfonie in H Moll*" (B minor) has become one of the most beloved classics of the entire literature.

Before we get to the recordings of the score, let us touch upon the "unfinished" aspects of the symphony. The lack of a Scherzo and Finale has given posterity a handy title by which to identify the score. If one insists upon the four-movement format of the classical symphony as an unalterable model, then Schubert's B Minor Symphony may be said to be unfinished. On purely aesthetic grounds, however, the work is a unified whole, a thing of beauty and completeness in itself, no more unfinished as an artistic masterpiece than the Venus de Milo, missing arms and all. Schubert must have felt this instinctively when—having penned nine bars of Scherzo—he put the work aside with only two movements completed.

The first movement, *Allegro moderato*, opens with a questioning five-measure phrase in the lower strings, which is answered immediately by the second part of the first subject in unison oboes and clarinets while the strings are busy with a repeated-note figure. The first subject is extended and developed and then, against a gently syncopated rhythm in the violas and clarinets, the cellos announce the famous second subject of the movement, a gloriously lyrical effusion that is the essence of Schubert. The structural development of the movement is in the purest classical tradition, with the three sections of sonata-allegro form clearly observed. The second movement, *Andante con moto*, begins with a few measures of sustained horn notes over pizzicato strings, followed by the first principal theme stated by all the strings. The second subject is a long, sustained song for the clarinet over syncopated strings. In describing this movement the scholar Alfred Einstein wrote: "The whole movement, in its mystery and unfathomable beauty, is like one of those plants whose flowers open only on a night of the full moon."

In general there are two alternative interpretative approaches to the performance of the "Unfinished" Symphony: one is a kind of demonic attack upon the score that elicits sharp contrasts of dynamics and mood and makes of the symphony a bold, defiant thing; the other approach is what might be called the Viennese attitude —a spontaneous and casual warmth and mellowness, in which the listener is left spellbound by the inevitability of Schubert's lyrical outpouring. The very prototype of the forceful and dynamic approach is the Toscanini recording (RCA Victrola VICS 1311), made in NBC's old Studio 8-H in 1950. The sound matches the performance: it is hard, dry and unresonant. There is no denying its power, but of grace and charm and easy flow there is precious little. My own predilections are for the other kind of performance, hence it is to several of these that I should briefly like to turn. My favorite among the budget-priced recordings is the performance conducted by the lamented Guido Cantelli (Seraphim 60002, mono only)—a superbly disciplined, smoothly recorded performance that still sounds very well despite its early recording date (in the mid-1950s). Despite Cantelli's Toscanini orientation, he is much more plastic in his reading of this score than Toscanini was, and this account is one of the most cherishable surviving mementos of the art of this tragically lamented conductor. Also in the budget-priced category is a surprisingly gentle performance of the score conducted by Charles Munch (RCA Victrola VICS 1035)—a surprise because I have heard Munch drive the music unmercifully in the concert hall. At the time he prepared this recorded performance, however, he was content to take a more leisurely approach. What emerges is a beautifully shaded, if slightly heavy-handed treatment. The recorded sound is a bit on the boomy side.

Of the more than two dozen currently available stereo recordings, my own favorites are those conducted by Casals (Columbia MS 7262) and Walter (now available on disc in Columbia's low-priced Odyssey series, Y 30313; tape Columbia MQ 391).

Of the available cassette performances, Klemperer's would be my
first choice (Angel 4XS 36164).

SYMPHONY NO. 9 IN C MAJOR, D. 944, "THE GREAT"

Schubert's first six symphonies were all for comparatively small orchestra, and all derived in large measure from the musical language
of Haydn and Mozart. The first three were composed while Schubert was a student at the School of the Vienna Imperial Choir; the
next three were designed for the immediate uses of the amateur
musical society that grew out of regular musical gatherings at the
home of Schubert's father. Although Schubert is believed to have
composed four more symphonies during the remaining ten years of
his life, only two of these have survived: the "Unfinished" in B
minor, and the Dionysiac "Great" C Major.

The two missing symphonies are a work in E major fully sketched
in 1821 and another symphony thought to have been composed in
the small town of Gastein in 1825. The manuscript of the sketch for
the E Major Symphony is in the possession of the Royal College of
Music in London. Sir George Grove, who examined it carefully,
stated (in *Grove's Dictionary of Music and Musicians*) that the
memoranda in Schubert's sketch

> are, in their own way, perfectly complete and orderly to the end of
> the finale. Every bar is drawn in; the tempi and names of the instru-
> ments are fully written at the beginning of each movement; the
> nuances are all marked; the very double bars and flourishes are
> gravely added at the end of the sections, and "Fine" (The End) at
> the conclusion of the whole. . . . There is not a bar from beginning
> or end that does not contain the part of one or more instruments: at
> all crucial places the scoring is much fuller; and it would be no doubt
> possible to complete it as Schubert himself intended.

The symphony was indeed completed by no less a figure than the
great conductor Felix Weingartner in 1934. According to the scholar
Alfred Einstein (*Schubert: A Musical Portrait*), Weingartner's reali-

zation of Schubert's sketch is accomplished "with a delicate sense of style, leaving the second and third movements untouched, and tightening up the first and last movements, i.e. shortening them a little." The Schubert-Weingartner Symphony in E Major has not, however, penetrated into the active performing repertoire—though it was once recorded by the Vienna State Opera Orchestra under Franz Litschauer's direction (Vanguard 427, mono only, still available).

Concerning the missing "Gastein" Symphony, the situation is much more confused. A onetime widely held theory speculated that Schubert's Grand Duo for Piano, four hands, was nothing less than a four-hand arrangement by Schubert himself of the missing symphony. Sir Donald Francis Tovey, one of the principal promulgators of this theory, wrote:

> The Grand Duo is unique among Schubert's four-hand works in the disconcerting nature of its orchestral style. . . . [It is] full of the kind of orchestral things the pianoforte obviously cannot do, and deficient in the things, pianistic or orchestral, that it can do with enjoyment. . . . The autograph of the duet, in the possession of the late Mr. Edward Speyer, is one of the most flawless fair copies Schubert ever wrote; and it is impossible to imagine that it represents the process of composition. Nevertheless, the special authorities on Schubert are very unwilling to entertain the suggestion that the Grand Duo may be the lost Gastein Symphony; though they do not seem to have very conclusive arguments against the idea.

Like the E Major Symphony, the Grand Duo, too, was orchestrated by a distinguished musician—in this case a great violinist and conductor of the nineteenth century, Joseph Joachim. Of Joachim's orchestration Tovey wrote: "Joachim's orchestration is exactly right, and differs from what Schubert would have written only in so far as Joachim had become, at an early age, one of the most experienced living masters of the orchestra, so that he avoids, almost instinctively, many a difficulty that arises from Schubert's idiosyncrasies." Like the Weingartner orchestration of the E Major Symphony, Joachim's orchestral treatment of the Grand Duo was also once recorded, with Felix Prohaska conducting the Vienna State Opera Orchestra (Vanguard VRS 417—no longer available).

Having said all the foregoing, it must now be added that the most recent scholarship tends once and for all to lay to rest all the speculation concerning Schubert's missing "Gastein" Symphony. In the October 1959 issue of the London publication *Music and Letters* an interesting article by John Reed was published under the title "The 'Gastein' Symphony Reconsidered." Introducing a wealth of evidence, Reed tends to confirm the theory of Schubert's recent biographer, Maurice Brown, that the symphony Schubert composed during the summer of 1825 in the town of Gastein was nothing else but the "Great" C Major Symphony (to distinguish it from the composer's far slighter Sixth Symphony, also in the key of C Major). Reed speculates that the date of March 1828, which appears on the autograph of the "Great" C Major Symphony and which had always given rise to the belief that Schubert composed the symphony in the last year of his life, was actually the date of a final revision of the score rather than the period of composition. A Schubert letter of 1826 mentions a new symphony he was offering for performance, and Reed concludes his argument stating that the new symphony was indeed the one he had recently composed in Gastein—the "Great" C Major. If Reed's research is correct, then we must readjust our thinking concerning the number of symphonies Schubert composed: the total now becomes nine, with the "Great" C Major as the Ninth. I, for one, am ready to accept this thesis without reservation.

In any case, whatever the circumstances of its composition and whether or not it is the real Gastein Symphony, Schubert's "Great" C Major Symphony came into existence with no special commission, fee or performance in mind. Difficulty, length, orchestration—these were not ordered by the limitations of any particular orchestra or group of players. The composer by now was motivated only by his own soaring fancy. Rather casually, Schubert offered the score of the new work to the Musikverein in Vienna, and just as casually, the parts were copied out and distributed for rehearsal. An early biographer of Schubert, Kreissle von Hellborn, reports that ". . . The

Symphony was soon laid aside as too long and difficult and Schubert advised them to accept and perform in its stead his Sixth Symphony [the so-called "Little" C Major]." Some musicologists have tended to doubt this account of Schubert's ready willingness to abandon his newborn symphony, but the fact remains that the work never was performed during the composer's lifetime. Ten years later, Robert Schumann, visiting Vienna, called upon Schubert's brother, Ferdinand, and went through a pile of manuscripts of Schubert's music in Ferdinand's possession. Schumann came upon the C Major Symphony and sent a copied score to his friend in Leipzig, Felix Mendelssohn, who was the conductor of the Gewandhaus Orchestra. Mendelssohn promptly conducted it at a Gewandhaus concert in March 1839 and wrote to his friend Moscheles: "We recently played a remarkable and interesting symphony by Franz Schubert. It is without doubt one of the best works which we have lately heard. Bright, fascinating and original throughout, it stands quite at the head of his instrumental works." When Mendelssohn visited England sometime later, he scheduled the symphony for performance with the London Philharmonic Society. The orchestra musicians, however, balked at what they called the unreasonable difficulty of the music and laughed openly at the oft-repeated triplets in the last movement. The same reaction came from Paris when Habeneck attempted to introduce the symphony there. To us in this latter day of orchestral virtuosity the complaints of orchestral players a century ago seem grotesque and perverse and the famous triplets in the Finale are the inevitable couriers of Schubert's message of swift and inexorable propulsion.

Sir George Grove, in his masterly essay on the C Major Symphony, written after he had studied the manuscript score, notes numerous changes and corrections in Schubert's own handwriting in the first three movements, but very few in the Finale, as though "the pen seems to have rushed on at an impetuous speed, almost equalling that of the glorious music itself." Concerning the triplets in the Finale, Grove writes fascinatingly:

Here is what happened in Schubert's autograph—he had got as far as the four premonitory notes of the horns: and then he dashed

off into a schoolmasterly little fugue from which the only possible
reaction would have been a schoolboy's practical jokes. By good luck
almost unique in Schubert's short career, he lost interest in this
project before he had written nine bars of it—or perhaps the real
gigantic inspiration came before he developed interest in the frivolity
which he had started. Whatever the mental process was, it cannot
have taken three-quarters of a minute: the dingy little fugue subject
was struck out before the answer had well begun: the danger was
past, and instead of a weak facility, we have the momentum of a
planet in its orbit.

So it is that the Schubert "Great" C Major stands with Mozart's
"Jupiter," Beethoven's "Eroica" and Brahms' Fourth as one of the
monumental touchstones of major artistic aspirations.

The first movement opens with an *Andante* introduction: horns
in unison and unaccompanied have a noble theme that is destined
to play a very prominent part in the following *Allegro ma non
troppo*. From the horns the theme is passed to various woodwind
instruments, and then the violas and cellos continue it. The section is built to a mounting crescendo and then the main body of the
movement begins with a vigorous and rhythmic motive in the strings,
answered by echo-like frills in the horns. Oboes and bassoons have
the contrasting second theme, gentler, more idyllic in character but
no less rhythmic. Other woodwinds join in and soon the whole orchestra reaches a grand climax. During the development section the
original horn theme of the introduction appears in unison trumpets,
while the rest of the orchestra plays with elements of the second
theme. There is an elaborate development and a normal return of
the original themes. The movement ends with a stunning coda in
which our old friend, the horn theme of the introduction, dominates
the proceedings heroically, first in the brass and woodwind instruments, then finally in the strings.

The second movement, *Andante con moto*, begins with a rhythmic
chanting in the strings, followed immediately by a plaintive melody
in the oboe. The second subject appears pianissimo in the strings
and closes with a melting horn passage. Robert Schumann wrote of
this section: "All is hushed, as if a celestial host were moving about

the orchestra." The two themes are varied and repeated and then the movement ends calmly with the rhythmic march chanting.

The Scherzo, a vigorous *Allegro vivace*, begins with a headlong rush in the strings, answered more delicately by a figure in the woodwinds. The pattern is repeated until the second theme of the movement appears—a wistful, waltz-like section, with bassoons and clarinets accompanying the strings. The Trio, in sharp contrast to the boisterous rhythms of the main section, is introduced by horns and clarinets; its character is song-like and gentle. The dynamism of the Scherzo proper returns and the movement ends boldly.

The last movement, *Allegro vicace*, is a headlong, impetuous rush. It begins in fanfare fashion in the brass, followed by rapid string flourishes and then the principal theme erupts in proclamative, heroic style. The second theme is given to the woodwinds over rushing triplet figures in the strings. The sense of momentum is absolutely irresistible throughout as the music proceeds on its winged flight to the heavens. At the end, Schubert insistently drives home the rhythmic pulse that has served as the motor for the entire movement.

Several among the many available recordings of the symphony deserve special attention. The most deeply personal of all the performances is the one by Wilhelm Furtwängler and the Berlin Philharmonic Orchestra (Turnabout TV 4364). This mono Turnabout recording derives from a wartime broadcast performance. At one time there was also available a superb Furtwängler studio recording of this score (Heliodor S 25074), a performance that was a masterly example of the conductor's expansiveness at its most persuasive and of his mesmeric power as an interpreter.

Among modern stereo recordings, my first choice is the performance Szell recorded with the Cleveland Orchestra in the spring of 1970, just a few months before his death (Angel S 36044; cassette 4XS 36044). This is a heroic account of superb discipline, yet with a plasticity and easy flow that is the essence of this sublime score.

Among other stereo recordings, rewarding performances are those conducted by Klemperer (Angel S 35946), Krips (London STS 15140, tape L 80043) and Walter (Columbia MS 6219). Klemperer's has a monolithic nobility that sometimes tends to take itself rather too seriously; Walter's, a relaxed ease and poetry that at times borders on the edge of slackness; and Krips' combines some of the rugged grandeur of Klemperer's approach with some of the grace of Walter's.

Of the two available performances on tape, my preference is for the geniality of Krips.

Robert Schumann

Born: Zwickau, Saxony, June 8, 1810
Died: Endenich, near Bonn, July 29, 1856

Robert Schumann was the fifth and youngest child of a highly cultured bookseller, publisher and author. His first musical studies were with the local organist, who quickly predicted immortality for his young pupil. Schumann's first compositions came when he was six; by the time he was seventeen he was setting his own poems to music. When he was eighteen he enrolled at Leipzig University to study law and philosophy and at the age of nineteen he left the University to enroll at the University of Heidelberg, where he also studied music. At the age of twenty Schumann returned to Leipzig and took up residence in the home of his piano teacher, Friedrich Wieck. He was obsessed with the thought of becoming the outstanding piano virtuoso of his day and used to spend long hours of practice in trying to strengthen his fingers with trick exercises. One of them consisted of suspending the fourth finger of his right hand in a sling while playing with the others—with the result that the finger became permanently disabled and Schumann had to give up all thoughts of a life as a virtuoso.

He then focused all his energies on composition—and on Wieck's young daughter Clara. From rather tentative beginnings there developed a truly passionate love affair, which Wieck did everything to discourage: he loved Schumann as a son, but not as a prospective son-in-law. Finally, in 1840, after all manner of difficulties, including a year's lawsuit, Wieck was forced to consent and the two lovers, both now embarked upon distinguished careers (Schumann as a composer and writer, Clara as a pianist), were united in one of the happiest marriages known in art. For the rest of her life Clara performed Schumann's music widely in her popular concert tours; Schumann, in turn, was intensely devoted to her and he dedicated much of his best work to her.

In 1834 Schumann had founded the *Neue Zeitschrift für Musik* and he was its editor for the next ten years. His essays and criticisms —signed Florestan, Eusebius, Meister Raro and other such fanciful names—are among the most important works in the history of criticism, particularly in the matter of recognizing new genius and heralding it fearlessly and fervently. (Chopin, Brahms and Berlioz all profited from early recognition by Schumann.) In his writings Schumann constructed an imaginary band of ardent young Davids attacking the Goliath of Philistinism. The group was called Davids-bündler. His pen name Eusebius represents the gentle and poetic side of his nature; Florestan, the vehement side.

The year of his marriage, 1840, was the year of his most important song composition; 1841 became his orchestral year and 1842 his chamber-music year, with 1843 the choral year. Also in 1843, at the invitation of his close friend Mendelssohn, Schumann joined the faculty of the Leipzig Conservatory of Music, teaching piano and composition. Between 1844 and 1850 the Schumanns lived in Dresden, where Robert taught and composed, and in 1850 they went to Düsseldorf, where Schumann had the post as music director. From 1833 onward there were disturbing signs that Schumann's mental stability was sometimes questionable: he was given to spells of irritability and moodiness. Then in 1854 came a total collapse; in a thoroughly irrational state Schumann threw himself into the waters of the river Rhine. He was rescued by some boatmen and taken at his own request to an asylum at Endenich near Bonn. There he remained in acute melancholia, with a few flashes of complete rationality, until his death in July 1856.

Schumann was an extraordinarily prolific composer. His principal works are concertos for piano, violin and cello; four symphonies; many songs; much chamber music, including the marvelous Piano Quintet in E-flat Major; many works for solo piano, including sonatas, the *Carnaval* Suite, *Fantasiestücke, Kinderscenen, Kreisleriana*, the C Major Fantasy and *Faschingsschwank aus Wien*.

CONCERTO IN A MINOR FOR
CELLO AND ORCHESTRA, OP. 129

In the first days of September 1850, Robert and Clara Schumann moved from Dresden to the Rhineland city of Düsseldorf, where Robert was to assume the post of municipal music director. The move was not undertaken without considerable apprehension, for Schumann had been warned by his friend Felix Mendelssohn that the musicians in Düsseldorf were a pretty shoddy bunch. Nevertheless, the post's duties appealed to Schumann and seemed to present no serious threat to his fragile health. Therefore, the Schumanns established themselves in Düsseldorf. The musical community there welcomed them with a serenade, a concert of Robert's works, a supper and a ball. At first things went well enough. Schumann threw himself into his new position with extraordinary enthusiasm. He conducted the subscription concerts of the orchestra, rehearsed and conducted the local choir, led performances of church music, gave private music lessons, and organized a chamber-music society. He was everywhere at once, and to every project he brought great energy and vitality.

His creativity as a composer flowered too. On the twenty-ninth of September he visited the city of Cologne and its majestic cathedral, a visit whose echoes are to be heard in the fourth movement of the "Rhenish" Symphony, composed just a few weeks later. In addition, during the early period of his Düsselfdorf residence, Schumann composed many songs, the scenes from Goethe's *Faust*, the overture to Schiller's drama *The Bride of Messina*, and several other works.

In the week between the tenth and the sixteenth of October he sketched out a cello concerto, and by the twenty-fourth of the month the full score was completed. In a diary entry dated November 16, Clara wrote, "Last month [Robert] composed a concerto for violoncello that pleased me very much. It seems to me to be written in true violoncello style." A year later (October 11, 1851) there is another reference to the cello concerto in Clara's diary:

I have played Robert's Violoncello Concerto again, and thus gave to myself a truly musical and happy hour. The romantic quality, the vivacity, the freshness and the humor, and also the highly interesting interweaving of violoncello and orchestra are indeed wholly ravishing, and what euphony and deep feeling there are in all the melodic passages!

The Düsseldorf idyll was short-lived, however. There soon arose friction between Schumann and the orchestra's personnel and management. Charges of mental instability were leveled against him, and finally the orchestra committee instituted proceedings to relieve him of his position. Schumann complained to Clara that he was being cruelly vilified; she must have known that he was perilously close to a mental breakdown.

The Cello Concerto seems to have given Schumann some postcomposition problems. It was more than two years after he completed it that he wrote to the publisher Härtel saying that the score was finally ready for publication. He was still correcting proofs of the printed music some fifteen months later, in February 1854, just a few days before the desperate act that led to his being confined in an asylum.

Schumann had already been confined to the Endenich asylum when the Cello Concerto was finally published, in August 1854. What seems to have been the first performance did not take place until nearly four years after Schumann died, at a concert given at the Leipzig Conservatory to celebrate the fiftieth anniversary of his birth. Despite such inauspicious beginnings, however, the concerto has grown in popularity over the past hundred years until it now rivals the Dvořák concerto for the position of the most frequently performed concerto for cello and orchestra in the entire literature.

The concerto is in three movements played without pause. The first, marked *Nicht zu schnell* (Not too fast), begins with a short introductory passage in the winds and pizzicato strings. The cello then enters with the first principal theme, accompanied by the strings. The second theme, also first heard from the solo instrument, moves the tonality up to the bright sunshine of C major. Both themes are developed extensively and after the recapitulation and coda the solo cello has a bridge passage that connects the movement directly with the second movement.

Langsam (Slow) is the marking on the second movement, which is essentially a long and moving song for the solo cello, with string and wind accompaniment. Near the end of the movement the marking changes to *Etwas lebhafter* (Somewhat livelier) and again the solo cello has a passage that serves as a bridge to the final movement without interruption.

The Finale, *Sehr lebhaft* (Very lively), tosses phrases back and forth from the solo instrument to the orchestra. As in the first movement, the cello introduces both the first and second themes, there is a lively development and at the end the cello has a virtuoso cadenza.

By and large the available recordings of the concerto serve the music well. Three different performances by the Soviet virtuoso Mstislav Rostropovitch are available; the finest of them is the collaboration with Gennadi Rozhdestvensky and the Leningrad Philharmonic Orchestra, remastered and reissued by Deutsche Grammophon (2538025; cassette 923107). It is coupled with Richter's somewhat wayward account of the Schumann Piano Concerto. In phrase after phrase Rostropovitch reveals a matchless sensitivity for nuance, shading and dynamic contrast. This performance, in short, places emphasis upon the "Eusebius" side of the composer's nature, the poetic aspect. The "Florestan" side—the rebellious reformer—comes alive in the collaboration between the two Leonards—Rose and Bernstein (Columbia MS 6253). Theirs is an impassioned, dramatic reading that is quite stunning in its virtuosic impact. There are also two different recordings of the score by Janos Starker—an earlier performance with Carlo Maria Giulini and the Philharmonia Orchestra (Angel S 35598) and a later one with Stanislaw Skrowaczewski conducting the London Symphony Orchestra (Mercury SR 90347, now withdrawn). Surprisingly, it is the earlier one that seems to be the more successful fulfillment of this artist's intentions. The team of Jacqueline du Pré and Daniel Barenboim (Angel S 36642; tape L 36642; 4XS 36642) also offers a finely detailed, warmly Romantic performance.

A curiosity is the performance by Pablo Casals (Odyssey 32160027, mono only—budget-priced, of course). Recorded during the early 1950s at Casals' Prades Festival in France, the performance took place at a time when Casals' technical command of the mechanics of playing the cello was much less secure than it became when Casals was in his eighties and nineties! Phrases are pulled out of shape and there are patches of painful intonation. The conductor of the Prades Festival Orchestra (he is unnamed on the record jacket) is Eugene Ormandy.

CONCERTO IN A MINOR FOR PIANO AND ORCHESTRA, OP. 54

Several times during the 1830s, when he was in his twenties, Robert Schumann thought of composing a piano concerto, but nothing ever came of the project. During May of 1841, eight months after his long-deferred marriage to the brilliant pianist Clara Wieck, Schumann composed especially for her a *Fantasie* in A Minor for Piano and Orchestra. At the same time, he worked on his First Symphony in B-flat Major, and on the score that was to become his Fourth Symphony in D Minor. In August of that year the Gewandhaus Orchestra in Leipzig was preparing a performance of the First Symphony, and Clara seized the opportunity to read through the *Fantasie* twice with the orchestra. "Carefully studied," she wrote in her diary, "it must give the greatest pleasure to those that hear it." There was no great rush among publishers, however, to secure the work for their catalogs. The score was set aside for four years.

In 1845, while Schumann and Clara were in Dresden, he made a concerto out of his *Concerto Allegro*, as he had intended to call it, by adding an Intermezzo and a Finale to it. "Robert has added a beautiful last movement to his *Fantasie* in A Minor," wrote Clara in her diary when the work was finished, "so that it has now become a concerto, which I mean to play next winter. I am very glad about it, for I always wanted a great bravura piece by him." The first performance was conducted by Ferdinand Hiller, to whom the score was dedicated, in Dresden in December 1845; Clara, of course, was the pianist. She repeated it in Leipzig just a few weeks later at a concert of the Gewandhaus Orchestra with the Schumanns' friend Felix Mendelssohn conducting. And then she took it to city after city. Early reactions to the concerto were on the cool side, but for more than a century now it has been the delight of pianists and audiences who are attuned to its near-perfect evocation of the age of Romanticism.

In his *Essays in Musical Analysis* Sir Donald Francis Tovey points out that the first movement of the concerto, betraying its origin as an independent concert piece, is not structured along formal lines:

> The orchestra makes no attempt to muster its forces for its own full connected statement of the themes. At the climaxes it bursts out with a short triumphant passage in the manner of a ritornello; but for the most part it behaves very much as the strings behave in Schumann's quintet: though it has far more color, and is, for all its reticence, much above Schumann's normal achievement in its purity and brightness of tone.

The first movement is marked *Allegro affettuoso*. After an opening flourish in the orchestra and piano, the first theme is heard as a plaintive oboe solo. Throughout the movement this melody is the dominating force, subtly shaded and transformed. One of the loveliest sections is a duet in the development between the solo piano and the clarinet; later in the development much dramatic impact is obtained from repetitions of the material heard at the very beginning of the piece. Schumann wrote out his own cadenza for the movement; it emphasizes lyrical poetry rather than bravura display. The movement comes to an end with a coda of great brilliance.

The second movement is an Intermezzo marked *Andantino grazioso*. It begins with a dialogue between the piano and the orchestra that is at once playful and tender. The middle section is ushered in by a meltingly lovely theme in the cellos. Then the first part of the movement is repeated, and in a bridge passage we hear a hint of the theme of the first movement. Suddenly, without pause, there are upward-leaping runs in the orchestra and we are into the final movement of the concerto, marked *Allegro vivace*. The principal theme is a jaunty, proclamative one, the second subject a study in rhythmic displacement. A fugato section is introduced in the development, along with some new thematic material. After the recapitulation of the two main themes, there is an extensive coda that inexorably sweeps soloist and orchestra along to a breathless conclusion. Professor Tovey wrote of the concluding pages: "Never has a long and voluble peroration been more masterly in its proportions and more perfectly in character with the great whole which it crowns with so light a touch. . . . Fashion and musical party-politics have tried to play many games with Schumann's reputation, but works like this remain irresistible."

Likewise irresistible is the recording of the concerto made in 1948 by the lamented Romanian pianist Dinu Lipatti, who died two years later at the age of thirty-three. A tribute to the wisdom of the people at Columbia Records is the fact that Lipatti's performance has never been out of the catalog ever since it was first released in this country: for many years it did yeoman service as ML 4525 in the Columbia Masterwork catalog; now it is available in the company's budget-priced Odyssey line (32160141, mono only). The performance has enormous strength, meltingly beautiful tone, a matchless sensitivity to form, and an emotional rapport with the score that gives the reading a tremendously exciting sense of urgency. Herbert von Karajan conducts a vigorous yet supple and lyrical performance of the orchestral part and the Philharmonia Orchestra plays exceedingly well. The still serviceable recorded sound offers convincing testimony to the high level of technical skill that the British Columbia engineers had achieved in the years just following the war. Without question the Lipatti performance of Schumann's Piano Concerto is one of the important landmarks in the history of recorded music and it remains a monument to the memory of one of the master music-makers of the twentieth century. Now another Lipatti performance that, despite some wrong notes in the first and last movements, is simply overwhelming in its emotional impact has been added to the recordings available. It derives from Swiss Radio tapes of a broadcast performance given in February 1950—less than ten months before Lipatti's tragic death at the age of thirty-three—with Ansermet and the Suisse Romande Orchestra (London STS 15176). And the "electronic stereo" sound is surprisingly good. Here is truly an instance of buried treasure rediscovered!

Two performances of the concerto that are similar in their small-scale, intimate approaches to the music are those by Myra Hess (Seraphim 60009, mono only) and her compatriot Solomon (Pickwick S 4034, 4034)—both now on budget-priced labels. Each performer imparts his own particular charm to the score, but in the end one misses some of the dynamic impetus of the music.

A good many younger performers have recorded the concerto, including Van Cliburn, Leon Fleisher, Fou Ts'ong, Friedrich Gulda, Julius Katchen and Peter Katin. Fleisher's is the best of them, for my money (Odyssey Y 30668). His performance (with George Szell and the Cleveland Orchestra) has a real feeling of emotional involvement, with genial responsiveness to the lyricism of the score as well as to the more impulsive sections. Further, Szell has an instinctive feeling for Schumann's musical personality and the technical quality of the recording is fine.

My own preference among the modern recordings of the score, however, lies with two sovereign artists from the older generation— Artur Rubinstein (RCA LSC 2997) and Rudolf Serkin (Columbia MS 6688). Rubinstein's performance with Carlo Maria Giulini conducting the Chicago Symphony Orchestra is a welcome antidote to his earlier performance conducted by Josef Krips in which the pianist seemed curiously inhibited and ill at ease. The newer version finds Rubinstein at his most lyrical and rhapsodic, Giulini's conducting is a perfect match and the recorded sound is full-bodied. Serkin, for his part, delivers a passionate, highly charged performance, in which Eugene Ormandy and the Philadelphia Orchestra are co-equal partners. Again, the recorded sound is excellent.

On tape I would single out Katchen's volatile and exciting performance (London L 80104); and Anda's (DGG 923016) among the cassette versions.

SYMPHONY NO. 1 IN B-FLAT MAJOR, OP. 38, "SPRING"

In January of 1841 the house at No. 5 Inselstrasse in Schönefeld, a suburb of Leipzig, was occupied by a young newly-wed couple. The bridegroom, Robert Schumann, was a brilliantly gifted pianist, teacher and composer, and his bride, Clara Wieck, was one of his former pupils.

On the seventeenth of January Clara wrote in the diary she and her husband kept jointly: "It is not my turn to keep the diary this week, but when a husband is composing a symphony, he must be excused from other things." A few days after that Clara wrote further: "The symphony is nearly finished, and though I have not yet heard any of it, I am infinitely delighted that Robert has at last found the sphere for which his great imagination fits him." On the twenty-fifth of January Clara noted: "Today, Monday, Robert has about finished his symphony; it has been composed mostly at night. . . . He calls it 'Spring' Symphony. . . . A spring poem by Böttger gave the first impulse to this creation."

Felix Mendelssohn conducted the first performance of the new symphony a few weeks later at a Leipzig Gewandhaus concert. The audience was cordial, if not really enthusiastic, but Schumann's great good humor at the time led him to consider the symphony a major triumph. To a friend he wrote that the score had a success "as no other had since Beethoven!"

Schumann himself has left us a graphic account of his own feelings about the score. In a letter written on January 10, 1843, Schumann had these things to say to a conductor who was scheduled to give a performance of the music in Berlin:

Could you infuse into your orchestra in the performance the sort of longing for the Spring which I had chiefly in mind when I wrote in February, 1841? The first entrance of trumpets, this I should like to have sounded as though it were from high above, like a call to awakening; and then I should like reading between the lines, in the rest of the Introduction, how everywhere it begins to grow green, how a butterfly takes wing; and, in the Allegro, how little by little everything appears that in any way belongs to Spring. True, these are fantastic thoughts, which came to me after my work was finished; only I tell you this about the Finale, that I thought it as the good-bye of Spring.

At one time the composer had intended to fix descriptive titles upon each of the four movements: I. The Dawn of Spring; II. Evening; III. Merry Companions; IV. Spring at the Full. Finally he decided against the idea. To his composer-friend Louis Spohr he wrote: "I do not wish to portray, to paint; but I believe firmly that the period in which the symphony was produced influenced its form and character, and shaped it as it is."

An oft-repeated canard of music criticism holds that Schumann was an ineffectual orchestrator. However true this may be of the other symphonies, the "Spring" Symphony is as light and transparent in texture as anything in symphonic music. The scoring calls for woodwinds in pairs, four horns, two trumpets, three trombones, three tympani and the usual strings. A triangle is used in the first movement to brilliant coloristic effect.

Until Schumann came upon the scene, the accepted aim of composers of symphonies was the creation of a musical entity in which a central idea informs all the movements and makes them seem inseparable parts of an integrated organism. Schumann expanded this idea so that literary and even pictorial elements found their place in his symphonies. Mosco Carner, the distinguished English musicologist, has written: "It is this very intrusion of poetic ideas that gives Schumann's symphonic work its special place. . . . He opened to the Symphony a world of Romantic imagery and lyricism which was at once new and personal."

The symphony begins with an introduction marked *Andante*. Horns and trumpets in unison sound a buoyant fanfare which is echoed by the orchestra. The pace quickens and the movement proper, *Allegro molto vivace*, bursts upon the scene with a bright, dance-like rhythmic vigor. The second theme, graceful and easy, is first stated by the clarinet with low string accompaniment. The development section plays with the rhythmic outlines of the principal theme, but it also introduces a brand-new theme, heard first from the oboe. The climax of the development is reached with the reappearance of the opening fanfare, ushering in the recapitulation. The movement ends with an accelerated coda which introduces yet another new and tender theme at the end. But the ultimate resolution comes with another triumphant repetition of the opening fanfare. The second movement, *Larghetto*, concerns itself chiefly with an expansive melody first stated by the violins, later taken up by the

horn and oboe. Toward the end of the movement there is an unob-
trusive entrance of the trombones, the color changes and the movement leads without pause into the Scherzo, *Molto vivace*. The
prinicipal theme is a variant of the principal theme of the slow movement and it has been characterized by Edward Downes as "a full-
blooded, masculine counterpart to the feminine charm of the
Larghetto." There are two Trios, the first a rhythmic distribution of
chords between the winds and the strings, the second full of bustling
energy. The coda has a brief reminiscence of the theme of the first
Trio. The concluding movement, *Allegro animato e grazioso*, begins
with an ascending scale and leads to a main theme that has been
characterized by Professor Tovey as "slight as a daisy-chain." The
development is dramatic and rhythmic and the return to the recapitulation is ushered in by an unaccompanied flute cadenza. The
concluding coda whips up to a triumphant finish.

The "Spring" Symphony has been recorded many times over the
years. Of currently available performances, the superior ones in my
opinion are those by Bernstein (Columbia MS 6581), Krips (London STS 15019), Kubelik (Deutsche Grammophon 138860) and
Szell. All are well played by the respective orchestras and well recorded by the engineers. Kubelik's, it seems to me, has more of a
Romantic glow about it than the other three, but each has its own
special excellences and any one of them will give the listener a
generally fulfilled experience. Columbia has now restored to currency the more thoughtful but slightly more rigid Szell performances
of all the Schumann symphonies in the low-priced Odyssey series
(Y3 30844, three discs). The Kubelik performance is also available
on both tape (Deutsche Grammophon L 8860) and cassette
(Deutsche Grammophon 923022).

Dmitri Shostakovich

Born: St. Petersburg, September 25, 1906

Shostakovich studied at the St. Petersburg Conservatory, where his principal teachers were Glazounov and Maximilian Steinberg. His graduation thesis from the Conservatory was his First Symphony, an astonishing work full of sardonic bite, melodic invention and harmonic tension. The symphony carried the name of the nineteen-year-old composer far and wide. Two more symphonies followed in the next two years and each bore a descriptive title (Symphony No. 2 was called "A Dedication to October," and the Third Symphony, "A May Day Symphony").

Shostakovich made his next big noise with his first opera, *The Nose* (1928–29), based on the fantastic tale by Gogol in which a man who has lost his nose appeals to the police to help him find it. Between 1930 and 1932 Shostakovich worked on his second opera, *Lady Macbeth of Mzensk*—a bloody tale of adultery and murder which was withdrawn from circulation by order of Stalin after he had seen a production of it in the 1930s. Many years later Shostakovich made some revisions in the opera and retitled it after the principal female character, *Katerina Ismailova*. This version has enjoyed some success in recent years, especially in the repertoire of the New York City Opera.

Stalin's denunciation of the original work led to the composer's complete isolation from the Soviet musical community during the mid-1930s. The work that restored him to favor was his Fifth Symphony of 1937, greeted by the arbiters of Soviet musical culture as the work by which Shostakovich had at last freed himself from "individualistic chaos and formalistic experimentation." The Fifth

Symphony has since become the most frequently performed symphony written since the end of the First World War.

At last count Shostakovich had composed ten more symphonies, for a total of fifteen. His rehabilitation in 1937 was followed eleven years later by another denunciation, this time by the Central Committee of the Russian Communist Party; the charge was much the same as the first one: Shostakovich was guilty of composing decadent, bourgeois music. All was forgiven a few years later, but the trials and tribulations suffered by Shostakovich and some of his other distinguished Soviet composer colleagues—Prokofiev and Khachaturian among them—seem to have drained the creative individuality out of his music. Where once his was a vital, impetuous, challenging voice, much of his later work is homogenized and formula-ridden.

Despite a severe heart attack in the mid-1960s, he has been able to continue to compose—a Second Violin Concerto written for David Oistrakh was introduced to this country by Oistrakh early in 1968 with Leonard Bernstein and the New York Philharmonic. Aside from the symphonies and operas already mentioned, Shostakovich has composed several ballets; much incidental and film music; two piano concertos; two cello concertos; a large amount of chamber music, including a brilliant piano quintet and about a dozen string quartets; much music for solo piano; and a growing list of songs. In 1939 and 1940 he also made a new orchestration of Moussorgsky's opera *Boris Godounov*.

When the history of twentieth-century music comes to be written, the name of Shostakovich will certainly figure in it—not as prominently, however, as seemed certain in the two decades between 1926 and 1946.

SYMPHONY NO. 1 IN F MAJOR, OP. 10

Dmitri Shostakovich was only nineteen years old when he completed his First Symphony. The year was 1925; the young musician had recently graduated from the piano class of the Leningrad Conservatory, and was completing his final studies in composition there.

Nicolai Malko conducted the premiere of the work in Leningrad in May 1926; from there it was taken up by Bruno Walter, who gave the symphony its initial hearing in Berlin in November 1927. A year later it was played in the United States for the first time, by Leopold Stokowski at concerts of the Philadelphia Orchestra. Thus the symphony, the first large-scale composing venture by Shostakovich, propelled him into international prominence very quickly.

A biography of Shostakovich published in this country in 1943 contains a fascinating account of the composer's early years as recalled by an aunt, Mrs. Nadejda Galli-Shohat, who had left the Soviet Union for America in 1923 (*Dmitri Shostakovich*, by Victor Seroff in collaboration with Mrs. Galli-Shohat). In the book Mrs. Galli-Shohat remembers young "Mitya" Shostakovich as a boy "who liked fairy tales, and often asked me to tell them to him." He was a "very serious and sensitive child, often rather meditative, very modest about his music, and rather shy. . . . His favorite composer at the very beginning was Liszt. He liked to read, and his favorite author was the great Russian novelist Gogol. His first opera, *The Nose*, was based on Gogol's story."

Mrs. Galli-Shohat's recollections also provide an interesting view of what Shostakovich may have had in mind as he wrote the First Symphony. Mr. Seroff writes:

> The melodies reminded her of those in *The Dragon-Fly and the Ant* which Mitya had composed in 1922 and which he used to play to his family. According to Nadejda, the themes from this composition as well as [an] early Scherzo were used in his First Symphony. In the first movement, she says, one hears the recitative of the flighty, irresponsible dragon-fly and the mutterings of the laboring ant. Then comes a march of all the insects, with the fireflies leading the way; they range themselves in a semi-circle in the amphitheater and the dragon-fly performs a dance on the stage. The Scherzo is inserted in full. In the last movement, the second theme for violin and cello is taken from an unfinished piece that Mitya was composing at the time of *The Dragon-Fly and the Ant*; he was writing it around [Hans Christian] Andersen's story of the Mermaid, an idea that had been suggested to him by his mother. With the last movement of the symphony, Nadejda remembers how Mitya described to his family

the Mermaid swimming up through the waters of the lake to the brightly lit castle where the Prince is holding a festival.

Whatever may have been the inspiration for the First Symphony, the music is extraordinary. Listening to it, one has the feeling that it sprang full-grown out of the depths of its creator's being. It is an impudent score, in the best sense of that word—it is full of boyish exuberance and vitality; and yet there are moments, especially in the slow movement and in the Finale, when Shostakovich moves us deeply by the power and poignancy of his music. Though it is numbered Opus 10, the symphony was only the second work that Shostakovich released for publication (the first was Three Fantastic Dances for Piano, Opus 5); its equal as an inaugural orchestral statement would be hard to find among the music of the past half century, no matter who the composer.

The first movement is marked *Allegretto*, then it becomes an *Allegro non troppo*. In the introduction epigram-like motifs are tossed back and forth among solo brass and woodwind instruments. Finally the solo clarinet announces what is unmistakably the first theme. It is a jaunty, nose-thumbing melody that could serve as background for a Chaplin film. The second theme is introduced by a solo flute over pizzicato strings; it is taken up by the clarinet and then the basses. For the remainder of the movement Shostakovich deals with these musical materials. There is some hectic scurrying around as the strings and brasses proclaim the material of the very opening in the most impassioned manner, but the movement ends quietly in the clarinet and cellos. The Scherzo that follows is marked *Allegro*. After a false start in the basses and clarinet, the violins finally announce the main subject, to a pizzicato accompaniment. Then the theme is taken up by the piano, which plays a very prominent part in this movement, with cymbals, horns and basses in the background. There is a Trio of oriental flavor, with two flutes carrying the principal melodic burden, and then the bassoon steers us back to the material of the main body of the movement. In the climax, the melodic material of the Trio is intoned fortissimo by the brass and the movement ends in a whisper.

The slow movement begins *Lento* with an oboe solo of deep melancholy. This soon leads to a *Largo* of similar emotional coloring in the strings and then there is another plaintive oboe solo with a rather serpentine melodic outline. This material is then developed by the brass, fortissimo, and a clarinet solo brings back the theme of the opening of the movement. A muted trumpet repeats the plaintive oboe solo and the movement ends in a pianissimo passage for the divided strings. There is a drum roll, crescendo, which leads without pause into the final movement, marked *Allegro molto*. After a single dramatic measure of arresting power the music subsides into a twenty-nine-measure *Lento* introduction. When we finally arrive at the main body of the movement, the clarinet has another of those typically jaunty Shostakovich themes. This is brought to a furious climax by the violins and then there is a change of mood. The second theme is presented by a solo violin, then a solo horn. The furious matter of the *Allegro molto* returns and is brought to a shattering climax. After a suspense-laden pause, Shostakovich introduces a kettledrum solo of great rhythmic significance while a muted solo cello muses on the second subject. The music then gathers momentum and concludes in a bold and proclamative F major.

The magnetic account by Stokowski and the Symphony of the Air, once available on the United Artists label, has now been withdrawn. Dare we hope that he may be given an opportunity to re-record the symphony for London Phase 4? In the meantime, among rather slim pickings these days, Ormandy's is the version I would most recommend (Columbia MS 6124).

Ormandy's recording with the Philadelphia Orchestra manages to get the entire symphony onto a single record side (on the overside is a performance of Shostakovich's First Cello Concerto featuring Mstislav Rostropovich as soloist). The Philadelphia maestro delivers a richly-hued, romantic reading and there can be no denying the sensuous appeal of the playing of the Philadelphia Orchestra. Columbia's engineers have captured the orchestra's sound superbly.

The only available tape performance these days in a monophonic recording of a particularly stark and angular reading of the music by Toscanini (included on RCA TR3 5010). On cassette there is no performance of any kind available.

SYMPHONY NO. 5, OP. 47

Following upon the instant success of his First Symphony Shostakovich almost immediately turned his attention to the Second Symphony, which he composed in homage to the Soviet Republic on its
tenth anniversary. This score was performed for the first time in
Leningrad in November of 1927, but this time Shostakovich did not
enjoy the triumph he had a year earlier.

During that period in his life Shostakovich was active in the Leningrad Association for Contemporary Music, an organization that
presented performances of some of the latest works from the West.
Exposed to the cynical stage works of Berg, Křenek and Hindemith,
Shostakovich decided to compose a satirical opera of his own. For
his subject he chose Gogol's *The Nose*, and he produced a score of
extraordinary complexity, full of atonality and intricate polyrhythms.
There was a Leningrad performance in January of 1930, and the
Russian Association of Proletarian Composers promptly branded the
opera "bourgeois decadence." *The Nose* was quietly removed from
the repertoire after a few performances.

Shostakovich then turned again to the symphony, and produced
his Third, with a choral ending modeled after the form of Beethoven's Ninth. As text he took a May Day hymn, but, despite the
patriotic inspiration, this work, too, was a failure with the public.

During the next few years Shostakovich turned out two satirical
ballets, *The Age of Gold* and *The Bolt*, and a social opera, *Lady
Macbeth of Mzensk*. The last work enjoyed a great vogue in Russia
from the time of its initial presentation in January of 1934 until two
years later. On the 28th of January 1936, there appeared an un-
signed article in *Pravda* condemning the opera as theatrically vulgar
and musically formalistic. This was apparently the first salvo in a
general Soviet volley aimed at artistic "formalism," for the campaign
was soon taken up in other parts of the Russian press.

Shostakovich was not the only Soviet artist attacked, but for a
time it appeared that he would be the principal victim. He was
faced with a difficult decision: to take seriously the words of his

critics and thus consciously stifle his natural creative instincts, or to go his own way and risk possible artistic liquidation.

Shostakovich chose the former course. He had begun a Fourth Symphony before the *Pravda* attack was printed, and he completed it. However, he withdrew it from performance after it had been placed in rehearsal in Leningrad in December of 1936, and he immediately began work on another symphony, his Fifth, staking his career (and perhaps his very life) on its acceptance. The symphony was performed for the first time in November of 1937 in Leningrad.

From the beginning, the Fifth Symphony was hailed with enthusiasm. An article in the Moscow *Daily News* is typical:

> The composer, while retaining the originality of his art in this new composition, has to a great extent overcome the ostentatiousness, deliberate musical affectation, and misuse of the grotesque, which had left a pernicious print on many of his former compositions. Shostakovich's Fifth Symphony is a work of great depth, with emotional wealth and content, and is of great importance as a milestone in the composer's development.

Ever since Artur Rodzinski introduced the Fifth Symphony to the United States in a broadcast concert with the NBC Symphony Orchestra in April of 1938, it has been the composer's most admired and most frequently performed symphony in this country. It is a big, bold score in the heroic nineteenth-century tradition, with an especially memorable *Largo*, a movement of searing intensity that Serge Koussevitzky once called "the greatest symphonic slow movement since Beethoven's Ninth."

The first movement, *Moderato*, opens with an intervallic theme stated alternately by the low and high strings. Out of it there grows a theme in the violins which becomes increasingly elaborated and cumulative. Horns and trumpets sound a repeat of the first theme, which then is returned once again to the violins. The tempo grows faster and the rhythm becomes more propulsive as the principal melodic material is now handed to the brass choirs. In the recapitulation the original slow tempo is suddenly restored, with the entire orchestra repeating the opening theme in unison. The movement closes as a calm, reminiscent mood takes over, with the woodwinds now prominently to the fore. The second movement, *Allegretto*, is clearly a Scherzo in the traditional sense. The lumbering opening soon gives way to a satirical theme in the clarinet, which is answered by the bassoon. The second theme is a mock-heroic pronouncement in the French horns. The Trio is introduced by a solo violin and it has the character of an Austrian Ländler such as those used by Mahler in his symphonies. The traditional formal pattern of Scherzo structure is observed and the movement ends in a broadly satirical vein.

The slow movement, *Largo*, is the very heart of the symphony. Like the first, it gradually develops melodic growth out of modest string beginnings. Woodwinds enter gradually and a searing emotional tension is built up. The strings soar to their highest registers and the climax attains an overwhelming sonority without a single brass instrument involved. The concluding movement, *Allegro non troppo*, has as its principal material a theme of unmistakable martial character, first stated in the trombones and trumpets. There is a slow section with reminiscences of themes from the first movement, and then the roll of a distant snare drum brings back the march-like theme of the opening of the movement—except that now it has the character of clumsy heavy-footedness. The end is an explosive peroration in the form of overwhelming fanfares using the martial theme of the movement's opening.

This is a symphony more than ordinarily pretentious, brooding, mystical, sardonic and sometimes vulgar. In short, it has many of the same virtues and faults one finds in the symphonies of Mahler. It is no accident, then, that one of the finest recordings of the score comes from the conductor who is also the leading interpreter of Mahler in our time—Leonard Bernstein. The New York maestro wrings every measure of drama and passion from the music, and the close-to microphone pickup reveals it all in most vivid detail. Interestingly, the recording (Columbia MS 6115, tape MQ 375) was made in Boston's Symphony Hall while Bernstein and the New York Philharmonic were on tour. It is one of the best examples of Symphony Hall's superb acoustical qualities.

The cumulative drama of the Bernstein performance makes it a standout version. But it has now been superseded by an absolutely stunning account conducted by the composer's son, Maksim (Angel/Melodiya SR 40163). The younger Shostakovich invests the music with an incomparable breadth and dignity that elevate the entire work to a level of unexpected grandeur. As of the writing of these lines, the performance has not yet been released on either tape or cassette; chances are, however, that it soon will be.

The pioneer recording of Shostakovich's Fifth Symphony was made in the late 1930s by Leopold Stokowski and the Philadelphia Orchestra. In the late 1950s Stokowski re-recorded the symphony for Everest with the Stadium Symphony Orchestra of New York (a *nom de disque* for the New York Philharmonic). The resulting performance (Everest SDBR 3010), though similar in concept to Bernstein's, lacks the latter's tightly controlled tension and power.

Another splendid performance is André Previn's with the London Symphony Orchestra (RCA LSC 2866). Previn quite obviously believes in this symphony and his performance of it is a deeply committed one. It is played magnificently by the orchestra and superlatively well recorded by the engineers.

In addition to the Bernstein recording on tape (Columbia MQ 375), there is a very serviceable performance conducted by Kiril Kondrashin on disc, tape and cassette (Angel/Melodiya S 40004; M 40004; 4XS 40004 respectively).

Jean Sibelius

Born: Tavastehus, Finland, December 8, 1865
Died: Järvenpää, September 20, 1957

Sibelius' father was an army surgeon and as a result of the comfortable family circumstances the boy received an excellent classical education. His first instrument was the piano but at the age of fifteen he began to study the violin with a local bandmaster. When he was twenty he was entered as a student of law at the University of Helsingfors, but he gave it up and in 1889 he went to Berlin for further musical studies. A period in Vienna followed, under the tutelage of Karl Goldmark, and then in 1892 he returned to his native land.

Nationalism was much in the air in the closing years of the nineteenth century and Sibelius determined that his music would be an expression of the Finnish national character and aspirations. The national epic, *Kalevala*, served as an inspiration to him and he composed several scores based upon material from it, including such works as *Kullervo*, *En Saga*, and the *Lemminkäinen* tone poems. In 1893 he became an instructor at the Helsingfors Conservatory and within a few years had so impressed himself upon the cultural life of the country that in 1897 the Finnish government granted him an annual stipend. This made it possible for Sibelius to free himself of all other entanglements and to concentrate upon composition. The most famous of all Sibelius' works was unveiled at a concert by the Helsinki Philharmonic Orchestra in July 1900—the symphonic poem *Finlandia*, which then became such a rallying cry of Finnish nationalism that its performance was banned by the Russian Czarist regime during times of political unrest. In 1904 Sibelius moved his family to the country seclusion of Järvenpää, near Helsinki, and there he lived for the next half century until his death.

Sibelius became a legendary figure in his own lifetime. In the quarter century between 1899 and 1924 he produced seven mighty symphonies; a Violin Concerto; a String Quartet (titled *Voces Intimae*) and other chamber music works; numerous symphonic poems, including *Pohjola's Daughter*, *Night Ride and Sunrise*, *The Bard* and *The Oceanides*; and much incidental music for the theater, including *Kuolema*, *Pelleas and Melisande*, *Belshazzar's Feast* and *The Tempest*. An Eighth Symphony was long rumored as imminent, but it was never forthcoming and apparently Sibelius stopped composing entirely after 1929.

It was perhaps inevitable that the lionization of Sibelius, so much a part of American musical life in the 1930s and 1940s, would ultimately induce reaction. And so it did, with the result that the music of Sibelius almost disappeared from our concert halls for more than two decades, from the mid-40s to the present—a period during which this composer was considered terribly old-fashioned, with little of value to communicate to new generations.

Happily, that period now seems to be over. There are indications that the pendulum of public favor is starting to swing back in his direction.

In his larger compositions Sibelius developed an original method of construction, with themes growing out of short units that later coalesce into their final form. His inspirations were drawn very largely from nature and there is the feel of the North about much of his music. It is not true, however, that his personality was essentially a gloomy or mystical one: on the contrary, many of his works display a boisterous humor and rude strength.

SYMPHONY NO. 1 IN E MINOR, OP. 39

Sibelius has been a unique and important creative force in twentieth-century music. In one sense he may even have been a seminal influence, in the manner of Anton Webern; for, like the music of Webern, much of the music of Sibelius grows out of short, epigrammatic figures and phrases. Unlike Webern, however, Sibelius worked these musical epigrams into vast formal structures, and it was into these—his symphonies and tone poems—that he poured his most deeply felt and personal musical thoughts. The magic spell of the North is evoked with passionate power and intensity in the orchestral music of Sibelius; his heroic and noble style speaks a language that should certainly have meaning for the ages.

Paul Rosenfeld, in *Musical Portraits*, wrote a vivid and picturesque description of Sibelius' music in general that seems particularly applicable to the First Symphony:

> Others have brought the North into houses and there transformed it into music. And their art is dependent upon the shelter, and removed from it, dwindles. But Sibelius has written music independent of roof and enclosure, music proper indeed to the vast open, the Finnish heaven under which it grew. And could we but carry it out into the Northern day, we would find it undiminished, vivid with all its life. For it is blood-brother to the wind and the silence, to the lowering cliffs and the spray, to the harsh crying of sea-birds and the breath of the fog, and, set amid them, would wax and take new strength from the strength of its kin. . . . The orchestral compositions of Sibelius seem to have passed over black torrents and desolate moorlands, through pallid sunlight and dim primeval forests and become drenched with them. The instrumentation is all wet grays and blacks, relieved only by bits of brightness, wan and elusive as the Northern summer, frostily green as the polar lights. The works are full of the gnawing of bassoons and the bleakness of the English horn, full of shattering trombones and screaming violins, full of the sinister rolling of drums, the menacing reverberation of cymbals, the icy glittering of harps. The musical ideas of those compositions that are finally realized recall the ruggedness and hardiness and starkness of things that persist in the Finnish winter. The rhythms seem to approach the wild, unnumbered rhythms of the forest and the wind and the flickering sunlight.

The First Symphony was composed in the last year of the nineteenth century. In many ways it epitomizes the musical influences that were to manifest themselves in much of Sibelius' later output. This is a mercurial symphony, full of impetuous enthusiasm. Following a brief, mysterious introduction (*Andante ma non troppo*) that has as its chief distinction a lonely and bleak clarinet solo, the main portion of the first movement bursts forth in a rush (*Allegro energico*.) There are wide interval leaps in the strings and insistent punctuation by the tympani. The second theme is of a gentler cast, with the flutes taking the major role. The movement ends with a growl in the low strings. The second movement is a sustained and lyrical *Andante*, the chief material of which is a pulsating melody in the strings. Harp arpeggios are also prominent here. The third movement, the Scherzo, is marked *Allegro* and is the most distinctly individual section of the symphony. It is wild, almost barbaric music, with a throbbing rhythm that is first announced by the kettledrums and then taken up by the first violins; the Trio offers music of sharp contrast, and then the movement ends, as it began, in a rhythmic frenzy. The last movement is in the form of a free fantasia. It begins *Andante* and then becomes *Allegro molto*. There are reminiscences of the clarinet melody that began the symphony, and also of the first theme of the slow movement. The development of this and much new material is stormy and highly involved. The end is a broad and moving hymn of sadness.

The three best stereo recordings are by Barbirolli and the Hallé Orchestra (Angel S 36409), Ormandy and the Philadelphia Orchestra (Columbia MS 6395) and Maazel and the Vienna Philharmonic (London CS 6375). Barbirolli's credentials as a Sibelius conductor go back to the '30s and '40s, when he was in the vanguard of Sibelius partisans as the conductor of the New York Philharmonic. (He recorded the first two symphonies with that orchestra.) This performance of the First with his Hallé Orchestra of Manchester, England, is a very good one. The sound is just a little deficient by the latest standards, but Barbirolli responds intuitively to the noble pages of the score and on the whole delivers a very persuasive account of the symphony. Ormandy's is a very romantic performance, with some exaggerated heavings and sighings. He has even gone to the length of re-orchestrating (or having someone else re-orchestrate) some of the music in order to arrive at a more luscious sound. If juiciness is what you are looking for in this work, the Ormandy recording will deliver it.

The most recent recording of the three is, in my opinion, the one to be preferred—the performance by the Vienna Philharmonic Orchestra conducted by Lorin Maazel. Unlike many conductors of today, Maazel is concerned with more than just the notes of a score and the problems of getting them properly organized for a clear performance. He seeks the implications of the music and its emotional meaning. The result is that, more often than not, a Maazel performance is a vibrant, passionate communication. Such is indeed the case with his recording of Sibelius' First Symphony. Though he too does not deliver quite the wallop that Collins does, he nevertheless succeeds in revealing to an extraordinary degree the headlong impulsiveness of this music. The recorded sound provided by London's engineers is equally brilliant.

A final word for tape buffs: the Maazel-Vienna Philharmonic recording is available on 7½ ips four-track stereo tape in two "double-play" versions from Ampex: LCK 80137 presents the reading as the second sequence in a coupling with Tchaikovsky's Fifth Symphony performed by the same forces; LCK 80162 presents the Sibelius First (and the *Karelia* Suite) as the first sequence on a tape that includes, as sequence two, Maazel's superb account with the Vienna Philharmonic of Sibelius' Second Symphony. The sound quality of both tapes is extraordinary, among the finest examples of orchestral reproduction this reviewer has ever heard. There is no version currently available on cassette.

SYMPHONY NO. 2 IN D MAJOR, OP. 43

It may come as a shock to the average listener, but Jean Sibelius, as he is painted in Karl Ekman's excellent biography, was something of a "beatnik" during his late twenties. Around 1890, when he was twenty-five, Sibelius was drawn into a youthful circle in Helsinki which boldly waved the banner of Swedish and Finnish solidarity against Eastern influences. Young intellectuals they were, who met regularly to debate the problems which seem to be the perennial concern of their kind: political freedom, the individual versus the mass, the place of the artist in society and so forth. They were authors, poets, teachers and painters and they called themselves "The Symposium." A painting by one of the group (Gallen-Kalela) once shocked all Helsinki because of the frank "Bohemianism" of its subject: the members of "The Symposium" are shown sitting gloomily around a restaurant table brooding over their wineglasses. In the foreground is to be seen a disheveled, scowling Sibelius and around the figures there hover ghostly wings and a partially obscured moon.

If all this sounds terribly arty, the fact remains that the association with "The Symposium" was a vital and dynamic one for Sibelius. " 'The Symposium' evenings were a great resource to me," he once said, "at a time when I should otherwise have stood more or less alone. The opportunity of exchanging ideas with kindred souls, animated by the same spirit and the same objects, exerted an extremely stimulating influence on me, confirmed me in my purposes, gave me confidence."

The group broke up about 1895, but not before the stimulation from "The Symposium" had turned Sibelius to the folklore of Finland for his musical inspiration. The First Symphony of 1899 and the Second Symphony of two years later may be considered to be the culmination of this romantic and highly charged emotional period in Sibelius' life.

The Second Symphony is in bold, heroic vein. Like Beethoven in the "Eroica" or Tchaikovsky in his Fourth Symphony—both, incidentally, composed at similar age periods in their composers' lives —Sibelius in this Second Symphony speaks with a supremely self-confident voice; here is the artist in full command of his resources hurling his thunderbolts with devastating accuracy. It is a symphony bursting at the seams with irrepressible vigor and strength.

In his analysis and description of the Sibelius symphonies Cecil Gray writes:

In outward appearance the Second Symphony would seem to conform to the traditional four-movement formula of *allegro, andante, scherzo* and *finale,* but the internal organization of the movements reveals many important innovations, amounting at times, and particularly in the first movement, to veritable revolution, and to the introduction of an entirely new principle into symphonic form. . . . Instead of presenting definite, clear-cut melodic personalities in the exposition, taking them to pieces, dissecting and analyzing them in a development section, and putting them together again in a recapitulation, which is roughly speaking the method of most 19th century practitioners of symphonic form, Sibelius inverts the process, introducing thematic fragments in   exposition, building them up into an organic whole in the development section, then dissolving and dispersing the material back into its primary constituents in a brief recapitulation. The peculiar strength and attraction of this method of construction consists in the fact that it is the method of nature and of life itself; Sibelius' most characteristic movements are born, develop, and die, like all living things.

The first movement of the symphony is marked *Allegretto* and it begins with a gently pulsating rhythm in the strings, followed immediately by a nostalgic theme in the woodwinds whose last notes are taken up and expanded by the horns. The fragmentary introduction of motifs is continued throughout the exposition. In the words of Gray, "one can detect several distinct groups of thematic germs, none of which can claim the right to be regarded as the most important." The second movement, *Andante ma rubato*, opens with a distant rumbling of the kettledrums followed by the steady pizzicato tread of eighth notes in the low strings. Soon a melancholy theme is introduced by the bassoons. There are explosive interruptions from the strings, who have a variant of the bassoon melody, and the atmosphere grows more tense and violent. Peace is restored —temporarily—in an *Andante sostenuto* for strings, accompanied by flutes and bassoons, but again the turbulence boils over. The end is a calm, exhausted reverie, but not before once again there is some violent buzzing from the strings and hysterical trills from the woodwinds.

The third movement is a classic Scherzo, *Vivacissimo*, that opens with the whirring of strings, then presents various woodwind instruments with fragments of a melody. The Trio begins with the oboe repeating the same note no fewer than nine times before the reiteration finally takes on the shape of a gently lyrical theme. There is a repeat of the Scherzo proper, then the Trio, and then one begins to detect the intervention of foreign material. Before we know it and without pause we are into the Finale, *Allegretto moderato*. The principal theme is a heroic one, noble and grand; there are two subsidiary themes ultimately disclosed, but it is the triumphant principal theme that sets the mood and character of the movement and that brings the symphony to its victorious conclusion.

"In these days of cynicism and disillusion," wrote Gray of the Second Symphony,

> it is of course the fashion to sneer at the convention of the "happy ending" . . . and it is certainly true that most modern attempts to conform to it ring hollow and insincere. We of the present generation simply do not feel like that; we find it difficult to be triumphant, and we have no doubt excellent reasons for this. Yet the fact remains that that is a weakness and deficiency in us; and there is something of sour grapes in the contemporary attitude towards those artists of an earlier generation who have achieved the state of spiritual serenity, optimism and repose which makes it possible for them to conclude a work convincingly in this manner. Sibelius is one of them: his triumphant final movements, so far from being due to a mere unthinking acceptance of a formal convention, corresponds to a definite spiritual reality.

In a bygone era Sibelius' Second Symphony found its ideal interpreter in Serge Koussevitzky, the conductor and music director of the Boston Symphony Orchestra from 1924 to 1949. Koussevitzky was able to pierce to the very core of the score and reveal it to us anew at each successive performance. Koussevitzky was the supreme and absolute master of the French and Russian symphonic literature and his efforts on behalf of the American composer almost singlehandedly brought into being a significant repertoire of native symphonic composition. His demonic drive and passionate intensity created in the Boston Symphony Orchestra of his era what was probably the most responsive and supple symphonic instrument in the history of the art.

The tragedy is that Koussevitzky passed from the musical scene in 1951, just before high-fidelity recording techniques began to be perfected. Even though he made many recordings with the Boston Symphony Orchestra, very few of them remain available today. RCA Victor was perspicacious enough to record Koussevitzky's performance of Sibelius' Second Symphony twice—in January 1935 and again in December 1950 (at what proved to be his last recording sessions). The second recording is back in circulation again (RCA Victrola VIC 1510, mono only). How long it will remain available depends upon the RCA cost accountants who figure these things with no regard to artistic principle. My advice is: grab Koussevitzky's recording while it is still grabbable. The 1935 recording, a miracle of sound reproduction in its time, now sounds quite undernourished, but that performance has never been equaled by any subsequent recording. One minor criticism may be directed at the slightly deliberate tempo for the first movement (the tempo in the 1950 recording is a shade faster, incidentally) but for the rest, here is Sibelius' Second Symphony in an intense, passionate presentation of nobility and sweep. Koussevitzky's extraordinarily brilliant account of the climax of the symphony used to lift me out of my seat in Boston's Symphony Hall and it does so here, too. The 1950 recording is a great improvement in the sonics department but there is not quite the same degree of tension and classic nobility in the performance. Still, in perception and penetration it is in a class by itself.

Half a dozen of the currently available recordings are quite good: Barbirolli, himself a long-time Sibelius champion, brings to his latest recording of the symphony (Angel S 36425) a dignity and respect born of long association with the music; Ormandy (Odyssey Y 30046) has a steady grip on the score and keeps it moving; Maazel (London CS 6408), Monteux (London STS 15098) and Szell (Philips 835306; cassette PCR4 900092) turn in performances of great vigor and dynamism, and all are very well recorded. There is also available on the imported Odeon label a performance of the symphony recorded at an actual concert presentation in London's Royal Festival Hall by the BBC Symphony Orchestra conducted by Sir Thomas Beecham (Odeon PALP 1947, mono only). The excitement of concert conditions pervades this performance, even though the recorded sound is not up to the best of the others.

Maazel's (London K 80162—coupled with the conductor's splendid account of Sibelius' First Symphony) is my recommended tape version.

SYMPHONY NO. 5 IN E-FLAT MAJOR, OP. 82

For Sibelius the urge to compose was a deep inner compulsion unaffected by external circumstances. The creation of the Fifth

Symphony, a work of heroic affirmation, is a perfect example. Sibelius began it during the darkest days of the First World War, but it was four years before he was finally satisfied with it. A first version was performed in Helsinki on December 8, 1915, at a gala concert celebrating the composer's fiftieth birthday. About a year later Sibelius took up the Fifth Symphony again and rewrote it in a more concentrated form. This revision was performed in Helsinki in December of 1916, the composer conducting. The following summer Sibelius was thinking of a new symphony, his first important work of the war period other than the Fifth. At the same time he contemplated a "new and final revision" of the Fifth. It was not until the spring of 1918, however, that he was able to return to his scores with renewed energy. The Sixth and Seventh Symphonies were sketched, and a complete revision of the Fifth was begun. How drastic the final revision was Sibelius tells in a letter of May 20, 1918: "The Fifth Symphony in a new form, practically composed anew, I work at daily. Movement 1 entirely new, Movement 2 reminiscent of the old, Movement 3 reminiscent of the end of the first movement of the old, Movement 4 the old motifs, but stronger in revision. The whole, if I may say so, a vital climax to the end. Triumphal."

John N. Burk, in the Boston Symphony Orchestra concert bulletin, wrote of the Fifth Symphony:

> To a world steeped in lavish colorings, tending toward swollen orchestrations, lush chromatizations, Sibelius gave a symphony elementary in theme, moderate, almost traditional in form, spare in instrumentation. The themes at first hearing are so simple as to be featureless; the succession of movements makes no break with the past. However, any stigma of retrogression or academic severity is at once swept aside by the music itself. It goes without saying that Sibelius set himself exactly those means which the matter at hand required, and using them with consummate effectiveness created a sound structure of force, variety, and grandeur which no richer approach could have bettered.

The symphony is in four movements, with the first two connected without pause: the opening *Molto moderato* becomes an *Allegro moderato*. And though they are two distinct movements in mood and character, they are bound together by virtue of sharing a common theme—the bucolic ascending horn motif heard at the very beginning. Out of this motif evolves much of the germination of ideas. The second theme is a fragmentary figure in the woodwinds, with melancholy commentary from the bassoons. A variant of the opening horn motif is given to the principal trumpet, then other brass instruments take it up. The music builds in intensity and passion and there is an extraordinary section that pits a bleak bassoon melody against whirring strings. Suddenly there is a broadening and lightening of the texture and the trumpets in unison repeat the motto theme four times as introduction to a whirring Scherzo section. The music builds to an impassioned climax. The next movement, *Andante mosso, quasi allegretto*, begins in the flutes with a simple, naïve melody. The music is in the form of Theme and Variations, with a constantly repeated rhythmic underpinning. The last movement, *Allegro molto*, begins with another whirring and buzzing in the strings. The effect is intensified as woodwinds are attracted to it. Then horns intone a droning theme which is recognizable as a variant of an accompaniment figure from the slow movement. There is a development of these various elements and then the first theme is repeated in the muted and divided strings, misterioso, before the magisterial coda, *Un pochettino largamente*, brings the symphony to an emphatic and heroic conclusion.

The classic recording of Sibelius' Fifth Symphony for many years was the one made in the late 1930s by Serge Koussevitzky with the Boston Symphony Orchestra. It was also available for a time as a long-playing disc reissue (RCA LCT 1151). To his performance of the Fifth, as to his performances of all the Sibelius symphonies, Koussevitzky brought an intuitive perception and understanding. The brooding, mystical quality of much of the music struck a sympathetic chord in Koussevitzky's own make-up—as did the pages of triumphant heroism—and the Koussevitzky readings of the Sibelius symphonies will never be forgotten by any who were fortunate enough to hear them. It is significant that until the recent upsurge in the fortunes of Sibelius' music, sparked by the centennial celebrations in 1965, there was a slackening in Sibelius' popularity that followed immediately upon Koussevitzky's death in 1951.

The outstanding Barbirolli and Gibson performances are no longer available, which leaves the field clear for Bernstein's firm, noble and poetic account (Columbia MS 6749). Not far behind Bernstein's reading in emotional perception is Maazel's (London CS 6488).

Maazel's is my choice among the available tape versions (London L 80185). On cassette, the only available performance is Karajan's rather turgid account (DGG 923039).

Bedřich Smetana

Born: Leitomischl, Bohemia, March 2, 1824
Died: Prague, May 12, 1884

Though Smetana's musical talents were manifest at a very early age, his father, who managed the brewery on the estate of Count Waldstein, discouraged any serious musical study. It was through a childhood friend, Katharina Kolar, that Smetana came to the attention of the piano teacher Proksch in Prague. Smetana began studying piano and theory with him and then he obtained a position as music teacher in the family of Count Thun. After four years of this he went out on a concert tour that proved to be a financial disaster. With the help of Franz Liszt, to whom he turned in despair, Smetana then opened a piano school in Prague that flourished. In 1849, at the age of twenty-five, Smetana and Katharina Kolar were married.

Smetana was an intense Bohemian nationalist. The abortive revolution of 1848 only succeeded in clamping down tighter restrictions on free national expression and Smetana quickly found it impossible to exist in this environment. When the conductorship of the Philharmonic Society in Göteborg, Sweden, was offered to him in 1856, he accepted. He remained there five years and during that period he composed three symphonic poems, strongly influenced by Liszt, that were inspired by non-Bohemian cultures—*Richard III* (after Shakespeare), *Wallenstien's Camp* (after the play by Schiller) and *Haakon Jarl* (after a tragedy by a Danish poet).

Following the defeat of the Austrian forces by the Italian armies in 1859, Bohemia was granted political autonomy in the following year and the subterranean Bohemian national aspirations were allowed to surface in full flower. Agitation began quickly for the establishment of a national opera house in Prague and in May 1861

Smetana left Göteborg to take up residence in Prague once again and to become one of the leading spirits in the new movement. Between 1863 and 1874 Smetana composed eight patriotic operas for the new national theater and between 1866 and 1874 he also functioned as the principal conductor at the opera. *The Bartered Bride*, his second opera, was an immediate success and it carried Smetana's name far and wide.

Smetana encountered growing resistance and opposition to his direction at the opera house, which soon led to a serious nervous disorder. In the spring of 1874 he resigned his conductorship and by the following October he had become completely deaf. It was then that he returned to the symphonic-poem form and produced the six works that collectively are known as *Má Vlast* (*My Country*): *Vyšehrad* (the ancient castle of the Bohemian kings) and *Vltava* (*The Moldau*) in 1874. *Šárka* (a valley north of Prague, named after a mythological character) and *From Bohemia's Meadows and Forests* in 1875; *Tábor* (*The Camp*; introducing the Hussite warsong) in 1878; and *Blanik* (the hollow hill to which the Hussite heroes retreated in order to regroup for their ultimate battle of liberation) in 1879. To this period also belongs Smetana's First String Quartet, "From My Life" (1876).

At the end of his opera, *The Devil's Wall*, completed in April 1882, is this note: "Achieved in spite of terrible and constant hindrances." Those hindrances were nerve-shattering noises in the head and recurring states of restlessness and depression. On his sixtieth birthday in March 1884 a concert was organized to celebrate the event. Smetana, however, was too ill to participate in it and a letter he wrote at about the same time revealed a dangerous state of mental deterioration. Within a few weeks he was persuaded to enter an asylum, and there he died two months later.

THE MOLDAU (FROM MÁ VLAST)

Smetana dedicated his cycle *My Country* to the city of Prague. Indeed, the first two of the six symphonic poems in the cycle, *Vyšehrad* and *Vltava* (*The Moldau*), deal with sights in and around the city—the Vyšehrad rock which rises out of the river Moldau on the outskirts of Prague, and the Moldau itself.

Smetana completed *The Moldau* late in 1874, utilizing as his principal "river" theme an old Czech folk song. The program affixed to the score declares that the music traces the scenes through which the beloved river passes—the forests and meadows, the historic sites —and other associations with it, such as the revelry of water nymphs.

Four of the individual recordings of the score seem to me to have unusual merit: the versions conducted by Leonard Bernstein (Columbia MS 6879, tape MQ 805), Istvan Kertesz (London CS 6330, tape L 80115), Leopold Stokowski (RCA Victor LSC 2471) and George Szell (Odyssey Y 30049). Since *The Moldau* lasts only about eleven minutes in performance, the individual recordings of the score all include various other orchestral works: the Bernstein, Kertesz and Szell performances are all part of collections of Bohemian music, with selections from *The Bartered Bride* and Dvořák's *Slavonic Dances*; the Stokowski disc ranges over a wider field, containing, in addition to *The Moldau*, performances of Liszt's Second Hungarian Rhapsody, Enesco's First Roumanian Rhapsody and the overture to *The Bartered Bride*.

Bernstein's recording is typical of that conductor at his best: the performance has a characteristic surge and sweep, and there is no doubt whatsoever concerning his deep involvement with the music at hand. But Columbia's engineers, in spotlighting the important piccolo figures in the climactic pages, have rather overdone it, to the point of transforming those pages into a veritable piccolo concerto. Otherwise, the recorded sound is fine, and the New York Philharmonic plays sensitively.

The recordings by Kertesz and Szell have many points in common. Both give readings that are more objective than Bernstein's, but both are eminently persuasive nonetheless. Szell's orchestra receives a better acoustical *ambience* from the recording engineers than Kertesz does—there is more warmth and shading to the sound of the Cleveland Orchestra than there is to that of the Israel Philharmonic under Kertesz.

And so we come to the Stokowski recording. As I recall the circumstances of the sessions that produced his disc, the scores were rushed into the studio literally at the last minute. Stokowski and the RCA Victor Symphony had originally been scheduled to record a concerto with a distinguished soloist; a day before the sessions, when it was too late to cancel them, the soloist became unavailable for the assignment. There followed a mad scramble to come up with repertoire for the sessions. Several Stokowski specialties were selected, and *The Moldau*, for which Stokowski was not particularly noted, was thrown in too. Nonetheless, the performance of *The Moldau* that Stokowski recorded that day is not only one of his finest recordings, but is also one of the touchstones of recorded performance of any kind. The great river theme near the beginning, taken at a tempo somewhat slower than that of most conductors, seethes and soars with passion; conversely, the dance episodes are a little faster than usual, so that the contrast between the various sections of the score is intensified. The whole performance is one of extraordinary cumulative impact, and the playing and the recorded sound are all one could reasonably hope for.

Of the performances of *The Moldau* that are contained in recordings of *My Country* complete, it is the London set (CSA 2222) by Vaclav Neumann and the Leipzig Gewandhaus Orchestra that I find the best. It has a stylish elegance that is quite winning, and it is very well played and reasonably well recorded. But anyone interested in *The Moldau* alone is urged to go on a voyage of rediscovery with the redoubtable Stokowski at the helm.

Unfortunately, the Stokowski performance is not available, apparently, either on tape or cassette. In those departments my recommendations would be Bernstein's reel (Columbia MQ 805) and Kubelik's cassette (DGG 3881008—devoted to the complete cycle of six symphonic poems that together form *My Country*).

Richard Strauss

Born: Munich, June 11, 1864
Died: Garmisch-Partenkirchen, September 8, 1949

Richard Strauss' father, Franz, was a famous horn player in the Munich Opera Orchestra; indeed, he is supposed to have reduced, at Wagner's request, the well-nigh unplayable horn-call of Siegfried to its nearly playable final shape. The father supervised young Richard's earliest musical studies, and then he came under the tutelage of several other leading musicians in Munich. At the same time he received a traditional general education and he attended the University of Munich in 1882–83. He had already begun to compose: in March 1881, a Symphony in D Minor was performed in Munich; two years later his Violin Concerto was given, also in Munich, and before the end of 1884 another symphony, in F minor, was played by the New York Philharmonic under Theodore Thomas.

The winter of 1883–84 was a crucial one for Strauss: he came to the attention of Hans von Bülow, who engaged him as his assistant in Meiningen. When von Bülow left Meiningen, Strauss succeeded him. The one season (1885–86) that Strauss spent in Meiningen as the principal conductor was perhaps the turning point in his career, for he became closely associated with the poet and musician Alexander Ritter, who had a profound influence on him. Ritter urged upon Strauss the concept of music as expression and it was from the association with Ritter that Strauss became interested in composing music with a literary or philosophical outline.

A journey to Italy in 1886 resulted in a large-scale symphonic fantasy, *Aus Italien*, which was first performed at Munich in the spring of the following year. In rapid succession other symphonic poems followed—*Macbeth, Don Juan, Death and Transfiguration*, all before 1890. Strauss was passionately praised by some, just as

passionately condemned by others for his "musical modernism."
Hans von Bülow left no doubt as to where he stood: he dubbed
Strauss "Richard II" as a legitimate heir to the mantle of Wagner.
Strauss composed his first stage work, the opera *Guntram*, during
1892–93. It was first performed at Weimar in May 1894, with
Strauss himself conducting. The leading role was sung by a soprano
named Pauline de Ahna; four months later she and Strauss were
married and she remained by his side for the rest of his life, surviving
him by only a few months.

Over the decade between 1894 and 1904 Strauss produced five
more large symphonic poems—*Till Eulenspiegel's Merry Pranks,
Thus Spake Zarathustra, Don Quixote, Ein Heldenleben* and the
Symphonia Domestica. One more large-scale orchestral work was
to come from his pen, the *Alpine Symphony* of 1915. And in his last
years (1945–49) there was a sudden burst of orchestral creativity
again, albeit for smaller instrumental forces (the *Metamorphosen*
for twenty-three solo string instruments; the Duet-Concertino for
Clarinet and Bassoon with Strings and Harp; the Oboe Concerto).
For the most part, however, the last forty-five years of Strauss' life
were devoted to opera composition.

Guntram was succeeded in 1901 by *Feuersnot*, which attracted
little attention. Then in 1905 came Strauss' setting of the Oscar
Wilde play *Salome*; the erotic story was supplemented by a vivid
and sensuous score and a real *scandale* erupted: *Salome* was de-
nounced where it was not censored and censored where it was not
banned. There was a production of it at the Metropolitan Opera in
New York in 1907 and then it was withdrawn from the repertoire
not to return for many years. Strauss' next opera, *Elektra* (1909),
was no less sensational: its lurid story of matricide was decked out
with music of tremendous power and strength. The *Elektra* libretto
was written by the dramatist Hugo von Hofmannsthal and the collaboration thus begun was continued in five more operas until
Hofmannsthal's death in 1929: *Der Rosenkavalier* (1910), *Ariadne
auf Naxos* (1911–12), *Die Frau ohne Schatten* (1914–17), *Die
Ägyptische Helena* (1924–27) and *Arabella* (1930–32). *Der Rosenkavalier* is unquestionably Strauss' masterpiece for the stage; its
heroine, the Marschallin—a handsome woman in her thirties who

fears she will lose her good looks as she grows older—is one of the great figures in all operatic literature and the music that Strauss composed has a transparency and character that have caused comparison of Strauss with Mozart. After Hofmannsthal's death, Strauss continued to compose operas—*Die Schweigsame Frau* (1934–35), *Friedenstag* (1935–36), *Daphne* (1936–37), *Die Liebe der Danae* (1938–40) and *Capriccio* (1940–41). None of the five, however, has penetrated into the international operatic mainstream.

Strauss was famed throughout German-speaking countries as an extraordinary conductor also. There are those who say that his performances of the standard German symphonic literature were unequaled by any conductor of his time. He recorded some Mozart and Beethoven, but these performances have long been unavailable. There are available a few discs of Strauss-conducted performances of his own music; unfortunately, the best of them all—an absolutely magnificent performance of *Till Eulenspiegel*—has long since passed out of circulation.

Early in the Nazi regime in Germany Strauss was appointed to the all-important post as Reichsmusikkammer: in effect he was the dictator of all musical activities. Though he resigned in June 1935, he still maintained rather cozy relations with the Nazi government during its entire rule. A court de-Nazified him in June 1948, but his slate could never be wiped completely clean and the image that persists of Strauss during the dozen years of the Hitler scourge is one of equivocation, opportunism and moral weakness.

DON JUAN, OP. 20

In 1630, one of the most universal and indestructible characters in literature was created by a Spanish playwright, Tirso de Molina. Molina's play was titled *El Burlador de Sevilla* and its "hero," Don Juan, has long since become synonymous with unprincipled and calculating libertinism. Call someone a "Don Juan" in most cultures and no further description of him is necessary.

The image of Don Juan has fascinated artists for more than three hundred years; he has served as a figure to fire the imagination of

dramatists from Molière to Shaw, and his dashing exploits were un-
forgettably portrayed on the silent motion picture screen by Douglas
Fairbanks. The Don Juan figure served as a musical stimulus for
countless composers, chief among whom were Gluck (a ballet),
Mozart (the opera *Don Giovanni*), Dargomizhsky (the opera *The
Stone Guest*) and Richard Strauss.

Strauss' *Don Juan* was the first of the composer's tone poems to
be published. A product of Strauss' twenty-fifth year, *Don Juan* is
an extraordinary score: exuberant, supremely self-confident and exhibiting a command of form and substance which stamp it as
probably the most inspired orchestral score Strauss gave us.

Strauss' *Don Juan* erupted upon the musical scene in November
1889, when the composer conducted his second concert as the newly
appointed assistant Kapellmeister of the Grand Ducal Court Orchestra at Weimar. Even when it was new, there was no resisting the
headlong brilliance of the music: Strauss was called back for five
curtain calls and there were demands for an immediate repetition.
Hans von Bülow, who was present at the premiere to witness the
success of his protégé, wrote home to his wife: "Strauss is enormously popular here. His *Don Juan*, two days ago, had a most un-
heard-of success." When he was preparing a Berlin performance of
the score a year later, von Bülow wrote to Strauss: "Your most
grandiose *Don Juan* has taken me captive." *Don Juan* was not long
in reaching these shores; Artur Nikisch conducted the American premiere at a concert with the Boston Symphony Orchestra in October
1891. So secure is the niche of *Don Juan* in symphonic literature
that its performance at least once a season by every major orchestra
in the world is practically mandatory.

Strauss took his literary inspiration for *Don Juan* from a poem by
Nikolaus Lenau, an early-nineteenth-century Austrian philosopher
and poet. Where the *Don Juan* of Byron or Da Ponte (Mozart's
librettist) was a ruthless sensualist, Lenau's hero was motivated
by more complicated psychological factors. Lenau himself is supposed to have explained his Spanish nobleman as follows:

My Don Juan is no hot-blooded man eternally pursuing women. It is
the longing in him to find a woman who is to him incarnate woman-

hood, and to enjoy in the one all the women on earth whom he cannot possess as individuals. Because he does not find her, although he reels from one to another, at last Disgust seizes hold of him, and this Disgust is the Devil that fetches him.

This Don, in his final disillusion, throws his sword away as he is engaged in a duel and allows his opponent to run him through. His final words, in Lenau's poem, are: "My deadly foe is in my power, and this, too, bores me, as does life itself." A final clue to the character of this Vienna-flavored Don Juan is contained in his will: he has provided for all the women he has seduced.

The stirring opening of the tone poem, *Allegro molto con brio*, seems to depict the youthful, vigorous Don Juan in all his virile robustness—an irrepressible adventurer. In the words of Tovey, the opening section culminates "in a superb gesture of welcome to Love wheresoever it may be found." This "searching" music of Don Juan alternates with love episodes for some time; the first of them appears in the solo violin after a harp cadenza, the second as an oboe solo of melting lyricism and warmth. Then comes the second characteristic theme of Don Juan himself—a heroic proclamation from the four horns in unison. A repeat of the opening "searching" theme brings us to the middle section of the score. The increasing brilliance and color of the music builds to a bacchanalian climax, and then there are snatches of the violin and oboe themes and others associated with the seducer's previous exploits. Near the very end of the score there is a tremendous climax followed by complete silence: bitterness and despair seize hold of the hero and there is a shuddering section of desolation where the strings and winds have an A-minor chord which is pierced by the almost painful dissonance of trumpets in F major. One commentator has described the ending as "laconic, tightlipped; there is no wild complaint . . . only abandonment of life."

One of the classic recordings of *Don Juan* is the performance by the NBC Symphony Orchestra conducted by Arturo Toscanini (RCA Victrola VIC 1267, mono only). The fiery intensity of Toscanini produces a performance of enormous thrust and brilliance, and the clarity of the orchestral texture is awesome. Clearly, it should be in everybody's record collection. The recorded sound, dating from 1951, is still quite acceptable.

Among the many stereo versions available, my current choice would be the impetuous performance conducted by Henry Lewis (London SPC 21054; cassette M 94054). Three others that I find particularly gratifying are Bernstein's (Columbia MS 6822), Stokowski's (Everest SDBR 3023) and Szell's (Odyssey Y 30313). Bernstein's has a whip-lash brand of dynamism, with plenty of poetry in reserve for the more Romantic sections; Stokowski's has an uncommonly keen appreciation of the musical architecture of the score; and Szell's is an impetuous, exciting reading. All three are very well recorded, too.

For the reel-to-reel collector my suggestion would be Maazel's well-organized performance (London L 80158) now that the tape versions by Bernstein, Stokowski and Szell have all been withdrawn.

TILL EULENSPIEGEL, OP. 28

Six Novembers after the 1889 premiere of *Don Juan* there was introduced in Cologne another new symphonic poem by Richard Strauss. At first the composer refused to amplify his intentions in the new score in any way, preferring to allow the title to stand by itself without an embellishing program: *Till Eulenspiegel's Merry Pranks, After the Old-Fashioned Roguish Manner—In Rondo Form.* To a conductor about to perform the score, however, Strauss wrote a letter that reveals a little more:

It is impossible for me to furnish a program for *Eulenspiegel*; were I to put into words the thoughts which its several incidents suggested to me, they would seldom suffice and might even give rise to offense. Let me leave it, therefore, to my hearers, to crack the hard nut which the Rogue has prepared for them. By way of helping them to a better understanding, it seems sufficient to point out the two Eulenspiegel motives, which, in the most manifold disguises, moods, and situations, pervade the whole up to the catastrophe, when, after he has been condemned to death, Till is strung up to the gibbet. For the rest, let them guess at the musical joke which a Rogue has offered them.

Strauss then noted three themes: the beginning of the introduction, the horn motive of Till and the ominous descending interval of the hero's final condemnation.

Some historical facts may help in setting the mood and character of the piece. Till Eulenspiegel was a German folk-hero, a peasant who was born sometime around 1300 and who died near Lübeck in 1350. His exploits, centering around his unprincipled practical jokes and generally riotous behavior, became legendary in the half century after his death—the time of the flowering of German folk poetry and folk song. During the period of the mastersingers, Till flourished as a folklore figure. Stories about him were collected and published late in the fifteenth century and his exploits were immediately translated into half a dozen different languages. Editions continued to be published, often in new translations, and an English version of Till's merry pranks appeared in 1890. Perhaps the most celebrated modern version of the Eulenspiegel legend is the colorful *Glorious Adventures of Tyl Ulenspiegl* by the Belgian poet-novelist Charles de Coster, first published in 1869 and issued here in 1943 in a handsome English-language version by Pantheon Press, New York. Till even found his way onto the ballet stage, when Vaslav Nijinsky did a ballet of the Strauss tone poem.

The music begins with a phrase in the strings that sets the atmosphere in "Once upon a time" fashion. The strings are joined by the clarinet, and then the theme of Till himself appears in a fiendishly difficult French horn solo that is full of mischief. This material is brought to a climax and then the woodwinds announce a variant of Till's theme, this time mocking and saucy. There follows a very graphic section in which Till rides his horse through the market place, shattering the displayed crockery as he goes. A whip is heard in the orchestra in this section. Next there is a growling from the bassoons as Till is seen impersonating a monk. A lyrical theme for the solo violin, culminating in a dizzying downward slide, suggests that Till has fallen madly in love. The girl will have no part of him, however, and so he stalks off in search of his next adventure accompanied by mock heroics in the brass instruments. Till's next encounter is with a group of university professors, whom he befuddles with his mock seriousness. Bassoons and bass clarinet paint a particularly vivid portrait. In the middle of the argument Till suddenly decides he has had his fun and he runs off. There is an elaborate development of material and then a doom-laden drum roll is heard announcing Till's trial. Once, twice, three times Till's bravado asserts itself as his perky clarinet theme strives bravely to be heard, only to be summarily dismissed by the imperious trombones. There is no escaping his fate: Till is strung up. In an epilogue, the original "Once upon a time" theme returns, but Till does indeed have the last laugh as at the very end his theme erupts in a great orchestral belly laugh.

Of the recorded performances, Bernstein's is the version to have for snap and spirit (Columbia MS 7165, but also available on at least three other discs with different couplings). Rudolf Kempe's performance (Seraphim S 60122) has a rare wit and charm, and Szell's (Odyssey Y 30313) a brilliant polish and virtuosity. Tape collectors have available only the rigid Karajan performance (London L 80078 or L 80128, coupled differently); cassette collectors have Lewis' quite adequate reading available (London M 94054)—dependable if not quite so exhilarating as his *Don Juan* performance.

Igor Stravinsky

Born: Oranienbaum, Russia, June 17, 1882
Died: New York, N.Y., April 6, 1971

Stravinsky's father, Feodor Stravinsky, was a celebrated bass singer at the Imperial Opera in St. Petersburg. The boy grew up in a household full of music, but he was intended originally to pursue a career in law. A chance meeting with Rimsky-Korsakov in 1901 pointed the nineteen-year-old Stravinsky on the road to composition and six years later Stravinsky was taking private lessons in St. Petersburg with Rimsky-Korsakov himself. In January of the following year Stravinsky's First Symphony was performed in St. Petersburg and it revealed a remarkable technical mastery. In June of 1908 Rimsky-Korsakov's daughter was married to Maximilian Steinberg, the Russian teacher and composer, and Stravinsky composed his orchestral fantasy *Fireworks* for the occasion. Rimsky-Korsakov died just a few days later and Stravinsky composed a *Chant Funèbre* in tribute to his master.

The turning point in Stravinsky's early career as a composer came with the first performance of his next orchestral work, a *Scherzo Fantastique* performed in St. Petersburg in February 1909. In the audience was the great ballet impresario Diaghilev, who was so impressed with Stravinsky's powers that he invited him to compose music for a forthcoming ballet on a Russian subject. The work that resulted was *The Firebird*, a brilliant impressionistic use of orchestral color, exploiting exotic timbres and instrumental effects. As a result of the success of *The Firebird*, Stravinsky transferred the base of his operations to Paris, where Diaghilev's company was the reigning dance troupe. In June 1911 Stravinsky's second ballet for Diaghilev, *Petrouchka*, was premiered and again the music was an immediate success. Here Stravinsky extended even further the range of orchestral color he had exploited so dazzlingly in *The Firebird;* and to the explosive rhythms and vivid orchestral colors he also introduced the novel concept of simultaneous tonality in more than one key (C major and F-sharp major—the "Petrouchka Chord"). The first phase in Stravinsky's creative life came to an end two years later, with the introduction of his even more revolutionary ballet score *Le Sacre du Printemps—The Rite of Spring.* Here the harmonic daring, the propulsive rhythmic subtleties and the extraordinary orchestration were quite unlike anything that had gone before. *The Rite of Spring* is surely one of the most boldly original and imaginative works in the whole literature of music. Another work from this period is the Chinese fairy opera *Le Rossignol,* after a story by Hans Christian Andersen, produced in Paris by Diaghilev in May 1914.

The period of the First World War found Stravinsky spending most of his time in Switzerland, where he composed his unorthodox ballet score *Les Noces,* written for chorus, four vocal soloists, four pianos and seventeen percussion instruments. Another important work from the Switzerland period of the First World War is the danced pantomime with narrator, *L'Histoire du Soldat—The Story of a Soldier.* Here Stravinsky required only seven players to give him the full color range of strings, winds, brass and percussion. After the war there was a resumption in Stravinsky's association with Diaghilev and in 1920 came the composer's score for Diaghilev's *Pulcinella,* with musical material based largely on themes by the eighteenth-century Italian composer Giovanni Battista Pergolesi. For Diaghilev Stravinsky also composed two one-act operas from Russian literature—*Mavra,* after Pushkin, and *Renard,* a sort of animal fable in chamber style.

During the 1920s and '30s Stravinsky's music evidenced a tendency to compose in the manner of composers from the past—what has been called his Neo-Classic period. To these years belong such scores as his Concerto for Piano and Winds; the pantomime for string orchestra, *Apollon Musagète* (commissioned by the Elizabeth Sprague Coolidge Foundation); the *Capriccio* for Piano and Orchestra; the opera-oratorio *Oedipus Rex;* the *Symphony of Psalms* (composed for the fiftieth anniversary of the Boston Symphony Orchestra in 1930–31); the Violin Concerto; the melodrama *Perséphone* (to a text by André Gide); the "ballet in three deals," *Card Game*; the chamber concerto *Dumbarton Oaks*; and the ballet *The Fairy's Kiss*.

Stravinsky visited the United States for the first time in 1925, when he appeared as soloist in his Piano Concerto with the Boston Symphony Orchestra under Serge Koussevitzky. He maintained his residence in Paris, and became a French citizen in 1934, but he continued to make regular visits to the United States both as conductor and pianist in his own works. In 1939 he left France and emigrated to the United States, settling in Hollywood. The following year he composed his Symphony in C for the fiftieth anniversary of the Chicago Symphony Orchestra, and three years later, for the centennial of the New York Philharmonic, he composed his Symphony in Three Movements. A renewed association with George Balanchine of the New York City Ballet brought into being the score for *Orpheus* in 1948, and in 1951 Stravinsky produced a full-length, three-act opera, *The Rake's Progress*, after the famous series of engravings by Hogarth, to a libretto by W. H. Auden and Chester Kallman. *The Rake's Progress* was produced by the Metropolitan Opera in the early 1950s but it failed to make an impact, principally because of a wildly inferior production. Other opera companies have incorporated *The Rake's Progress* into their active repertoires with enormous success—especially the Stockholm Opera, whose production (directed by Ingmar Bergman) is one of the great experiences in today's theater.

Stravinsky's music since *The Rake's Progress* has found him more and more an adherent of the serial principles espoused by the Austrian composer Anton Webern, a pupil of Schönberg. In this idiom Stravinsky has written extensively, including such works as the ballet *Agon*, the *Canticum Sacrum* for the glory of St. Mark's Church in Venice, and the Movements for Piano and Orchestra; there is also a considerable body of short pieces for various small instrumental forces, all employing the serial technique. None of these works has achieved the success of Stravinsky's earlier scores; what the future holds for them only time can tell.

It is also significant that Stravinsky is the first great composer in music history who will have given us documented evidence concerning how he wished his music to be played: Columbia Records has recorded all his larger works and many of the smaller ones either with Stravinsky conducting or with his disciple Robert Craft in charge while Stravinsky supervised the proceedings.

PETROUCHKA

It was during his early twenties, while he was studying law, that Stravinsky made the acquaintance of Vladimir Rimsky-Korsakov, the youngest son of Russia's most prominent composer. Through the son Stravinsky soon met the great man himself, and for about half a dozen years, until the death of Rimsky-Korsakov in 1908, a close bond of affection and respect existed between the two (not unlike the relationship that developed in his later years between Stravinsky and Robert Craft).

The influence of Rimsky-Korsakov permeates Stravinsky's early output: Stravinsky's first published score, a Symphony in E-flat Major, was composed under Rimsky's supervision and is dedicated to him; the *Fantastic Scherzo, Fireworks* and *The Firebird*, all composed between 1907 and 1910, are direct descendants of *Scheherazade*, "Antar," and *Le Coq d'Or*. Not until the music of *Petrouchka* seized hold of his imagination did Stravinsky speak out in his own unique and personal manner.

The writing of *Petrouchka* seems to have been one of those inexorable artistic compulsions that could not be denied. Stravinsky was supposed to be working on a score for Diaghilev's Ballets Russes, which eventually became *Le Sacre du Printemps*. But work on this piece had to be suspended temporarily while Stravinsky gave himself over completely to the concert pieces for piano and orchestra, which had invaded his subconscious. "I had in my mind," Stravinsky writes in his autobiography, "a distinct picture of a puppet, suddenly endowed with life, exasperating the patience of the orchestra with diabolical cascades of arpeggios. The orchestra in turn retaliates with menacing trumpet blasts. The outcome is a terrific noise which reaches its climax and ends in the sorrowful and querulous collapse of the poor puppet."

After Diaghilev suggested that this score also should become the basis for a ballet, the work took shape rather quickly. The original concert pieces for piano and orchestra became the music for the second scene of the ballet; for the rest, Stravinsky composed new music of extraordinary color and brilliance, incorporating some half-dozen Russian folk songs along the way. Two levels of human experience seem to exist in *Petrouchka*, one actual and tangible, the other dream-like and almost hallucinatory.

The score describes the music as a "Burlesque in Four Scenes." As described in the full score, the scenes and action are as follows:

Scene I. *People's Fair at Shrovetide.*

Introduction. A group of drinkers pass dancing by—An old man on a platform engages the crowd—An organ-grinder appears with a dancer —He begins to play—The dancer performs, marking the beat with a triangle—The organ-grinder, while continuing to turn his handle, plays a cornet—At the opposite side of the stage a music box begins and another dancer performs—They cease—The old man resumes— A merry-making crowd passes—Two drummers draw attention to the little theater—The old showman appears before it and plays his flute—The curtain of the little theater is drawn and the crowd perceives three puppets: Petrouchka, a Moor and a Ballerina—The showman's flute gives them life—Russian Dance—All three begin to dance, to the astonishment of the public.

Scene II. *At Petrouchka's.*

The door of Petrouchka's room opens suddenly; a foot kicks him on stage; Petrouchka falls and the door slams—Maledictions of Petrouchka—The Ballerina enters—Despair of Petrouchka.

Scene III. *At the Moor's.*

The Moor dances—Dance of the Ballerina (cornet in her hand)— Waltz (the Ballerina and the Moor)—The Moor and the Ballerina listen—Petrouchka appears—Quarrel of the Moor and Petrouchka; the Ballerina disappears—The Moor pushes Petrouchka out.

Scene IV. *People's Fair at Shrovetide* (toward evening).

Nurses' Dance—Enter a peasant with a bear—The crowd separates —The peasant plays the chalumeau and the bear walks on his hind legs—There appears a rakish holiday merchant with two gypsies— He tosses bank notes among the crowd—The gypsies dance while he plays the accordion—Dance of the coachmen and grooms—The nurses dance with the coachmen and grooms—The masqueraders—

A masker dressed as a devil incites the crowd to fool with him—
Altercation of maskers dressed as goat and pig—The crowd joins the
maskers—The dance is interrupted—Petrouchka comes out from his
booth pursued by the Moor while the Ballerina tries to hold him back
—The Moor strikes him with his sword and Petrouchka falls, his head
broken—He moans and dies—The crowd surrounds him—The police-
man is sent for to find the Charlatan—The Charlatan arrives and lifts
the body of Petrouchka, shaking him—Alone on the stage the Charlatan drags the body toward the booth—Above the booth, the shade
of Petrouchka appears, threatening, and makes a long nose at the
Charlatan—The Charlatan drops the puppet in terror and goes out
quickly, glancing behind him.

Petrouchka has been one of the most frequently performed of all
ballets for more than fifty years, and the concert suite Stravinsky
extracted from the full score has been a staple of international concert life for nearly the same length of time. Leopold Stokowski once
recorded the full score during his halcyon days as the conductor of
the Philadelphia Orchestra, but it remained for a remarkable and
widely noted recording of 1947, by Ernest Ansermet and the London
Philharmonic Orchestra, to make the complete *Petrouchka* as familiar to our concert-going public as it is to our balletomanes.

The 1947 Ansermet recording of *Petrouchka* served to introduce
the new FFRR technique of English Decca (London), and twice
since then the firm has had Ansermet re-record his inimitable
version of the music as a demonstration of successive advancements
in the recording art. Ansermet's first re-recording of the score, made
in the early 1950s for the newly developed long-playing medium, is
still carried in London's low-price Richmond series (19015), while
London itself now proudly distributes a more recent Ansermet performance which is one of the glories of stereophonic reproduction
(CS 6009). What makes all of Ansermet's three recordings precious
gems is the conductor's effortless spontaneity and naturalness, his
total immersion in the score, and his uncanny ability to make the listener part of it. In these respects, Ansermet's performance of *Petrouchka* is unique. His most recent recording also has the benefit of
extraordinary recorded sound; and this is my favorite of all the
Petrouchka recordings.

Pierre Monteux, in his version with the Boston Symphony Orchestra (RCA LSC 2376) has the same virtues as Ansermet but not to such an overwhelming degree. Both conductors, for example, achieve real poignance in the concluding pages when the ghost of Petrouchka hovers above the scene of the action, but Ansermet's interpretation is the more moving. Ansermet has slightly the better of it in recorded sound, too, with pellucid reproduction that outshines the slightly hazy Monteux version.

The late Sir Eugene Goossens recorded a fine performance of the complete score with the London Symphony Orchestra for Everest (SDBR 3033), but both Ansermet and Monteux outrank him in authority. All three conductors employ the original 1910 orchestration.

Thirty-five years later, after he had completed his Symphony in Three Movements, Stravinsky returned to *Petrouchka* and reorchestrated it. Ostensibly the new orchestration—which was mostly a thinning-out process—represented the composer's mature improvements on a masterpiece of his youth. In my view, however, any dilution of *Petrouchka's* brilliance and color is no improvement, and the nagging thought remains that among Stravinsky's motives in reorchestrating the music was a financial one: the composer never collected royalties from performances of the 1910–11 orchestration because it was never copyrighted (Russia never signed the international copyright agreements). But the new (1947) orchestration is protected by the copyright law, and a royalty payment automatically accrues to the composer from each public performance of the work.

Two conductors—Zubin Mehta (London CS 6554) and, not unexpectedly, Stravinsky himself (Columbia MS 6332) have recorded the 1947 orchestration of *Petrouchka*. Mehta's is rather frenetic, with an almost constant straining after effect. It is brilliantly played and recorded, but superficial in its approach and attitude. The composer's, on the other hand, is an eloquent statement of the subject matter and will be a valuable document in the years to come.

New recordings of *Petrouchka* appear with numbing regularity. Of the very recent bunch (including performances conducted by Boulez, Bernstein, Leinsdorf and Ozawa) the Boulez performance

(Columbia M 31076) is remarkable for its linear clarity, unremarkable for its slighting of the music's dramatic energies. Boulez employs the original 1911 version. Bernstein's (Columbia MC 30269 —a specially priced two-disc set that also includes the conductor's discussion of Stravinsky and *Petrouchka*) makes more of the score's irony and menace than any other known to me; he uses the 1947 version, as does Ozawa in his clear but rather antiseptic recording (RCA LSC 3167; cassette RK 1164). Clear and antiseptic are also the words for the Leinsdorf recording (London SPC 21058; tape L 75058; cassette M 94058)—another performance that employs the original instrumentation of 1911. Of the recordings of the original orchestration, Ansermet's—on tape as well as disc (London R 80205) —satisfies me most.

LE SACRE DU PRINTEMPS

In the spring of 1910, the Ballets Russes of Serge Diaghilev unveiled simultaneously two new phenomena: a new ballet based on the ancient Russian folk tale, *The Firebird*, and a brilliant new composer in the person of Igor Stravinsky. Both Stravinsky and his music scored a sensation. Fresh from this triumph, Stravinsky soon became absorbed in thoughts for another ballet based on primitive rites in which a young girl would dance herself to death as a sacrificial offering. Diaghilev was delighted with the idea and encouraged Stravinsky to pursue it. The following year Diaghilev visited Stravinsky at Clarens on Lake Geneva to see how work on *Le Sacre du Printemps* (*The Rite of Spring*) was progressing. Instead he found the composer absorbed in a new idea: a concert piece for piano and orchestra that was to become his second ballet, *Petrouchka*, pushing all thoughts of *Le Sacre du Printemps* into the background.

Stravinsky returned to his ballet on pagan rites after *Petrouchka* was produced for the first time at the Châtelet in Paris in June 1911. In 1912, Pierre Monteux became the regular conductor for the Ballets Russes and it was decided that he would be in charge of the musical preparation for the premiere of the next Stravinsky ballet. Monteux has written (*Dance Index*, 1947):

One day Diaghilev summoned me to a tiny rehearsal room in a theater of Monte Carlo where the ballet was at that time appearing. We were to hear Stravinsky run through the score of his new work, *Le Sacre du Printemps.*

With only Diaghilev and myself as audience, Stravinsky sat down to play a piano reduction of the entire score. Before he got very far, I was convinced he was raving mad. Heard this way, without the color of the orchestra, which is one of its great distinctions, the crudity of the rhythm was emphasized, its stark primitiveness underlined. The very walls resounded as Stravinsky pounded away, occasionally stamping his feet and jumping up and down to accentuate the force of the music. Not that it needed such emphasis.

I was more astounded by Stravinksy's performance than shocked by the score itself. My only comment at the end was that such music would surely cause a scandal. However, the same instinct that had prompted me to recognize his genius made me realize that in this ballet he was far, far in advance of his time and that while the public might not accept it, musicians would delight in the new, weird, though logical expression of dissonance.

Monteux was right in immediately sensing the shock value of the music but not even he could have foreseen the absolute riot which occurred when *Le Sacre du Printemps* was presented for the first time at the Théâtre des Champs-Elysées in Paris on May 29, 1913. The scene has been vividly described by those who were there. The audience squirmed at first, then began to murmur, and then the whole theater erupted into a monstrous cacophony of hoots, catcalls and hisses. People pounded on the heads and backs of their neighbors and then began a mass stampede to the exits. Stravinsky had created a monumental *scandale.* Not quite a year later, on the fifth of April 1914, Monteux conducted a concert presentation of the music at one of his concerts at the Casino in Paris and the colossal stature of the music began to be revealed. It took nearly eight years for *Le Sacre* to reach this country. It did so in March 1922 at a concert of the Philadelphia Orchestra conducted by Leopold Stokowski.

Pierre Monteux introduced the score to Boston and New York audiences toward the end of his last season (1923–24) as music director of the Boston Symphony Orchestra. After the initial Boston presentation, the distinguished critic of the Boston *Transcript*, Mr. H. T. Parker, wrote:

> It is believable that a future historian of the Boston Symphony Orchestra will note in particular the Symphony concert of January 25, 1924. Then and there, he may write, was first heard in Boston a masterpiece that had altered the whole course of music in our time, that had become beacon and goal to a whole generation of composers up and down the European and American earth.

Parker's words have come to have about them the ring of prophecy. The elemental drive, the rhythmic vitality, the psychologically perceptive power, the mass of the full weight of the gigantic orchestra, and above all, the irresistible power of the music to communicate stamps Stravinsky's *Le Sacre* as *the* single most important contribution to symphonic literature during the first half of our century.

The score is divided into two continuous parts, separated by a brief pause. The first part is titled *The Fertility of the Earth*, the second *The Sacrifice*. Stravinsky himself has written a vivid description of the action of the ballet and its music:

> In the *Introduction* before the curtain rises I have given to the orchestra alone the idea of that great sense of fear which weighs upon all sensitive spirits before a controlled power, and this develops through the entire instrumental texture. It is a profound mystic sensation which comes to all things at the hour when nature seeks to renew its various forms of life; it is this vague, yet profound discord which affects all at puberty. Even in my orchestration and in the play of the melody I desire to evoke this quality. . . .
>
> The musical material itself swells, expands and is then diffused; each instrument is like a bud which grows on the bark of a venerable tree; it becomes part of an immense ensemble. And the entire orchestra, the entire ensemble, must take on the meaning of a rebirth of Spring.
>
> In the first tableau (*The Fertility of the Earth*) some adolescents are seen with an old, old woman, a woman whose age is not known, nor even from what century she comes, but who understands the secrets of nature and who is teaching their meaning to her sons. She

runs, bowed down toward the ground, as if neither woman nor animal. These adolescents near her are the Augurs of Spring who evoke with the pulsating beats of their dance the very rhythm of Spring's awakening.

During this time the adolescent girls come down to the river. They form a circle which mixes with that of the boys. The groups merge; but in their rhythm one feels a straining toward the formation of new groups; and they divide to right and left. Now a new form has been realized, a synthesis of rhythms, and then from this a new rhythm is produced (*Dance of the Youths and Maidens; Dance of Abduction; Springs Rounds*).

The groups separate and begin to fight. Messengers go from one to another and struggle . . . signifying, so to speak, that aspect of brute force which is also play (*Games of Rival Towns*). The arrival of a procession is heard. It is the Sage, the oldest man of the clan. A great fear surges through the crowd. Then the Sage, face down on the ground, becoming one with the soil, gives a benediction to the earth (*Entrance of the Celebrant; Kiss to the Earth*). Then all cover their heads, run in spirals, and leap as though endowed with renewed energy from nature . . . the *Dance to the Earth*.

The second tableau, *The Sacrifice*, begins with a quiet and obscure play among the adolescent girls. At the opening the musical prelude (*Introduction—The Pagan Night*) is based on a mysterious song which accompanies the dance of the young girls. They mark within their circle the signs showing where the Glorified One will finally be enclosed never to come out again. She it is who is being consecrated to the Spring and who will thus return to Spring the vitality which Youth has taken from it (*Mystic Circle of the Adolescents*).

Around the Chosen One, who is immobile, the young girls dance a ritual of glorification (*Dance to the Glorified One*); then follows the purification of the soil and an *Evocation of the Ancestors*. The Ancestors group themselves around the Chosen One (*Ritual Performance of the Ancestors*) and she commences the *Sacrificial Dance*.

As she is about to fall exhausted, the Ancestors glide toward her like rapacious monsters. So that she should not touch the soil as she falls, they seize her and raise her toward the sky.

Once again is fulfilled in its primeval rhythm the cycle of forces which are re-born and which fall again into the lap of nature.

Two notable recordings of *Le Sacre* were released in the 1940s: the composer's own detached but starkly earthly reading with the

New York Philharmonic, and Monteux's more plastic yet no less dynamic reading with the San Francisco Symphony Orchestra. With the advent of the microgroove record both performances were transferred to the LP format.

In January 1951, Monteux returned as a guest to conduct the Boston Symphony Orchestra for the first time since April 1924. There was a good deal of nostalgia attached to this return and to the fact that Le Sacre figured on his program. On a very snowy Sunday evening following the Friday-Saturday concerts, Monteux and the Boston Symphony Orchestra again gathered on the stage of Symphony Hall, Boston, to perform Le Sacre du Printemps—this time for the RCA Victor recording microphones. It could be the fact that I was present at the sessions and overcome by the drama and sentiment of the occasion, but this particular recording (RCA LM 1149, mono only) has always seemed to me to have just the right combination of elements where this work is concerned: virtuoso orchestral playing of peerless perfection mated to an inspired reading of drive, passion and sensitivity from the conductor. I am dismayed to find this performance has been withdrawn from the catalog. Monteux's re-recording of the score with the Paris Conservatory Orchestra for stereo (RCA LSC 2085) may have been newer and may have benefited from more modern recording techniques, but as a performance it remains inferior to his 1951 recording with the Boston Symphony Orchestra.

Le Sacre du Printemps obviously calls for the ultimate in reproduction and is thus a natural for the flexing of stereo muscles. Half a dozen of the recordings of the music are in one way or another absorbing listening experiences—the performances conducted by Ansermet (included in London CSA 2308), Bernstein (Columbia MS 6010), Boulez (Nonesuch S 71093—budget-priced), Markevitch (Angel S 35549) and Stravinsky himself (Columbia MS 6319).

Ansermet's is a thoroughly unorthodox reading, stressing the lyrical elements in the music and making of it virtually a new experience. But Ansermet must be firm in his conviction that this is really what the score is all about, for he turned in the same kind of performance in a London disc of the early microgroove era. London's stereo sound for Ansermet is a little diffuse and distant. The Boulez recording is a rarefied intellectual exercise—cool and detached, transparently, indeed microscopically reproduced, but lacking in warmth and involvement. The Markevitch issue is a repeat of the conductor's earlier triumphant recording (once available on an HMV imported disc, HMV 1) with the Philharmonia Orchestra—a solid, exciting reading, highly charged and with great cumulative power. Stravinsky's own recording is a taut, elemental one, like the Boulez largely impersonal, but packing a considerable wallop nonetheless.

The Boulez-Cleveland Orchestra performance (Columbia MS 7293; cassette 16110154) has been highly praised by others; I find it undernourished in the dramatic department.

And so finally to what seems to me unquestionably *the* choice among available modern recordings of the score—Bernstein's. *Le Sacre du Printemps* is one of those works that ignites a particularly responsive spark in Bernstein's make-up. The music consumes him and he gives us a reading of overwhelming drive, rhythmic vitality and visceral excitement. The recording was made during the 1957–58 season—before Bernstein became the Philharmonic's music director—but already he had the orchestra playing for him like 110 possessed demons. The discipline of the performance is extraordinary and Columbia has contrived stereo sound that is rich and resonant, yet with carefully delineated detail.

Tape-reel collectors are offered only the very pallid account by Ansermet (London R 80205). DGG has a performance awaiting release by the Boston Symphony Orchestra conducted by Michael Tilson Thomas. There is also a re-recording of the score conducted by Bernstein (this time with the London Symphony Orchestra) awaiting release on the Columbia label.

There remains one other recording of the *Sacre* that I should like to mention briefly: Karajan's (Deutsche Grammophon 138920). Here is the perfect example of everything that is wrong with this conductor's music-making. Careful study and dissection of the score succeed in completely eviscerating it and rendering it bloodless. No more telling indictment of the whole Karajan philosophy exists than this terrifyingly anti-human account of Stravinsky's fiery and passionate music.

Peter Ilyitch Tchaikovsky

Born: Votkinsk, Russia, May 7, 1840
Died: St. Petersburg, November 6, 1893

The son of a mining inspector in the Ural Mountains, Tchaikovsky received a traditional education that included French and music studies. In common with many other scions of middle-class Russian families he seemed destined for a life as a law practitioner; at the age of nineteen he was graduated from a school of jurisprudence and went to work as a government clerk. Two years later, however, he was accepted as a student at a newly opened musical institution that was to become the famed St. Petersburg Conservatory. Upon his graduation four years later he won a silver medal for his cantata setting of Schiller's "Ode to Joy," the same text that served as the basis for the final movement of Beethoven's Ninth Symphony. In the following year he became professor of harmony at the Moscow Conservatory under the direction of Nicholas Rubinstein, brother of Anton, who had been Tchaikovsky's mentor in St. Petersburg.

Tchaikovsky was in his mid-twenties before he applied himself seriously to composition. His first works were a symphony (subtitled "Winter Daydreams"), some overtures and pieces for chamber ensembles, but it was not until 1869, when he was twenty-nine, that the first indications of his own individual style were revealed in the symphonic poem *Fatum:* this score has a highly developed feeling of nostalgic longing, it is mainly in the minor mode and it throbs with vitality and rhythmic excitement. In the same year also Tchaikovsky first undertook to compose an orchestral work inspired by Shakespeare's *Romeo and Juliet;* in 1870 Tchaikovsky met the composer Balakirev in St. Petersburg and discussed the *Romeo and Juliet* project with him, but it was not until 1879 that Tchaikovsky finally finished the score to his own satisfaction. It became almost immediately the vehicle by which Tchaikovsky's name came to be widely known.

During the years 1868–74 he was also active on the Moscow scene as a music critic, contributing articles to various newspapers and periodicals. For one of them, the *Russky Viedomosti*, he visited the first Bayreuth Festival in 1876 and reported back his impressions. Despite his active musical life as teacher, composer and correspondent, Tchaikovsky was beset with serious financial problems, and his plight came to the attention of a wealthy widow, Madame Nadejda von Meck. At first Madame von Meck commissioned Tchaikovsky to compose several works at rather high fees; then she arranged to pay him a handsome annual annuity. For thirteen years there was a steady correspondence between the two of them, but they never met —at Tchaikovsky's insistence.

One of the most bizarre episodes in Tchaikovsky's life occurred in 1877 when he entered briefly into a marriage for which he was emotionally and temperamentally not equipped. After a nightmare attempt at cohabitation, he fled from his bride and attempted suicide by walking in the Moskva River in hopes he would contract pneumonia. All he got for his efforts was a slight chill, but he never returned to his wife. His brother Anatol drew up the legal papers for their separation but they were never divorced; the unfortunate young lady, who had been a student at the Moscow Conservatory, died in an insane asylum in 1917.

Tchaikovsky spent much of the next few years traveling in Italy, Switzerland, Paris and Vienna and it was during this period that he composed his Fourth Symphony, dedicated to Madame von Meck. In the autumn of 1878 he resigned from his teaching position at the Moscow Conservatory and from that time onward he was able to devote his full-time energies to composition, thanks to the continued subsidy from his benefactress. In 1879 he completed his most successful opera, *Eugene Onegin*, and in the ensuing years a steady flow of masterpieces came from his pen, including the First Piano Concerto, the Violin Concerto and the Fifth Symphony. In the autumn of 1890 the long friendship with Madame von Meck came to an abrupt end: Tchaikovsky received a letter from her declaring that she had lost her fortune, would be unable to continue to send him money and would henceforth have no further contact with him. Tchaikovsky wrote back to her the same day, deeply concerned for her well-being, but his letter was never answered. His pain was compounded some time later when he discovered that her story was a complete fabrication: she had suffered no financial setback but had invented the story as a means of breaking off their correspondence. To this day no satisfactory explanation of her abrupt action has been forthcoming.

Tchaikovsky weathered this storm, too, and in 1891 he journeyed to the United States to participate in the opening ceremonies that inaugurated Carnegie Hall in New York. He led four concerts of his works in Carnegie Hall and one each in Baltimore and Philadelphia. Early the next year he went on a concert tour of Russia, Poland and Germany and he began to work on two disparate scores —the music for the ballet *The Nutcracker*, one of his most amiable and gay works, and his Sixth Symphony, which was titled "Pathétique" by his brother and intimate associate, Modest. At the time of the premiere of the symphony in October 1893, a cholera epidemic was raging in St. Petersburg. The populace was warned against drinking unboiled water—and yet that is precisely what Tchaikovsky did, out of carelessness, presumably. He quickly developed symptoms of the disease and within ten days of the first performance of the "Pathétique" Symphony its composer was dead.

CONCERTO NO. 1 IN B-FLAT MINOR FOR PIANO AND ORCHESTRA, OP. 23

It was during the late fall of 1874 that Peter Ilyitch Tchaikovsky gave birth to his First Piano Concerto. The analogy is intentional, for the labor pains attendant to its final production and public baptism left an indelible impression upon the psyche of the composer.

Tchaikovsky was in his thirty-fifth year, a teacher of harmony at the Moscow Conservatory, music critic for the *Russky Viedomosti* and an important figure in the cultural life of the Russian capital. Nicholas Rubinstein was the reigning baron of Russian musical life and Tchaikovsky decided to seek his opinion of the concerto.

In a letter to Madame von Meck, Tchaikovsky described the experience most vividly:

In December 1874 I had written a pianoforte concerto. As I am not a pianist, I thought it necessary to ask a virtuoso what was technically unplayable in the work, thankless, or ineffective. I needed the advice of a severe critic who at the same time was friendly disposed toward me. Without going too much into detail, I must frankly say that an interior voice protested against the choice of Nicholas Rubinstein as a judge over the mechanical side of my work. But he was the best pianist in Moscow, and also a most excellent musician; I was told that he would take it ill from me if he should learn that I had passed him by and shown the concerto to another; so I determined to ask him to hear it and criticize the piano part.

On Christmas Eve, 1874 . . . Nicholas asked me . . . to play the concerto in a classroom of the Conservatory. We agreed to it. . . . I played through the first movement. Not a criticism, not a word. You know how foolish you feel, if you invite one to partake of a meal provided by your own hands, and the friend eats and—is silent! "At least say something, scold me good-naturedly, but for God's sake speak, only speak, whatever you may say!" Rubinstein said nothing. . . . I did not need any judgment on the artistic form of my work; there was question only about mechanical details. This silence of Rubinstein said much. It said to me at once: "Dear friend, how can I talk about details when I dislike your composition as a whole?" But I kept my temper and played the concerto through. Again silence. "Well?" I said, and stood up. There burst forth from Rubinstein's mouth a mighty torrent of words. He spoke quietly at first; then he waxed hot, and at last he resembled Zeus hurling thunderbolts. It appeared that my concerto was utterly worthless, absolutely unplayable; passages were so commonplace and awkward that they could not be improved; the piece as a whole was bad, trivial, vulgar. I had stolen this from that one and that from this one; so only two or three pages were good for anything, while the others should be wiped out or radically rewritten. "For instance, that! What is it, anyhow?" (And then he caricatured the passage on the pianoforte.) "And this? Is it possible?" and so on, and so on. I cannot reproduce for you the main thing: the tone in which he said all this. An impartial bystander would necessarily have believed that I was a stupid, ignorant, conceited notescratcher, who was so impudent as to show his scribble to a celebrated man.

The original dedication of the concerto was to Rubinstein, but after the incident of December 1874 Tchaikovsky indignantly tore Rubinstein's name from the title page and inscribed instead the name of the pianist and conductor, Hans von Bülow, the renowned German musician whom Tchaikovsky had not yet met but who was enthusiastically making known the composer's piano pieces throughout Europe. Von Bülow eagerly accepted the dedication of the concerto and wrote to Tchaikovsky a letter whose phrases stand in grotesque contrast to those of Rubinstein:

> The ideas are so original, so noble, so powerful; the details are so interesting, and though there are many of them they do not impair the clarity and the unity of the work. The form is so mature, so ripe and distinguished in style, intention and labor being everywhere concealed. I would weary you if I were to enumerate all the characteristics of your work, characteristics which compel me to congratulate equally the composer and those who are destined to enjoy it.

Von Bülow was the soloist at the world premiere performance of the Tchaikovsky B-flat Minor Piano Concerto—in Boston, Massachusetts, of all places, on October 25, 1875. The reception of both audience and critics was tumultuous. Bülow telegraphed Tchaikovsky the news of the wild audience response and Tchaikovsky spent his last ready cash answering the cable. In a letter sometime later to Rimsky-Korsakov, Tchaikovsky wrote: "Think of the healthy appetite these Americans must have: each time Bülow was obliged to repeat the whole Finale of my Concerto! Nothing like this happens in our country!"

The reasons for the popularity of the concerto are not too difficult to pinpoint. For one thing, it fairly bursts with tuneful melodies—extraordinary even for so prolific a tunesmith as Tchaikovsky. For another, the solo part is bold and fluid. The work is cast in big contours and it makes for a Bunyanesque, larger-than-life effect. And then there is that introduction, quite possibly the most arresting opening in the entire concerto literature.

The introduction is marked *Allegro non troppo e molto maestoso*. After imperious horn flourishes and orchestral punctuations, the solo piano enters with a series of chords and then the strings introduce the principal theme of the introduction—a long-breathed, sweeping melody that once was set to the words "Tonight we love, while the moon is shining bright" and in that form achieved popular Hit Parade stature. The theme, in a slightly altered rhythm, is repeated by the solo piano, then there is a piano cadenza and the theme is repeated once more by all the strings (minus the double basses). After this the introduction comes to a conclusion and the great theme is heard no more. The main body of the movement is marked *Allegro con spirito* and it begins with a rushing phrase in the piano that Tchaikovsky is supposed to have heard sung by a blind beggar. To his patroness, Madame von Meck, Tchaikovsky wrote: "It is curious that in Little Russia every blind beggar sings exactly the same refrain. I have used part of this refrain in my pianoforte concerto." The horns and woodwinds first announce the second principal subject (*Poco meno mosso*) and the piano then takes it over. These elements are thoroughly worked over and the movement ends in a blaze of pianistic fireworks.

After some preliminary string pizzicato, the flute announces the first principal subject of the second movement (*Andantino semplice*). The second theme appears first in the oboe and clarinets, while the bassoons drone away on a single note. There is a dancelike middle section marked *Prestissimo* given to the strings with the solo piano decorating it with all kinds of frills and runs. The movement ends with the simple melody with which it began.

The last movement, *Allegro con fuoco*, is a brilliant tour de force for the piano and the orchestra. There are three principal themes. The first appears immediately in the piano after a brief and explosive orchestral introduction. Having the character of a wild Cossack dance, this piano theme will dominate the coda at the end of the movement. The second main theme is given to the orchestra and it, too, has a syncopated dance rhythm. The third theme, assigned first to the violins, will also take on a heightened importance and significance in the concluding coda. The elaboration and development of the material is masterful and the conclusion is guaranteed to lift an audience right out of its seats.

Ever since Van Cliburn won the first Tchaikovsky Piano Competition in Moscow in April 1958, the recording industry has rushed the winners of this competition into the recording studios to engrave their performances of the Tchaikovsky concerto for posterity. Thus, beginning with Cliburn (RCA LSC 2252), there are recordings available by many of the first- and second-prize winners of the Tchaikovsky competition: Vladimir Ashkenazy and John Ogdon, who shared the first prize in the 1962 contest (London CS 6360 and Angel S 36142, respectively), and Grigory Sokolov (Angel/Melodiya S 40016) and Misha Dichter (RCA LSC 2954), the first- and second-prize winners in the 1966 competition. Truth to tell, all the young artists turn in outstanding performances and a choice between them is exceedingly difficult. All are well supported by their respective orchestras, conductors and recording teams (though Sokolov has it less good in these departments than his colleagues); any one of them will give lasting pleasure. If I continue to favor Cliburn's, it is because the nostalgia of his triumphant return to this country after his extraordinary victory is still very fresh in my memory. And the collaboration between Cliburn and the Soviet conductor Kondrashin pries loose from the score a wide range of musical values. Especially successful are the first and last movements, which emerge as models of controlled dynamism. In the slow movement there are a few instances of rhythmic unsteadiness but they do not detract from the impact of a presentation granitic in its solidity and exemplary in its musicality.

Among the other available recordings of the score, three are deserving of special comment: Gilels' with Reiner and the Chicago Symphony Orchestra (RCA Victrola VICS 1039), Horowitz' with Toscanini and the NBC Symphony Orchestra (RCA LM 2319, mono only) and Rubinstein's with Leinsdorf and the Boston Symphony Orchestra (RCA LSC 2681). Gilels delivers an uninhibited virtuoso account, but one with enough leavening of poetry to make it satisfying on both digital and musical levels. The presentation is essentially a dramatic one. There are moments of untidy ensemble, but they do not affect the sweep of the whole. The Horowitz-

Toscanini collaboration—a recording of the concert they played as a War Bonds benefit in New York's Carnegie Hall on April 25, 1943—is an astonishing document: a demonic, fire-spewing performance that tears up the turf in its visceral energy and excitement. Though the sound is barely acceptable, this performance must be heard. Finally, Rubinstein's account is a steady, unruffled one with a kind of masterful dignity that not many artists can find in this often-abused masterpiece. Some recent very worthy entries are the performances by Argerich-Dutoit (DGG 2530112) and Davis-Lewis (London SPC 21056; tape L 75056).

Cliburn's (tape TR3 1011, 3¾ ips; cassette RK 1002) would be my first tape recommendation, with Ashkenazy's (London K. 80125—coupled with a splendid performance by this artist of Rachmaninoff's Third Concerto) a good alternate choice.

CONCERTO IN D MAJOR FOR VIOLIN AND ORCHESTRA, OP. 35

Critical vituperation and invective run through all the annals of music history and there is hardly a composer of note who at one time or another has not had his head chopped off in print by a coeval representative of the Fourth Estate. A particular target of his contemporary music critics and fellow musicians was Tchaikovsky. Take this slashing attack from the pen of Vienna's Eduard Hanslick:

> For a while the Concerto has proportion, is musical and is not without genius, but soon savagery gains the upper hand and lords it to the end of the first movement. The violin is no longer played; it is yanked about; it is torn asunder; it is beaten black and blue. I do not know whether it is possible for anyone to conquer these hair-raising difficulties, but I do know that Mr. Brodsky martyrized his hearers as well as himself. The Adagio, with its tender national melody, almost conciliates, almost wins us; but it breaks off abruptly to make way for a Finale that puts us in the midst of a brutal and wretched jollity of a Russian kermess. We see wild and vulgar faces, we hear curses, we smell bad brandy. Friedrich Vischer once asserted in reference to lascivious paintings that there are pictures that "stink in the eye."

Tchaikovsky's Violin Concerto brings us for the first time to the horrid idea that there may be music that stinks in the ear.

Hanslick wrote these words in December 1881, after the violinist Adolf Brodsky introduced the Tchaikovsky concerto to Vienna. To Tchaikovsky, who had suffered many slings and arrows in creating the concerto in the first place, this commentary came as a blow below the belt and he remembered Hanslick's critique word for word for the rest of his life.

The concerto came into being three years before Hanslick had delivered his denunciation. On the twenty-seventh of March 1878, Tchaikovsky wrote to his benefactress that he found a "freshness, piquant rhythms, beautifully harmonized melodies" in the recently completed *Symphonie Espagnole* for Violin and Orchestra by Edouard Lalo. These were more than words of professional admiration; the *Symphonie Espagnole* apparently turned Tchaikovsky to thinking about a violin concerto of his own. At about the same time, coincidentally, Tchaikovsky was visited at Clarens, on the shore of Lake Geneva, by a young violinist friend from Moscow, Joseph Kotek. When the two of them sat down to make music, Tchaikovsky showed Kotek sketches in manuscript for a violin concerto. Before the end of April Tchaikovsky was able to write to his Russian publisher: "The Violin Concerto is hurrying toward its end. I fell by accident on the idea of composing one, but I started the work and was seduced by it, and now the sketches are almost completed."

Within a matter of weeks Tchaikovsky had sent a copy of the concerto, prior to publication, to Madame von Meck. With the slow movement, the *Canzonetta*, she was "delighted beyond description"; but there apparently were things in the first movement which she found less immediately attractive, for on June 22 Tchaikovsky wrote to her:

Your frank judgment on my Violin Concerto pleased me very much. It would have been very disagreeable to me if you, from any fear of wounding the petty pride of a composer, had kept back your opinion. However, I must defend a little the first movement of the Concerto. Of course it houses, as does every piece that serves virtuoso purposes, much that appeals chiefly to the mind; nevertheless, the themes are not painfully evolved. The plan of this movement sprang suddenly in my head and quickly ran into its mould. I shall not give up hope that in time the piece will give you greater pleasure.

When Tchaikovsky completed the concerto, he dedicated it to the ranking Russian violinist of the day, his friend Leopold Auer, who was also head of the violin department of the St. Petersburg Conservatory. Tchaikovsky, not unreasonably, must have hoped that Auer would see fit to introduce the concerto to the world. To the dismay of the composer, however, Auer shook his head over the concerto and pronounced it unplayable, hence the three-year delay before the piece finally came to the attention of the aforementioned Adolf Brodsky. Brodsky seized upon it as "wonderfully beautiful" and wrote to Tchaikovsky: "One can play the Concerto again and again and never be bored; and this is a most important circumstance for the conquering of its difficulties."

It goes without saying that in the near-century since it was composed, Tchaikovsky's concerto has become "repertoire" for every self-respecting violinist in the civilized world. And here is a neat bit of irony: some of the greatest exponents of the concerto—Seidel, Zimbalist, Elman, Heifetz and Milstein—studied with Leopold Auer!

The first movement, *Allegro moderato*, begins in the strings and woodwinds. It builds to a crescendo of excitement before the solo violin enters with an improvisatory sequence followed immediately by a statement of the first theme (*Moderato assai*). This is worked up elaborately and then the second theme appears, also in the solo instrument. Instead of a formal development section, there is a rhapsodic cadenza for violin, unaccompanied, and a long and brilliant coda concludes the movement.

The second movement, *Canzonetta: Andante*, begins with chords in the woodwinds followed by a motif in the clarinet and bassoon. The solo violin enters, muted, singing a nostalgic melody in musing discourse. The first phrase of this theme is then taken up by the flute and clarinet before the second subject is stated by the violin, *con anima*. When the first theme returns in the violin, the clarinet embroiders it with an obbligato of arpeggios.

The Finale, an *Allegro vivacissimo*, is ushered in without pause by a bridge passage and then it suddenly explodes upon the scene. The two principal melodies of this Finale have a folk-like character —the second one, a broad theme first stated by the solo violin, exhibiting definite Russian gypsy characteristics. Tension and excitement build and the end is a brilliant climax.

That the Tchaikovsky Violin Concerto has been one of the most frequently recorded of all works in this genre is no surprise. As a matter of fact, several of the virtuosi of the past generation have recorded it more than once. From among the many available recordings I would cite as pre-eminent the performances by Francescatti (Columbia MS 6758), Heifetz (RCA LSC 2129), Milstein (Angel S 35686), Perlman (RCA LSC 3014), Stern (Columbia MS 6062) and Szeryng (RCA Victrola VICS 1037). Francescatti's is a performance of silken elegance, very well recorded. The Heifetz performance is a dazzling display of violin pyrotechnics, with a frankly exhibitionistic and eye-popping approach. Not another violinist alive could generate this kind of electric excitement and dramatic tension. Unfortunately, the recorded sound, both mono and stereo, is not good. The microphones were placed so close to Heifetz that there is a pinched quality to the whole acoustic and his tone sounds coarse and harsh; too, there is distortion in some of the louder passages. Stern, in his recording, takes a view of the concerto almost exactly opposite from that of Heifetz. Stern's is a lyrical, more relaxed, warmer performance, lacking the astounding brilliance of the Heifetz version, but with plenty of its own kind of quieter excitement. Columbia's recording is rich-sounding, well balanced and spacious. As for Milstein's recording, it takes him the better part of the first movement to warm into the work, but from near the end of the first movement until the very end of the concerto, this is vintage Milstein: steady, assured and deeply felt. The recorded sound is less resonant than Columbia's for Stern, but it is crystal-clear and bright. Perlman's is sweet-toned and sensuous, and he plays the concerto absolutely complete, restoring the sections in the first movement and Finale that are sometimes cut. Finally, Szeryng's account is gently lyrical and thoroughly musical; also, it is available at budget prices. Other recent worthy recordings are those by Pinchas Zukerman (Columbia MS 7313; tape MQ 1197; cassette 16 11 0162)—fiery and impassioned, with a leavening of rhapsodic lyricism—and Kyung-Wha Chung (London CS 6710)—altogether gentler than either the Heifetz or Zukerman performances, but genuinely satisfying nonetheless.

THE NUTCRACKER, OP. 71

In December 1960 the Bookspans, *en famille,* were sitting in the New York City Center of Music and Drama watching a performance of Tchaikovsky's ballet *The Nutcracker.* The children were hypnotized by the events on stage. They registered terror at the appearance of the mice and the gunshot in Act I, rapturous disbelief at the blooming of the Christmas tree before their eyes in the "Midnight Scene," a frenzied partisanship for the Nutcracker in his battle with the bewhiskered Mouse King, and sheer blissful happiness at the joyful ending and the general merrymaking.

Yet, despite all the stage activity, and the children's complete involvement in what they were seeing, it was what they were hearing that apparently made the more lasting impression. For weeks afterward, Shellie paraded around the house trumpeting the music of the March while David, behind her, conducted an imaginary orchestra. "The Dance of the Sugarplum Fairy" with its delicately colored celesta solo, came to be called, in our household, the "tinkling music." And "The Dance of the Toy Flutes" was known affectionately as "Doriot's music," the children's frame of reference for flute sound being the Boston Symphony Orchestra's distinguished soloist Doriot Anthony Dwyer. The music of Tchaikovsky's *Nutcracker* had again woven its spell and drawn young and old alike into its wonderful world of fancy.

Tchaikovsky composed *The Nutcracker,* his third and last ballet, in 1891–92 on commission from the Director of St. Petersburg's Imperial Theatre, Prince Vsevolozhsky, and the celebrated choreographer Marius Petipa. The scenario was prescribed in advance: Alexandre Dumas' French adaptation of E. T. A. Hoffman's fanciful tale, "The Nutcracker and the Mouse King." Tchaikovsky accepted the commission unenthusiastically, feeling that the Hoffman story

was not suited for ballet treatment. His work on the score was interrupted by his highly publicized journey to the United States to participate in the opening concerts dedicating Carnegie Hall. *The
Nutcracker* was completed nine months later, in February of 1892.

The ballet itself is in two acts. Act I begins at a gala Christmas
party attended by children and mechanical dolls. The heroine is
little Marie Silberhaus (Tchaikovsky calls her Clara), daughter of
the host and hostess, who receives a marvelous German Nutcracker
shaped in the form of an old man with huge jaws. During some
rough play, the Nutcracker is broken by two boys. Later at night,
Clara is unable to sleep because she is possessed with pity for the
broken article. She climbs out of bed to take another look at her toy
and wondrous things begin to happen: the Christmas tree grows, the
toys come to life, as do the various cakes and pastries—and of course
the Nutcracker is healed and alive. Suddenly a terrific battle breaks
out between the tin soldiers, who are led by the Nutcracker, and the
mice. The Nutcracker and the Mouse King engage in a hand-to-
hand battle and for a time the Mouse King appears to have the
upper hand, but a well-aimed toss of Marie's slipper puts the Mouse
King out of commission and the battle is over as suddenly as it began. The most miraculous adventure of all now begins: the Nutcracker is transformed into a handsome young Prince who thanks
Clara for saving his life and invites her to journey with him to his
enchanted Kingdom of Sweetmeats and Lollipops.

Act II of *The Nutcracker* takes place in the fairyland of the realm
of the handsome young Prince. Clara and the Prince are welcomed
by the Sugarplum Fairy and all her court and there is a series of
dances by the several sweetmeats to celebrate the liberation of their
Prince.

On March 19, 1892, Tchaikovsky led a concert of his music at the
Imperial Russian Musical Society. The hit of the evening was a suite
he had fashioned from his score for *The Nutcracker* ballet, made
up of the overture, the March of the children from the first act and
the characteristic dances from the second. In the years since, this
Suite from *The Nutcracker* has probably introduced more people
to a serious interest in concert music than any other orchestral piece
ever written.

The Suite from *The Nutcracker* is, and probably will remain, one of the most frequently recorded of all orchestral works. There are about two dozen available recordings of the Suite. Even more surprising is the growing number of recordings of the complete ballet score, where not too many years ago there were none.

The pioneer recording of the complete ballet was Mercury's in 1954, with Antal Dorati conducting the Minneapolis Symphony Orchestra (OL 2101, two discs—now available in a six-disc album that also contains Dorati-Minneapolis Symphony performances of Tchaikovsky's remaining two great ballets; *Swan Lake* and *The Sleeping Beauty:* SR 6-9014) To his *Nutcracker* recording Dorati brought a keen sense of vivid theatrical effect and an enlivening imagination. The familiar sections of the Suite throbbed with a fresh vitality, and the entire score was revealed as one of Tchaikovsky's most inventive, especially for orchestral color. About ten years after that pioneer recording Dorati was given an opportunity to re-record his matchless interpretation of the complete ballet score, this time with the London Symphony Orchestra and in stereo (Mercury SR 2-9013). The resulting two-disc album is in a class by itself among the recordings of the complete score.

The recorded performances of the familiar Suite may generally be arranged into three categories: those with a conductor bored by the whole affair; those, at the opposite extreme, whose conductor agonizes over the music and bends it out of shape in a misguided effort to find new meanings hidden in it; and those whose conductor meets the score on its own ground, responding to the sparkle, wit and imagination of Tchaikovsky's muse with an enlivening sense of wonder and spontaneity. For all the proliferation of *Nutcracker* Suite recordings, there are only a relatively few that can properly be classed in the third category: Bernstein's (Columbia MS 6193; tape MQ 468; cassette 16 11 0030), Dorati's (Mercury SR 90528), Ansermet's (London CS 6097) and Steinberg's (Command S 11027).

A unique if variably interesting recording of the Suite, and one for rather special tastes, is the one by André Kostelanetz and his Orchestra for Columbia (M 30677), with specially created verses for the music by Ogden Nash (à la his *Carnival of the Animals* treatment) spoken by Peter Ustinov.

SERENADE IN C MAJOR FOR STRINGS, OP. 48

One would expect that the overwhelming popularity of Tchaikovsky's Fourth, Fifth, and Sixth Symphonies and the ballets *The Swan
Lake, The Sleeping Beauty* and *The Nutcracker* would extend to the
other examples of his orchestral creativity. Yet performances of the
First and Third Symphonies are extremely rare—the Second, the
so-called "Little Russian" Symphony, fares a little better. And Tchaikovsky's four orchestral suites, which contain some of his freshest
and most inventive music, appear almost to have passed from the
orchestral repertoire.

But there is one orchestral work of Tchaikovsky's, other than the
late symphonies and ballets, that maintains a strong hold on the
affections of the concert-going public: the Serenade for String Orchestra in C Major. Tchaikovsky's own attitude toward the work is
revealed in a letter to his benefactress written in October of 1880:

> You can imagine, dear friend, that recently my Muse has been
> benevolent, when I tell you that I have written two long works very
> rapidly: a Festival Overture and a Serenade in four movements for string
> orchestra. The Overture will be very noisy. I wrote it without much
> warmth of enthusiasm; therefore it has no great artistic value. The
> Serenade, on the contrary, I wrote from an inward impulse: I felt it;
> and I venture to hope that this work is not without artistic qualities.

The festival overture to which Tchaikovsky made reference was the
1812 Overture, a work whose bombast and posturing Tchaikovsky
well knew would not find favor with Madame von Meck. Just as
surely, however, Tchaikovsky knew that the Serenade, particularly
the middle two movements, would strike a responsive chord in the
emotional make-up of his friend. In another letter to Madame von
Meck about a year later, Tchaikovsky wrote:

> I wish with all my heart that you could hear my Serenade properly
> performed. It loses so much on the piano. I think that the middle
> movements, as played by the strings, would win your sympathy. As

regards the first and the last movements, you are right: they are
merely a play of sounds and do not touch the heart. The first movement is my homage to Mozart: it is intended to be an imitation of
his style, and I should be delighted if I thought I had in any way
approached my model. Do not laugh, my dear, at my zeal in
standing up for my latest creation. Perhaps my paternal feelings are
so warm because it is the youngest child of my fancy.

The first performance of the Serenade was given at a private
gathering in the Moscow Conservatory in the spring of 1881. The
occasion was arranged by Nicholas Rubinstein, who had displayed a
keen interest in the score and who himself conducted the student
orchestra. In his last illness, and unable to stand, Rubinstein led
the performance from a chair on the podium.

The official premiere of the Serenade for Strings was given in
Moscow in January of 1882, and the score served Tchaikovsky well
on his debut tour as a conductor in Hamburg, Prague, Paris and
London in 1887. The piece was especially successful in the French
and English capitals, and after a London performance Tchaikovsky
wrote: "The Serenade pleased most and I was recalled three times,
which means a good deal from the reserved London public." During
the course of his American tour in 1891, Tchaikovsky conducted performances of the Serenade in two cities, Baltimore and Philadelphia.
At the concert in Philadelphia's Academy of Music, the audience
cheered Tchaikovsky until the rafters rang.

The Serenade is in four movements. The opening movement bears
the curious designation *Pezzo in forma di sonatina*. It is in shortened
and simplified sonata form, with a slow introduction that is like a
chorale. The main part of the movement is an energetic and vigorous *Allegro molto*. At the end of the movement the broad and imposing theme of the introduction returns. The second movement is
a waltz, one of Tchaikovsky's most delicate and charming. The third
movement (*Larghetto elegiaco*) is a slow elegy, and the concluding
Finale makes use of some Russian folk tunes. The main theme of
this last movement bears a family resemblance to the chorale-like
melody heard at the beginning in the introduction. Near the close
of the Finale Tchaikovsky recalls the music of the introduction, but

the exuberant folk tune that serves as the principal material of the movement brings the score to a resounding close.

In the late 1940s Serge Koussevitzky recorded a performance of the Tchaikovsky Serenade, with the strings of the Boston Symphony Orchestra, that was a miracle of suave, polished playing. The incandescent quality of the Koussevitzky-era Boston Symphony strings was never shown to greater advantage. In addition, Koussevitzky brought to the score that unique quality of personal involvement with this composer that made such extraordinary experiences of his Tchaikovsky performances. The Serenade recording originated in the 78-rpm era, of course, but it was an early transfer to the long-playing medium, where it graced the RCA Victor catalog as LM 1056. Some years ago this incomparable performance was withdrawn, along with all the other Koussevitzky recordings. No matter what other salutary projects RCA plans, reissue of the remarkable series of recordings made by Koussevitzky and the Boston Symphony between 1929 and 1950 should take precedence.

Of the several available recordings of the score I would recommend Barbirolli's (Angel S 36269), Ormandy's (Columbia MS 6224) and Solti's (London STS 15141). All work with superior string sections and all are sumptuously recorded. My own favorite among them is Barbirolli's, an absolutely first-class, emotionally committed, deeply moving presentation of the music.

The more matter-of-fact performance conducted by Ormandy (rather severely cut) is my choice in the tape medium (Columbia MR 30447), with Karajan's refined version the pick of the cassette crop (DGG 923046).

SYMPHONY NO. 4 IN F MINOR, OP. 36

"I may be making a mistake, but it seems to me this symphony is not a mediocre work, but the best I have done so far. How glad I am that it is ours, and that, hearing it, you will know how much I thought of you with every bar."

An impassioned outpouring by a love-smitten composer to his beloved, she who was the inspiration for his latest and "best" sym-

phony? Well, not exactly. The words are Peter Ilyitch Tchaikovsky's
and they are contained in a letter written to his unseen benefactress
in November 1877. The symphony he was writing about was his
Fourth, just completed in Italy. And, as you might suspect, thereby
hangs a tale.

The previous May, Tchaikovsky had become engaged to Antonina
Ivanovna Miliukov, a chance admirer whom he scarcely knew. In
writing to Madame von Meck and acquainting her with his intention
to marry, he confided that he felt honor-bound to go through with
his promise of marriage. "We cannot escape our fate," he wrote, "and
there was something fatalistic about my meeting with this girl." The
wedding took place on July 18; six days later Tchaikovsky fled from
his house. On the twelfth of September he returned, and there was
a two weeks' farce of "conjugal" life (September 12–24) which
ended with the composer attempting to catch a fatal cold by standing waist-deep in the frigid waters of the Moscow River. When this
failed, he again made a precipitate flight and never saw his wife
again. Suffering from a nervous collapse, which "bordered upon insanity," he was taken by his brother Anatol to Switzerland for a
complete rest and change. During the entire period of turmoil between May and September Tchaikovsky was yet able to complete
his sketches for the Fourth Symphony and to complete the orchestration of the first movement. At Lake Geneva, as soon as he had regained some of his stability, he was able to take up his pen and work
happily on the remaining movements, which contain some of his
most lyric writing.

In discussing Beethoven's "Eroica" Symphony and "Emperor"
Piano Concerto, we found that work upon these scores served for
their creator as cathartic escape during periods of severe personal
trauma. Certainly the fact that Tchaikovsky was able to concern
himself with work upon the Fourth Symphony hastened his rehabilitation from the crisis of his marriage, and may well have saved him
from a total and irrevocable collapse. Not many months later, in
January 1878, he was able to write to Madame von Meck that the
circumstances under which the symphony came into being seemed
like

a strange dream; something remote, a weird nightmare in which a man bearing my name, my likeness and my consciousness acted as one acts in dreams: in a meaningless, disconnected, paradoxical way. That was not my sane-self, in possession of logical and reasonable will-powers. Everything I then did bore the character of an unhealthy conflict between will and intelligence, which is nothing less than insanity.

The miracle is that the Fourth Symphony betrays none of the self-doubt with which Tchaikovsky tortured himself at the time of its creation. Depression, fears and emotional imbalance are not here; rather, this is music of supreme assurance and self-confidence, bold and heroic in its extroverted vitality. Tchaikovsky himself wrote a long and detailed "program" for the score, but little of it is important to an understanding of the music. What does emerge as pertinent is his characterization of the brass fanfare which opens the symphony, plays an important part throughout the first movement and then recurs near the end of the Finale. Tchaikovsky says this symbolizes his "vain terrors" and "fear of the unknown," akin to the sword of Damocles hanging over his head. He continues: "Although there is no actual musical resemblance, the work is modelled after Beethoven's *Fifth*." Here it is, then, another symphony in which the underlying motivating force is Man and his eternal struggle with his Destiny.

At its Moscow premiere, in February 1888, the symphony was received rather casually. It did not take long, however, for it to gain a secure hold on the affections of the mass public, and it has remained a cornerstone of the international symphonic repertoire for nearly a century.

The first movement opens with the brass fanfare stated imperiously in the horns and bassoons, later joined by the trombones and then by the trumpets. The motto theme is developed to an impressive climax and then the main body of the movement begins, *Moderato con anima*, with a long, chromatic theme in the strings that has the character of a sigh. The theme is passed from strings to winds, is heard fragmentarily and alternately from each instrumental group and then works up to a powerful climax. The second theme is first heard from the clarinet, a nostalgic waltz-like melody that is ac-

companied first by woodwind flourishes, and then by a lyrical coun-
termelody on the cello. When the theme is passed on to the violins,
it is accompanied by soft drumbeats. The excitement mounts and
the exposition section ends with another stormy climax. The development is heralded by a return of the motto theme but the main
concern is manipulation of the first theme. Another climax returns
the motto theme to the fore and the recapitulation follows a fairly
traditional course, with the fanfare theme returning yet again to
introduce the fiery coda.

The second movement, *Andantino in modo di canzona,* opens
with a sorrowful oboe theme accompanied by pizzicato strings. The
cellos then take up the theme and there is an impassioned orchestral follow-up. A contrasting middle section, march-like in its springi-
ness, is introduced by the clarinet, is taken over by the violins and
then other woodwind instruments, and rises to an impressive climax.
The material from the beginning of the movement returns—passed
from one instrument to another—and the movement ends in deepest
melancholy.

The third movement is a satirical Scherzo, with the strings playing
pizzicato throughout. The principal marking of the movement is
Allegro. The Trio middle section is given over principally to the
woodwinds, who play what can only be described as "tipsy" music;
following upon the dizzy embellishments of the piccolo, the focus
then shifts to clipped brass figures before the pizzicato strings again
take over. The various elements are then reworked and combined
and the movement ends with a flourish and then a whisper. The
Finale, *Allegro con fuoco,* opens brilliantly in the brass, cymbals and
drums with a unison flourish in the strings. The first principal theme
is a variant of an old Russian folk song, which then is treated at
considerable length. Finally there are ominous forebodings, the
tempo broadens and suddenly the motto theme from the first movement reappears, shouted out defiantly by the trumpets. But the
atmosphere grows calmer and over rumbling drums the second part
of the movement's opening flourish is heard in the horns. From there
until the end of the movement the mood becomes one of exultant
triumph and affirmation.

Among the many recordings of the symphony currently available,

an excellent and dramatic account is the Maazel-Vienna Philharmonic performance (London CS 6429). Razor-sharp orchestral execution, superb recorded sound and a magnificently vibrant conception on the conductor's part make this one of the best Tchaikovsky
symphony performances ever recorded. It is also available on tape
(London L 80161), coupled with a performance by the same artists
of Tchaikovsky's Third ("Polish") Symphony. Barenboim's carefully
inflected and highly individual reading may not be to everyone's
liking (Columbia M 30572; tape MR 30572; cassette MT 30572). I
think it is a masterly re-creation of a cornerstone of symphonic literature, superbly played by the New York Philharmonic and expertly
recorded. It is now my unquestioned favorite among all available
recordings of this score.

One of the most perverse recordings of any music at all is
Stokowski's account of this score with the American Symphony
Orchestra (Vanguard Cardinal VCS 10095), in which tempi are
pulled all over the lot, phrasings are incomprehensible, dynamics
are exaggerated beyond all limits, and the whole thing has an aura
of incredible self-indulgence. This Stokowski recording is near the
very top of my own list of recorded horrors.

SYMPHONY NO. 5 IN E MINOR, OP. 64

The Fifth Symphony was an extremely crucial one for Tchaikovsky.
Six years earlier, at a Moscow performance of his Violin Concerto,
one of the critics had suggested that Tchaikovsky was "written out";
that his music was tired and uninspired and generally the work of a
man past his creative prime. Tchaikovsky was especially sensitive to
this sort of criticism, for, during the ten years that separated the
Violin Concerto (1878) and the Fifth Symphony, he produced no
symphonic work of major importance.

During the summer of 1888, Tchaikovsky wrote to his benefactress: "I am exceedingly anxious to prove to myself, as to others,
that I am not played out as a composer. . . . Have I told you that I
intend to write a symphony? The beginning was difficult; but now
inspiration seems to have come. However, we shall see."

The symphony was performed for the first time at St. Petersburg in November, and a month later, after a repetition in St. Petersburg and a performance in Prague, Tchaikovsky wrote to Madame von Meck: "I have come to the conclusion that it is a failure. There is something repellent, something superfluous, patchy, and insincere, which the public instinctively recognizes. It was obvious to me that the ovations I received were prompted more by my earlier work, and that the symphony itself did not really please the audience."

Time, of course, has negated the harshness of Tchaikovsky's appraisal of his score. The Fifth Symphony is one of the cornerstones of the repertoire and is yet another work in the "victory through struggle" tradition of Beethoven's Fifth. And yet Tchaikovsky's words are not as unduly self-deprecating as they might seem at first blush. If he was unhappy with the architectural structure of the symphony, one must agree that he had sufficient cause for his unhappiness: the Fifth Symphony is certainly the most episodic and least organically unified of his last three symphonies. Much of the music is balletic in character, and indeed it has been treated choreographically by Massine in a work called *Les Présages* (*Destiny*) presented in 1933 by the Ballet Russe de Monte Carlo. It is interesting to note that the Fifth Symphony is Tchaikovsky's Op. 64, while his ballet masterpiece, *The Sleeping Beauty*, is Op. 66.

No matter what weaknesses one may find in its construction, however, Tchaikovsky's Fifth Symphony seems assured of enjoying eternal popularity. The reasons are not hard to find: first, there is the impact of the aforementioned victory-through-struggle concept. The motto theme in E minor, stated at the very outset of the symphony by the clarinets in a subdued, reflective manner, recurs in the succeeding movements as a kind of sinister *idée fixe*. At the beginning of the last movement, and with startling but masterful psychological effect, Tchaikovsky shifts the tonality of the motto theme from the minor to the major. It thus assumes a completely new, heroic aspect and the symphony comes to a triumphant conclusion in E major. Tchaikovsky also endowed the symphony with some of his most effulgent melodic inspiration. It is small wonder that during the discovery of Tchaikovsky by Tin Pan Alley some decades ago the

French horn solo in the slow movement of the Fifth Symphony took on a new identity in jukeboxes around the country as "Moon Love."

The first movement opens with an *Andante* introduction, the clarinets stating a somber theme over chords in the strings. This, in the course of the unfolding of the symphony, is the motto theme of the whole work, returning in each of the three subsequent movements —indeed, reaching an apotheosis in the last movement. The main body of the movement, *Allegro con anima*, begins with a theme in octaves from the clarinet and bassoon, which is then taken up by the strings. Two more brief episodes are heard before the principal second subject appears in the strings, a yearning melody ornamented by the flutes and then taken over by other woodwind instruments. There is a comparatively short development section but a highly dramatic one. The return of the first principal theme in the bassoon heralds the arrival of the recapitulation. Then there is a long coda and the movement sinks back to its original mood of melancholy.

The second movement is marked *Andante cantabile, con alcuna licenza*. After a brief introduction of chords in the low strings, the horn sings the principal melody and it is later joined by the clarinet. The second theme is entrusted to the oboe, which is answered by the horn, and this theme is taken up by the violins and violas. The cellos then have a noble statement of the first theme and then the strings repeat the second one, building to an impassioned climax. Clarinet and bassoon return the music to its nostalgic, bittersweet atmosphere, there is a long working out of this material and suddenly the storm clouds gather and the trumpets thunder out the motto theme of the first movement. The two principal themes of this second movement are then once again worked over and the music again builds to a tremendous climax, with the motto theme returning to sound its ominous warning. The movement subsides into a troubled peace.

The third movement is a waltz, *Allegro moderato*, whose principal theme is presented by the strings and then repeated by the woodwinds. There is a middle section with running figures in the strings against woodwind chords and interpolations. Then the first section returns, but near the end clarinets and bassoons bring back, as if from a distance, the motto theme: the inescapable shadow once again hovers over the proceedings. The last movement begins with a long introduction, *Andante maestoso*, in which the motto or Fate theme undergoes a transformation: it is now in the major and the tempo is slightly martial. The main *Allegro vivace* section begins with a crescendo roll on the tympani and a vigorous, march-like theme in the strings. The woodwinds and then the violins have a more tuneful theme. The development section assigns the motto theme to the brass, there is much storm and fury and a great climax is prepared and reached. Then the music suddenly comes to a halt, and after a pregnant pause a magisterial coda begins: now the motto theme is unfurled in all its aggressive grandeur. Gone is the morbid brooding and in its stead the symphony ends on a note of triumph.

Two extremely personal accounts of the symphony exist on recordings—Koussevitzky's (included in RCA VCM 6174, 3 discs) and Stokowski's (London SPC 21017; tape L 75017), the former available only in monophonic sound, the latter only in stereo. Both are "personality" performances in the truest sense of the word. Neither conductor hesitates to shape the music in his own image. In Koussevitzky's case this takes the form of numerous tempo changes and rhythmic shifting of gears; so persuasive is the conductor's over-all concept, however, that I for one am not bothered in the slightest by these interpretative quirks. The recorded sound, dating from 1944, leaves much to be desired, but enough of the sound of Koussevitzky's imaginative approach to this symphony is there to sweep aside any other considerations. Stokowski's recording, with London's New Philharmonia Orchestra, is a much more recent accomplishment—hence it is blessed with much finer reproduction. Even more flagrantly than Koussevitzky, Stokowski toys with the score, reorchestrating it in many places, disregarding score markings in others—as an example, he has his tympani player roll right through the "pregnant pause" mentioned above just before the start of the coda in the last movement—and otherwise stamping the symphony with his own unique brand. Nevertheless, I am prepared to go all the way with Stokowski. These idiosyncrasies are the idiosyncrasies of genius—a commodity rare indeed in the music markets of today.

Those seeking a more traditional performance are directed to either Ozawa (RCA LSC 3071; tape TR3 5043, 3¾ ips) or Mehta

(London CS 6606; tape K. 80217). Incredibly, there does not seem to be a cassette version available of any performance of this work.

SYMPHONY NO. 6 IN B MINOR, OP. 74,
"PATHÉTIQUE"

The summer of 1892 was a busy one for Peter Ilyitch Tchaikovsky. He conducted at the Vienna Exhibition and then went on to Salzburg and Prague, returning in November to St. Petersburg for gala performances, in the presence of the Czar and his court, of his opera *Iolanthe* and ballet *The Nutcracker*. Thoughts of a new symphony began to occupy him, and on February 23, 1893, he wrote to his nephew Vladimir Davidov:

> Just as I was starting on my journey [a visit to Paris in December 1892] the idea came to me for a new symphony. This time with a program; but a program of a kind which remains an enigma to all— let them guess it who can. The work will be entitled "A Program Symphony" (No. 6). This program is penetrated by subjective sentiment. During my journey, while composing it in my mind, I frequently shed tears. Now I am home again, I have settled down to sketch out the work, and it goes with such ardor that in less than four days I have completed the first movement, while the rest of the Symphony is clearly outlined in my head. There will be much that is novel as regards form in this work. For instance, the finale will not be a great *allegro*, but an *adagio* of considerable dimensions. You cannot imagine what joy I feel at the conviction that my day is not yet over, and that I may still accomplish much.

The symphony was scheduled for its first performance on October 28, 1893, in St. Petersburg, with Tchaikovsky himself conducting. He arrived in St. Petersburg on October 22 and was met by his brother Modest and his favorite nephew, the aforementioned Davidov. (Davidov, incidentally, served for many years as curator of the Tchaikovsky Museum in Klin.) As rehearsals for the premiere progressed, Tchaikovsky became discouraged with the lack of enthusiasm on the part of the orchestra players and feared that their coldness might affect the performance. The premiere itself proved to be a *succès d'estime*, but little more.

The day after the premiere, before sending the score to his publisher, Tchaikovsky decided to give the symphony some descriptive title. "No. 6" seemed to him too isolated by itself and "Program Symphony" was meaningless. Modest offered the title "Tragic" but this, too, was rejected. "I left the room before he had come to a decision," Modest tells us. "Suddenly I thought *Pathetic*. I went back to his room—I remember it as though it were yesterday—and I said the word to Peter. 'Splendid, Modi, bravo, *Pathetic*' and he wrote in my presence the title that will forever remain."

On the first of November, complaining of stomach upset, Tchaikovsky joined Modest and his nephew at lunch. He ate no food, but took a long drink of unboiled water, to the dismay of his companions. By nightfall his condition had deteriorated considerably and Modest sent for a doctor. Cholera was the diagnosis. After rallying slightly the following day, Tchaikovsky lapsed into another state of depression, grew progressively weaker, and at 3 A.M. on the morning of November 6, 1893, he died.

It has been customary to associate the dark melancholy of the "Pathétique" Symphony with what may have been Tchaikovsky's presentiments of his impending death. However, we have it on the authority of Modest that "from the time of his return from England until the end of his life, Tchaikovsky was as serene and cheerful as at any period in his existence." Here again, then, is dramatic proof of the ability of the artist to dissociate himself from immediate reality and to lose himself in his art, for surely there is no more deeply brooding, passionately resigned music than this.

The first movement opens with its famous bassoon solo, *Adagio* and very quiet in ascending notes. The violas pull the melody into the depths and then, after a suspenseful pause, the music becomes very agitated and rhythmic in an *Allegro non troppo*. When this has run its course there is another powerful pause and then a tranquil, lyrical melody in D major is introduced, which has since found its way to the Hit Parade ("This Is the Story of a Starry Night.") The balance of the movement is concerned mainly with developing these two themes. A most remarkable moment occurs when the whole orchestra explodes with the agitated *Allegro* theme after the D-major melody has been whispered by the clarinet in its lowest register. The movement ends calmly and quietly.

The second movement is a flowing *Allegro con grazia* in 5-4 meter; its steady, even assurance is clouded only by the Trio section with its constant descending motion and repeated drumbeats.

The third movement, *Allegro molto vivace*, is a vigorous March that begins in a whirlwind of alternating strings and woodwinds. It gathers momentum gradually until the clarinet announces a distinctly martial theme. This is then taken up by the strings. There is a constant building with climaxes of hair-raising excitement, until at the very end the frenzy is hammered home with four notes belched out in unison by the full orchestra.

The last movement, *Adagio lamentoso*, begins with a threnody in the strings. Again, as in the first movement, the melodic pattern is a descending one, but now the cry is one of utter despair. Consolation comes in D major once more as it did in the first movement in a theme directed by Tchaikovsky to be played "with gentleness and devotion." The lament of the opening returns, however, and builds to another shattering climax. Silence follows, then an ominous stroke on the tam-tam ushers in a chain of soft trombone chords. The symphony ends in a mood of resignation, calm and at peace.

It is a budget-priced version—Giulini's with the Philharmonia Orchestra (Seraphim S 60031)—that I unhesitatingly recommend as my own first preference among all the available "Pathétique" Symphony recordings. Giulini delivers a deeply moving, sensitively felt account of this symphony, without falling into the trap of bathos that has ensnared so many conductors in this work. The playing of the Philharmonia Orchestra is simply magnificent and the sound is excellent. All told, Giulini's performance is in the nature of a restorative. To the excellent straightforwardness of the Giulini account may now be added the similar excellence of Haitink's recent performance (Philips 6500081).

Also quite good is Ormandy's recording (Columbia MS 7169), a direct and compelling statement that strikes a delicate balance between objectivity and overstatement.

Tape addicts are directed to Ormandy's Columbia version (MQ

368), an earlier and finer performance and recording of this work than his subsequent re-recording of the score for RCA. The choice among cassette editions is the lean and stark performance conducted by Markevitch (Philips PCR4 900225).

Antonio Vivaldi

Born: Venice, possibly on June 11, 1669 (but an
indeterminate year between 1675 and 1678
is usually given)
Died: Vienna, July 1741

As the inconclusive information concerning the birth- and death-
dates of Vivaldi would indicate, comparatively little is known about
his life. He was the son of a violinist at San Marco in Venice and his
first music teacher was his father. Young Antonio was a precociously
gifted musician, but he entered the priesthood and received the holy
orders some time before 1703. In that year he became a teacher at
the famous school for girls, the Seminario musicale dell' Ospitale
della Pietà in Venice. He must have had red hair, for he quickly
came to be called *"il prete rosso"*—"the red priest." In 1709 he became director of concerts at the Ospitale and he remained nominally
in that position until 1740 despite widespread travels through Italy,
Germany and possibly France.

For the Ospitale Vivaldi composed an enormous bulk of compositions, including two concertos a month, which he was obliged to
provide to the seminary even when he was away. In 1740 Vivaldi
went to Vienna to join a number of his colleagues at the court of
Charles VI, hoping to prosper there because of the many opportunities offered to performers and composers. Vivaldi's hopes were
frustrated, however, and he died in Vienna the following year. A
contemporary of his wrote: "The Abbé Don Antonio Vivaldi, greatly
esteemed for his compositions and concertos, made in his day more
than 5000 ducats, but from excessive prodigality died poor in
Vienna."

One of the greatest admirers of Vivaldi's music was his German
contemporary Johann Sebastian Bach, who adapted several of Vivaldi's works for different instrumental combinations. The sheer bulk

of Vivaldi's output is astonishing: dozens of violin concertos, more than three dozen bassoon concertos, nearly the same number for flute, many for oboe, viola d'amore and for different instrumental combinations; much choral music for the church; other sacred and secular compositions for voice; and many operas.

The great Baroque explosion of the 1950s and '60s brought about an enormous new interest in the music of Vivaldi and has caused much of it to be exhumed from oblivion. Some of it has proven to be extremely worthwhile and interesting; some of it has turned out to be formula-ridden note-spinning. It probably will be some time yet before we can arrive at a true assessment of Vivaldi's stature; his rediscovery, however, has been one of the most dynamic elements in recent musical history and it promises to enliven the musical scene for years to come.

THE FOUR SEASONS, OP. 8

In 1948 knowledgeable record critics were hailing "the superb *Four Seasons* series" of violin concertos by Antonio Vivaldi which had just been released in an expanded orchestral version edited by Bernardino Molinari. At the time, the Molinari recording was the only one generally available—a performance for the Concert Hall Society by Louis Kaufman being restricted to that organization's Limited Editions subscription list. Today *The Four Seasons* is unquestionably the best-known musical work of the Italian Baroque period.

Two reasons, it seems to me, are paramount in accounting for this phenomenon. The first is the appearance during the postwar years of small instrumental ensembles in many different parts of the musical world: the Stuttgart Chamber Orchestra, the Virtuosi di Roma, I Solisti di Zagreb and I Musici among foreign groups; the Zimbler Sinfonietta and others like it in this country. These small orchestras in search of a repertoire found in Vivaldi's *The Four Seasons* an ideal vehicle for the display of musical and technical virtuosity. The voice of the turtledove and goldfinch, of the birds and the dogs as Vivaldi portrayed them in *The Four Seasons* began to be heard throughout the land. Secondly, any record company could add a version of the score to its catalog for a rather modest capital investment: fewer than twenty players are needed to bring Vivaldi's tone painting to vibrant, throbbing life. With these two built-in advantages, *The Four Seasons* has become the *Scheherazade* of chamber-orchestra literature.

Generically, *The Four Seasons* title is attached to the first four of the twelve violin concertos of Vivaldi's Opus 8, published in Amsterdam around 1725 under the collective title *Il Cimento dell'Armonia e dell'Invenzione* (*The Conflict Between Harmony and Invention*). David Johnson has speculated that by the title Vivaldi meant to indicate the "intransigence of 'harmony' or music when 'invention' or the imaginative faculty tries to impose extra-musical meanings upon it. Harmony wishes to be a simple F Minor scale; invention wishes that scale to 'be' a man slipping on the ice. Significantly, seven of the concertos bear titles, five do not: Invention wins the conflict."

Music explicitly notated for programmatic purposes generally conjures up composers of the late Romantic period—Strauss and Mahler, for example. In point of fact, however, composers of the seventeenth and eighteenth centuries were given to the invention of fanciful programs and titles the likes of which composers a couple of centuries later would scrupulously have avoided as being too lurid. What composer, for example, no matter what his Romantic excesses, would think of writing music descriptive of a gall bladder operation? Yet that is precisely what Marin Marais did in a piece written at the turn of the eighteenth century. Another composer of the period, Johann Kuhnau (1660–1722), composed a Biblical Sonata that specifies each incident in the struggle between David and Goliath.

For his own part, Vivaldi attached to the head of each of the concertos of *The Four Seasons* a sonnet—probably of his own writing—that sets the mood and outlines the pictorial content of the music to follow. Further, throughout the entire score there are phrases and sections labeled in the most explicit manner imaginable: *Languidezza per il caldo* (Languidly, because of the heat) reads the notation over the opening bars of the second concerto, *L'Estate* (*Summer*); the sonnet that precedes the music describes a hot,

scorching landscape. The music is representational in the highest
degree, as in the slow movement of the *Spring* Concerto where the
solo violin portrays the sleeping goatherd while the first and second
violins express the rustling of leaves and the violas characterize a
barking dog.

Despite all these programmatic devices, Vivaldi maintained in
each section the strict form of the solo Baroque concerto. Fast-slow-
fast is the scheme for the progression of the successive movements,
and the basic mood of each piece is set by the orchestra. The solo
violin serves, naturally, as the chief protagonist and occasional re-
vealer of individual details. Perhaps the most interesting writing of
all occurs in the slow middle movements, where there is little "action" as such, for here Vivaldi develops a more abstract and lyrical
style of writing for the solo violin. Other considerations aside, Vivaldi's *The Four Seasons* is of enormous historical interest and importance; for, in the emotional intensity of the slow movements and
in the flashing virtuosity of the outer ones, these are true concertos
in the nineteenth-century sense of the term. And it is fascinating to
note that they enjoyed a wide popularity at the time of original
publication, not only in Italy but in other countries as well. As was
the custom of the period, there appeared transcriptions of the music
for various instrumental combinations: *La Primavera* (*Spring*), the
most popular of the four, was adapted as a flute solo by none other
than Jean Jacques Rousseau in 1755 and ten years later the same
concerto appeared as a motet for large chorus in an arrangement by
Michel Corrette.

The *Spring* Concerto (*La Primavera*) has an *Allegro* first movement that opens with a joyous spring theme that returns throughout
the movement in all the tutti sections. Birds are heard twittering in
trills that alternate between the solo violin and the violins of the
orchestra. A murmuring stream is heard in rushing figures in the
lower strings and there are flashes of lightning in the violins and
claps of thunder in the broken chords of the solo violin. The movement ends as it began, with the return of the birds and the breezes.
The second movement, *Largo*, paints a blissful sleeping scene in the
calm repose of the solo violin while the orchestral violins represent
"gently rushing leaves." Completing the pastoral picture are sharp

notes in the violas that Vivaldi identifies as "the barking dog." The concluding movement, *Allegro*, is a rhythmic dance of nymphs and shepherds in the brilliant sunshine.

L'Estate, the *Summer* Concerto, begins with a humid, languorous introduction, *Allegro non molto*. The cuckoo is heard in the solo violin, then the turtledove and the goldfinch. A triplet figure in the violins describes the blowing of soft breezes and then suddenly the north wind moves in with vigorous violin figures. The movement ends with the summer storm in full force. The slow movement, *Adagio*, represents a restful scene interrupted by the swarming of insects (dotted violin figures) and the distant rumbling of thunder (the low strings tremolando). The concerto ends with a concluding *Presto*. The storm now rages furiously, the winds are wild and the crops are destroyed. There are no extended solo violin passages in this movement but there is a virtuoso cadenza with flashing arpeggios.

L'Autunno (*Autumn*) begins with a vigorous first movement marked *Allegro*. The opening section alternates between passages for the orchestra and the soloist as the harvest is celebrated. The second solo passage for the violin introduces music that is unmistakably tipsy in character, and Vivaldi drives the point home by labeling the supporting instruments as "*ubriachi*" ("drunkards"). A sustained note on the solo violin at the end of the movement signifies sleep. The second movement, *Adagio molto*, describes "sleeping drunkards" (Vivaldi's own phrase). Everything is quiet and peaceful, with the violin and violas muted. The final movement, *Allegro*, is unmistakably a hunt. The orchestra makes galloping noises and the first violin solo has the character of a horn call. The chase grows in intensity and at the end the capture and death of the prey is depicted in the final violin solo.

The concluding concerto, *L'Inverno* (*Winter*), begins with an *Allegro non molto* that conveys winter's icy chill to perfection. The "fierce and biting winds" are portrayed in the violin's swift arpeggios and even the chattering of teeth is suggested by the rapid double-stops. The second movement, *Largo*, is a brief respite from the icy surroundings. Here the solo violin sings a long and contemplative song, supported by pizzicato violins in the orchestra. The final movement, *Allegro*, brings a return of the wintry blasts and at the end there is an increase in momentum until the full fury of the winds is unleashed.

Two among the many available recordings of Vivaldi's fascinating score seem to me to be particularly outstanding—Goberman's (Odyssey 32160132) and Bernstein's (Columbia MS 6744). The Goberman performance is a highly imaginative one with keen awareness of Baroque performing practices, and there is no question that the stylistic authority and inventive ornamentation place it in a class by itself. No tape of the Goberman performance has been released, which makes Bernstein's (Columbia MQ 736) my recommended first choice for the tape collector. The Virtuosi di Roma carry the day in the cassette field (Angel 4XS 35877).

Glossary of Musical Terms

A cappella: Unaccompanied vocal music, either solo or choral.

Accelerando: Accelerating in speed.

Accent: Emphasis on a tone, chord or beat.

Accidental: A sharp, flat or natural sign that is foreign to the home key.

Accompaniment: A part or parts added to the principal part or parts.

Adagio: Slow—slower than *Andante*, not so slow as *Lento*.

Affectueux: Affectionately, tenderly.

Affettuoso: Affectionately, tenderly.

Agitato: Agitated, stormy.

Air: A melody or tune.

Alcuna: Some—as *Con alcuna licenza*, With some license.

Allargando: Gradually slower and broader.

Allegretto: Animatedly, but slower than *Allegro*.

Allegro: Fast, but not as fast as *Presto*. This is often modified by other descriptive phrases—*Allegro ma non troppo* (Fast but not excessively), *Allegro con moto* (Fast and fiery), *Allegro moderato*, *Allegro non molto*, *Allegro non troppo* (Moderately fast), etc.

Allemande: A dance movement in 4-4 time, derived from a German national or peasant dance.

Anacrusis: Upbeat.

Ancora: Once more.

Andante: Moving moderately slowly. Again, this is often modified by other descriptive phrases—*con moto, maestoso, cantabile*, etc.

Anima: Animation; *con anima*: with animation.

Animato: Animatedly.

Antiphony: Responsive singing or playing by parts of divided performing forces.

Appassionato: Passionately.

Appoggiature: A "leaning" or grace note.

Arco: The bow.

Arpeggio: The individual tones of a chord played in rapid succession one after the other.

Assai: Very. As *Allegro assai*, Very fast.

Atonality: Music without a definite key center or tonic.

Attacca: To attack immediately the next bar, phrase or movement.

Augmentation: A repetition with note values lengthened (opposite of diminution).

Bagatelle: A trifle.

Bar: A vertical line denoting the end of a measure; also the measure itself.

Bass: The lowest note of a chord; the lowest line of a part; the deepest-voiced instrument of a class.

Basset horn: An obsolete clarinet.

Basso ostinato: A figure in the bass obstinately repeated.

Baton: The stick used by the conductor to beat time.

Battery: The percussion instruments.

Bel canto: Beautiful song; the art of singing beautifully and artistically.

Binary: Two-part.

Bitonality: Two keys employed simultaneously.

Bravura: With dash and brilliance.

Brio: Vigor, fire.

Buffa: Comic.

Caccia: A hunt.

Cadence: Literally "a fall," therefore a concluding strain.

Cadenza: A passage of great virtuoso display for the solo instrument in a concerto, unaccompanied.

Canon: A form of strict musical imitation; e.g. "Three Blind Mice" is a canon.

Cantabile: Singing, lyrical.

Cantando: In a lyrical, singing style.

Cantilena: Melodic, singing line.

Canzona: Song.

Capriccio: A whimsical work.

Cassation: A serenade-like work consisting of several instrumental movements.

Cavatina: A one-subject melody.

Cembalo: A harpsichord.

Chaconne: A dance, probably of Spanish origin, in 3-4 time with a repeated bass figure, usually in the form of variations.

Chanson: Song, ballad.

Chord: A combination of three or more notes sung or played together.

Chromatic: Literally "colored," hence a scale proceeding in half tones.

Clarino: A small trumpet.

Clavier: Keyboard instrument usually referring to the clavichord or harpsichord.

Coda: The section that concludes or rounds off a movement or composition.

Coloratura: Brilliant ornamental passages in vocal or instrumental music; also florid singing style.

Concertante: A piece with more than one principal solo instrument.

Concertino: The small group of solo instruments in a concerto grosso.

Concerto: A composition for one or more solo instruments, usually with orchestral accompaniment.

Conductor: The time-beater and shaper of a musical performance.

Consonance: A pleasant combination of sounds, agreeable and restful.

Contrapuntal: Dealing in counterpoint.

Counterpoint: Notes were originally called "points"; counterpoint, therefore, is note against note, or the simultaneous combination of more than one melody.

Courante: Literally, "running," hence a fast dance movement.

Crescendo: Sound increasing in loudness.

Crotchet: A quarter note.

Cue: Notes from another part inserted as a guide.

Czardas: A Hungarian dance in duple meter (usually either 2-4 or 4-4 time). It is also usually in binary form, with the moderate first part called *lassú* and the quicker, more exhilarating second part called *friss* or *friska*.

Da capo: From the beginning, signifying that the first part is to be repeated.

Deciso: Decisively, boldly.

Decrescendo: Diminishing in loudness (same as diminuendo).

Deliberato: Deliberately.

Delirio: Frenzy, delirium.

Demiquaver: A sixteenth note (or semiquaver).

Demisemiquaver: A thirty-second note.

Diapason: An octave.

Diatonic: A regular scale uncolored by sharps, flats or natural marks foreign to its key signature.

Diminished: Intervals a semitone smaller than minor intervals; chords containing diminished intervals.

Diminuendo: Diminishing in loudness (same as decrescendo).

Diminution: A repetition with note values shortened (opposite of augmentation).

Disaccentato: Without accent.

Discord: An unharmonious combination of tones.

Dissonance: Tones or combinations that demand resolution in some other tone or chord.

Divertimento: A musical diversion; hence a light, airy composition.

Divisi: Divided.

Dodecaphonic: Literally "twelve-toned"; hence music without a definite key center or tonic, repeating a tone row of twelve different notes of the chromatic scale.

Dolce: Sweetly.

Doloroso: Sorrowfully.

Dominant: The fifth tone of a scale, so called because it is the most important tone in the scale after the tonic.

Doppio: Double. *Doppio movimento* or *Doppio tempo*: Twice as fast.

Double: A repetition, a variation.

Double stops: Two notes bowed on a string simultaneously.

Douloureux: Sadly.

Doux, douce: Sweetly, softly.

Drammatico: Dramatically.

Drone bass: A monotonously repeated bass note suggesting a bagpipe.

Duet: A work for two singers or instrumentalists.

Dumb piano: A keyboard without strings or hammers intended for silent practice.

Dumka: A slow Bohemian dance.

Duo: Two, in two parts.

Duple time: Double time—two beats to a measure.

Durchdringend: Penetrating.

Durchkomponiert: Through-composed—a song with individual treatment of every stanza.

Dynamics: The contrasts between loud and soft.

Eclogue: A pastoral work.

Elegia, elegy: A mournful work.

Embellishment: Ornament, decoration (trill, grace note, etc.).

Encore: Again.

Enharmonic: Differing in name or notation but not in sound, as A sharp and B flat.

Ensemble: A combination of voices or instruments.

Entr'acte: Music played between acts.

Entrada, entrata: Introduction, entrance.

Espressione: Feeling, expression.

Exercise: A practice piece.

Expressif: Expressive.

Expressionism: A style whose principal aim is abstraction.

Fanfare: A flourish of brass instruments.

Fermata: A symbol either above or below a note (⌒ or ⌣) denoting that the note should be held.

Feroce: Fiercely.

Fervente: Fervently.

Festivo: Festively, gayly.

fff: Abbreviation of fortissimo (very, very loud).

Figured bass: Musical shorthand in which only the bass part is written out, with numerals to indicate the desired chords.

Finale: The last movement in a symphony, concerto, sonata, etc.; also, the concluding portion of an operatic act, usually very elaborate.

Fine: The end.

Finito: Finished.

Fioritura: Florid ornament.

Flat: A symbol (♭) that lowers the note before which it occurs by a semitone.

Flautando: Drawing the bow lightly across the strings near the bridge, thus producing a flute-like sound.

Forte: Loud (the abbreviation is f).

Fortissimo: Very loud (the abbreviation is ff, sometimes fff for emphasis).

Forza: Force, power.

Fughetta: A brief fugue.

Fugue: An imitative musical form with a recurring principal subject.

Fundamental: The root note of a chord.

Fuoco: Fire, energy, passion.

Furiant: A furious Bohemian dance with irregular rhythm and accent.

Galliard: An old dance resembling the pavan.

Galop: A hopping dance in 2-4 time.

Gamba: Leg—therefore, the viola da gamba, an instrument placed on the floor and played in an upright position cello-fashion.

Gavotte: An old French dance in 4-4 time.

Geschwind: Quickly.

Gigue: The English jig dance.

Gioco: A joke.

Giocoso: Merrily.

Giuoco: A joke.

Giusto: Exact, precise.

Glissando: Sliding the finger across the keys of a piano or on the strings of an instrument to produce a rapid ascending or descending scale.

Grace note: A musical ornament whose time value is not counted in the general rhythm and must be subtracted from either the note preceding or following.

Grave: Grave, slow.

Ground bass: A bass phrase or figure repeated throughout a piece.

Gruppo: A group, formerly an ornament (trill, shake or turn).

Harmonic: A high-pitched tone produced on a string instrument by lightly touching the string at a certain point instead of pressing it.

Harmony: The art of chord combinations and progressions.

Harpsichord: The forerunner of the modern piano whose strings are plucked by quills rather than struck by hammers.

Hemi: Half.

Hemidemisemiquaver: A sixty-fourth note.

Homophony: Music that is non-contrapuntal, with one melodic line predominant.

Idée fixe: A term coined by Berlioz for his *Fantastic Symphony* to signify a recurring theme or motive.

Imitation: Repetition in other voices of a figure, subject or theme.

Impressionism: A term used originally to describe painting. In music the impressionistic style seeks to express feelings and impressions rather than subjects or ideas. It is characterized generally by a subdued subtlety and delicacy.

Improvisation: Extemporaneous performance.

Improvise: To sing or play spontaneously.

Innig: Heartfelt, sincere.

Instrumentation: The art of writing or arranging a composition for instruments.

Interlude: A short piece played between acts, scenes or movements.

Interval: The distance or difference in pitch between two notes.

Intonation: Accuracy of pitch.

Invention: A short work, usually contrapuntal, with one theme.

Inversion: Transposition of the elements of chords, intervals, etc.; an inverted chord, for example, is one in which the bass note occupies a position other than the root.

Ironico: Ironically.

Istesso: The same. *L'Istesso tempo:* The same speed (as before).

Jig: A quick dance in 6-8 or 12-8 time.

Jongleur: A hired or strolling musician.

Jota: A quick Spanish dance in 3-8 time.

Key: A scale or chain of tones whose center and point of rest is the tonic, the tone that also gives the key its name.

Keyboard: The series of black and white keys on the piano or organ.

Keyboard instrument: Any instrument activated by a keyboard: piano, organ, harpsichord, etc.

Keynote: The tonic.

Klavier: Keyboard; a keyboard instrument, usually the clavichord.

Koto: A Japanese zither with thirteen silk strings.

Lamentabile: Mournfully.

Lamentoso: Sorrowfully.

Ländler: A slow German or Austrian waltz.

Langsam: Slowly, broadly.

Languendo: Languishing.

Largamente: Broadly.

Largando: Broadening.

Larghetto: Slow, but not so slow as *Largo*.

Largo: Very slow (slower than *Lento*).

Lebhaft: Lively.

Legato: Literally "bound"; therefore, smooth and connected (opposite of staccato).

Legatura: A slur.

Léger, légère: Light.

Leggiadro: Gracefully.

Leggieramente: Lightly.

Leicht: Light, easy.

Leise: Slow, gentle.

Lent: Slow.

Lento: Slow, between *Andante* and *Largo*.

Lesto: Lively.

Libretto: Text of an opera, oratorio, etc.

Licenza: License, freedom.

Linear counterpoint: Contrapuntal music with voices moving independently of harmonic relationships.

Lirico: Lyric.

L'Istesso: The same.

Lustig: Merry, cheerful.

Lyric, lyrical: Song-like ("Fitted to be sung to the lyre").

Madrigal: Loosely, a short, usually amorous or pastoral song; strictly, an elaborately contrapuntal, unaccompanied chorus in more than two parts.

Maestoso: Majestically.

Maggiore: Major.

Malanconia: Melancholy.

Malinconia: Melancholy.

Manual: Organ keyboard.

Marcando, marcato: Accented.

Marcia: March.

Mässig: Moderato, moderately.

Measure: A bar.

Mediant: The third note of a scale.

Melancolia: Melancholy.

Melisma: A vocal embellishment or turn.

Melodrama: Spoken drama with instrumental accompaniment, hence the music that accompanies action.

Meno: Less.

Meter: The arrangement of rhythmic units or pulses.

Mezzo: Medium, half.

Mode: A species of scale, such as major, minor, etc.

Moderato: Moderately, in time.

Modesto: Modestly.

Modulation: Change of key, tonality or mode.

Möglich: Possible.

Moll: Minor.

Molto: Very, much.

Monody: Non-contrapuntal music, with one melodic line predominant.

Mordent: A grace note.

Morendo: Dying away; diminishing in volume and speed.

Mosso: Rapid.

Motive: A brief melodic subject.

Moto: Motion, speed.

Movement: A part of a larger composition that is self-contained on its own.

Musetta, musette: A brief pastoral dance in duple or triple time with a drone bass.

Mute: A device to muffle the tone of an instrument.

Natural: A symbol (♮) that nullifies a sharp or flat.

Nel, nella, nelle: In the, at the.

Neume: Early musical notation by points, hooks, commas, etc.

Nocturne: A term first used by the Irish composer John Field to indicate a composition of dreamy, night-like mood.

Notation: Symbols representing musical sounds.

Note: A symbol representing a musical tone.

Notturno: A nocturne.

Nuance: Variety of color and shading of expression.

Obbligato: An accompanying vocal or instrumental solo.

Octave: A consecutive series of eight diatonic tones.

Opus: A work or composition; frequently indicating the number of a published composition.

Organ point: A tone sustained by the pedal or some voice while the other parts move independently.

Ornament: An embellishment.

Oscillation: Beating, vibration.

Ostinato: Obstinate, continuous; a ground bass.

Parlando: In recitative style.

Passacaglia: A chaconne, with a ground bass, always in the minor and in 3-4 time.

Passepied: A lively French dance in triple meter.

Passion: A dramatic or musical setting of the "passion" (suffering) of Christ.

Pastoral: A composition of rustic nature or subject.

Pavan: A slow dance in 3-4 time, stately and usually in three stanzas.

Pedal point: A tone sustained by the pedal or some voice while the other parts move independently.

Pentatonic scale: A scale of five tones, generally found in oriental music.

Perpetual motion, perpetuum mobile: A piece of great speed and no pause until the end.

Pesante: Heavily.

Peu: Little.

Pezzo: A piece or number.

Phrase: A musical clause.

Piacere, a: At pleasure.

Piangendo: Plaintively.

Piangevole: Mournfully.

Pianissimo: Very soft.

Piano: Soft, softly.

Pitch: The relation in sound of one tone to another.

Più: More.

Pizzicato: Strings plucked with the fingers rather than bowed.

Placido: Placidly.

Poco: A little, somewhat.

Polacca: Polonaise (a Polish dance).

Polichinelle: "Punch" (of Punch and Judy). Hence a clown dance.

Polka: A lively round dance in 2-4 time, originally from Bohemia.

Polonaise: A polish dance in moderate 3-4 time.

Polyphony: Simultaneous use of different melodies (same as counterpoint.

Polyrhythm: Simultaneous use of different rhythms.

Polytonality: Simultaneous use of different keys.

Ponderoso: Ponderous.

Ponticello: Bridge of a stringed instrument.

Portamento: Gliding through all the intermediate tones in an interval with a continuous sound.

pp: Abbreviation of pianissimo.

Prelude: A brief introductory phrase, section or composition; hence a short work of improvisational character.

Presto: Very fast (the fastest rate in music except for its own superlative).

Primo: First, principal.

Program music: Music that tells a story or describes a particular mood or situation.

Progression: A melodic (or harmonic) advance from one tone (or chord) to another.

Quasi: Like, as if.
Quaver: An eighth note.

Rallentando: Becoming gradually slower.
Rapido: Quickly.
Rasend: Raging.
Rauco: Rough, harsh.
Recapitulation: Restatement of the exposition section in sonata form and fugue.
Recitative: Musical recitation or declamation. In opera there are two kinds: recitativo secco ("dry" recitative—that is, unaccompanied except for occasional chords on the harpsichord to keep the singer on pitch) and recitativo stromentato or accompagnato (recitative accompanied by the orchestra).
Relative key: Major keys are related to the minor keys whose tonic tone is a third below their own; conversely, the relative major of a minor key has its tonic tone a minor third above.
Reprise: A repeat.
Resolution: The dissolving of dissonance into consonance.
Rest: A period of silence during which the tempo is continuously maintained.
Retard: To slow or lessen the speed.
Rhythm: The flow of accented and unaccented and of long and short sounds.
Ricercare: Literally, "to search out," therefore highly complex, learned and resourceful compositions, usually in fugal form.
Ricordanza: Remembrance.
Rigadoon, rigaudon: A brisk and humorous dance, generally in 4-4 time.
Ripieno: Literally, "full," hence the larger, contrasting body of instruments in a concerto grosso, as opposed to the concertina or solo instruments.
Riposo: Restfully.
Risposta: The "answer" in a fugue.
Ritardando: Gradual retarding.
Ritenuto: *Immediate* retarding, as distinguished from *Ritardando*.
Ritornello: The orchestral—as distinguished from solo—parts in a concerto; in seventeenth- and eighteenth-century music an instrumental prelude, interlude or postlude.
Rondo: A musical form characterized by good humor with one princi-

pal theme acting as a binding and recurring element between other melodic episodes.

Root: The fundamental tone on which a chord is built.

Rotondo: Round, full.

Rubato: Literally, "robbed," hence a varying tempo with long notes stealing time from the short ones but with no dislocation of the basic rhythmic pulse.

Run: A rapid sequence of notes, usually in scales.

Saltando: Proceeding by skips.

Saltarello: A very fast dance, usually in 2-4, 6-8, or 6-4 time.

Sanft: Soft.

Saraband: A slow Spanish dance in triple meter with castanets.

Scale: From the Latin *scala*, "ladder," hence the ordered succession of notes either ascending or descending.

Scherzo: A musical form, generally in triple meter, with elements of jocularity and humor.

Schnell: Fast.

Scordatura: Unusual tuning of a stringed instrument for special effects.

Score: The parts of an ensemble composition with the simultaneous measures all joined together.

Scorrendo: Gliding.

Secular music: Music for other than church purposes.

Seguidilla: A Spanish dance in 3-4 time, usually slow and in the minor.

Sehr: Very.

Semiquaver: A sixteenth note.

Semitone: A half tone.

Semplice: Simply.

Sempre: Always.

Sensibile: Sensitive, expressive.

Senza: Without.

Septet: A work for seven voices or instruments.

Sequence: Repetition of a melodic pattern.

Serenade: Evening music; an instrumental piece of an open-air nature.

Serenata: A serenade.

Serio: Serious.

Sfogato: Literally, "exhaled," hence a lightly executed note.

Sforza, sforzando: "Forced," hence a note or chord played with sudden emphasis.

Shake: A trill.

Sharp: A symbol (♯) that raises the following note a half tone.

Siciliana: A slow, pastoral Sicilian dance in 6-8 or 12-8 time.

Signature: The symbols at the start of a composition indicating its key and time.

Sinfonia: An instrumental composition; in early operas, the overture.

Slargando: Becoming gradually slower.

Slentando: Becoming slower.

Slur: A symbol (⌒) above or below two or more notes indicating that they are to be played legato or sung on one syllable.

Smorzando: Dying away.

Sognando: Dreamy.

Solenne: Solemn.

Solfège: Identifying notes by their interval relationships.

Solo: A passage or composition for a single voice or instrument.

Sonata: Music "sounded or played," as opposed to *cantata* ("sung"). The term was first applied to any instrumental piece.

Sonority: Richness of sound.

Sordino: A mute.

Sostenuto: Sustained, prolonged.

Sotto: Under, below.

Sotto voce: Undertone, subdued.

Spianato: Calm.

Spiccato: Separated staccato bowing.

Spirito: Spirit, energy.

Staccato: Literally, "detached," therefore short, crisp notes (the opposite of legato).

Staff: Five parallel, horizontal lines on which notes are placed.

Stretto: "Compressed," therefore applied to the closing treatment of a fugue in which subject and answer are so compressed as to overlap each other.

Stringendo: Accelerating.

Subdominant: The fourth tone of a scale or key.

Subito, subitamente: Suddenly, immediately.

Suite: A connected series of pieces. Originally a group of dances.

Sul: On the, near the.

Suspension: A harmonic clash created by holding a note or notes from one chord while the others move to another chord.

Swell: Gradual increase (sometimes also decrease) of sound.

Syncopation: The suppression of a natural accent or strong beat and its shifting to a normally weak beat.

Tacet: "Be silent!"; e.g. *flute tacet*—"let the flute be silent."

Tanto: So much, as much.

Tarantella: A wild dance in 3-8 or 6-8 time that grows in frenzy.

Temperament: A method of tuning in which the intervals in an octave are divided into twelve equal parts, giving up the "tempered" scale and allowing the establishment of major and minor keys.

Tempo: Time, rate of speed.

Tenero: Tender.

Tenuto: Held, sustained.

Tessitura: The general "lie" or pitch of a song, phrase or voice.

Thorough bass: Figured bass.

Timbre: Quality and color of tone.

Time: Tempo, rate of speed.

Toccata: From the verb "to touch." Hence, a display piece of brilliant virtuosity.

Tonal: Relating to a tone, key or mode.

Tonality: The key relationship of a tonal composition.

Tone: A musical sound.

Tone clusters: Harmonies produced by the repeated and extensive use of simultaneous seconds.

Tonic: The first note of a scale.

Transcription: A rearrangement of a composition for a different instrument or instruments.

Transpose: To change the pitch of a composition to a different key.

Treble: The highest register or group of instruments.

Tremolo: The rapid reiteration of a single note on a stringed instrument.

Triad: A three-toned chord.

Trill: The rapid alternation of a principal note with an auxiliary note, usually a major or minor second above it.

Trio: A composition for three voices or instruments; in the dance forms—minuet, scherzo, and so forth—the contrasting lyrical second section.

Triplet: A group of three equal notes.

Tritone: An augmented fourth.

Troppo: Too much.

Turco: Turkish.

Tutti: The full orchestra.

Twelve-tone system: Constructing a section or an entire composition according to a strictly determined sequence of the twelve tones in the chromatic scale.

Unison: Identity of pitch.
Upbeat: The raising of the hand or baton; hence an unaccented beat.

Valse: Waltz, used primarily referring to a concert piece.
Vamp: To improvise an accompaniment.
Variation: The fanciful treatment of a theme.
Veloce: Swift.
Verismo: Operatic realism or naturalism.
Vibration: The oscillation of a string or sounding board that changes the density of the air and is conveyed to the ear as sound waves.
Vibrato: A note of pronounced quivering.
Vif: Brisk, quick.
Vigoroso: Boldly, vigorously.
Villanella: "A village song"; therefore, a rustic folk-like melody.
Viola d'amore: An obsolete string instrument, larger than the viola.
Vite: Quick.
Vivace: Lively, animated faster than *Allegro*.
Vivo: Animated.
Vocalise: Vocal exercise.
Vorspiel: Prelude.

Waltz: A popular dance in 3-4 time whose speed and rhythm vary.

Zapateado: A Spanish dance whose rhythm is emphasized by heel-stamping.
Zarzuela: A two-act Spanish drama with music.
Ziemlich: Rather.
Zum: To the.

INDEX

Index

Index